Canine Body Language

A Photographic Guide

Interpreting the Native Language of the Domestic Dog

Brenda Aloff can be reached at:
www.brendaaloff.com

This book is available at Dogwise
www.dogwise.com

Also by Brenda Aloff:
Positive Reinforcement - Training Dogs In The Real World (2001).
Aggression In Dogs: Practical Management, Prevention and Behaviour Modification (2003).
Foundation Behaviours for Every Dog DVD (2005).
Get Connected With Your Dog: Emphasizing the Relationship While Training Your Dog; Book & DVD (2007)
Puppy Problems? No Problem!: A Survival Guide for Finding & Training Your New Dog (2011)

Illustrations by Brenda Aloff
Cover Design by Brenda Aloff & Joanne Weber

ISBN 1-929242-35-2

First Edition
First Printing, September 2005; Third Printing March 2006 Fourth Printing October 2007
The last digit is the print number 9 8 7 6 5 4 Thirteenth Printing July 2019

This book is dedicated first to the dogs. All dogs. They are my teachers.
Next to my incredible, dedicated and willing students. Thank you.
Betty Owen, for always being there for me.

Acknowledgments

Doing the Acknowledgements is the single most difficult thing in a book because it is incredibly frustrating to not be able to list everyone first!!!

I must first thank the people who did all the great photo shots. Those people are acknowledged again in the book as photographers, but, as always, my fantastic clients make me look good! When I called for photos, I was showered - no, deluged. I went through thousands of photos to choose the ones you will get to learn from. It was so hard to choose sometimes, but because I had such variety, the book is full and rich.

It is quite safe to say that without the stunning and professional photographs of Joanne Weber, who did the vast majority of photographs for this book, there would not be this book on the native language of dogs. The quality of the photographs is so incredible, as is Joanne's generosity. Joanne has the touch.

Other Dog Scout Camp photographers, Felicia and Ginger and Lonnie, also contributed great photographs. These girls are not just good photographers, but wonderful people who really have made caring about dogs and improving understanding of dogs their life's work.

A legion of dog trainer friends and clients also steadfastly took up their cameras at my request. Lori Saxe, Cherish DeWitt, Rashelle DeWitt, Tammy DeWitt (all the DeWitt photographs are listed under Cherish's name), Dave Schrader, Rachel Plotinski, Candy Smith, Abbey Palmer, Cheryl Ertelt and Amy Morris. These folks captured great moments in time in real settings - just like at your own house. Because of these photos, the content in this book gains a "real life" feel - stuff that happens under your nose all the time!

Once the vast quantity of photographs was collected, the writing started. Lori Saxe did the editing on this book. She is dedicated, skilled and diligent. I do not know how she does it, but she totally keeps my style and tone intact while improving my writing so much. I really could not do this without her, and my gratitude to her is immeasurable.

I owe a great deal to Lonnie Olson and Dog Scouts of America. Her camp is the location for Joanne's photographs. Without that venue, I would not have had the thousands of photographs of dogs coming together in numbers. Lonnie's Dog Scout Camp has been a source of inspiration and learning for me for many years. The first year I instructed at camp, I had been in dogs for many years already. Sometime during my first camp I had one of those emotional "Ah HA!" moments. Because of Lonnie and the other lovely instructors there, I, somewhat jaded at that point in time, remembered why I had gotten into dogs in the first place: because the activities you can do with your dog are FUN!!!! This is an easy thing to forget. Those of us who spend all of our time instructing, competing, and being with dogs do forget this frequently. Lonnie and the staff at camp serve an important function - they educate people about having fun with your best friend and thus open up possibilities for dogs. Thank you, Lonnie.

As always, Lori Saxe helped me to think through and explain things better. This was a big project, and discussions with Lori helped me over and over to clarify my thoughts. I am so glad that she was able to lend me her brain, a clear thinking brain, when my head was spinning.

At totally the last minute, Lori, who had the copy editing partially done, broke her elbow. Because of the pain meds and the surgery and the deadline, which all unfortunatly converged at the same time, we were in a bit of panic. However! Andi Plonka, another dear client, stepped in and finished the copy editing for me. This allowed me to be a good friend to Lori and not follow her into surgery and hound her after surgery, placing impossible demands upon her when she was in a helpless and weakened state. Thank you so much Andi!

The second edit, done for this fourth printing, was done by Priscilla Walker. I am so grateful for all of the help she provided me and all of the good advice. Priscilla, an excellent dog trainer herself, and (lucky for me) also literate, did a super job stepping in after Lori was injured to *finally* put a finished edit on this book.

I want to thank the many dogs and people who are in these photographs. The service I hope to render to dogs and their people with this book is possible because of you! If the world is to be a better place for dogs, people need to understand the species much better than we currently do. Dogs are misread all the time, and some of them die because of it. The lack of communication and the preponderance of miscommunication is frustrating for both species. If people can learn to be bilingual in human and dog, we are in a better position to help our dogs and enrich the lives of both species. This also prevents anthropomorphization, which creates impossible situations for dogs every day.

My daughter, Abbey, is always there in the background. Everything I do is flavored by my relationship with her, and her warmth and wit. An English major and now away at University (how did that happen? I am not old enough to have a daughter at University...), she encouraged me and also put up with less than intelligent phone conversations as I worked and talked simultaneously. I kept saying, "No, I'm listening." To which she would reply, "Mom, I can hear you typing. And your replies are not making sense." She also was a great sounding board for some of my technical inquiries, like, "How do you think I should spell Butt Sniff? Should it be one word or two or hyphenated, or what?"

On a more practical note, if it weren't for Steve, I would have starved to death while writing this book. Collecting, organizing, laying out the book - all these activities eat up vast, yawning spaces of time. Time where he is not just deprived of my company, but also takes on all my chores. Steve makes sure I have foot rubs, hot baths, and hot meals. He fed the dogs, fed the sheep, checked on my horse, and bottle-fed the orphaned house lamb during portions of the writing of this book.

Betty Owen is always there. For anything. Anytime. Enough said.

If there are any errors or omissions, they are mine alone, and cannot be placed at the doorstep of anyone else!

Canine Body Language

A Photographic Guide

Interpreting the Native Language
of the
Domestic Dog

Table Of Contents

Table Of Contents

Dogs & Language

You have probably noticed that your dog doesn't speak in sentences. Or, as I am fond of reminding my students, "If you have to explain it in a sentence, your dog will never get it." Dogs rely heavily on communication through body language, and much less through verbalization. The verbal communications that humans use are impossible for dogs to replicate, just as human imitations of dog verbalizations are pretty dicey.

Living with dogs means that you must work at establishing a common language between the two of you. This is frustrating in the extreme for both species. While humans are constantly trying to talk to dogs as if they were people, simultaneously, dogs are trying to talk to humans as if they were dogs. This causes endless misunderstandings, which is unfortunate for both parties.

With this book I have provided you with hundreds of photographs of dogs living their daily lives, interacting with each other and with people. (There are just as many photographs that are not included because one runs out of room.) With each photograph there is an interpretation of the dog's communication. These photographs are thought provoking and fascinating to those of us who are avid students of canine lore. I know you will enjoy perusing them and learning to Read Canine.

Communication

Communication, for all of us, arises out of how that species lives and *what they do.*

Dogs are social animals (they live in a pack or family) who hunt together and raise young together. To the dog, another animal is either of the in-group (family member) or an outsider. Outsiders are potential threats, competition for resources, or prey. Understanding this is crucial to understanding who dogs see themselves as *communicating with* and *what messages they are communicating.* Outsiders can be accepted into the group, and on occasion, Insiders can be cast out or dispersed from a group.

Communication, in the broadest sense, is the exchange of ideas, thoughts, feelings, or intentions using speech, signals, or writing. For dogs, communicating is primarily about intentions, especially intentions about what is "safe vs. dangerous" or about predation. "Come closer, let's do some mutual grooming." Or, "This bone is mine and if you come closer you'll be very sorry." Or, "Let's go get that deer!" Dogs communicate these messages largely through their body language. They don't write, of course, and their vocalizations are actually a minor part of their language. If you want to know a dog's intentions, look at the signals he is giving with his body.

Dog signaling will also involve many behaviours *that are not intended to be communication,* but are just "there" in the act of getting a job done. For instance, a shaking behaviour is just that – something the dog does to break the prey's neck or get meat loose from a bone or dry off after a swim. This kind of shaking is not a deliberate communication, even though it might incidentally signal to a nearby dog that prey has been caught or there is water nearby. Similarly, sometimes signals are exhibited as an *expression* of an inner state, like sniffing the ground as a Displacement Behaviour, because the dog is nervous and wishes to comfort herself by doing something familiar. Again, in this case, the sniffing is not necessarily intended as a deliberate communication; others can, however, still "read" this signal and know the dog is uncomfortable.

Unfortunately, in the real world of doggy interactions, this division of dog body signals into "deliberate communications" and "non-deliberate signals reflecting an inner state or a job to be done" is not so neat. Sniffing can also be a very *deliberate* communication to another dog: "Look, there is an interesting trail here, maybe we should hunt together" or "You are making me uncomfortable, but I still am in a negotiating state."

To make things even more complicated, some signals begin as emotional expressions (reflexive), but a dog can *learn* to use these as deliberate communications. For instance, is a Prey Sequence (the series of behaviours a dog engages in during the hunt, such as stalking and chasing) intended by the dog, initially, to be a communication? I don't think so. It is just an expression of the intense emotions of the hunt and of the physical requirements of competent killing. But other dogs in the area certainly recognize these behaviours and will often rush to get involved in the hunt, too.

Similarly, my Border Collie quickly learned that if she "eyes" a duck, or even another dog, she can make it move, which is satisfying to her. A dog will quickly learn that she can "do" a certain physical posture and it gains her positive results. One of my students has a dog that repeatedly lifts her butt on sits. After a veterinary exam to make sure the dog was comfortable and had good hips, we began to work on the problem. Why was this dog lifting her hips? It began as just an expression of her intention: "I am uneasy and I'm going to get up and come to you," and quickly became, when coming to the owner was discouraged, "I can get my owner to return to me when I am uneasy if I lift my butt." It became a deliberate communication.

So, for the sake of having some sort of organizing principle, I have separated the deliberate from the non-deliberate signals, but always remember that your dog is exhibiting both at all times, and that even the same signal may contain elements of both!

To add even more complexity, any particular behaviour or cluster of behaviours might have multiple intents and will vary according to context. Because of evolutionary parsimony, similar looking behaviours might serve different but distantly related purposes. That is, behaviours developed to correct the puppy, discipline the peer, and subdue the prey. But, in normal interactions, discipline directed toward a puppy has a very different flavor than discipline directed toward a peer. Or, you will see a head duck in both Resource Guarding and Stalking Prey. The head duck intention is related in both situations ("Move away!") - in one case, so the valuable resource is controlled by the guarder, in the other case, so the chase can be initiated. When reading your dog's body language, always be cognizant of the nuances of context that determine the precise meaning of the communication.

Basic Needs and Purposes

Let's return to the "safe vs. dangerous" idea for just a moment. A very basic emotional need of anyone, dog or human, is to determine that she is in a safe situation. This determination affects every behaviour that follows in that context. "Dangerous" doesn't have to mean life-threatening, such as someone pointing a gun to your head. It can mean a situation that is a bit socially awkward: you don't behave confidently because you don't feel completely "safe" or emotionally comfortable. When a dog first enters a context she has never seen before, the first thing she will likely do is determine if the environment is "safe" or comfortable. If she is a dog you are working with, for example, she may be preoccupied with the environment and unable to attend to you until she decides she is safe. Once she has determined she is safe, she can begin to listen to you again and respond to known cues. If the dog is so anxious about her safety that she cannot function normally, you might see a response that humans label as "aggressive: the dog might lunge and bark at any other dog or person approaching. Safety is so important to dogs that it can control their ability to be in Front Brain and think; the lack of it can keep them in their Hind Brain (reactive), where they will display defensive and aggressive displays until they feel safe again. Many signs of a dog feeling unsafe, however, are not nearly as dramatic as this - for most dogs in most "unsafe" situations, subtler discomfort is what you are likely to see, therefore, it will be useful to learn to recognize this.

Safety, for dogs, has a great deal to do with their personal space and their belongings (This, to a dog, may include things that we, as humans, would never guess. Your dog, for example, may think of you as "his object or belonging.") This concept is discussed further in Section 4, "Space Invaders," but the basic idea is that dogs are constantly concerned with and communicating about the safety and integrity of their personal boundaries and, by extension, the possession of their things. This makes a lot of sense when you think about wild canines. It is very important that wild canids protect themselves, their pack, and their territory from outsiders, as well as control insiders' encroachments on each other and decide what they will share and what they will not.

Predation is another vital arena of canine communication. Dogs and wolves hunt in groups, and the hunt is a tightly choreographed sequence in which every participant has a role, but the roles shift as the hunt evolves.

Hunting is both dangerous and necessary. Swift, accurate communication is crucial, and this is achieved through *body language*. A lot of what your dog is communicating is about predation in a general sense, but note that this broad "predacious" behaviour includes many activities you might not immediately assume relate to hunting, such as Herding (moving and controlling prey), Retrieving (carrying prey), and Playing (hunting practice).

Learning to recognize the signs of a dog going into "predator mode" can be very useful. On the one hand, a highly predacious dog can be difficult to work with when you need him to focus on something else: it's that Hind Brain thing[1], where the dog is being flooded with neural chemicals and is merely reacting, not thinking. Recognizing and interrupting an unwanted predatory sequence early, before your dog gets too fired up to respond to you, is obviously beneficial. On the other hand, engaging in predatory games with your dog is one of the best ways to bond with her. Tap into your dog's desire to "hunt together" and you will become a solid working team.

Themes and Variations

Our ancestors did not necessarily *want* to be dog trainers. Instead, they watched nature. They observed that dogs did things naturally that would benefit humans, such as barking when an intruder was sensed. Humans capitalized on this and became dog breeders. Selecting for specific traits to do a specialized job makes great sense if you don't want to be troubled with lengthy training.

If I wanted a dog to be a good alerting dog, I would choose a noisy animal that is reactive. This type of dog is a good candidate as a Hearing Dog in today's service work.

Now, if I wanted to leave my family for a few days and ensure their safety while I was gone, I would want a dog that doesn't just alert. I'd want a dog who is very suspicious of *anything new* and that will bite: a guard dog. A sub-category of this type is the flock guarding dogs, whom we imprint on the species they are to guard at a very young age. This dog is then sequestered from other dogs and people. Now the sheep are very safe because this dog identifies sheep as his pack, and he is a very suspicious dog.

Herding dogs have been selected specifically for gathering traits or driving traits - behaviours, it turns out, that are rooted in the canine Prey Sequence. You can teach both activities to most herding dogs, but they will definitely put their own stamp on it. Aussies, Corgis, and Australian Cattle Dogs tend to be "rougher" and are more driving specialists. Border Collies prefer to eye, stalk, gather and do huge outruns. These breeds were selected originally to move certain types of stock in certain types of terrain, and their tendencies reflect this. Herding, like hunting, is a cooperative venture, so these dogs are commonly described as "having a good work ethic" or "cooperative." Intelligent disobedience, however, is fondly prized in a good working-on-a-farm-type herding dog. This means the dog did the job in spite of your poor directions, and took your intent, while ignoring your signals, to put the stock where you wanted it to end up.

Retrieving and Gun dogs have been carefully selected for good impulse control and cooperation. They have to wait for you to bring down the prey and then go fetch it up for you. In the process of selecting for this patience and for a "soft mouth," it was necessary to truncate the dog's predatory sequence. These dogs have been selected for liking to hold and carry, which is why they are such destructive little chewers and tenacious "mouthers" when they are puppies. Gun dogs don't need to guard and, in fact, guarding is not handy because hunters like to hunt in groups, so friendly behaviour towards humans and dogs is needed. These dogs display more gregarious and fewer guarding behaviours, and seem less interested in status and rank than many other breeds. They also main-

---

1. Here is a very simplistic explanation of a complex subject, but since we are not doing neurosurgery it will do nicely for our purposes. Think of the dog's brain as divided into two basic sections: Front Brain, where cognition and thoughtful responses are governed, and Hind Brain, where reflexive, reactive behaviour is emitted. Again, oversimplified, these two do not pull as a double team - either one is leading or the other is. When the dog is working out of the Hind Brain you observe just the kind of behaviours we find difficult to deal with in dogs, because the dog is not "listening" and processing information in a thoughtful way, he is merely reacting to the environment.

tain the innocence of play behaviour well into adulthood. Water is a place where people don't like to go when it is cold to retrieve game, so most of these dogs really love the water. As an aside, the exception in this group is the Chesapeake Bay Retriever, which was selected for guarding and territorial behaviour.

Terriers were bred to work independently. People do not accompany the terrier down into the deep, dark, claustrophobic hole to direct her where to grab the badger or when to bark at the fox. If I humorously anthropomorphize Herding dogs into a role as being Book Smart types, I think of the Terriers as being Street Smart. They are original thinkers, tenacious problem solvers (as long as it is a topic that piques *their* interest!) very fierce, and easily switched into prey drive from any intense emotional state. "We are playing, you are beginning to look like prey;" "I am disciplining you, you are beginning to act like prey;" "There is somebody at the door, I am excited, you look like prey." They often have virtually no impulse control. If they did, these dogs would not do their job correctly. The average Golden looks down a deep, dark hole at some snarling creature and says, "They don't want a visitor right now." The average go-to-ground terrier sees this same situation as a big party: "Awesome! I'm coming in!" They tend to be physically tough, and have high tolerance for pain and low tolerance for stupidity (lack of prey drive) in humans. They are very precocious with adult-appearing behaviours, such as ranking and predatory behaviour.

Sled dogs capitalize on the "we love to run" aspect of the hunt. If you have ever seen sled dogs work, you know they *love* what they are doing. Running in groups is intrinsically satisfying to many dogs; it is how dogs naturally hunt, as well as play.

This is obviously a very brief and limited "history" of breed selection. My intent here is not to be complete, but to get you thinking about why breeds bear specific traits. Even if you did not get your terrier to rid the yard of vermin or your Cattle Dog to work stock, your dog still has all the genetic material to do his "original job."

The importance of this history is that this selection also impacts dogs' communication. While all of the signals discussed in this book can be used by all dogs, certain dogs will, of course, rely on some signals more than others; the dog's breed is one important determinant of this. While you can tell when both your terrier and your Lab are playing, the play might look rather different, emphasizing different behaviours, and, crucially, may be more likely to change quickly into unwanted predatory behaviour with your terrier. Warning and Guarding behaviours will probably be more often or more quickly seen in the Guarding breeds. Predatory behaviour in a Border Collie may involve a lot of eyeing and stalking, while an Australian Cattle Dog may chase and be more likely to bite. And so on. This book emphasizes the "themes" - those signals, behaviours, and communications that *all* dogs share. But, when you are observing your own or others' dogs, be conscious of the "variations," especially those that arise from breed-specific traits.

I'm Talking to You! Are You "Listening?"

If you take only one thing away from this book, let it be that, dog behaviour is not random, despite how it may initially look to us! While some behaviours may seem superfluous to people, the behaviour is serving a function for the dog. It is either a reflection of the dog's internal state or a deliberate attempt to communicate with you or someone else. Your dog is talking to you all the time. ALL THE TIME!

Recognition of your dog's signals, as well as an ability to recognize stress-related topography, will move you significantly forward in understanding dog language.

Attempting to modify behaviour (training your dog) when you don't know what your observations truly mean can be very, very difficult, and your relationship with your dog will suffer.

It can even lead to tragic errors - for example, when treating aggression. In order to modify behaviour in the aggressive dog, it is important to know such distinctions as: Is the dog sitting calmly or with a deliberate, and

potentially dangerous, stillness (the proverbial calm before the storm)? Although the difference in the body language may be subtle, there is a vast difference in meaning, and woe unto the person who does not realize this.

The more knowledge you have about dog body language - that is, dog language - the better the decisions you will make in both training and everyday life with your dog. It is important for your dog as it develops your dog's trust: your dog feels understood. It is important for you to know the meaning of the behaviour you see in order to decide which consequences to provide for it.

And mostly, it is an important window for seeing into the soul of this delightful alien creature.

How to Use This Book

My intent is that this volume will help people learn more about dogs and their native language.

I also wished that professionals or others "in the trade" would be able to have a reference manual. There were many times when I was a novice dog trainer that I would dearly have loved something more than the progressive picture of the wolf showing neatly pigeon-holed pictures of the animal from submission to dominance. Not that that isn't a fantastic tool, it just wasn't nearly enough. Also, it is the subtle language that is most often seen, not overt snarling and staring. In that respect, the photographs in this book are, for the most part, of the subtle and often quick and casual exchanges that occur between dogs constantly.

There is a Table of Contents, as well as an Index and a List of Photographs to help you locate a specific item. You can look up obvious categories like "Calming Signals," or a specific signal, such as "Sniffing" in the Index. In addition to this, use the "key words" in the list below to help you locate a specific "part" of the dog you are seeking information for.

List of Key Words Used In the Index:

- body lowered
- body orientation
- braced legs
- dilated pupils
- ears
- eyes
- head lowered
- lips
- mouth, closed
- mouth, open
- paw lift
- rounded topline
- silhouette
- stillness
- tail

Glance through the entire book. Then read through section by section. See how the behaviours are inter-connected. Learn how subtle combinations of signals indicate different intentions. For instance, all of the same signals, changing only Tail down to Tail up, indicate a possible difference between a Play Bow and a Prey Bow. This small difference indicates a very different intention to the other dog. The Play Bow is used to invite play from another dog, and very often, the Play Bowing dog will wait for a signal from the other dog to commence play. The Prey Bow, when used in play, says: "I am going to pounce on you! Get Ready!"

To describe a Play Bow: used to invite play	To describe a Prey Bow: most often used before a pounce after prey, can be used in already established play:
Elbows down	Elbows down
Rear up	Rear up
Ears up	Ears up
Tail down	Tail up

This brings us to an interesting point. For humans to effectively communicate we have devised an immense vocabulary. Millions of words. The dog is limited by his body parts. Because of this, the dog must re-use "words" and depend on context and combination to form the "sentence." Keep this in mind as you observe, because, "mouth, open" must be combined with other "words" in many variations to get the most out of communication efforts.

Have fun with this! Avoid anthropormorphization (attributing human traits to animals). It will only muddy the waters of clear communication and prevent you from understanding the species. You have to make the effort to think like the dog would, seeing the world through her eyes; not through emotional transference.

Training issues disappear when you can recognize that your dog is asking for help, (anxiety or confusion) as opposed to making a choice to disobey (I'll greet this dog, THEN I will respond to your cue of "Come," even though I clearly heard you.) The real prize is communication with your life-long friend can be even more rewarding as you become "bilingual," including "Dog" in your language repertoire.

Section I: Expressions of an Emotional State

Not all canine body language is a deliberate communication. Some language is reflexive in nature and is a reflection of what is going on in the dog's autonomic nervous system.

Stress signals, for instance, can be deliberate communications, such as a Look Away & Lip Lick, or they can be reflexive, such as sudden hair loss and increased respiration.

At least in theory, such signals can neatly be divided into deliberate, conscious communications and reflexive responses. In the Real World, it is not so cut and dried. When you are reading a dog, you will find that signals often contain mixed elements of both.

In this section are examples of language that are predominantly reflections of the autonomic nervous system. They may also contain an element of deliberate communication, but mostly they are just expressions of the dog's internal state.

These signals are a window into the dog's current emotional experience. Learning these signals can help you answer such questions as: Should I move closer to this dog? Should I touch him? Is that dog feeling uncomfortable and therefore more likely to become reactive? Why is my dog unwilling to work in this setting? Knowing whether your dog - or someone else's - is stressed, fearful, neutral, or friendly, for example, can be very useful in protecting your safety or in any problem solving you plan to do with behaviour problems.

illustrations by Brenda Aloff.

1
Relaxed & Neutral

#1.1: Relaxed or Neutral Facial Expression

- lack of tension
- lips loose
- eyes blinking and soft
- ears hanging relaxed

This dog is relaxed. Notice that the lips, ears and eyes are not deliberately "held" or forced into any particular position. The lips are hanging loose, the eyes are blinking and soft, the ears just "are." There is no tension held in the face.

Note also the softness of the dog's brow and the relaxed muscles on the forehead.

Compare this relaxed face with the tense face, below.

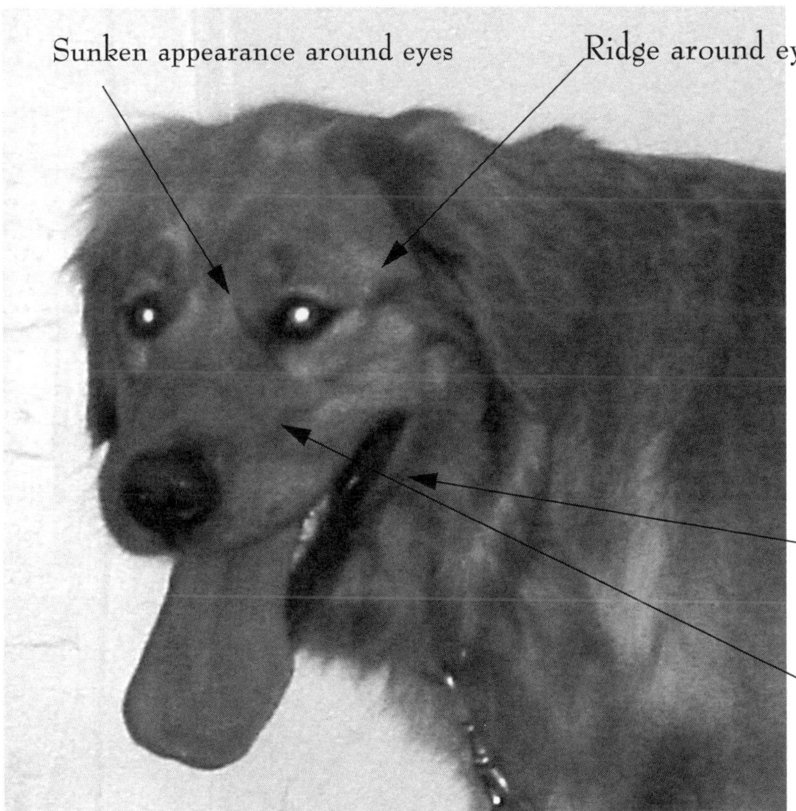

#1.2: Tense Facial Expression

- ridges around eyes and lips
- puckered forehead
- skin looks stretched tightly across the skull
- dilated pupils
- eyes wide
- spatualate tongue, wide at bottom (see also Photo #6.7)
- ears drawn back
- lips drawn back in an extreme manner

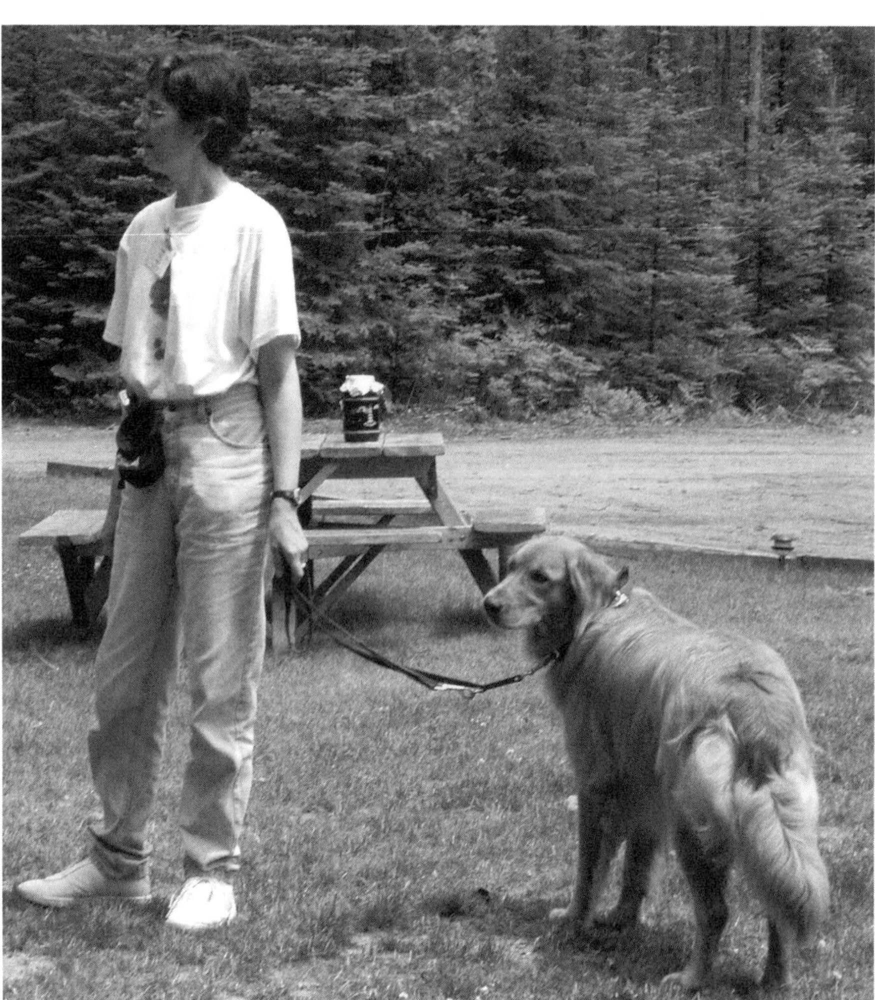

#1.3: Mirroring A Relaxed or Neutral Silhouette

- lack of facial tension
- eyes are soft and round
- mouth is closed, lips are long and loose
- ears just "are"
- lack of body tension
- tail is hanging in a relaxed manner at half-mast
- legs are not braced
- dog and human are mirroring (exhibiting similar relaxed postures)

I included the owner in this photo because the dog and the human are Mirroring each other. The woman is in as relaxed and neutral a posture as her dog. Coincidence? I don't think so. We know how easy it is to transfer emotional states between us and our animals.

Neutrality is evident in this dog's relaxed posture. None of his body parts are being forced into any particular position. His tail is held in a gentle curve, there is no facial tension evident. His ears are falling naturally and his eyes are going to be blinking. This dog is obviously comfortable and feels confident to cope with the current situation.

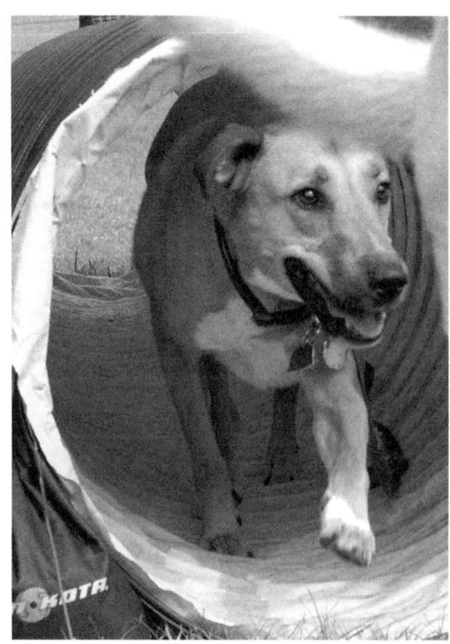

#1.4: Relaxed & On Task

- lack of tension
- lips loose
- eyes blinking and soft
- ears hanging relaxed

This dog is relaxed and confident while performing a task. The ears are at half-mast, the eyes are gently round, and there is no facial tension evident. The mouth is partially open and the dog is panting. Dogs in a medium panic don't pant; their mouths are closed. Dogs in a more frantic state are breathing in short, shallow breaths with that tell-tale second ridge above the lips indicating facial tension; they are panting, but often the tongue will take on a different shape.

You can see the tail of the dog just ahead of this dog. Obviously the dog in the tunnel is comfortable in the presence of this dog even though they are close together and in a tight space, which could make an animal feel trapped or socially pressured.

This group of dogs is comfortable with each other even though they are all confined (trapped) by being leashed.

#1.5: Comfortable In A Group
- lack of eye contact
- eyes blinking and soft
- tails & ears relaxed

Each dog has a slightly, but not exaggerated, lowered head. This is used to show "friendly" behaviour when it is accompanied by lack of facial and body tension. This kind of lowered head has an "I'm going somewhere and minding my own business" air about it.

Each dog has some form of half-mast ears.

Slightly open mouths indicate relaxation of the jaw when combined with the other signals. This is important because dogs are likely to hold tension in the jaw and in the tail. The two dogs with closed mouths have long lips visible (the Terv, far right) or the loosely hanging lips (on the Pariah dog, 2nd from the left).

Each dog has a relaxed tail carriage, varying from being held gently over the back, to horizontal, to slightly lowered to controlled by gravity. Even though the tails are held in varying positions, they all look gently swinging - the dogs are not "forcing" the tail into any extreme position, such as tucked or held rigidly over the back.

The dogs are all avoiding direct eye contact with each other.

Photo Credits: Photo #1: Joanne Weber;
Photo #2: Cherish DeWitt;
Photo #3, #4 & #5: Joanne Weber.

2 CONFIDENCE

I loved comparing the different reactions of the dogs with the stuffed bird. There were also several pictures of this same Papillon, and in each one he displays a relaxed confidence, regardless of the situation.

In this photo, it is clear by the slight lowering of his tail that he is concentrating hard. There is no evidence of braced legs in front or back. His nose is oriented directly at the bird and he is looking at it in a curious manner. He is in motion and still moving forward toward the bird, not standing still as a dog would if displaying Caution. Compare the dogs in the *Caution* Chapter (page 45) to the dogs in this Chapter for contrast.

2.1: Confident

- forward body orientation

2.2: Confident

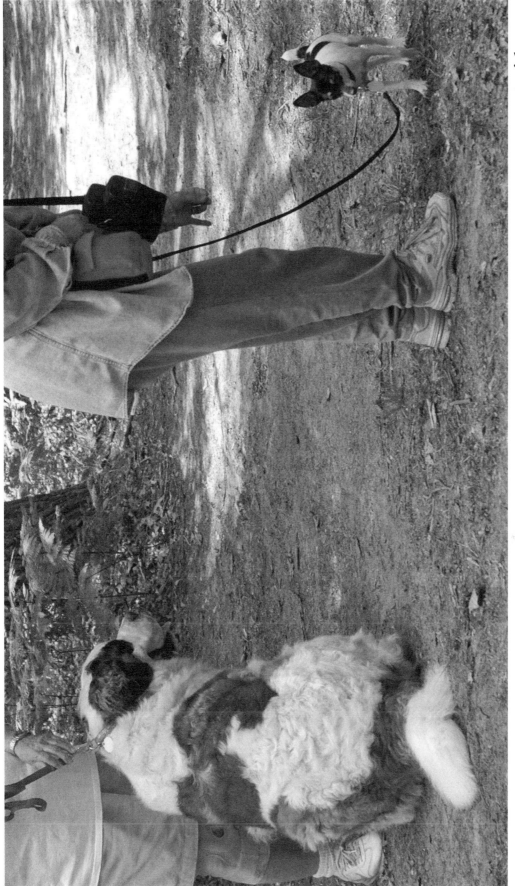

- forward body orientation

Who is the "big dog" in this picture? The tiny dog on the right! Look at the self-confidence in this dog's posture. Ears up, tail up, body orientation forward. Even the big dog is noticing! When I first looked at this photo, my eye was drawn to the right first and kept returning there.

For dogs who radiate "I am here, you may be seated," the phrase *in medias res* is perfect. Plunging into the middle of things, these dogs like to be involved and their body language indicates that.

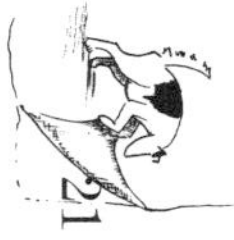

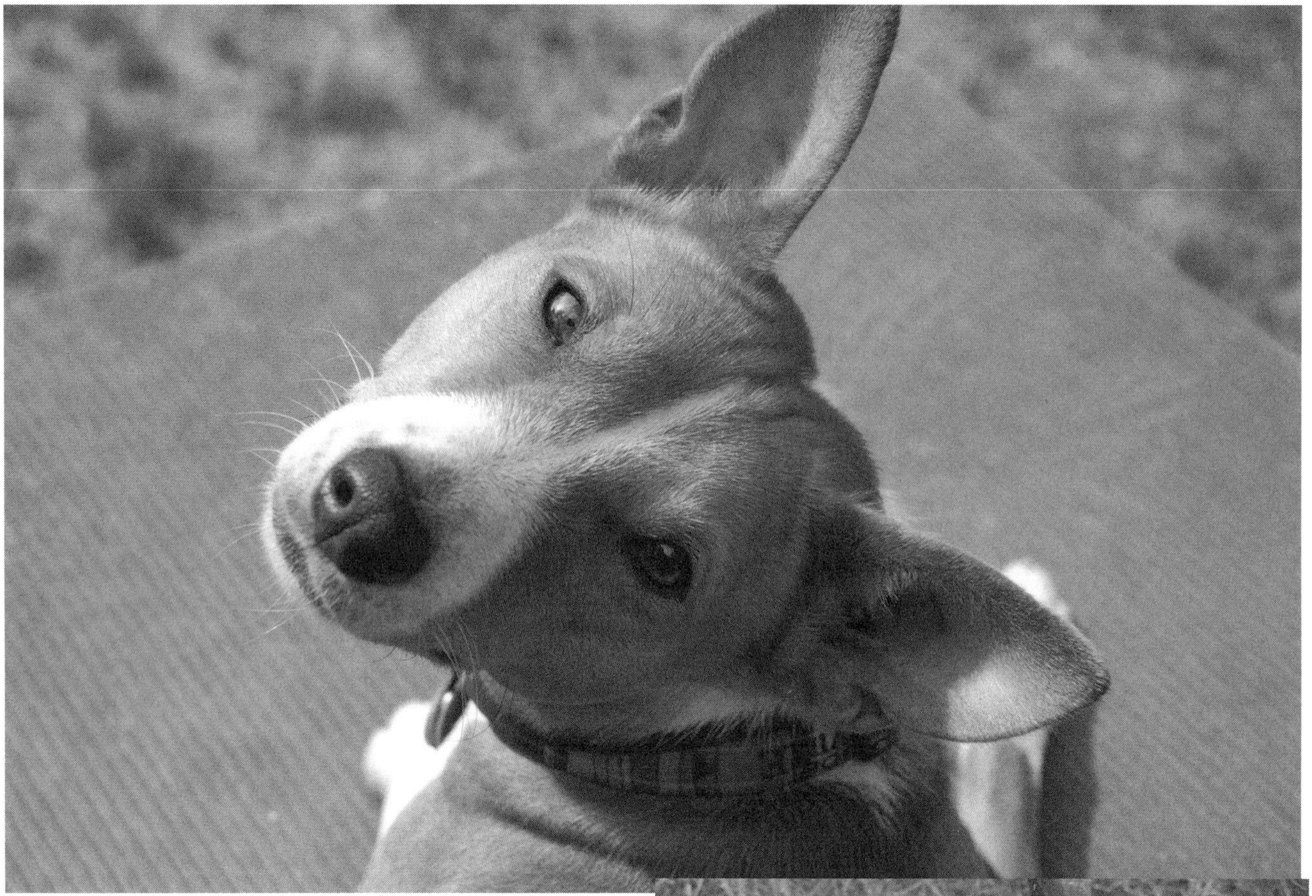

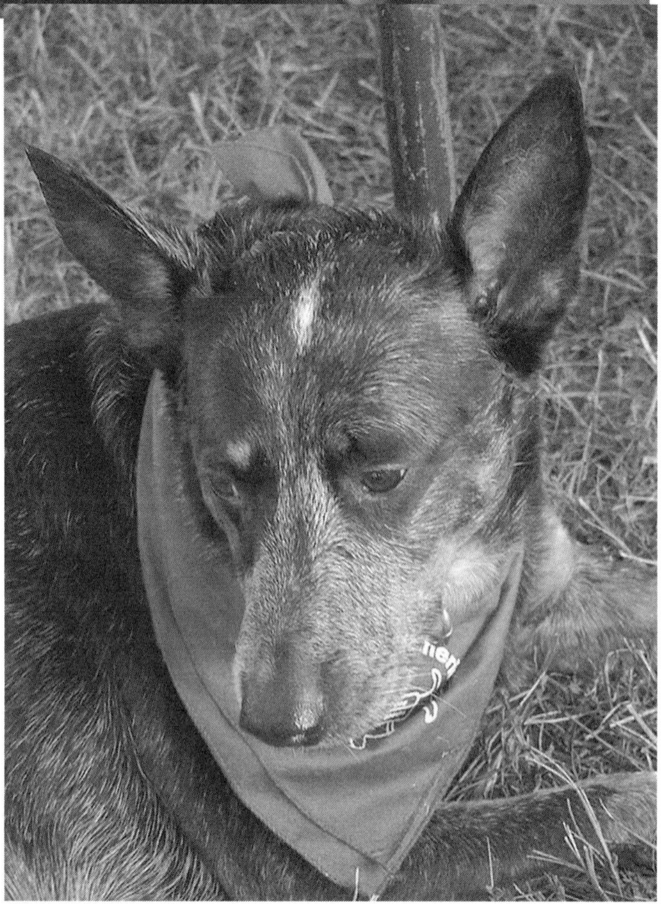

2.3: Confident (vs. Shy)

2.4: Shy, Apologetic

The difference in the way these two dogs react to having the photographer loom over and stare at them with the unblinking eye of the camera tells you how they feel about social pressure.

The Basenji is relaxed and confident: Hi, what are you doing?

The Cattle Dog is doing a Look Away, and is tipping his ears back slightly. He exhibits facial tension in the ridge under the eyes. Buster, a rescue, you will see in several photographs. He is a cautious, sweet dog and always seeks to be as invisible as possible.

Photo Credits:
Photo #1, #2, #3 & #4: Joanne Weber..

3 Curiosity

#3.1: Curiosity & Play

#3.2: Curiosity & Play

- engagement of dog to task
- use of paws
- ears, alert but not tense
- ears, assymetrical
- orientation of nose

A curious dog will often paw, mouth and/or sniff the object of curiosity. If the dog is comfortable with himself and the context, he will look very much like this dog.

The dog is looking at the object intensely, but the shape of the eye indicates confidence and interest - the eye is not held wide open in fear, nor is it squinting. The dog is blinking, not staring. The lips are relaxed but held back slightly in concentration and the dog's mouth is closed.

One thing I notice about dogs in a state of curiosity is that they often "place" that funny little fold in their ear, even though the ears are placed at half-mast. You can see in the second photograph that gravity is pulling the ears down, indicating that the dog is not holding the ears with tension. If the dog is holding the ears tensely, there will be a stiff, forced look. to them. There is a sloppiness or floppiness to this dog's ears.

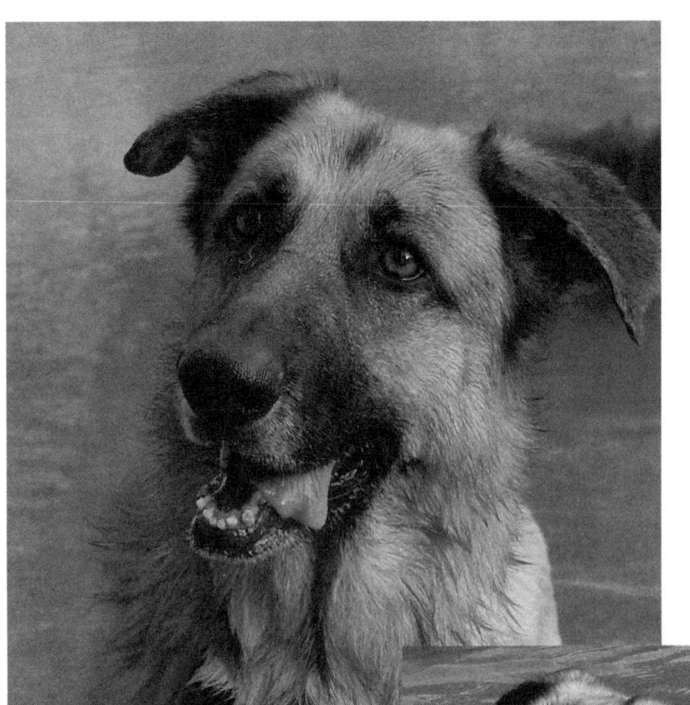

#3.3: Curiosity & Expectancy

- intensity of expression
- ears, alert but not tensely forwar
- ears, assymetrical
- orientation of nose and eyes is the same

#3.4: Interest

- ears up
- orientation of eyes & nose is the same
- poised to move, see the lowered rear
- forward "feel"

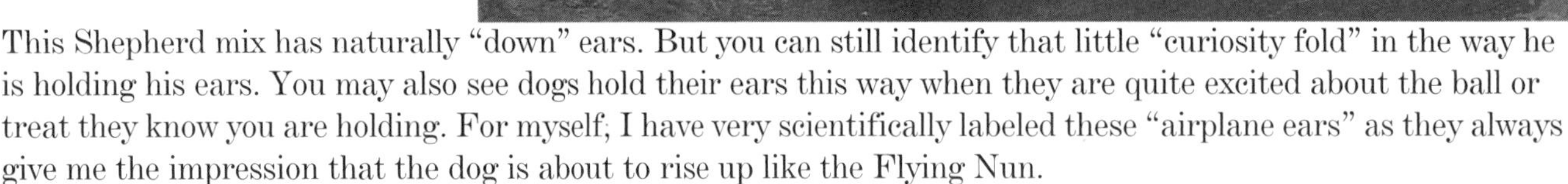

This Shepherd mix has naturally "down" ears. But you can still identify that little "curiosity fold" in the way he is holding his ears. You may also see dogs hold their ears this way when they are quite excited about the ball or treat they know you are holding. For myself, I have very scientifically labeled these "airplane ears" as they always give me the impression that the dog is about to rise up like the Flying Nun.

In Photo #3.4, the body language shows expectancy: "What will happen next?" You can tell this by the shape of the dog's back. Even though you cannot see them, the hind legs are drawn up under the dog's body slightly and the front legs are directly underneath the dog, not braced. This dog looks as if he would move forward toward whatever he is focused on; his energy is directed forward. The dog's general body language says to me: *in medias res.* "I am ready for action!"

In both photographs, the eyes are neither forced wide nor narrow. The lips are relaxed, the mouth is open, the tongue is relaxed and lolling, as opposed to flicking in a deliberate way. Also evident in this dog is the raise of the eyebrows - a sign of curiosity. It causes that cute little pucker in the forehead. In this dog it is a vertical line; in many with looser skin, such as Basenjis and Pit Bulls, you will often see a series of ridges.

Head Tilts indicate curiosity. Sometimes the Head Tilt is due to the dog trying to orient in order to *hear* a specific sound better. Many dogs will Head Tilt at a certain pitch of a sound. It can also be predatory - Many a time I have seen my Fox Terriers Head Tilt out in the field, then pounce and come up with some tiny dead creature. So if a dog is Head Tilting and the body posture is predatory or really tense, and not relatively relaxed as these dogs are, AND it is directed at a child or another dog, you might want to take note of that and be extra watchful until you determine the intent of the dog.

#3.5: Head Tilt

- Flying Nun ears

This dog has great "held out to the side" ears. The Flying Nun ears!

#3.5: Head Tilt

Head Tilt directed downwards, toward the object of interest. The eyes are following the nose.

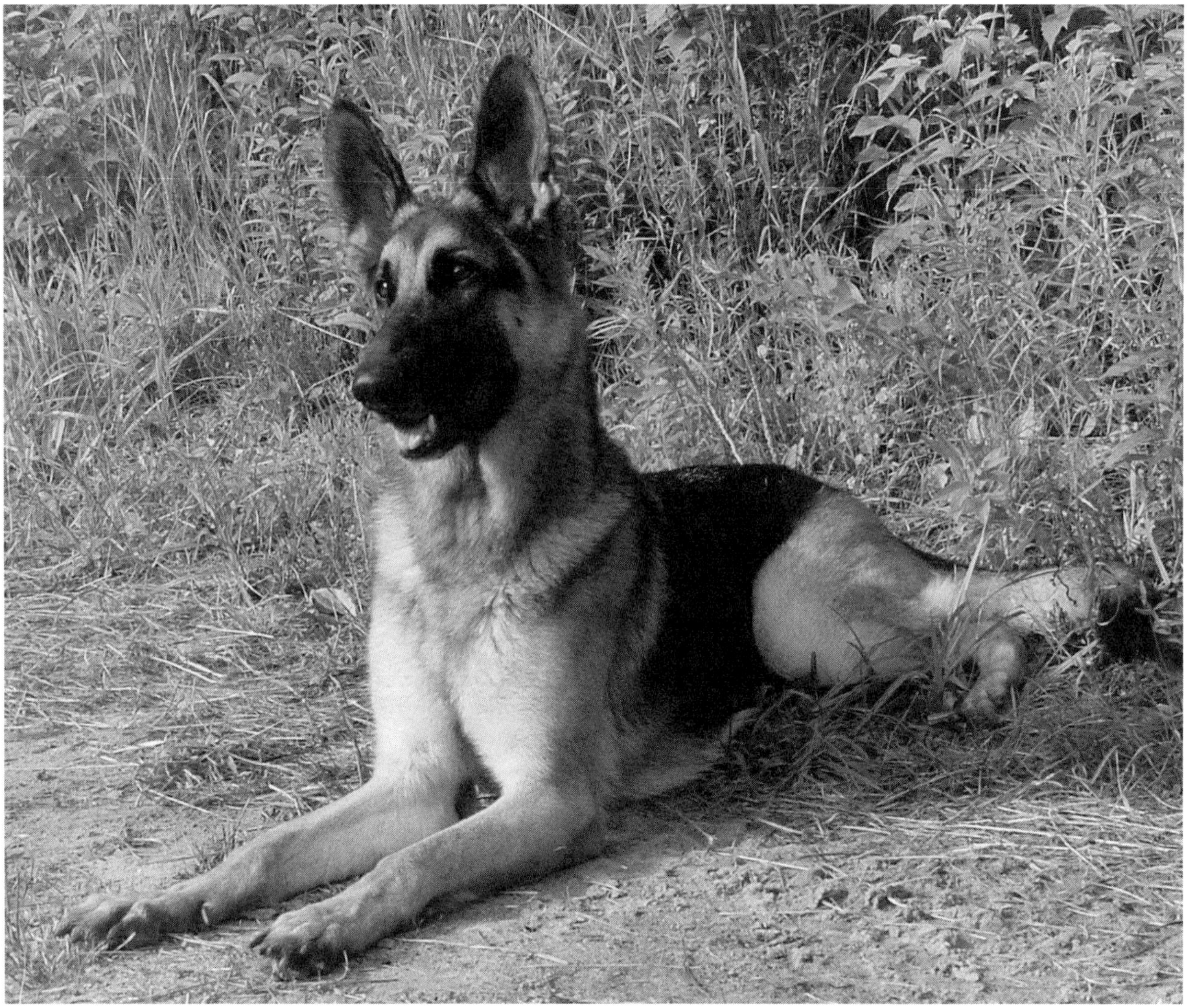

This dog is neutral, friendly, curious, and attentive.

#3.6: Head Tilt

- Head Tilt
- happy slightly open "grinning" mouth
- erect ears, but without excess tension

Photo Credits:
Photo #1, #2, #3, #4, #5, #6 & #7: Joanne Weber.

4 Rolling

Rolling is most often an activity unto itself rather than a specific communication.

Dogs roll in stuff all the time. My dogs roll in excrement, the runnier and more disgusting the better. They also roll in dead bugs and worms, happily scraping their faces and shoulders into the lovely perfume.

Dogs roll to scratch their bodies and give a self-massage. They roll wildly when they are wet or just out of the bathtub. Especially when just out of the tub, rolling is a big anxiety reliever: a displacement behaviour.

Any well-spoken dog would recognize rolling as a reflection of a happy, relaxed state of mind. Rolling is a non-threatening behaviour.

But Rolling can also serve as communication. One dog can take a scent-message from its original location to another dog. Sort of like lending a paperback to a friend.

Rolling excites other dogs because it means there could be interesting scents (even dead bodies!) where the rolling is taking place.

Dogs who are extremely predatory and not well socialized can become excited by watching another dog roll. To these dogs the motion and "down" position is stimulating, inviting attack.

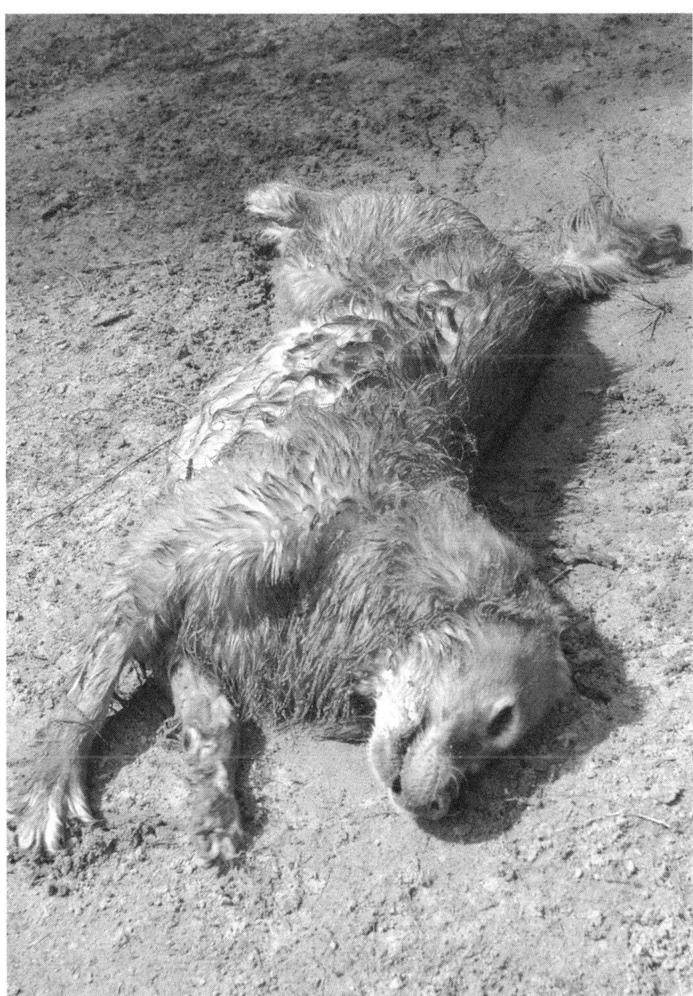

4.1: Wet Dog Rolling

- squinty eyes
- slightly open mouth
- relaxed body

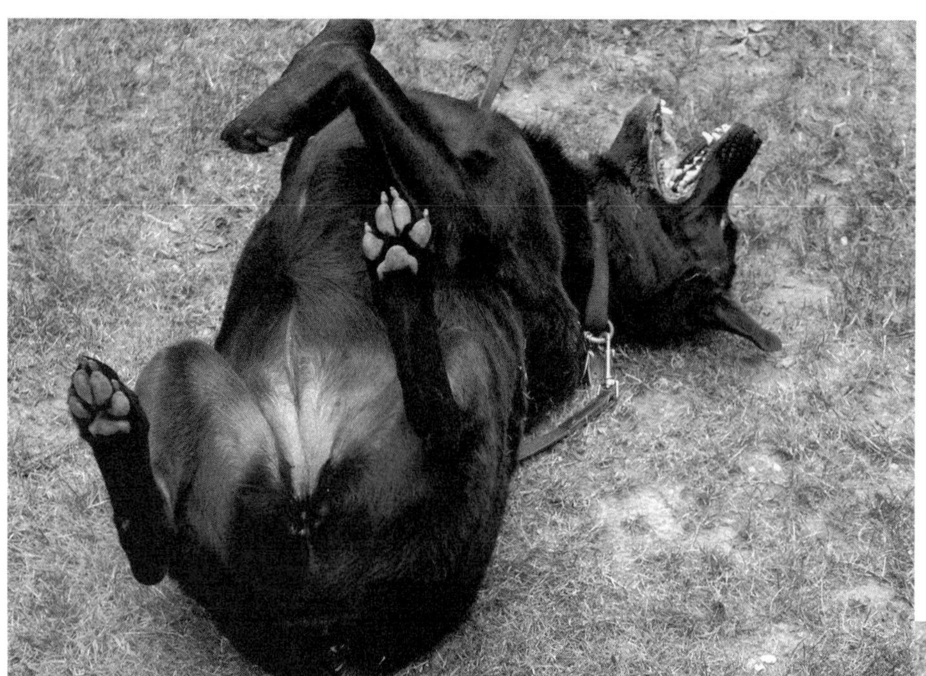

4.2: Abandonment & Ecstasy - Photo Essay

- happy open mouth
- lack of focus on any particular item or location

Photo Credits:
Photo #1 & Photo Essay #2: Joanne Weber..

Companionship

Companionship is an extreme version of relaxation. It is indicated by that willingness to violate another's personal bubble, as well as a relaxed acceptance of that same intrusion.

#5.1: Companionship

- proximity
- lack of tension

Notice that the puppies are lying companionably on each other. This kind of intrusion into personal body space is allowed only from those the dog feels comfortable with. Just like you. Note that these puppies are including the human in their Puppy Pile just as if she is another puppy. This is how a dog will always first try to communicate with you: as if you were another dog.

Contrast this photograph to the one following.

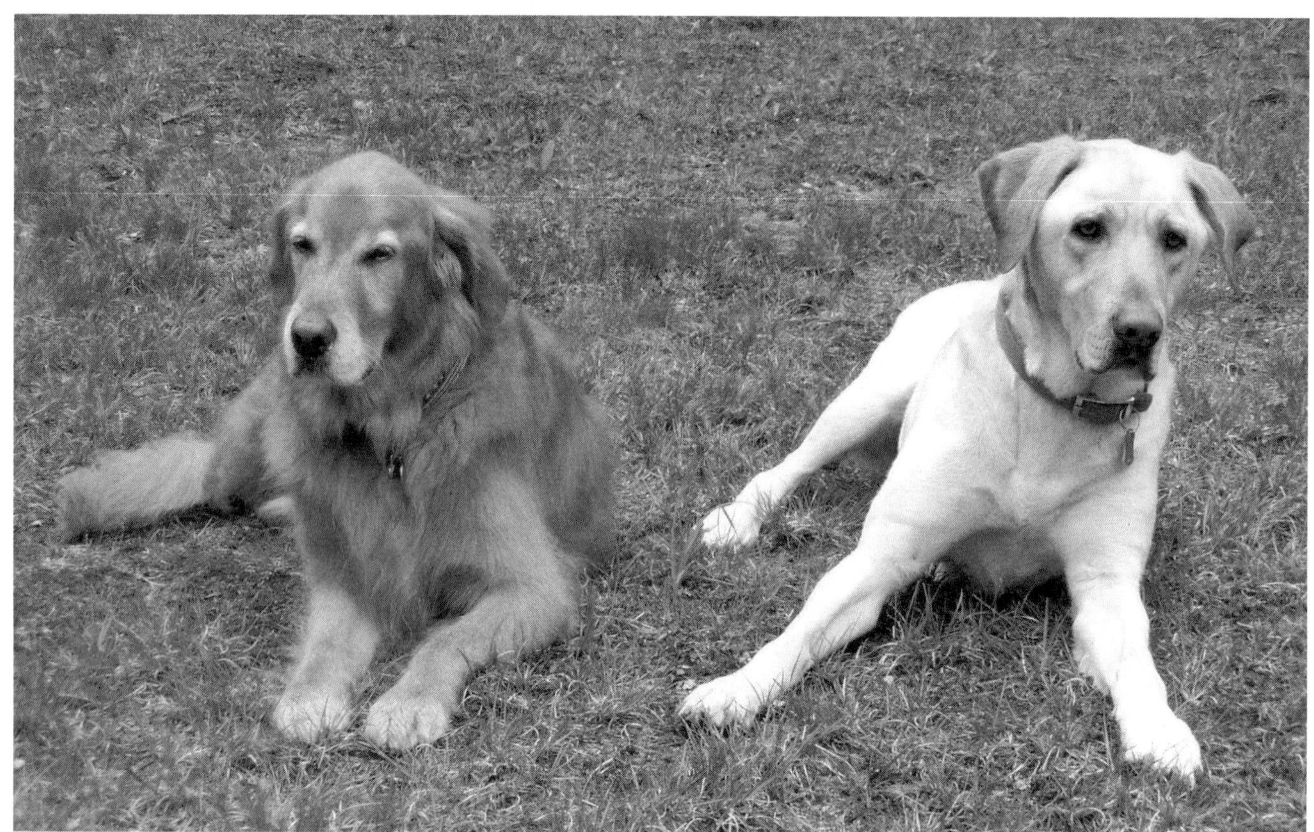

#5.2: Discomfort With Proximity

- proximity (how close the dogs are)
- how dogs are handling the space between them
- body orientation

Notice the unwillingness of both dogs to violate body space.

These dogs were put into a Down Stay to have their picture taken, so they were "forced" to be together.

Willie, on the left, is deliberately leaning his body away from the Lab. Willie has his head slightly averted and is Blinking.

The Lab appears to be interested in something out of our view, but his body is still markedly and deliberately leaning away from Willie.

Joanne, who owns Willie, told me that Willie is not thrilled about this young, rambunctious Labrador. There are several photos of these two dogs taken when they were spending the day together so Joanne could dog-sit the Labrador. In all of them, Willie is avoiding the Lab in some way. Not horribly, as in: "I am anxious and cannot bear to be near you," but rather more like many feel about toddlers: "I don't want you to behave outlandishly, and I don't want your sticky lollipop to get on my clothes."

I like the way this contrasts with the previous photograph. These dogs are choosing to stay OUT of each other's body space rather than accepting the relaxed intrusion of body space that indicates comfort with each other.

#5.3: Participating

- "leaning into" body posture
- happy open mouth
- sweeping tail
- lack of tension

This Siberian is accepting the restraint and touch of his owner. The man is leaning over his dog, his arms are restraining the dog in a hug, and his face is close to the dog's face. These are all signals of potential threat to a dog.

The Siberian isn't just tolerating, he is participating. He is leaning into the body of the man, his tail is doing the Friendly Sweep - a wagging tail at half-mast - and his mouth is open in a relaxed way. That relaxed open mouth is the doggy version of a primate grin. The dog's canines are exposed because he has drawn his lips up and back, but the lack of body tension communicates how comfortable the dog is with his owner.

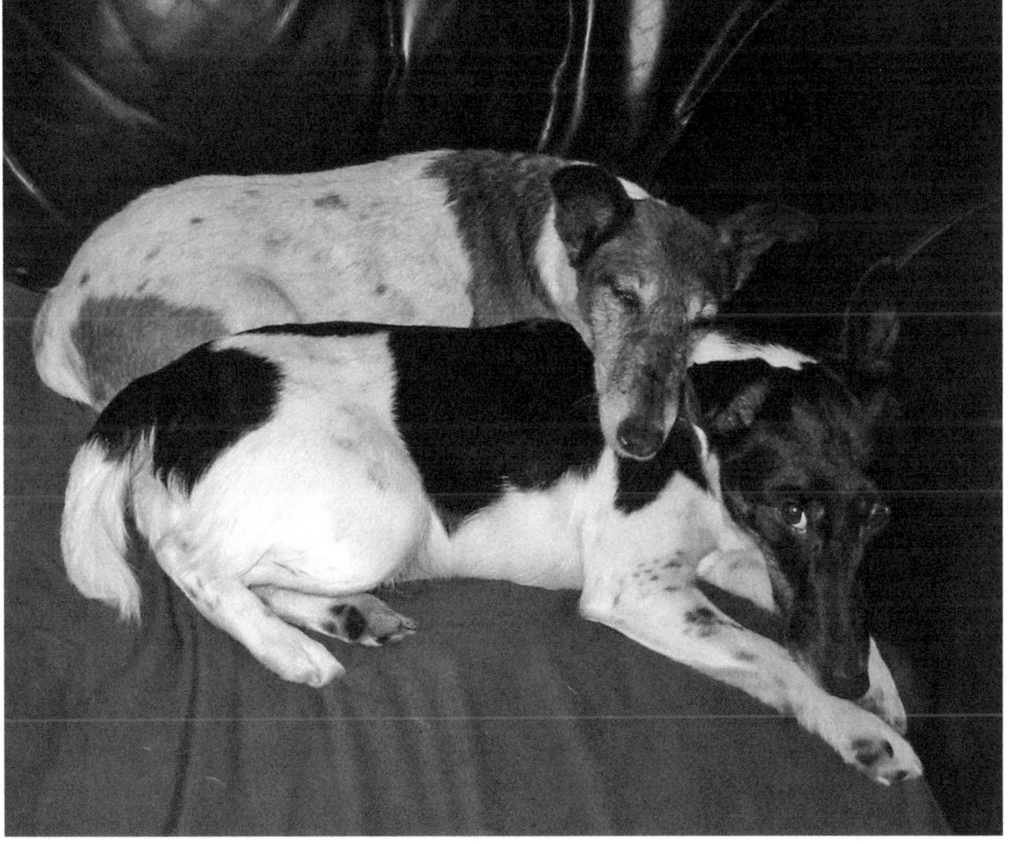

#5.4: Adult Dogs In Companionship

- proximity
- relaxation
- mirroring

Punch and Zoomer enjoy a nap together. The curled-up tails are typical of the resting, relaxed dog.

Photo Credits:
Photo #1, #2 & #3: Joanne Weber;
Photo #4: Brenda Aloff.

6 Stress Signals

Merlin came to the Training Center for some help with problem behaviour. He was described as a very hyperactive dog. When I met him, I could see that he was not just really lively - he was predominantly anxious.

Within a few minutes he displayed all of these things: scratching, panting, shallow breathing, hair loss and exfoliation (dander), sniffing. The following photos capture about 10 minutes of observation after he first walked into the Training Center.

The behaviours displayed in this photo essay are typical of a dog who is under stress. Sometimes you will see only one or two of them, other times the dog will, like Merlin, exhibit several.

Any of these stress signals can be used as deliberate communication and also as displacement behaviour. It stands to reason that certain behaviours could be used for both purposes simultaneously. A behaviour used as a Signal can also be a comforting behaviour for a stressed dog.

#6.1: Scratching

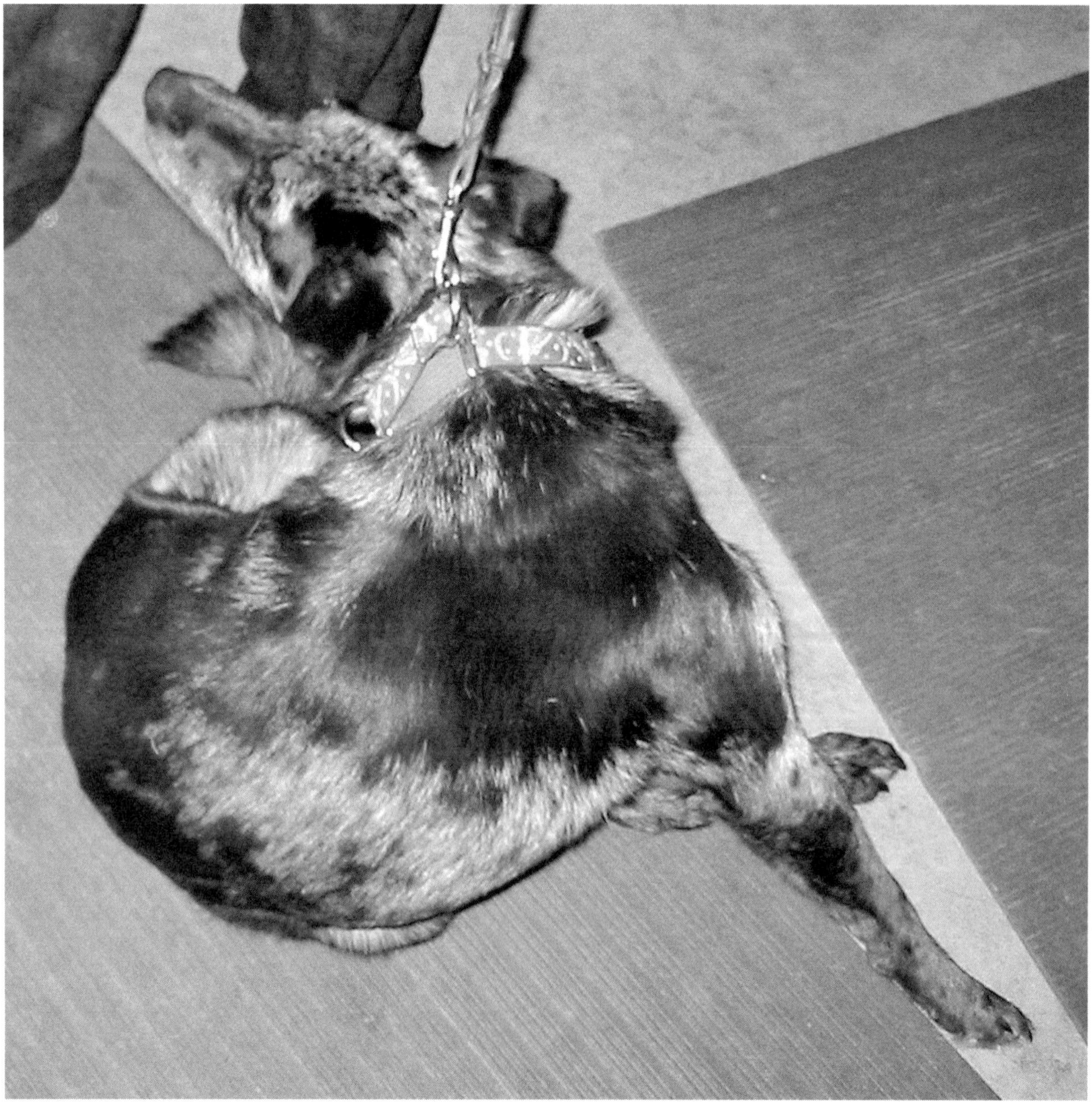

#6.2: Stress Indicators

- ears held in tension
- dilated pupils
- slightly spatulate tongue
- tongue way out
- braced legs
- tail down
- panting

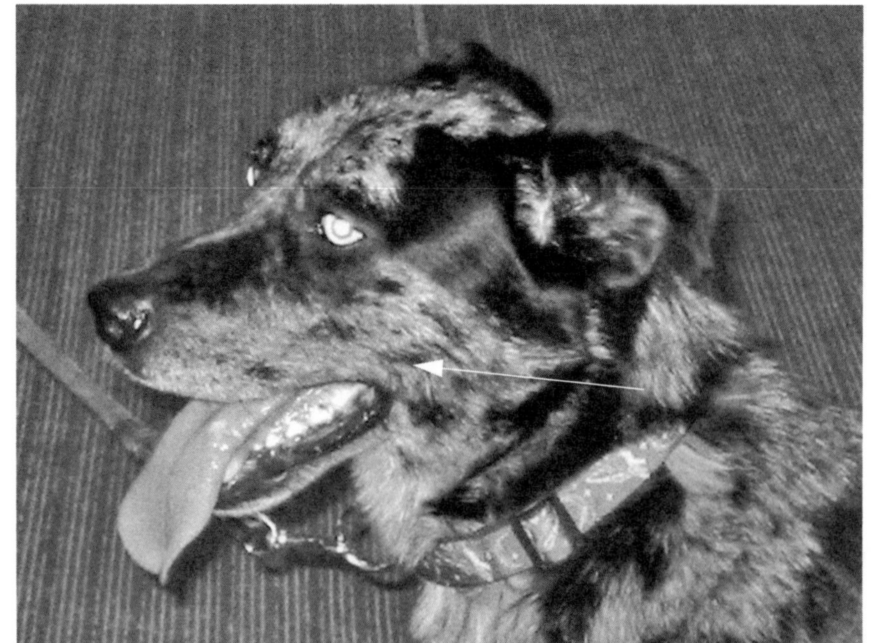

#6.3: Facial Tension

- tongue way out
- spatulate tongue
- ears drawn to the side and back
- lips drawn back
- tension ridges around the lips (see the arrow)
- Look Away of avoidance

#6.4: Tension Ridge By Eye

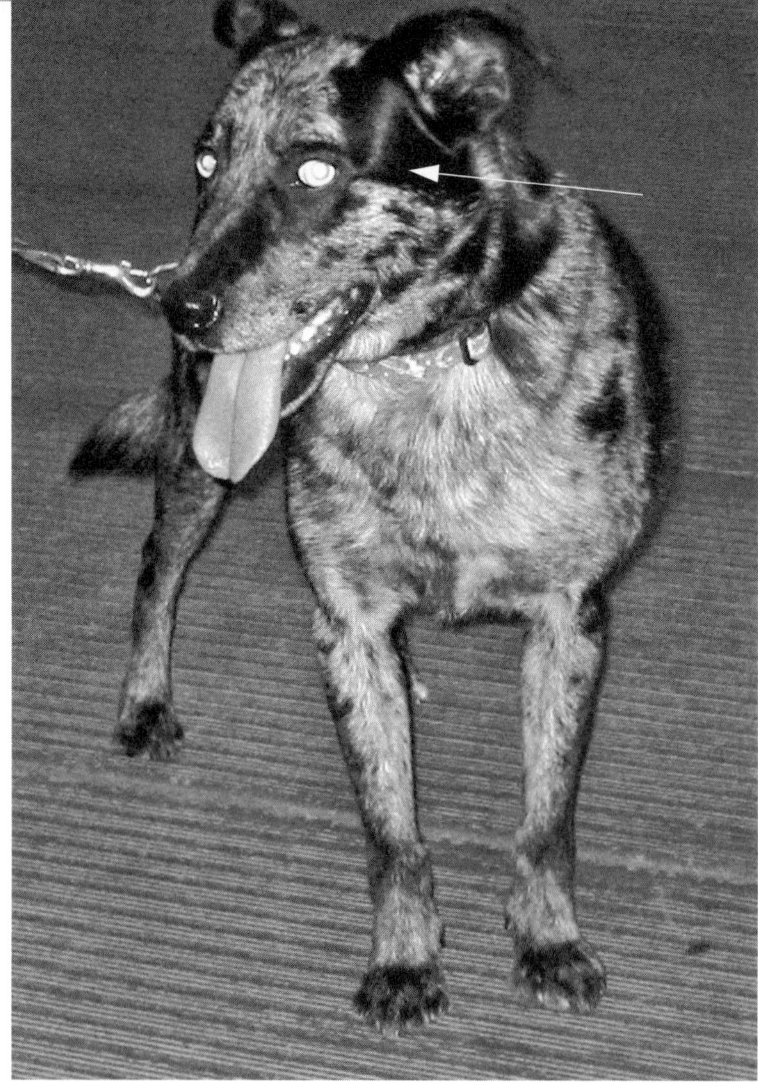

This photograph shows all of the same signals as in the photograph above. In addition, you can see the ridge indicating extreme facial tension above the eye (see the arrow). Merlin looks as if his skin is stretched tightly across his skull.

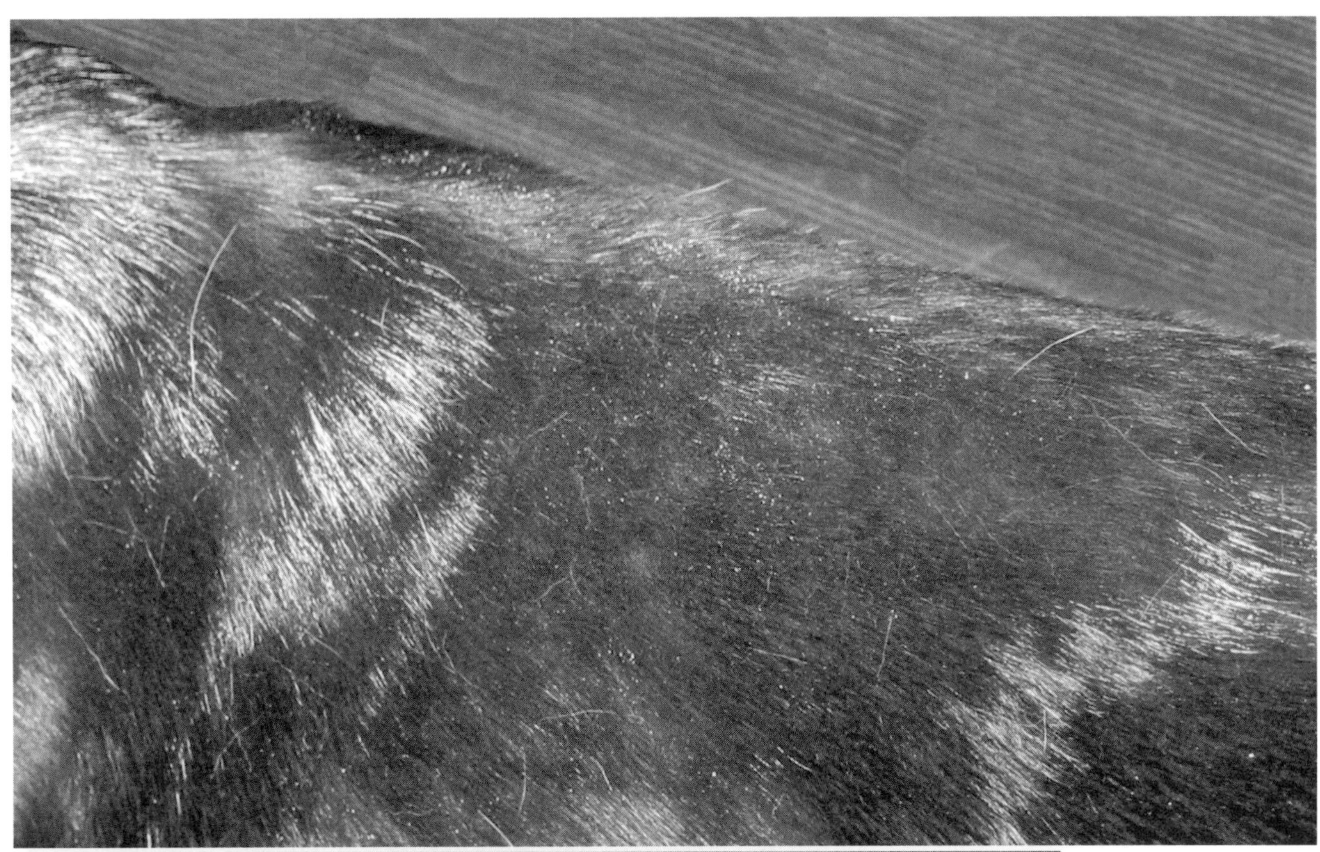

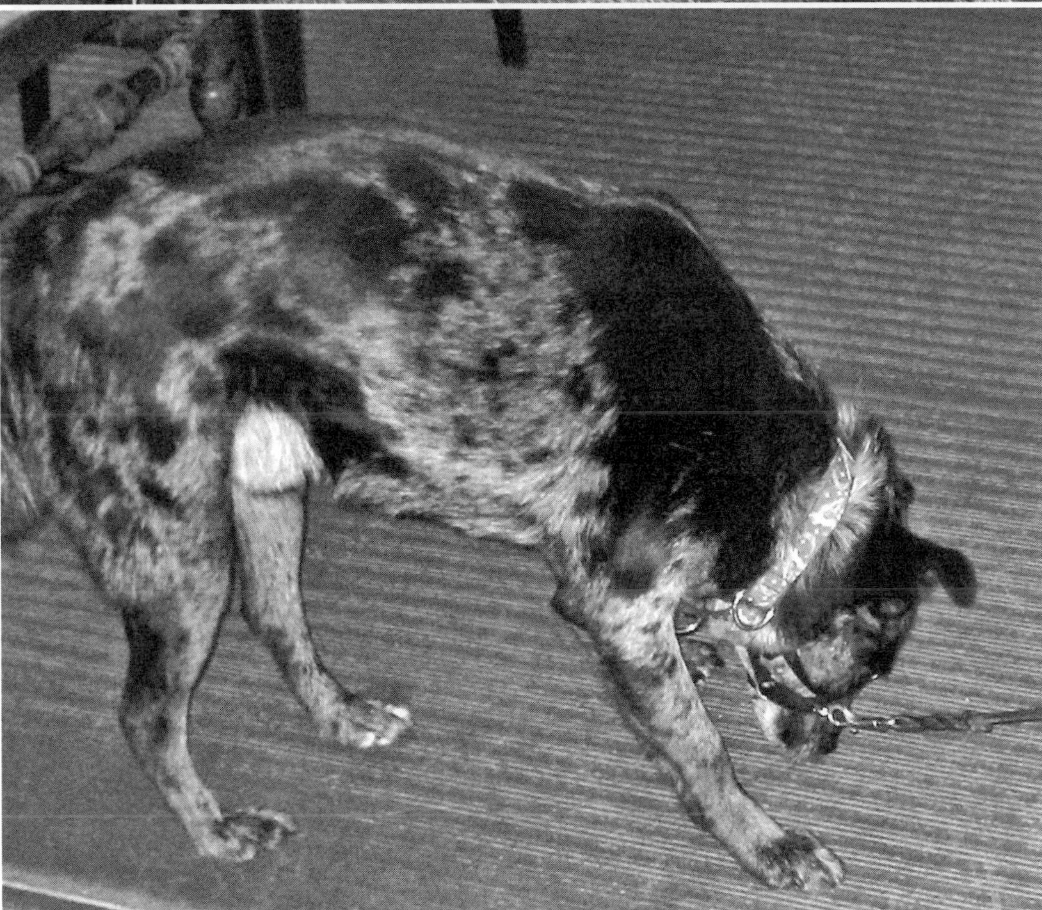

#6.5: Dander & Hair Loss

- sudden, visible dander
- excessive and sudden loss of hair

#6.6: Sniffing

#6.7: Spatulate Tongue & Facial Tension

- shape of tongue, particularly at the end
- ridges around eyes and lips

Here is an example of the spatulate tongue. This dog's tongue is held up tensely. The curling at the end is typical. The tongue is very wide at the bottom due to muscular tension.

#6.8: Stress Signs

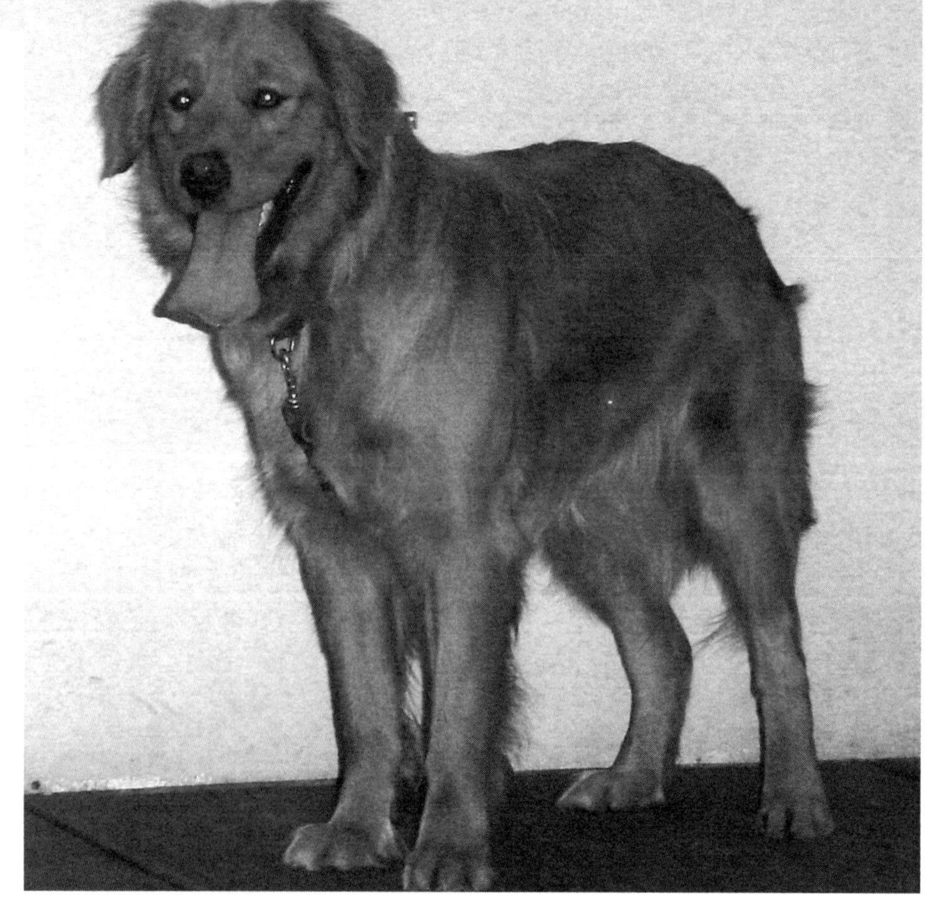

A stressed dog has a somewhat different appearance from a dog who is just hot and panting. In hot and panting dog, the tongue will be lolling out of the dogs mouth, sometimes even off to the side, and will be shaped more by gravity than by muscular effort.

Both photographs show the ridges around the eyes and lips very well. This dog is stressed and there is a lot of tension being held in her face. Notice the ridges below and to the sides of the eyes. Also note the way the lips are long, but, because of muscular tension, there is a forced look to the lips and they are puffed out around the edges. Legs are braced, topline is rounded.

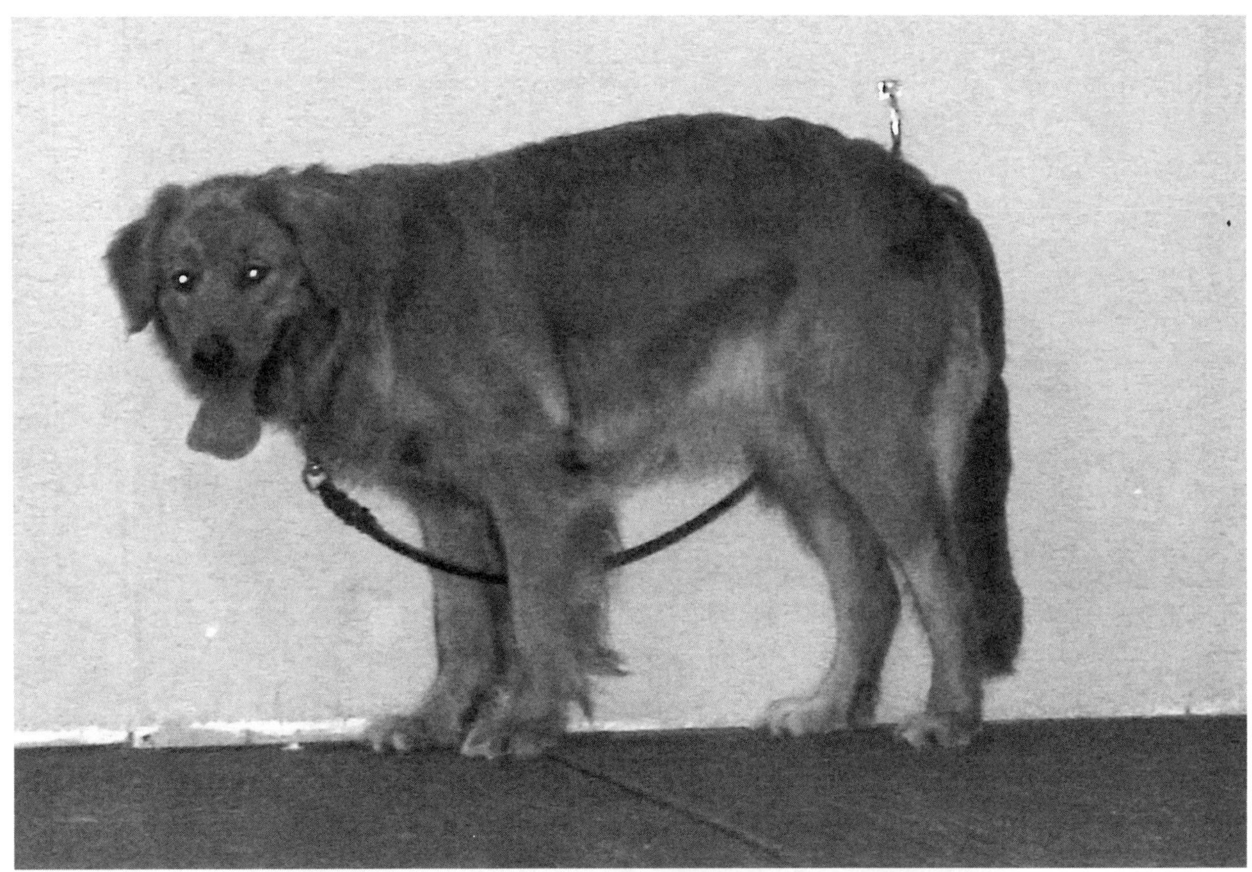

#6.9: Silhouette of stressed dog

- spatulate tongue
- rounded topline
- down tail

#6.10: Tired but Happy

Text for these photographs is on following page.

Text for Photo #6.9 & #6.10:

Photo #6.9: You do not have to see small details to know that in this is a dog who is very stressed. Look at the silhouette alone. The tongue is spatulate and curled up tensely. Her topline is rounded and she has a "hunched over" look. Her tail is not tucked, but just down and hanging limply. Her legs are braced under the body. Her head and neck are lowered.

Looking more closely, you can also see pupil dilation. Her lips are long, but there are ridges around the lips and eyes.

Compare the Golden in Photo #6.9 to Photo #6.10, a Chessie who is just tired and happy. See the differences in the way the body and head are held? Note the difference in the silhouettes, and the shape of the tongue and how the tongue is held.

The Golden in Photo #6.9 is under emotional stress; the Chessie in Photo #6.10 is exhibiting physical stress & exertion.

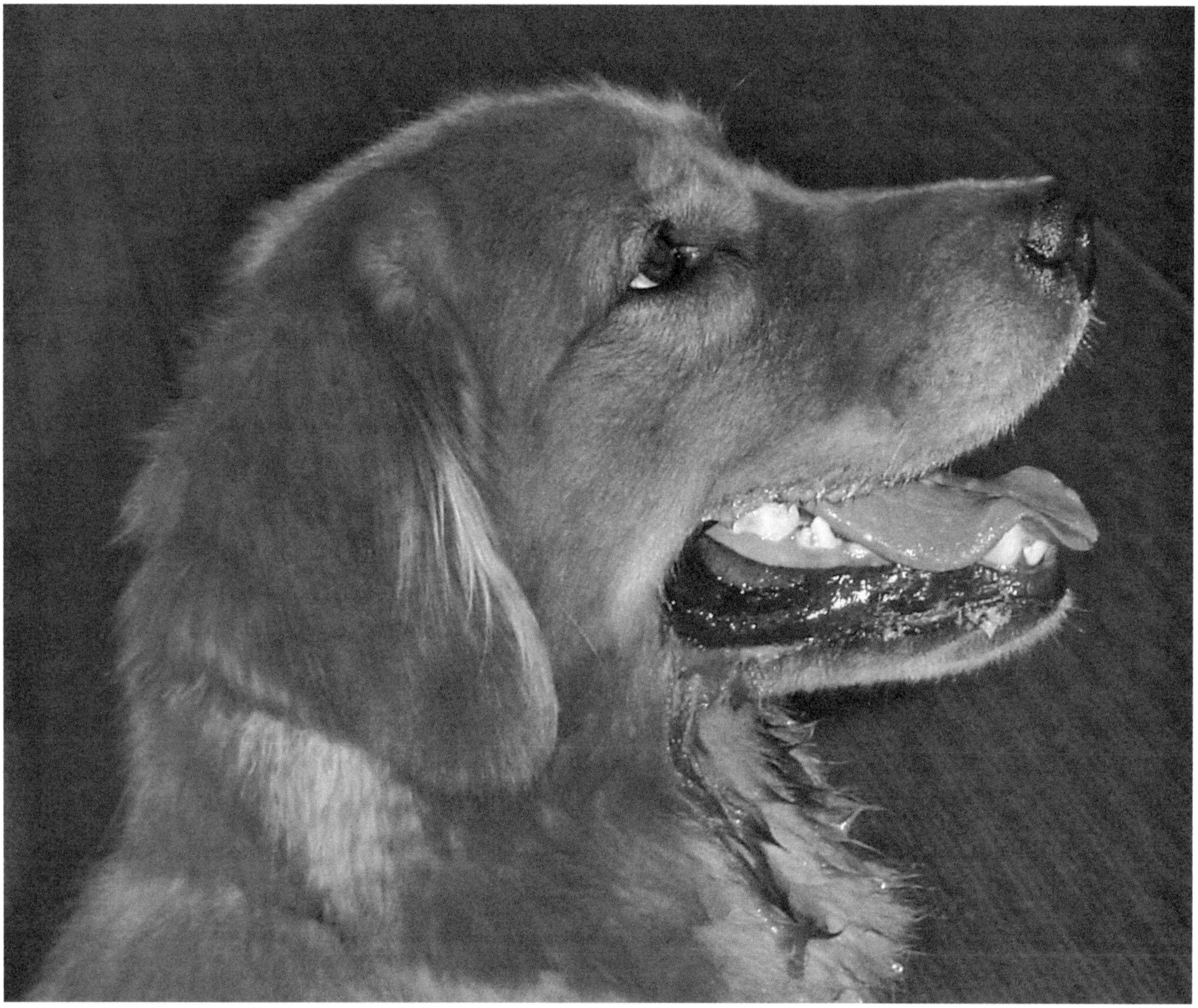

#6.11: Hypersalivation

Hypersalivation is sudden and excessive salivation. Drool will coat the dog. Sometimes dogs with Separation Anxiety will Hypersalivate so extremely, that when the owners come home, the dog is soaking wet and looks as if she had been sprayed with water.

You can see the evidence of hypersalivation from stress in the photo above. The dog doesn't otherwise look that stressed and wasn't acting horribly stressed. But this hypersalivation tells you that the dog was indeed under stress. If you look closely you can also see the ridge at the back of the lips that indicates tension.

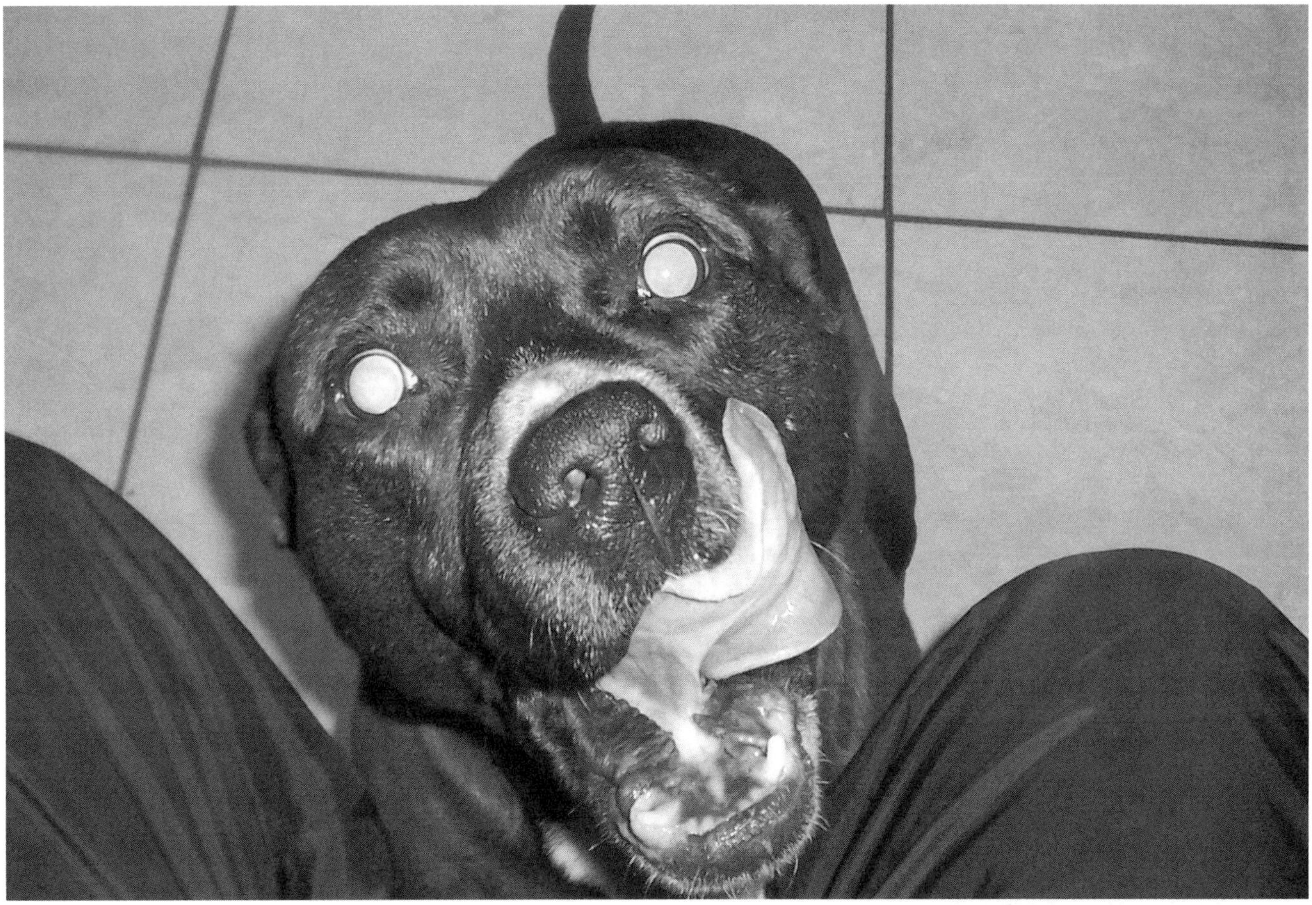

#6.12: What Are You Doing?

- dilated pupils
- Tongue Flick
- flattened ears

In this photograph, Buzz has extremely dilated pupils. She is also exhibiting very flattened ears. That's a pretty expressive Tongue Flick, too! And all this because she was told to Sit and then had a camera staring at her. We often underestimate what will cause a dog to feel extreme social pressure. It doesn't take much for many dogs - anything at all out of the ordinary will do it.

Photo Credits:
Photo #1, #2, #3, #4, #5 & #6: Brenda Aloff;
Photo #7, #8 & #9: Cherish DeWitt;
Photo #10: Joanne Weber;
Photo #11, & #12: Cherish; DeWitt
Photo #13: Rachel Plotinski.

7
FEAR

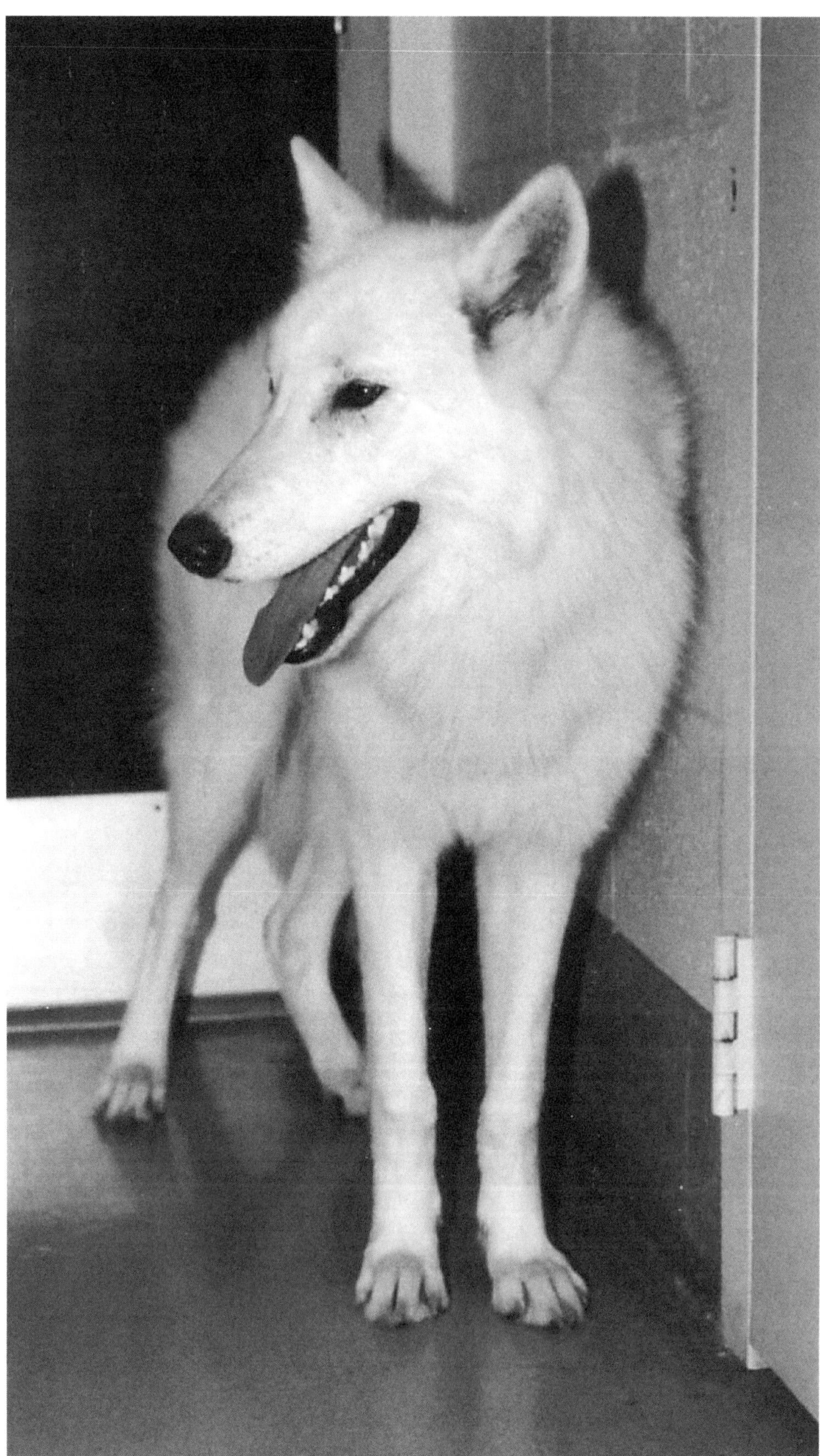

#7.1: Fear & Avoidance

- body is pressing into the wall (moving into pressure)
- ears, to the side
- squinting eyes
- Look Away
- braced front legs
- squatting rear legs
- down tail

This animal is stressed: eyes averted, ears held out to the side, tail down. There is a rigidity about her that tells us these are not signs of neutrality, but of anxiety. The Look Away is one of avoidance, not approachability. What tips me off mostly is the braced rear legs. I bet there are sweaty paw prints on the floor, too.

Her lips are drawn back, and you get a feeling of stillness.

She has pressed herself into the wall. When animals are anxious they will often Move *Into* Pressure. It seems odd, but it is why animals run through fences, or hurt themselves when they get confined and are panicky. It makes sense from a survival standpoint in some instances - if an aggressor has you cornered, blasting through him might be your last chance to save yourself.

In the second photo of this sequence, the dog has backed further into the corner and is giving definite "STOP your approach" signals.

In Photo #7.1, she says "I am anxious." Here, In Photo #7.2, upon closer approach, she went immediately into a defensive position. This is a posture of extreme fear. There are many Extreme expressions of body positions here. This "extreme-ness" indicates the strength of the dog's emotions.

When a dog gives you this kind of body language she is saying she feels trapped. This hallway presents an unfortunate circumstance which places her in a place of no options.

#7.2: Extreme Fear

- the extreme-ness of all theses elements of body posture:
- rounded topline
- ears flattened
- head lowered
- paw lift
- lips drawn way back
- tucked tail

Behaviour Tip: Fear makes an animal extremely unpredictable. If you reach in, the animal may fold, but very likely will explode into action when you ignore the demand to Stay Out Of My Bubble. For more examples of this, see Section 4: Space Invaders.

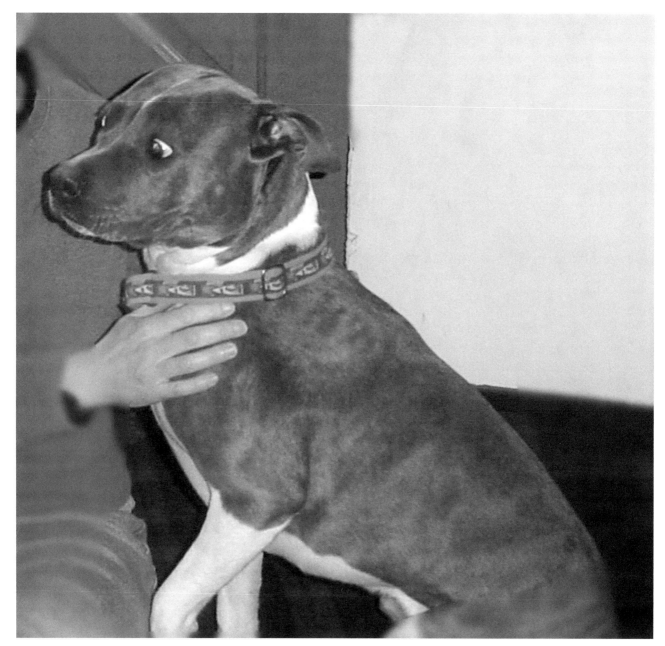

Other signals of fear are body tension and very wide open eyes, to the point where you can see the whites of the eyes. In this photograph, you can see Emma's Whale Eye. You can also see a lot of tension in her face. See the ridge under her eye? Emma is a sweet and soft soul, and has a fair amount of caution. Here, Lori is just asking her to sit still for a moment. Emma's reaction is all out of proportion to what Lori is doing, but that is not our call. Emma has decided she is in some trauma. There is a lot of action going on around her - I have loose dogs running around the kennel and two of us are standing there with a camera. This combination is enough to bother Em.

#7.3: Whale Eye

- wide open eyes
- whites of eyes visible almost all the way around the eye
- Paw Lift
- eyes oriented toward "concern," nose oriented away from

Photo Credits: Photo #1 & #2: Mary Wilmoth; Photo 3: Cherish DeWitt.

8
CAUTION

#8.1: Cautious Approach

- orientation forwards & backwards (conflict)
- braced front legs
- lowered tail

This dog, even though reaching forward, has his hind legs far out behind, as though to keep as much of his body away from the strange human (as in stranger, not weird). His ears are held close to his head, his tail is lowered. But you wouldn't have to look at anything but the general silhouette to see that the dog is approaching something warily. Note that the dog's energy is actually travelling Backward. We can assume the person has a pretty good treat, or the dog might be too wary to approach her at all.

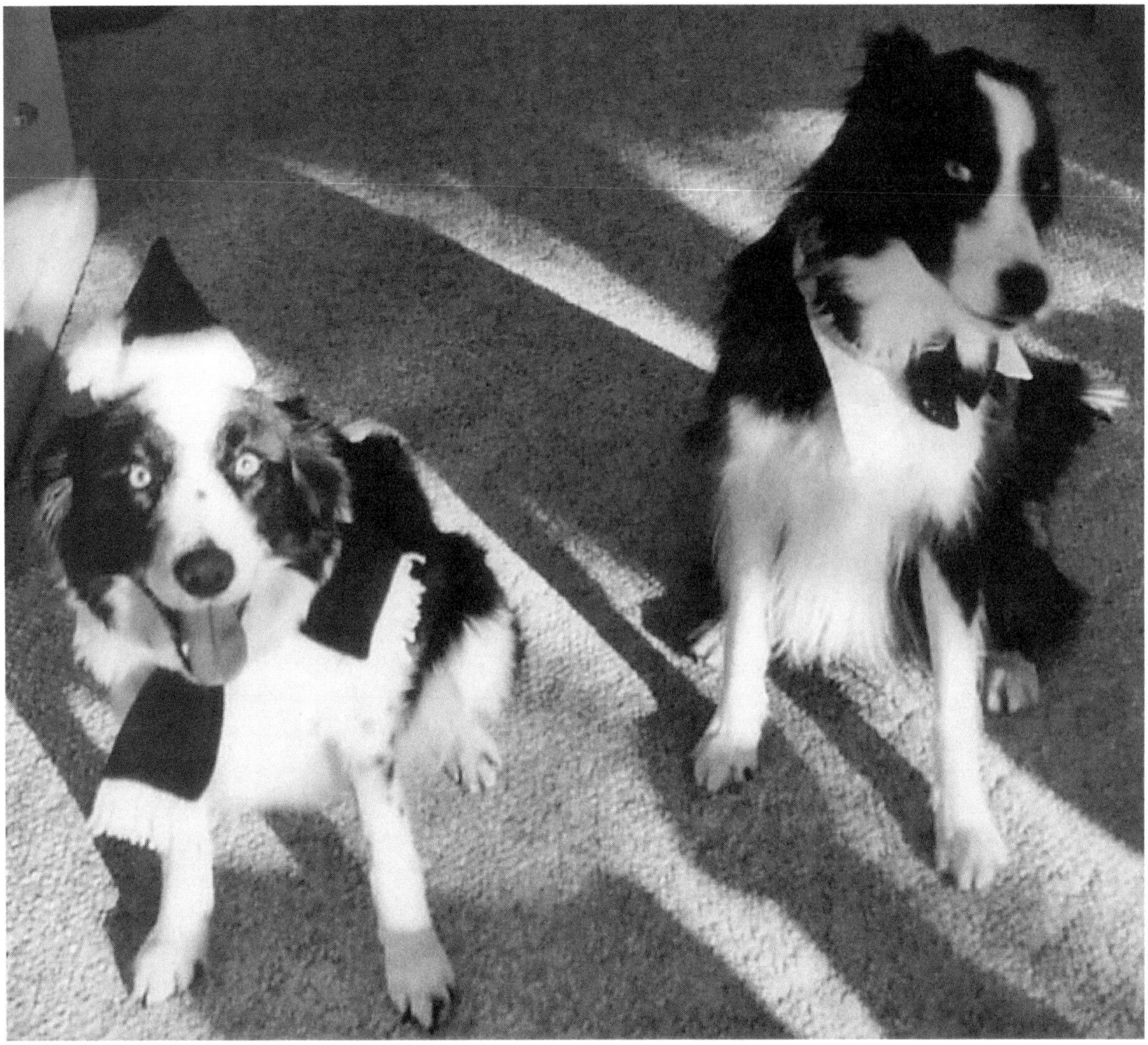

#8.2: Unbothered vs. Cautious

- body posture
- ears
- mouth
- orientation
- orientation of eyes and noses

Rylie, on the left, does not care, even a little bit, about the fact that she is wearing a hat and scarf. She appears to be totally unaware of the photographer as well. The dog on the right, Doc, is worried and uneasy. His ears are back, his mouth is closed, and his body orientation is Backwards rather than Forward. That is, were he to move, you get the distinct feeling that he would move Backwards, away from the direction he is facing, rather than Forwards, into the social pressure he is feeling.

Doc's nose is pointing to the left but his eyes are directed in another direction entirely. His nose tells you the direction he would likely move in as soon as he got up.

Compare that with Rylie, who gives the impression she would move towards the direction she is facing. Rylie's mouth is wide open in a happy grin and she is looking directly at something. Her nose is pointed towards it and so are her eyes.

It is always interesting to know the context, as this can help read the body language. In this case the dogs were placed in a Sit Stay. Rylie is staring at a tennis ball in my hand and Doc just wishes he were not dressed up and people weren't staring at him. Doc has played with Rylie many times and she takes the ball away from him when they do play. Because his eyes are looking at her, with his nose pointing away from her, she is the main cause of his concern. Add the stress of the staring eye of the camera and being told to stay in an uncomfortable social position. Doc is keeping a close eye on Rylie to see what her reaction will be. So I am not certain exactly how many things are bothering Doc, but it is clear he wishes he were somewhere else!

The stuffed bird is obviously an object of curiosity for this dog. Intense interest is evident by the dog's proximity and also in the orientation of the nose - towards the object - and forward-held ears. The dog has stopped moving and is standing still.

But the general impression is still one of caution. Notice the body has a feel of traveling Backward. This time it is not visible in the rear legs, as in the dog in Photo #8.1, but is instead evident in the braced front legs. There is a rounding of the back, as if the dog is ready to gather himself up to move quickly if need be.

Note also the tongue flick, indicating that the dog is Negotiating at this time, rather than using Predatory language. (For information about Negotiation see Section 2: Calming and Negotiation Signals).

Once the initial curiosity is satisfied, some dogs use a Curiosity Bite to test if there is prey potential.

#8.3: Cautious yet Curious

- orientation
- ears forward
- tongue flick
- rounded back

#8.4: Cautious Yet Curious

- braced legs
- body orientation

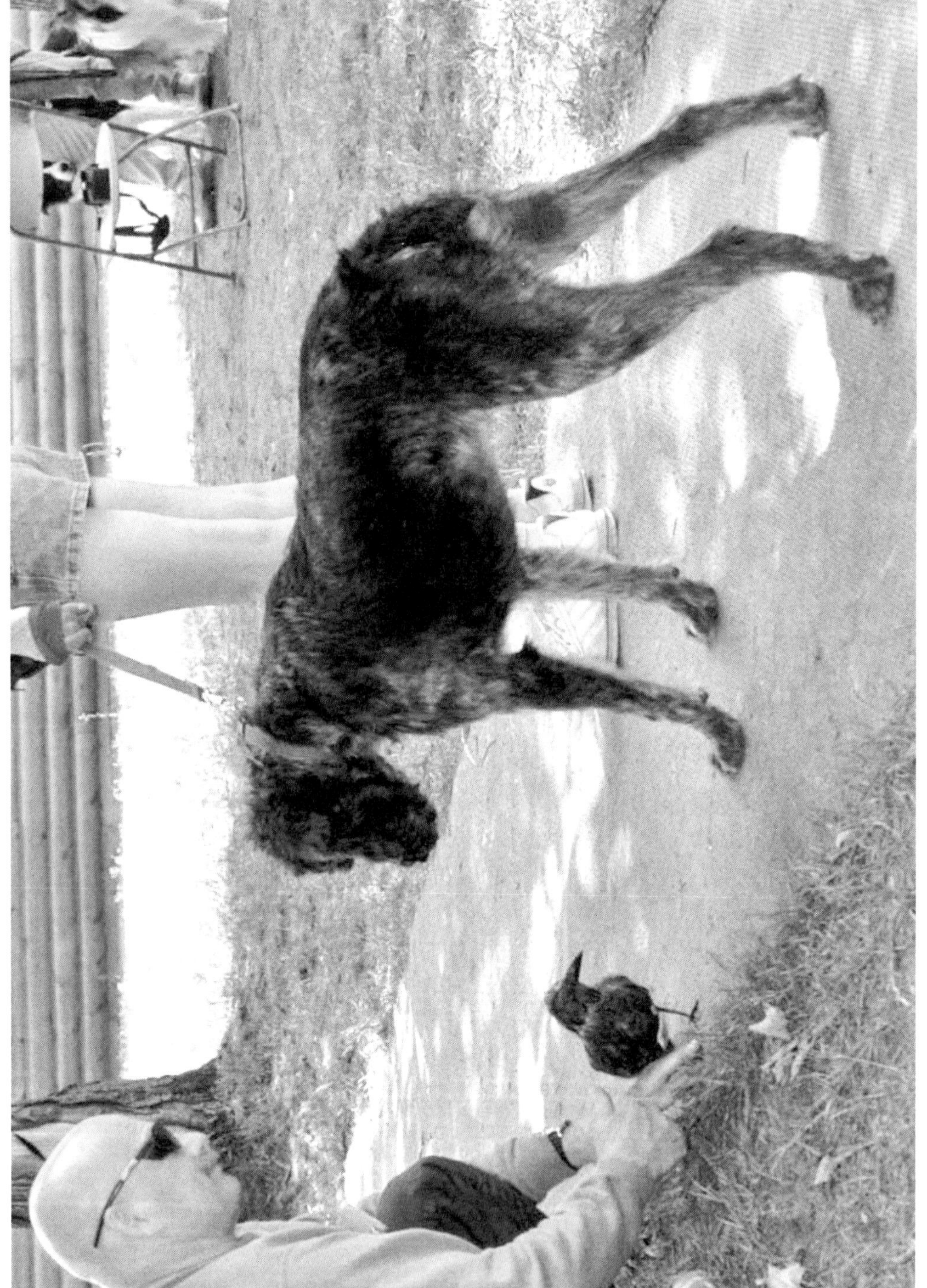

We know this dog is wary because, again, you can see that the dog's legs are braced. With this dog, the front legs are braced AND he has his hind legs out rather far behind. The tail is slightly tucked.

Dogs who are curious, but wary, will often have either a lowered back (here), or a slightly rounded back. (See Photo #8.3). This dog, too, has stopped moving forward and is standing still.

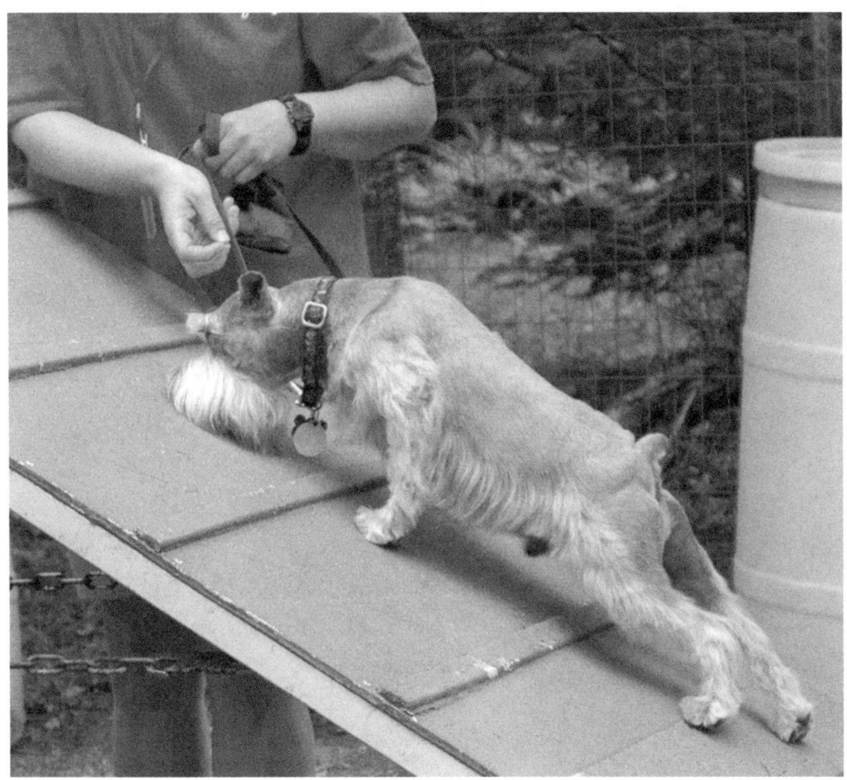

#8.5: Caution

- ears held back
- braced front legs
- sniffing and not paying attention to the food treat the owner is holding.

From Cautious to Confident. As this dog gains in his physical awareness and realizes he can easily cope with this new situation, his body language changes drastically. See him show more confidence in Photo #8.6, as he moves along the dog walk.

In this photograph you can observe all the signs of caution - keeping as much of his body Backward and Away as possible. Slow movement. The rear legs are stretched behind the dog, the front legs are braced. The ears are back. This dog is a pretty self-reliant boy, though. Look at that tail. Even though he is feeling cautious, his emotion is not so extreme it has caused the tail to drop level with the back. It is still at a jaunty angle.

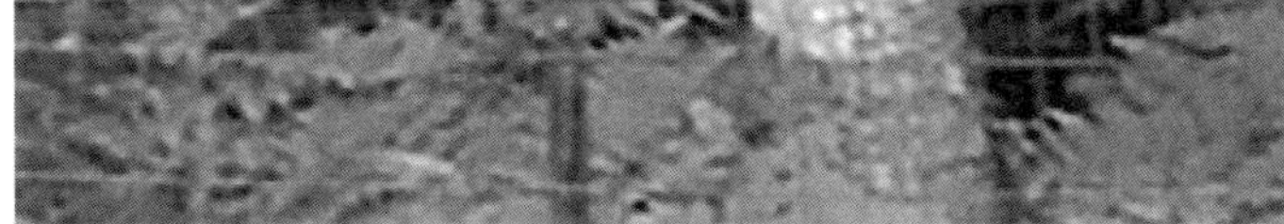

#8.6: Confident But Careful

- tail down slightly in concentration
- ears at half-mast

Here, you can see all the signs of a dog concentrating. He is confident, though - he is moving forward. The head is lowered, looking where he is about to place his feet. The tail is slightly below the "jaunty angle" of being held vertically, as in the photo above. Dogs often lower their tail, even curling it downward, when they are really concentrating on something. Sometimes people mistake this lowered tail during concentration for a form of submission. His back is neither roached nor lowered, and his ears are relaxed and in a neutral position, indicating comfort with the task at hand.

Photo Credits: Photo #1, #3, #4, #5, #6: Joanne Weber; Photo #2: Candy Smith.

9
Anxiety & Avoidance

#9.1: Anxiety & Avoidance

- "hiding"
- silhouette shows crouching
- rounded back
- bracey front legs
- paw lift
- proximity - moving INTO pressure

This is a dog I worked with at a clinic. Hiding her face is not the object for this animal. She is using Avoidance behaviours instead of confident coping behaviours. Feeling overwhelmed, vulnerable and anxious, she demonstrates Moving Into Pressure intensely. No one is threatening her in this context; she is uncomfortable with my proximity alone, even in the absence of threat. She is also very likely worried because I am not allowing her to "control" my movements.

Dogs may use this specific tactic in one of many ways. Hiding the face can be a form of not having to look at the environment. Although I see this as an extreme and dysfunctional (avoidance in the absence of threat) Look Away, it is better than lunging and barking.

Moreover, I see this as a way the dog can effectively change the subject. When she does not wish to follow through with a known cue, or if she feels the task is a bit unpleasant, she will use pushing into the handler as a distraction. This works really well, as it prevents the handler from moving forward. A dog will also use this strategy if she feels over-faced (no skill set for the current situation) or confused.

This behaviour demonstrates the tendency of many mammals to "Move Into Pressure" when they feel upset or panicky. It certainly indicates an animal that has just gone "Hind Brain" on you.

Another form of this behaviour is when the dog keeps repeatedly jumping and/or climbing on the handler.

> *Training Tip*: As a training issue, I treat this like I treat all anxiety: I discourage it. Instead, I encourage my dogs to "stand on their own feet" and do not allow them to lean on me when they are anxious. I ask the dog to do a simple task she already knows how to do, and then reinforce her heavily for Thinking and Responding rather than Reacting, as this dog is doing.
>
> By allowing the dog to remain in this position, you only validate her discomfort. It is just like cooing over the dog when she is afraid. What the human intends as reassurance, the dog takes as validation for the fear: "Oh, you like me to be silly and afraid and anxious."

#9.2: I Wish I Weren't Here

- Look Away
- ears held back
- white around the eyes
- lack of body tension

I had to chuckle when I saw this photo, as I have seen this expression on my own dogs' faces many a time! This is recognized by many dog owners as the "Nail Clipping" face.

I think of this dog's expression more as dismay than anxiety. It is clear that the dog is Quite Disappointed as regards the current status quo.

The owner is placing a small "mitten" on the dog's foot so he can teach the dog to dip the mitten in some paint and then create a painted picture by pawing or "targeting" a watercolor board or canvas. The pulled-back ears, the Look Away (averted eyes), and the closed mouth tell us that this little terrier can hardly believe his fate. Yet there is still a lack of tension in the body, and the eyes remain soft. This little dog obviously trusts his young owner and has learned that humans just do weird stuff sometimes!

The real intent here is Avoidance. The dog Looks Away and does not engage or participate: "I'm Not Listening." If he were human he would have his little hands over his ears and he'd be chanting "I can't hear you, I can't hear you..."

Background: This person raised the Border Collie on the left, but got the one on the right as a rescue. The rescue dog is still fearful due to past experiences. Life was not predictable for her until she moved into her lovely new home.

#9.3: Confidence vs. Uncertainty

- direction dog is looking
- compare body postures

Both dogs are interested in what the owner has. This photo shows the varied response of two dogs to the exact same stimuli. The dog on the left is very confident and self-assured.

The dog on the right is reticent about approaching and anxious, although there is no threat evident. You can tell this by the lowered body posture, the drawn back ears and the squinty eyes. She has that look of the dog who is in a classic Approach-Avoidance conflict: "I would like to come nearer, but I just can't see my way to it right now because 'something' internal is preventing me from approaching." Although her eyes and nose are oriented one way, her body is in conflict with that. You get the feeling that her body is going the opposite direction that her attention is going. When a dog is in conflict or uncertain, often his attention (nose & eyes) is focused one way, but his body orientation indicates Energy In The Opposite Direction. You get the feeling that if the person moved suddenly, the dog would move away from the person, not towards her.

#9.4: Anxiety

- orientation backwards
- rounded topline
- tucked tail
- ears forced back
- long lips
- braced legs behind
- paw lift in front

Here, shown nail clippers by her owner, Amy, Blaze immediately goes from a happy, wagging dog into one showing the first signs of anxiety. Her body orientation is Backwards even though she is still looking at Amy, that demon with the nail clippers. We can see the beginning of a paw lift on the right front. Her ears are down, her tail is tucked, but we don't even need these details - you can tell just by the silhouette of this dog that she is anxious and will probably go into some sort of avoidance behaviour.

And she does.

#9.5: Retreat

- ears drawn back
- tail down
- moving away from the "pressure"

Sure enough, when Amy said kindly, "Come here, Blaze," this is the view we got. Blaze moved away, just as her body language suggested she would.

Below is the sideways view of the retreat. Look at the lowered head, ears forced back and squinty eyes. The tail is tucked, and her rear quarters are tucked underneath her body, causing a rounded topline.

#9.6: Retreat

- held back ears
- tail tucked
- lowered head
- rounded hindquarters
- squinty eyes

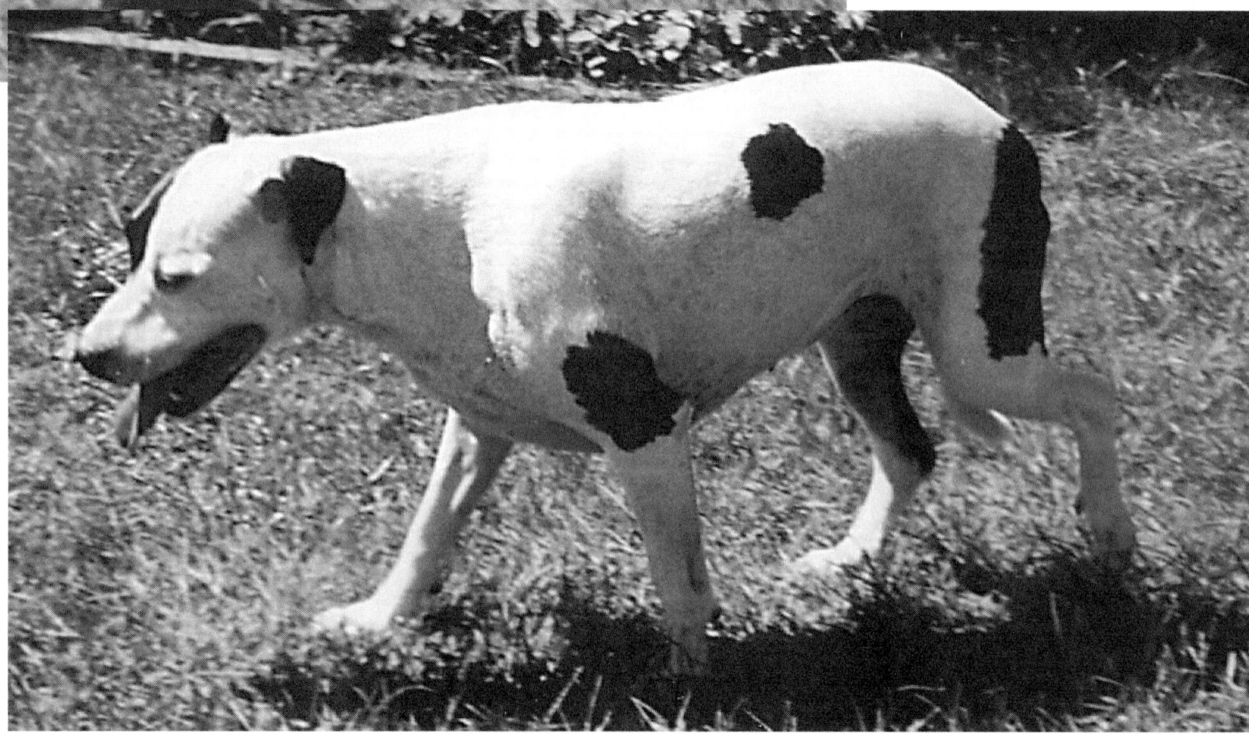

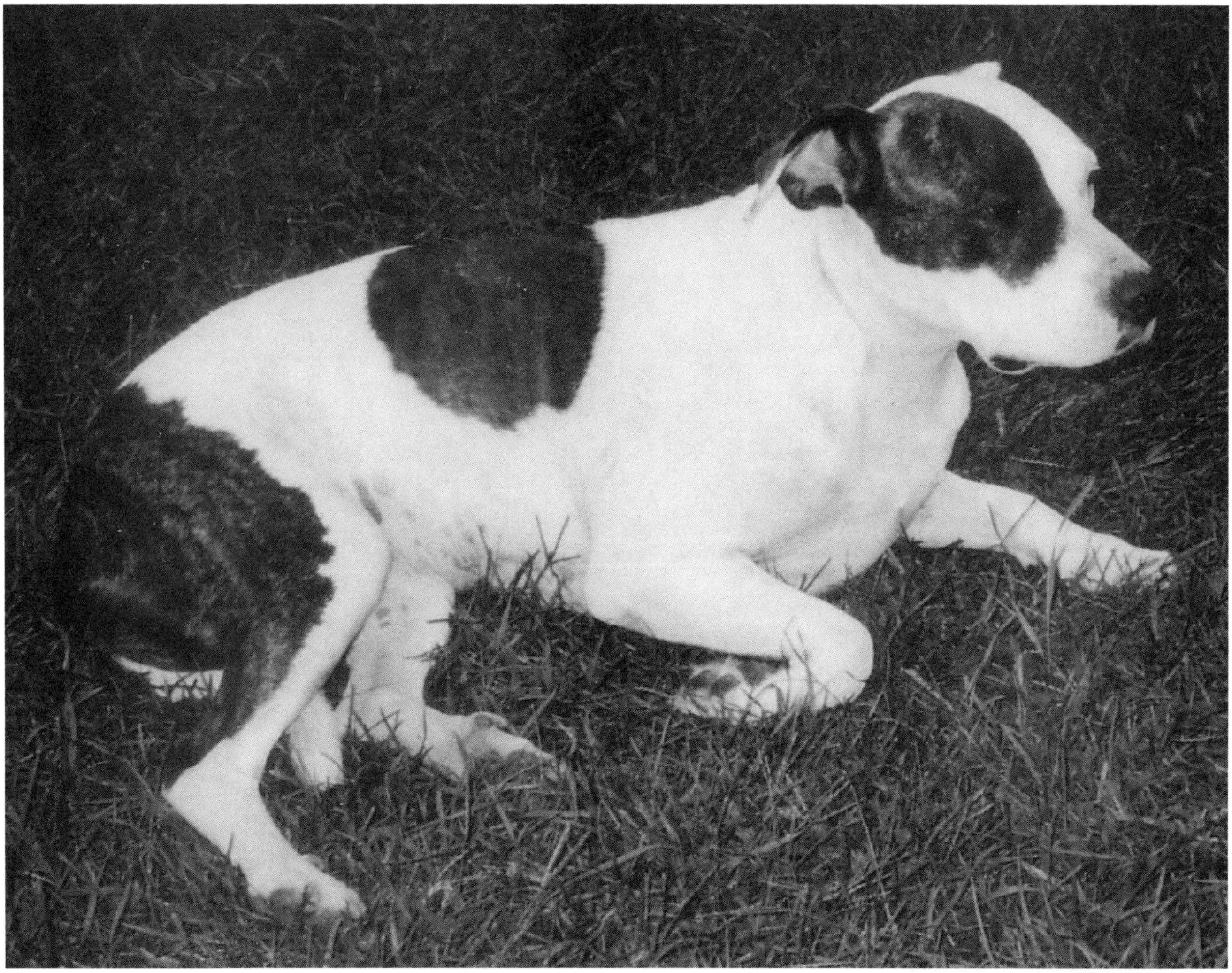

#9.7: Avoidance

- body position
- rounded back
- tucked tail
- avoidance of eye contact

When Amy followed her and caught up to her, Blaze laid down. Notice that Blaze clearly refuses to look at Amy (who is right in front of the photographer), as well as her rounded back and tucked under rear quarters. Her tail is tucked between her legs. Her paw is curled under, which, in this case, is a lying down version of a paw lift. The lying down is a Calming Signal.

Observation Tip: Avoidance is often accompanied by moving away with a lowered body posture, even if the dog is looking toward you.

Avoidance is also expressed by looking away from whatever is the bothering factor. You are the bothering factor if you are, for instance, holding the nail clippers. The moving away or looking away will often be accompanied by Tongue Flicking or Lip Licking.

Photo Credits: Photo #1: Brenda Aloff's Camera; Photo #2: Joanne Weber; Photo #3, 4, & 5: Brenda Aloff; Photo #6: Joanne Weber; Photo #7, 8, 9 & 10: Amy Morris.

Smile, Smile, Smile

These gruesome grimaces are happy dogs. While a dog smile can appear to be savage, the dog doing the smiling is communicating a happy, excited or submissive message - or a combination of all three.

Some individuals use a Smile at the drop of a hat, and others never use the "submissive grin" or smile at all.

#10.1: Smile

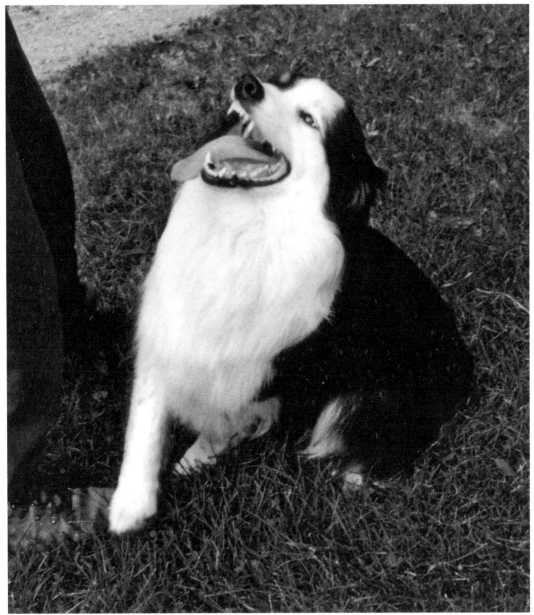

- Paw Lift
- lips long
- eyes squinty
- ears drawn back

Sky Smiles winsomely at her owner. Note the Paw Lift. Her ears are back, her tongue is hanging out of her mouth.

Sky is a super squishy, or submissive dog. She has been that way since she has been a puppy, and Janea, her owner, has worked very diligently to help Sky gain self-confidence. Sky Smiles upon a majority of human approaches, including when Janea approaches her.

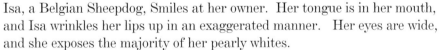

(Sorry about the photo quality, old photograph, and taken with a disposable camera...)

Isa, a Belgian Sheepdog, Smiles at her owner. Her tongue is in her mouth, and Isa wrinkles her lips up in an exaggerated manner. Her eyes are wide, and she exposes the majority of her pearly whites.

Isa is quite ferocious looking when she Smiles, but one of the give-aways is the Paw Lift. Another clue that this is not a nasty, vicious snarl, is the nearly Sitting position. Also, compare this silhouette to the silhouettes of the dogs who are in the *Puppy Licking* chapter.

Isa's personality could not be more different than from Sky. Isa is a bold, pushy, "I Am In Charge Of The Universe" kind of gal.

#10.2: Smile

- lack of tension
- lips long
- eyes wide
- ears half-mast

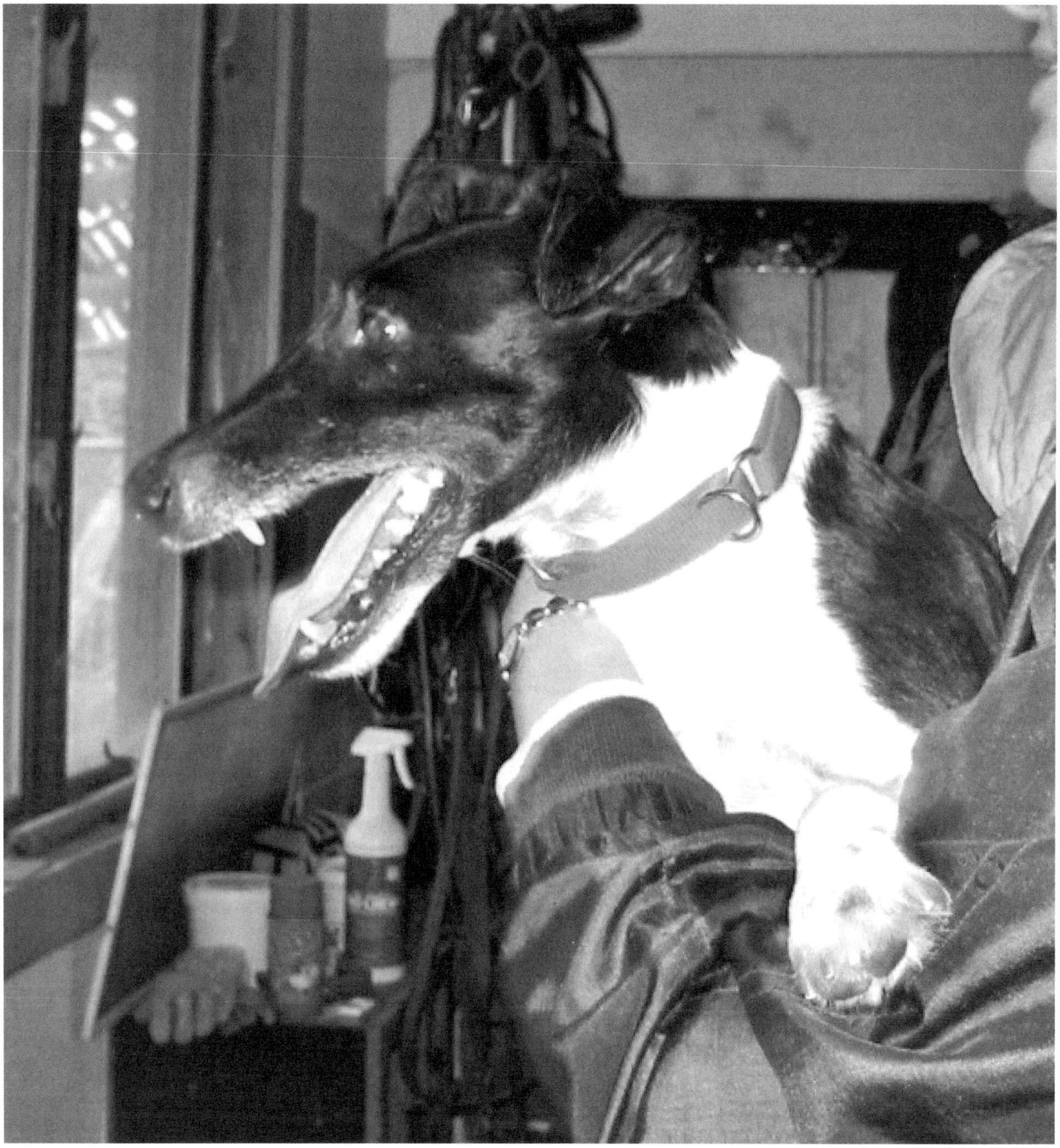

This is Dervish, whom I raised from a puppy and whose father was my daughter's Junior Handling dog. I kept Dervish until he was four-years old, and put a Championship and a Hunting title on him. Then, laboring under a huge volume of dogs that I had rescued (and who were "unplaceable"), I placed him with Karen Sirrine. He has a fantastic home with her. When she goes out of town I get to watch him. In this series of photographs, Dervish was beside himself. His old mom and his new mom, all at the same time! Overwhelmed with glee at seeing Karen (after a week without her) and having me there at the same time, set Dervish whirling from her to me in great excitement. When Karen scooped him up, he commenced with these great grins.

#10.3: Smile Variety - Photo Essay

- lips long
- eyes normal shape
- ears half-mast

Dervish uses a little Grin of delight. He raises his upper lip slightly to show the tips of his canines.

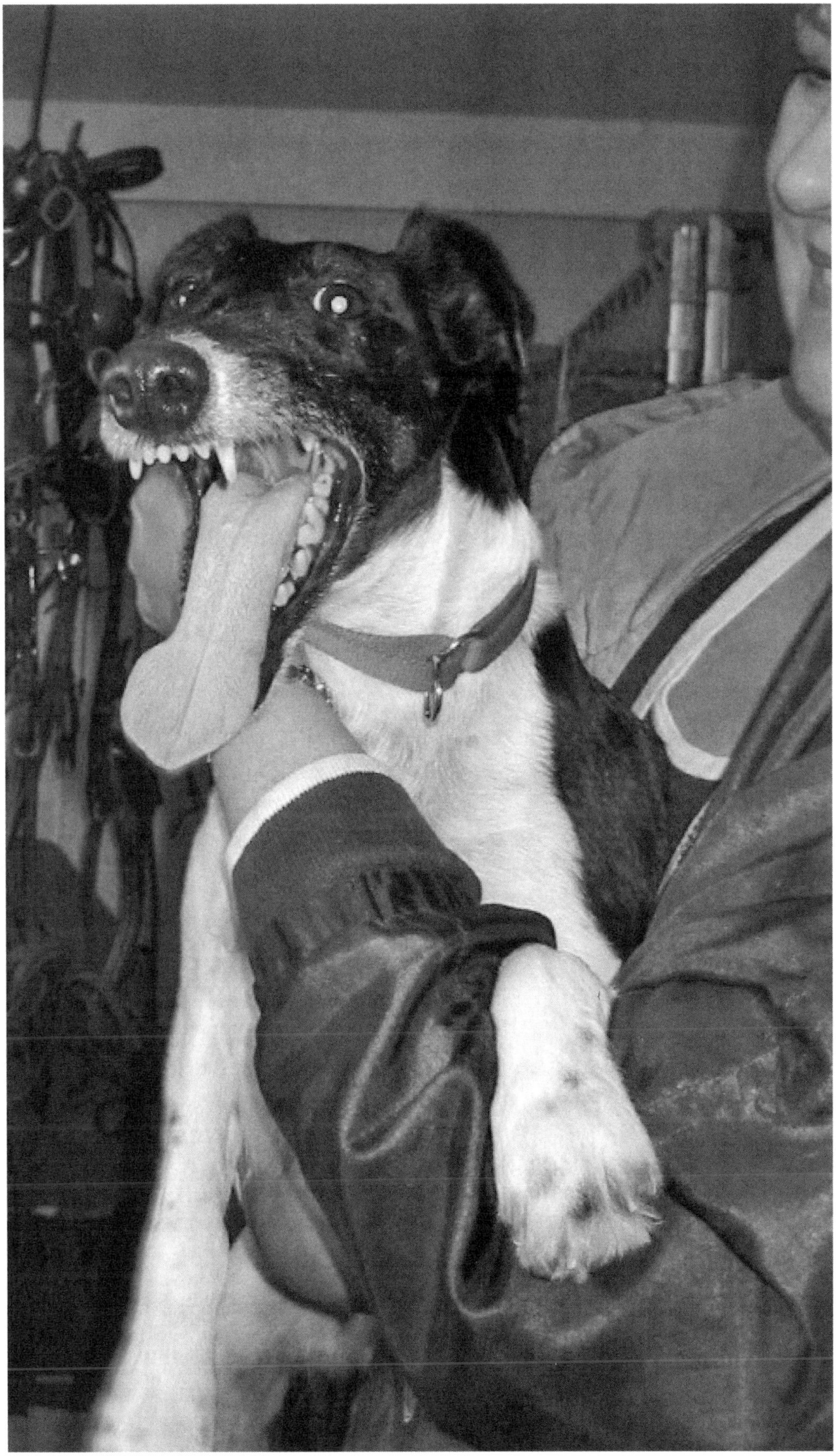

This photograph and the one immediately following were taken within about 2 seconds, so you get a good "front" and "side" view of the same behaviour.

Dervish has his ears held back at half-mast. His tongue is out and his eyes are Blinking. His upper lip is pulled up to show the canine teeth, and his lower lip is also pulled down to show the bottom teeth.

Just as an interesting bit of trivia: Dervish's father was also a big "Smiler," as is his daughter. Smiling tendencies run in breeds, too - ask any Belgian Sheepdog or Tervuren owner.

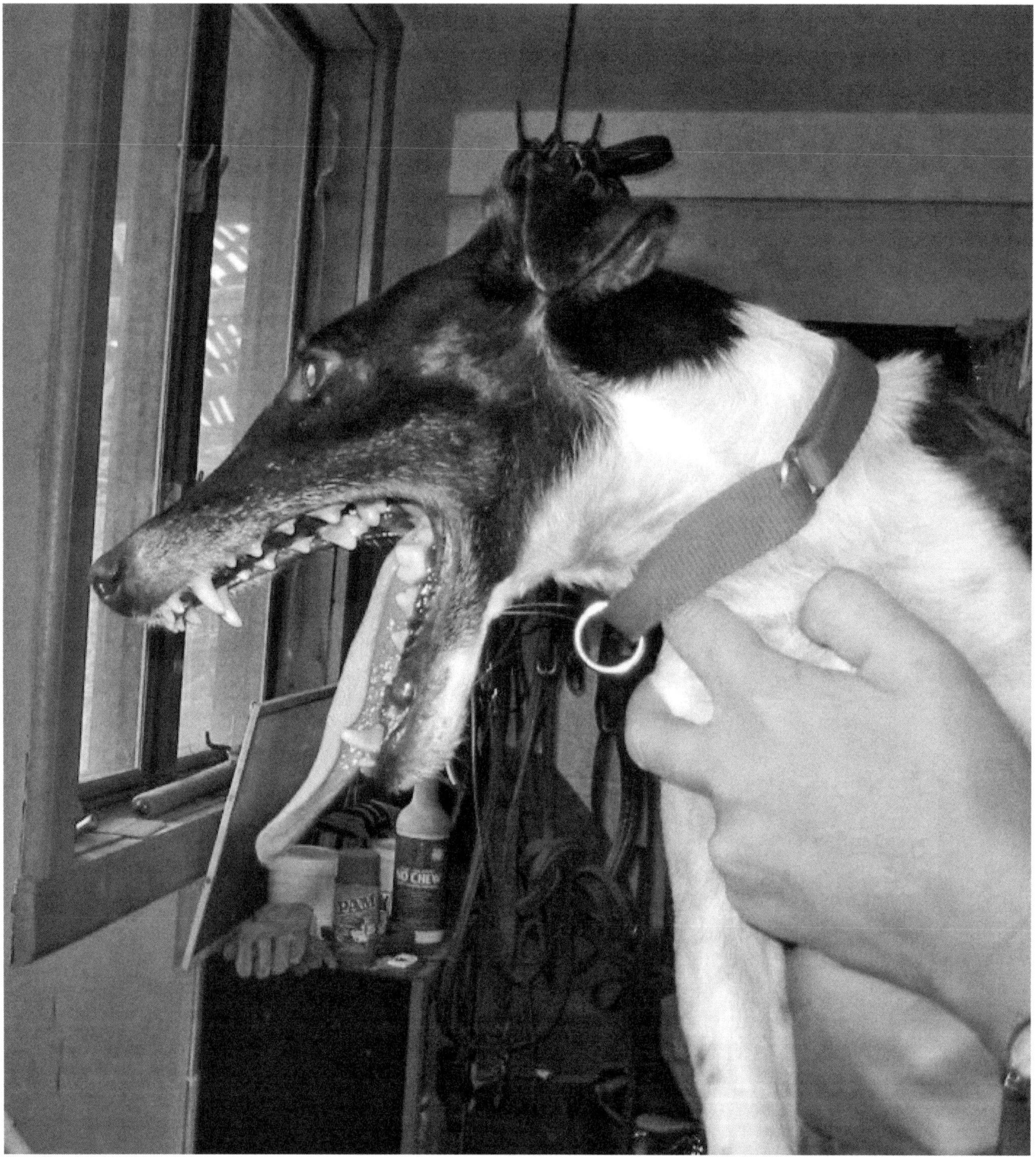

You can see how long Dervish's lips are in this photograph. He is beginning to squint his eyes a little in this photograph. His tongue is still out and he is panting in excitement.

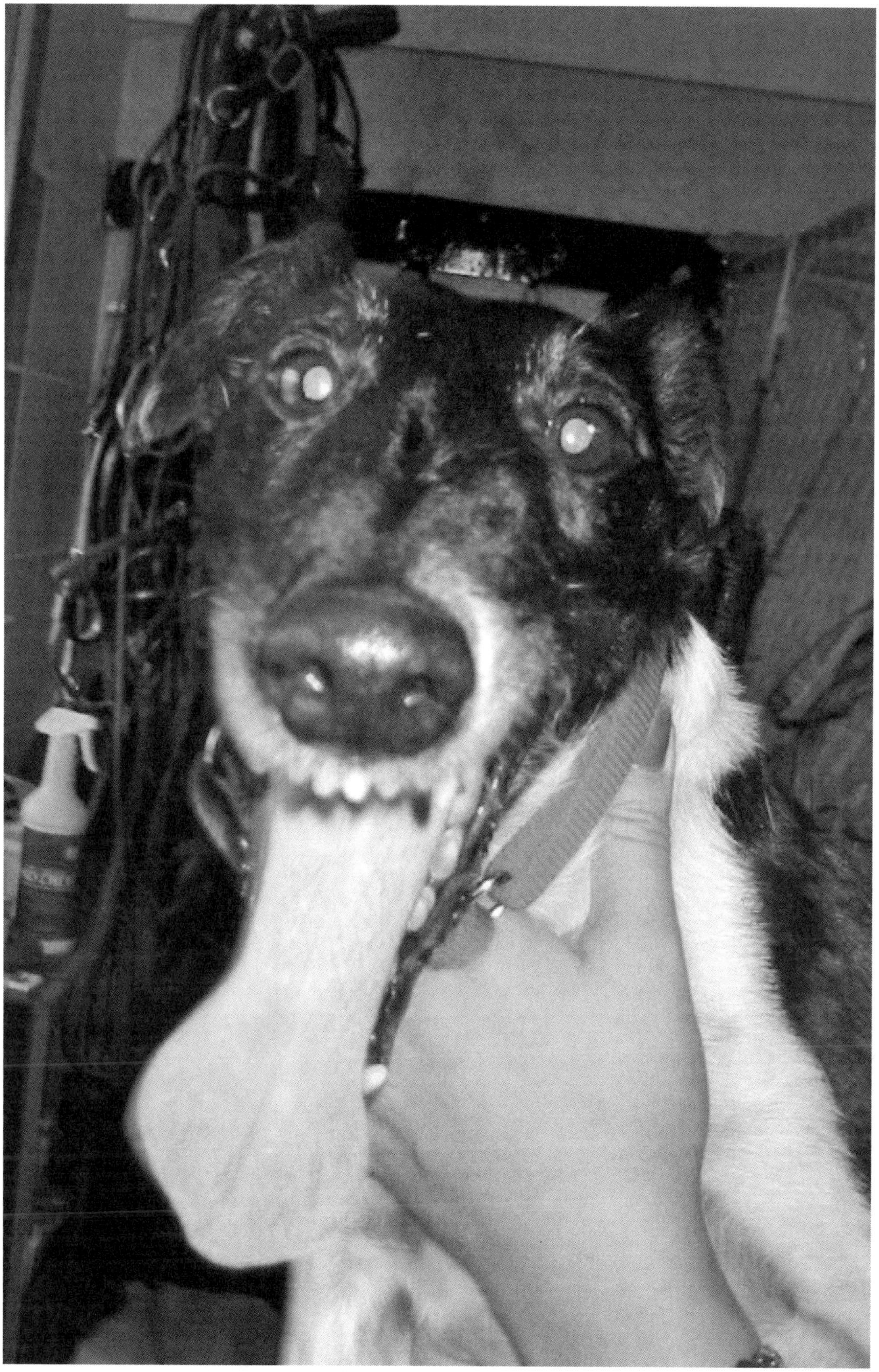

This is one deleriously excited and hap-hap-happy dog! You cannot help but share in his joy of being surrounded by people he likes. The spatulate tongue shows the stress. Remember, not all stress is "bad." The excitement is evident in the pupils, which are beginning to dilate.

Photo Credits: All photographs this Chapter: Brenda Aloff.

11
Larko Meets Sheep

In this photo essay, Larko, a five month old Malinois, meets sheep for the first time.

#11.1: Alerting & Uncertainty

- orientation of dog toward object of interest indicates Alerting
- slightly lowered body posture indicates uncertainty or caution
- body tension
- braced rear legs
- moving tail indicates the dog wishes to interact
- piloerector reflex

#11.2: Uncertain But Curious

Larko is obviously entranced, but is not certain what to do with the aliens. Sheep are not the passive and compliant creatures you might think, and Larko senses this. See in the photo to the right how the sheep are giving him direct eye contact? It is a challenge and indicates conflict.

In the top photo you can see the piloerector reflex. This does not, as many people think, indicate aggression. Rather, it indicates insecurity or, at least, that the dog is not certain of the outcome.

He is not frightened and retreating, but curious and yet a bit at odds about exactly how to handle the encounter.

#11.3: Sitting used as a Calming Signal

- piloerector reflex evident in both photos
- seated position
- intensity of orientation
- body tension

The ridge of hair standing along Larko's back is evident in both of these photographs. This is a reflexive action and comes from muscular tension along the spine. This dog shows intense interest in the sheep - his overall body tension and his orientation toward the sheep show an unwavering focus.

The dog was not cued to sit by the handler. As we were standing just watching the sheep, Larko chose to sit on his own. This indicates a desire to try to communicate with the sheep, using a Calming Signal, since he hasn't yet categorized them as prey or as companions. What the heck are they anyway?

#11.4: Piloerector Reflex evident

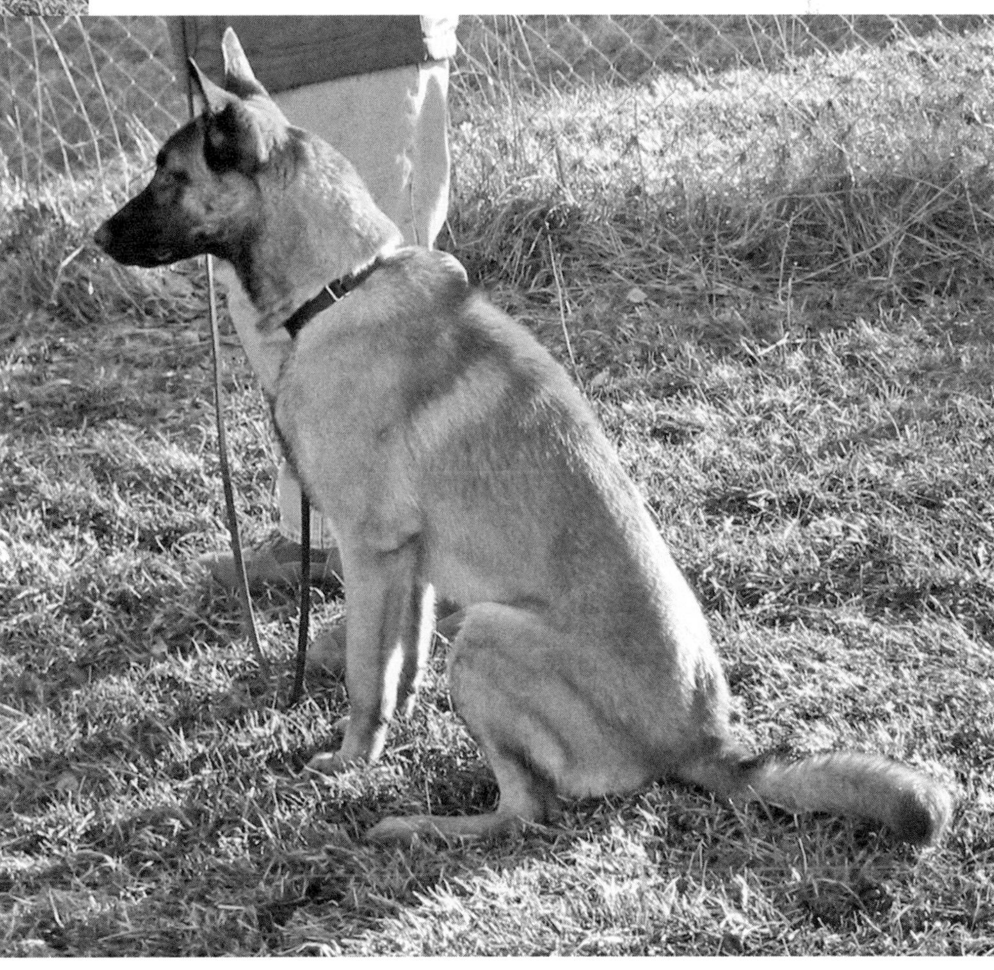

Photo essay by B. Aloff.

Section 2: Calming & Negotiation Signals

Turid Rugaas, in her ground-breaking book, *On Talking Terms With Dogs*, introduced many people to the fascinating world of dog communication. Her book was the first aimed at general readers that explained dog behaviours as deliberate communications. Rugaas classified dog signals in a very accessible way. Her primary classification is of Calming Signals: signals dogs use to "calm" others in the environment.

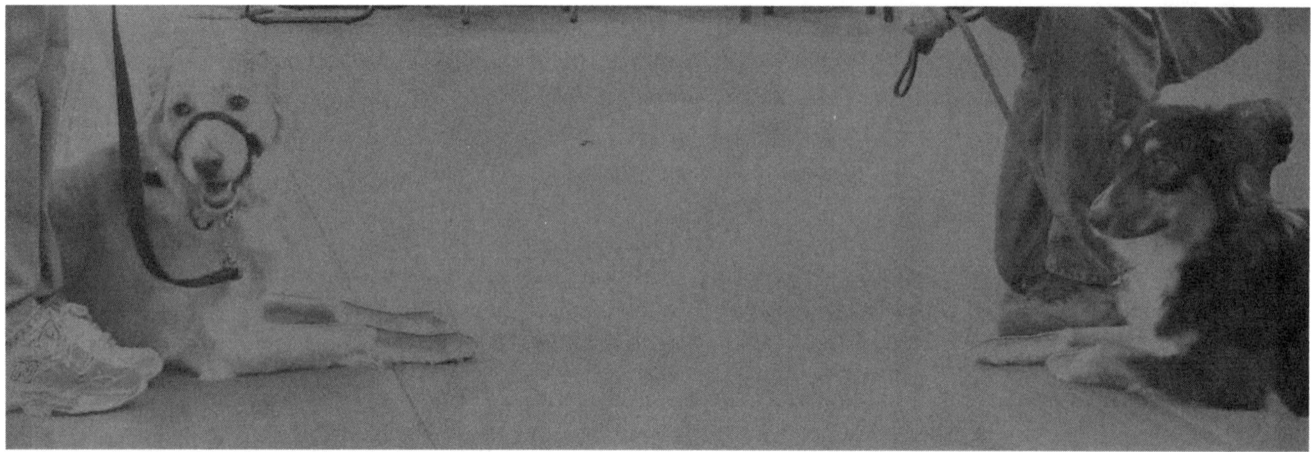

As I watched dogs over the years, I noticed that dogs use these deliberate signals in more than one way. That is, sometimes dogs are trying to create a calmer environment, but other times they are trying to negotiate other things. In particular, controlling personal space is of vital importance to dogs. (And to us as well, but that is a topic for another book!) Dogs are constantly aware of and negotiating the use of their space.

For example, a dog enters a room filled with strange dogs. He repeatedly licks his lips, avoids eye contact with the other dogs, and sniffs obsessively. This dog is using signals to say, "I am not threatening anybody. I wish I weren't here. I am not comfortable." These are classic Calming Signals. This dog is trying to keep himself safe and wants the environment to "calm down."

The obsessive sniffing is also a vacuum activity (displacement behaviour), a familiar behaviour the dog can engage in to avoid focusing on what is causing him stress (that is, to calm himself down as well). Finally, the Sniffing is also simply a sign of stress. In other words, as noted in the previous section, many of these behaviours are both deliberate communications and automatic reflections of the dog's internal state.

The example above is of a passive use of signals to communicate "I am not a threat" to anyone who might be watching. Calming Signals are broadcast to the entire environment and are a way of coping effectively with stress by the thinking (as opposed to the merely reacting) dog. They are deliberate signals, but are directed to a general audience. The dog is, fundamentally, trying only to keep his own personal space safe by calming down everyone around him.

In contrast, I began thinking of specific, deliberate interactions between one dog and another as involving Negotiation Signals. The difference is subtle and lies in the way the dog uses the signals for a more specific purpose. This purpose is less, "Let's all calm down, now" and more, "How are we going to Negotiate an intrusion into each other's personal space?" Negotiation Signals are directed to a specific individual or small group. The negotiation is taking place to avoid conflict over space or possessions.

Here are some examples of Negotiation Signals I have seen my own or friends' dogs use. Rylie, my Border Collie, has a tug toy. Zasu, my Smooth Fox Terrier, longs to play tug, but knows that if she goes up and just grabs at the toy, there will be conflict. Zasu knows this because she and Rylie are both very possessive and frequently

Resource Guard toys from each other. Rylie is lying down and chewing on the toy. Zasu approaches and stops two steps away. She stares at the toy for a couple of seconds - not at Rylie - then does a Look Away. Rylie responds with neutrality; that is, she continues with what she is doing. This allows Zasu to step closer, Look Away again, then orient her nose close enough to put her mouth on the toy. Rylie continues chewing on the toy (a deliberate communication of acceptance), and Zasu begins to tug. Rylie gets up and plays tug with her. Had Zasu stared at Rylie, instead of at the toy, and not used a Look Away, it would have been a direct Challenge. If Rylie had responded to either of the Look Aways or to the approach by Looking At Zasu, that would have constituted a Warning: "Back Off. Mine." The Warning Look is sometimes accompanied by a lip curl and a low growl. When Rylie issues such Warnings, Zasu just backs away and finds something else to do. In this case, though, Zasu and Rylie Negotiated a specific personal space violation and initiated play.

In the *Look Aways* Chapter, Photo #13.7, there is an excellent example of Negotiating a Pass By through another dog's personal space. Penny, the Sheltie, rules Rachel's household with an iron paw. Penny is lying on a rug in a hallway, chewing on a bone. The White Shepherd wishes to walk by, but it is a small, enclosed area. To walk by Penny, she must Negotiate passing through Penny's personal space, which Penny is likely to protect with some intensity because she has a valuable resource, the bone. The White Shepherd does not want the bone, just to get by. First and foremost, the White Shepherd must communicate that the bone does not exist as far as she is concerned! To obtain permission to enter Penny's space, she moves slowly through the hallway, using a beautiful Look Away: "I don't see you, I don't see the bone, I am non-threatening." As she Passes By, she keeps her head averted and stays as far away from Penny as possible. Penny acknowledges this communication by continuing her activity. The White Shepherd has Negotiated Safe Passage.

In another example, Zasu is lying on the sofa. Because she is there first, she is On Territory. Punch, my other Smooth Fox Terrier, wishes to get up on the sofa and lie down, too. Since all my dogs are very sensitive about personal space (I know how to pick 'em!), they use a lot of polite signals to each other and do not encroach without permission. Punch walks up to Zasu and looks at her with Blinking eyes. Zasu does not react. Punch Licks her Lips and then jumps up and lies down next to Zasu. Punch & Zasu have Negotiated sharing personal space.

Negotiations are essential to peaceful coexistence but their use does not guarantee a peaceful encounter. They can be rejected or fail. Take this incident: two of my male Smooth Foxies are nose-to-nose at the start of a personal space conflict. Sport uses a Look Away and a Lip Lick as Negotiation Signals. Evidently, by this point, Sherman wasn't interested in Negotiation because he continued to stare at Sport, giving Sport a definite refusal of the Negotiation. Sport, seeing this refusal and vulnerable now with his neck exposed to Sherman, was still for a second and then attempted a Grab-bite. Sport was smart to try Negotiation first because Sherman had more status and typically won any conflicts. (I stepped in here, of course, and separated the errant boys.) Just because dogs use Negotiation signals doesn't mean that they will, in fact, negotiate a peaceful agreement. Or that the dogs want to be "best friends." Sometimes a dog just wants to save his own butt.

I have had clients' dogs that I was restraining and doing something mildly unpleasant to, such as nail-clipping, use Negotiation Signals with me. Dogs do not *always* use these signals as their first communication. Instead, a dog might first snap at me. I remain non-reactive and continue to restrain the dog. When he is not successful in getting me to back off, he will immediately begin to use Negotiation signals: "Oh, since I cannot bluff or run roughshod over you, can we Negotiate?" Such dogs are accustomed to getting what they want through intimidation, threats, and bullying. When that fails, they use Negotiation as a last resort.

Dogs are potentially violent creatures. The sweet, friendly-to-every-living-thing animal that many like to think of as the iconic dog (Lassie, for example) does not depict the species' true nature. Dogs have a full emotional life, and status and possession are important to them. They are capable of settling conflicts with tremendous force. At the same time, they are social animals who must usually live together peacefully, and this involves constant communication about personal space.

Lest every dog-lover in the world protest in regards to the statement in the previous paragraph, remember that part of being a social creature means that the species has a basically cooperative nature, and strong fixed action patterns (instinctive behaviour) governing a desire to communicate with and get along with others. This means that dogs also have the capacity to be sweet, friendly and good companions.

Each individual dog is somewhere in that precious and complex mix: the predator, the status-aware, the guardian, and the socially gregarious, friendly, cooperative dog.

12 BLINKING

Blinking is always a good sign. If the dog is blinking faster than normal or is blinking slowly - holding the blink, so to speak - it is an intentional communication: "See, my eye contact is friendly."

This Chow is giving lovely clear signals, and we see the acceptance of them in the dog on the right, whose ears and tail are held neutrally and without tension, and whose mouth remains open with a relaxed jaw.

#12.1: Blink combined with Look Away

- blinking
- orientation of nose
- lack of body tension

Observation: Blinking is a Negotiation Signal. It is a Friendly sign, and indicates non-threatening intentions, as well as showing that the dog is relaxed.

It is used when making friendly or neutral eye contact, and, often, as in Photo #12.1, in combination with a Look Away.

The opposite of Blinking is Staring.

#12.2: Blink combined with Look Away

- blinking
- ears half-mast
- orientation of nose
- lack of body tension

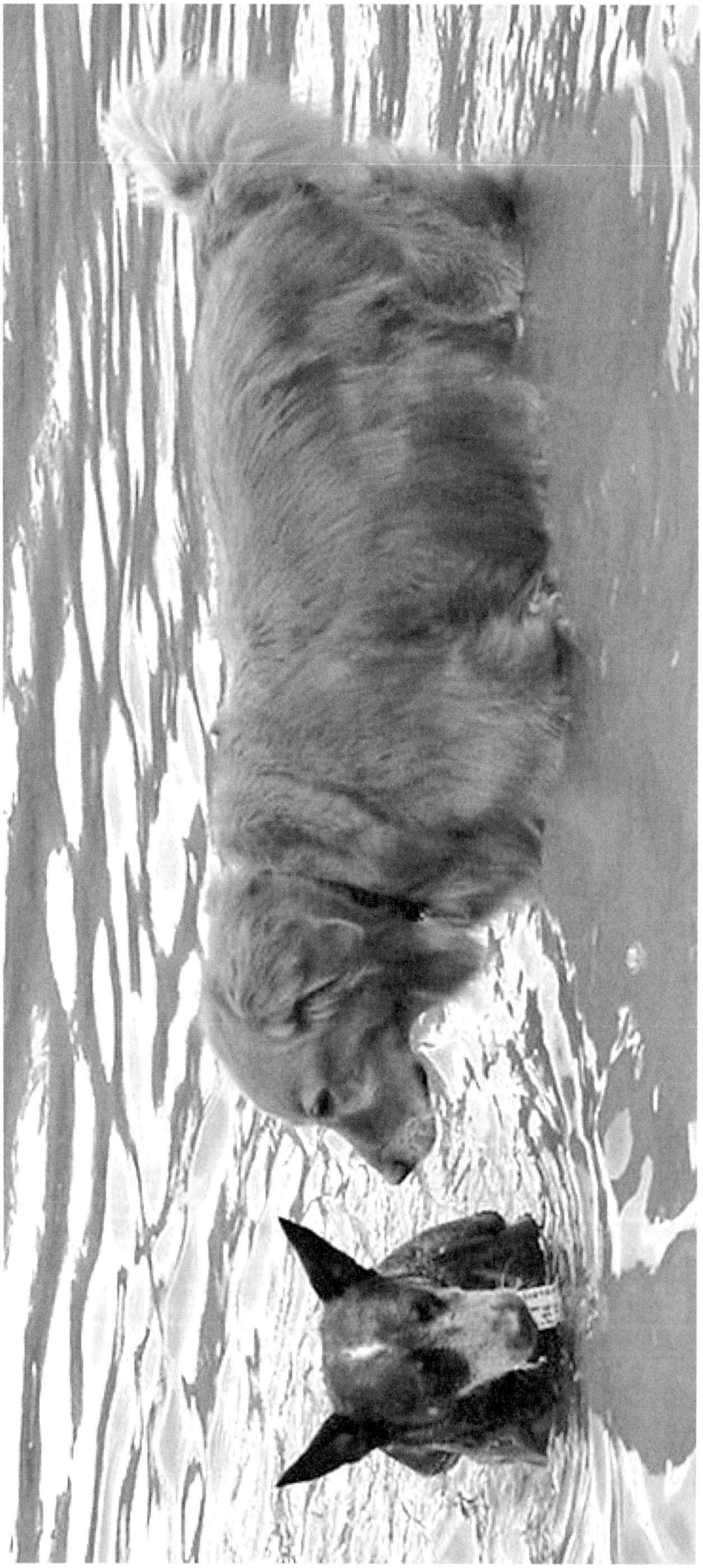

The Australian Cattle Dog on the left is tolerating the approach of the Golden. The Golden is using Negotiation Signals. He has his ears pulled back and has soft eyes. He is not squinting, but he is not holding his eyes wide open, which would be a signal of alarm or fear. His tail is half-mast and gently waving in Friendly Greeting mode.

The Cattle Dog is allowing the approach, and is using Negotiation Signals of his own to tell the Golden that he can approach. His ears are pulled back and he is Blinking in the typically exaggerated manner of Negotiating dogs. His nose is oriented in a neutral position, that is, not directly toward the Golden.

#12.3: Blink to Avoid Conflict

- eyes, blinking in exaggeration on the Golden
- ears half-mast
- long lips
- partially open mouth

When the Golden on the left finds himself in direct eye contact with another dog, either by design or by chance, he does the smart and polite thing: Blink. Blink in an exaggerated fashion, if need be.

Also note that the Golden's lips are drawn back so they are long, his ears are drawn back and his mouth is slightly open.

The dog on the right has some tension in his face and body. This is softened somewhat by the tail carriage. His tail is up over the back, although it is not forced up there, and looks relatively relaxed. He has his ears and eyes directed right at the Golden. His lips remain short, although his mouth is opened very slightly. What you can see is that he is Squinting slightly and is Blinking back. So, he is returning the signals, but very subtly. I get the feeling the dog on the right is just a wee bit on the muscle. He is holding himself with some Stillness and there is a rigidity about his demeanor. Perhaps the Golden was casually walking by and the other dog wishes to preserve a large area of personal space, and he is just letting the Golden know where the edges are.

Most significant is that we have two dogs in Direct Eye Contact, which is the big precursor to trouble, so all this Blinking on the part of the Golden is really important, because he is actively preventing this situation from escalating into something less friendly.

Remember, this encounter would be very quick in real time - maybe one or two seconds.

Photo Credits: Photo #1: Ginger Bross; Photo #2 & #3: Joanne Weber.

13
Look Away

The Look Away, when the dog's eyes are looking in the same direction the nose is pointed, and when accompanied by a happy, open mouth or relaxed jaw, is a friendly signal. This gesture is used to communicate: "I am no threat." It can be used as an invitation to "come into" personal space in play.

If a dog is stressed, she will often look in the opposite direction of the stressor. This kind of Look Away is avoidance, and it will be accompanied by body tension and facial tension.

If someone invades personal space, and it makes the dog uneasy, she will use a Look Away. This kind of Look Away will be accompanied by other signals of stress: lip licking, mild facial tension, ears held down or back.

There is an entirely different kind of Looking Away, too. It is wise to check both the orientation of the nose and the eyes. When the nose is oriented *away from*, but the eyes are looking *at*, it can be a Warning. I have seen two of my male Fox Terriers face off, and, just before physical contact is initiated, orient the nose away from with the eyes toward the other dog. With this type of "false" Looking Away there is tension in the jaw: the mouth is closed, the eyes are hard, and the eyes will be directed toward the threatening party. The ears are most often, but not always, held up; the ears could be flattened or drawn back, as well.

Therefore, when you are discussing or observing Look Aways, describe them well! Was it friendly or avoidance? Was it a Negotiation Signal or was it Guarding?

Looking At another indicates an array of intent and communication: interest, curiosity, Alerting, Targeting, Guarding, Predation, and Direct Threat.

#13.1: Look Away

- orientation of nose and eyes
- lack of body tension

This is not just a lovely picture of two beautiful Border Collies; it is a lovely picture of beautiful language usage as well. This depicts the perfect friendly Look Away.

Eyes are looking where noses are pointing. The ears are held in a relaxed, but attentive, manner. The dogs have their mouths partially open, with long lips. Their tails are held in a relaxed manner.

The general impression of the bodies of both dogs is neutrality. There is no tension; the front legs are not braced and the back is not hunched or rounded.

All signals indicate relaxed or neutral attitudes. No conflict here! These dogs are confident and comfortable with each other.

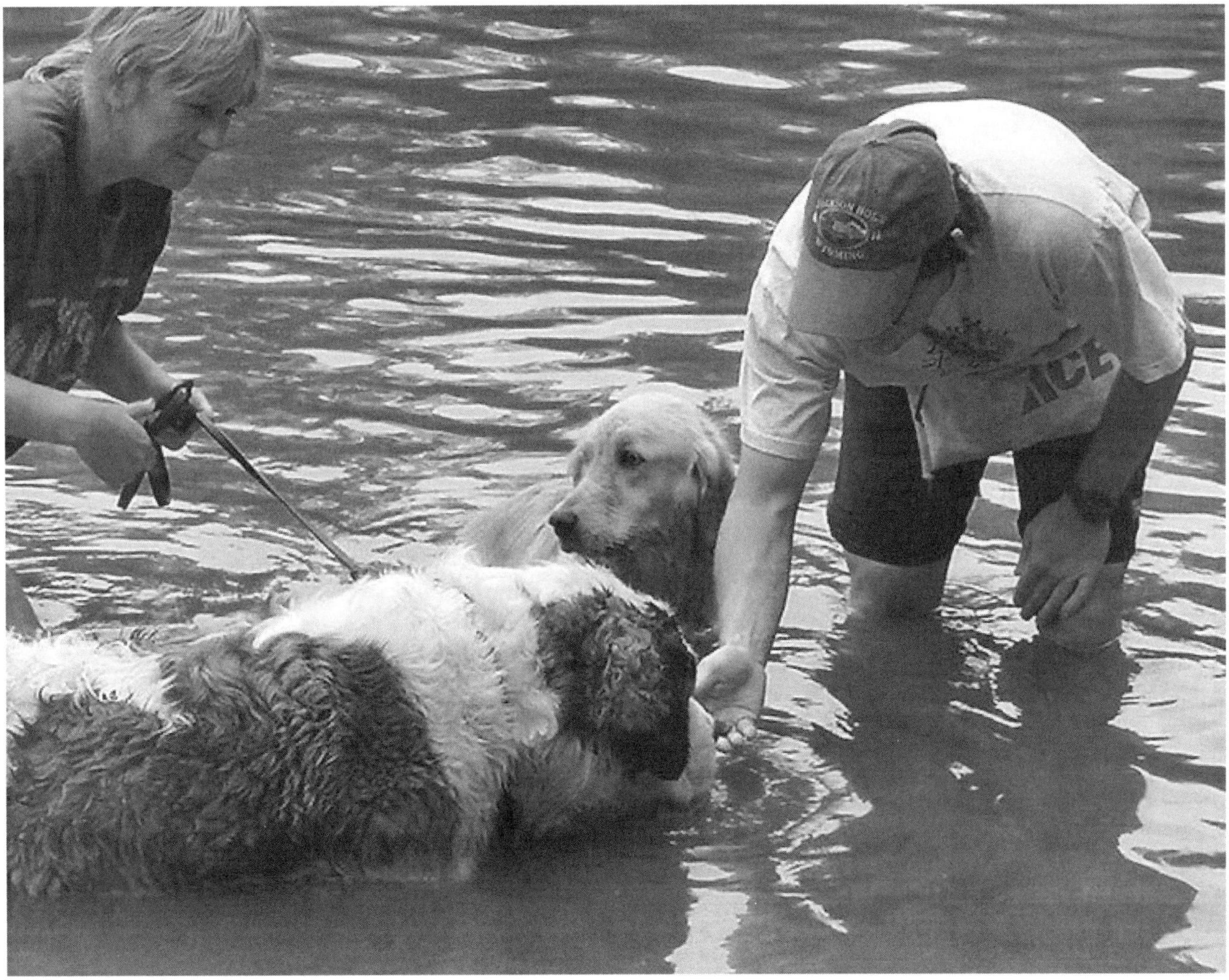

The St. Bernard is getting a treat from the person with the hat. The Golden in the background is giving the "intruder" a Look Away.

#13.2: Look Away

She is using the Look Away to keep the peace and to avoid direct eye contact. Her nose and eyes are oriented in the same direction. This is a Calming Signal, allowing the St. Bernard to come closer.

This Look Away tells the St. Bernard that the Golden intends to allow him into this space at this moment. There is some tension in the Golden: her ears are down, and her mouth is held closed. The Golden is "doing the right thing," but looks a bit uneasy about the invasion.

> *Observation & Tip*: When a dog gives a Negotiation Signal, she is expecting a signal back. This is polite behaviour and reassures the animal that the signal was received.
>
> An appropriate response may be as obvious as returning the signal received. Also appropriate is returning a signal of similar meaning: any one of the many Negotiation signals such as a Look Away or a Yawn, perhaps a Lip Lick. It may be as subtle as looking quickly at the other dog while Blinking, then appearing to ignore that dog.
>
> When you are training, as you approach a dog you do not know, if she gives you a signal, give her one back. A Look Away is easiest for humans; if you accompany it with Blinking, no Direct Eye Contact and Lip Licking, it is hard for the dog to miss, if she is capable of taking it in at that time.
>
> If your dog begins to give Negotiation signals, this alerts you to what the dog is concerned with at that moment - many times it is your own behaviour that concerns the dog.

#13.3: Look Away

- orientation of nose and eyes; both in the same direction
- lack of body tension
- low, waving sweep of tails

The Sheltie and the Golden are playing - or, at least, the Sheltie is attempting to initiate play. You can tell the Sheltie is playing because of the lack of tension in her demeanor. She is approaching with a lowered body. She has her ears back and an open mouth. Her tail is carried at half-mast. Even though she has used a head-on approach, she is not staring at Willie (the Golden), and she is in motion. She may be requesting that Willie be a substitute sheep.

Willie, the Golden, is maintaining a neutral and very relaxed body posture. His tail has the half-mast, Friendly Sweep and his ears are drawn back in "calming" mode. Willie is using a Look Away, with a partially open mouth (which means there is lack of tension in the jaw).

Willie is, at this moment, receiving the polite request to play sent by the Sheltie and acknowledging it. He is accepting the message as friendly, but not yet committing to play (he might not want to be a sheep). He communicates all that with a Look Away and a relaxed demeanor.

> *Observation*: When dogs are getting serious about conflict, they close their mouths. A closed mouth can also indication facial tension or tension in the jaw.

The Cattle Dog on the left is using a Look Away to avoid conflict with the Cattle Dog on the right. The Cattle Dog on the right is using a sideways approach, and is coming into the other dog's personal space slowly. This sideways approach is appropriate for Entering Personal Space, and is friendly. The contrast is what you so often see: a dog barging into another dog's space head-on and quickly. This behaviour is very inappropriate and rude.

#13.4: Look Away

- orientation of nose, eyes
- tails

Notice that the dog on the left has his mouth closed. This indicates a higher degree of tension than if the mouth were open. He has also lowered his tail. His ears are drawn back and toward the approaching dog. All of this says: Tension.

This kind of Look Away borders on something other than acceptance. The more extreme position of the head, and the lowered tail show, perhaps, some avoidance. If the body tension of the dog on the left dissipates over the next couple of seconds, the situation remains peaceful. If the dog on the left begins to escalate in body tension, the situation is going south. Increased body tension might be displayed by a lowering of the head (beginning to Guard personal space). Stillness is the crucial thing to look for. Sudden Stillness almost always ends in some sort of sudden release - an explosion of activity. An emotional Reaction rather than a thoughtful Response.

The Cattle Dog on the right has an open mouth, ears ever so slightly back and his tail is up in a normal and relaxed position. His lips are long. Both Cattle Dogs have eyes that are not forced wide open. All of this says: Friendly.

If the Cattle Dog on the right were to ignore the other's body tension, the dog on the left would feel more concerned, not less. Acknowledging the discomfort could be done by the dog on the right moving away after a quick sniff, or by giving a Negotiation Signal in return to the Look Away.

The Shiba is not involved at all; he is on his own mission. He is totally engaged with something in front of him. His motion is toward it, his eyes and nose are towards it, his ears and even his tail are all pointing in the same direction - towards whatever has captured his interest. It could be a scent or a frog, or the movement of the water. He is Alerting on something, not just avoiding the other two dogs.

The first thing to notice here is direct eye contact. The dog on the right is holding Still in that moment before the pounce. He has partially closed his mouth in preparation for this, but his lips remain long. He is staring intently and directly at the dog on the left.

The dog on the left knows what is going on: this is play conflict, not serious conflict. His mouth remains open. Both dogs have their ears slightly forward on Alert. Notice that, although direct eye contact is occurring, the dog on the left is oriented sideways and not head-on in "Chicken" position.

#13.5: Direct Eye Contact

- orientation of nose and eyes
- open or partially open mouth
- long lips
- Stillness
- degree of body tension
- ears up and forced forward

Note: This is an excellent example of using a Read on both dogs to determine how serious the situation is. If I looked only at the dog on the right, I would be uneasy. His look is predacious and intense. The only give-aways that this is not serious are quite subtle, and they might not be easy to pick up on if this were happening in real time. Even though his ears are forced forward, the tips are still a little floppy. His lips are long and his mouth is slightly open. The sideways approach is also an indicator of play, not war.

But it is the dog on the left, with the happy, open mouth, long lips, and tiny paw lift that really helps you determine these two dogs are not in conflict.

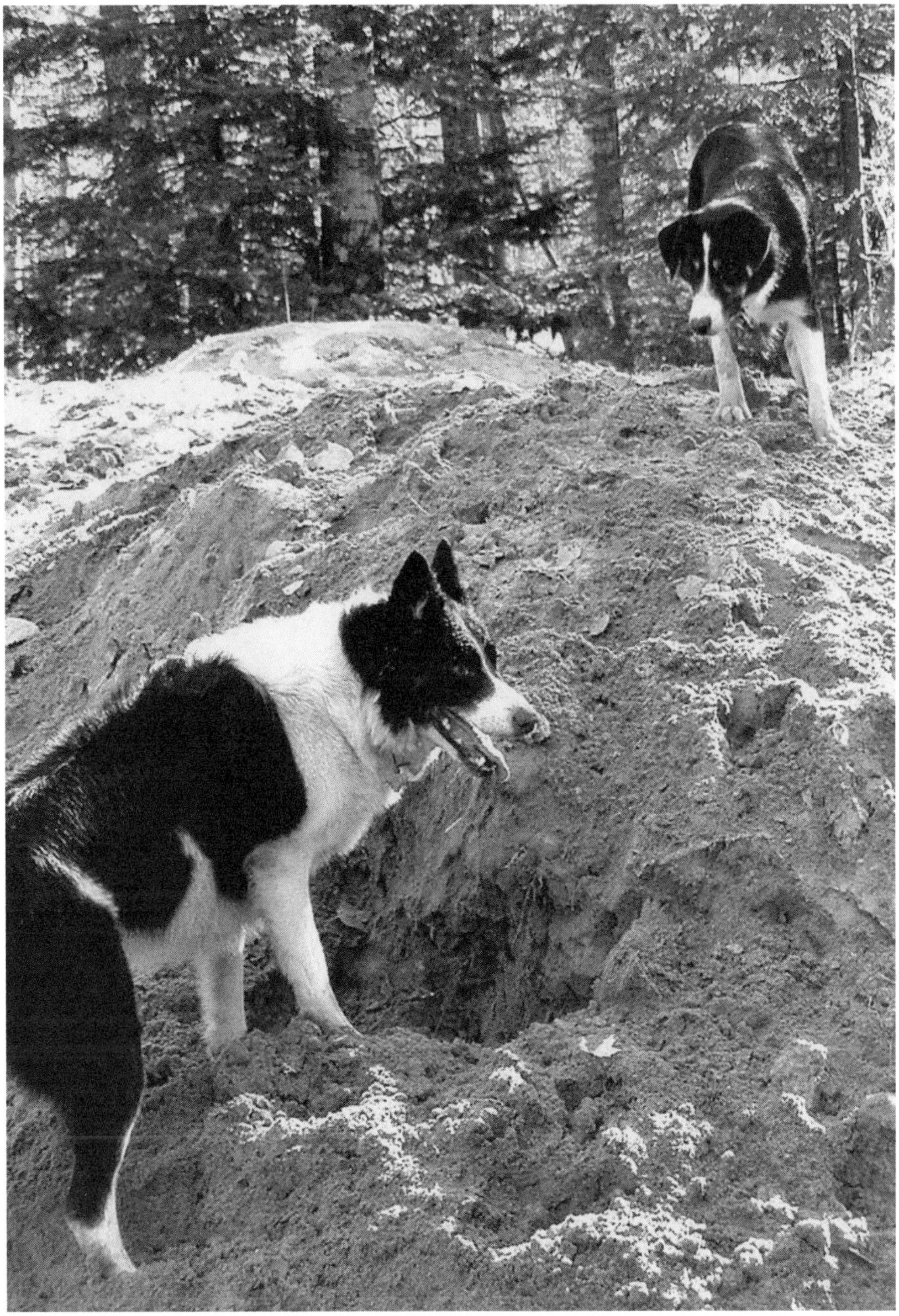

#13.6: Look Away vs. Eye Contact

- orientation of nose and eyes
- open or partially open mouth
- long lips
- Stillness
- degree of body tension

The dog on the right is getting ready to pounce, in play, on the Border Collie mix. The dog on the left is using a Look Away.

Her Look Away is not one of tension. Her ears are slightly back and relaxed, her mouth is open. She is accepting the invitation to play by using a relaxed and neutral body position.

This Look Away is a Negotiation Signal in play. An acceptance of the other dog's position as friendly, and not as a "real" attack position.

Contrast this photograph with the one preceding it. One photograph shows you dogs in direct eye contact, the other shows a similar situation, but with a Look Away.

Observation: Body tension or the lack of it are very important messages. Other dogs are very sensitive to changes in breathing and body tension.

#13.7: Look Away to Acknowledge Possession

- orientation of nose and eyes
- curved body

The Shepherd on the left wishes to Pass By in a physically restricted area. The Sheltie has a bone: A Possession. In order to make the Pass By peaceful, the Shepherd uses a Look Away, with a lowered head and half-mast ears, to communicate to the Sheltie that there will be no conflict. "I don't even *see* your bone."

Notice how the Shepherd's entire body is slightly curved away from the Sheltie. This is an extreme Look Away!

For dogs, "whoever gets there first" is relevant. The Sheltie is in current Possession of the area and the bone. The Shepherd is aware of this and is using good language skills to acknowledge both the Canine Rules and her respect for the dog In Possession.

Photo Credits: Photo #1: J. Reiss; Photo #2, 3, 4, 5 & 6: Joanne Weber; Photo #7: Rachel Plotinski; Photo #8: J. Weber.

14
Tongue Flick

#14.1: Tongue Flick While Learning a New Task

- Tongue Flick
- ears slightly back
- orienting nose toward "new" person

#14.2: Panting Tongue

- tongue drooping, not "flicked"

In each of these photographs, the dogs are doing an unfamiliar task. As they do the task, they are receiving help from an instructor, a person the dog is unfamiliar with. The instructor, as we instructors do, is touching the dog to assist in teaching the task.

If you compare the dog in the lower photograph to the dog in the top photograph, you can see that this dog is less bothered - you see no Tongue Flick here, just a panting tongue. The tongue is more "relaxed."

See how the tongue-flicking dog directs the Tongue Flick toward the instructor? It is a deliberate Signal.

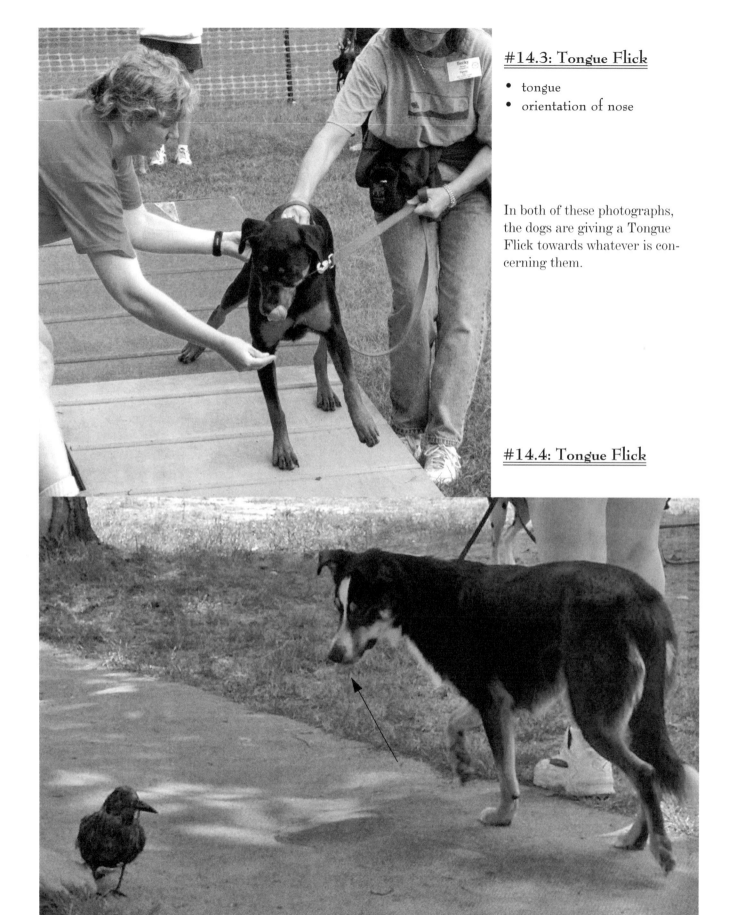

#14.3: Tongue Flick

- tongue
- orientation of nose

In both of these photographs, the dogs are giving a Tongue Flick towards whatever is concerning them.

#14.4: Tongue Flick

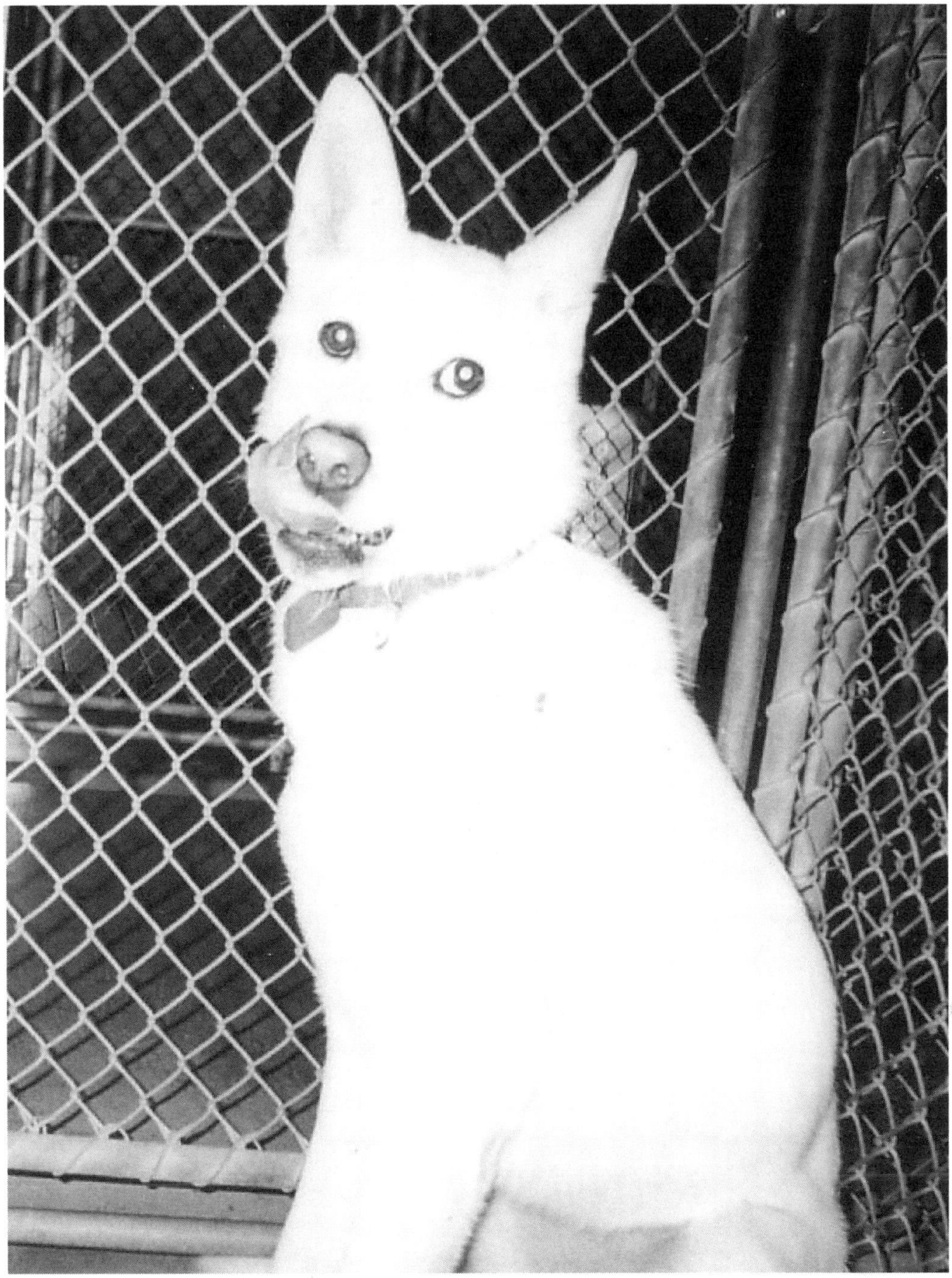

#14.5: Tongue Flick

- tongue
- body pressed INTO pressure

This is Rachel's dog at the animal shelter where she was being held prior to adoption.

In addition to the Tongue Flick, you can also see the Whale eye - the whites around the eyes. She is Moving Into Pressure, pressing her body against the fencing. Her back is rounded.

At least this story had a happy ending: Rachel rescued the dog from her stressful plight.

#14.6: "I Am Coming Through" Tongue Flick

- tongue
- orientation of nose

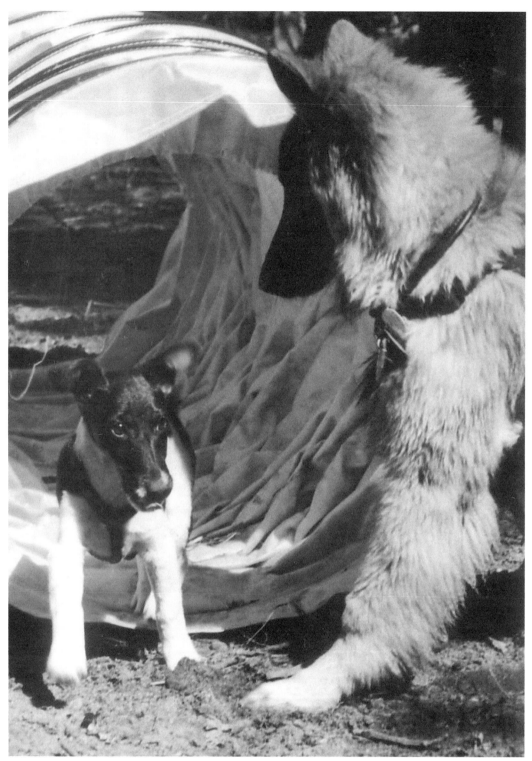

Zasu races through the tunnel to find, unexpectedly, a Tervuren puppy at the other end. As Zasu passes by the other dog, she gives a Tongue Flick.

Tongue Flicks are indications of personal space violations. It can be used for Negotiation or it could be indicating stress or an early warning. Here, because Zasu is racing into the other dog's space, she gives a Tongue Flick towards the oncoming dog. In this photograph, she is nine weeks old and already using sophisticated

#14.7: Avoidance with Tongue Flick

- tongue
- moving away

This Tongue Flick is coupled with apologetic and avoidant body language.

Note the lowered head, neck, and body. Her tail is down, and her pressed-down ears and squinty eyes all show the dog's discomfort. This dog is moving away from whatever is causing her discomfort.

Photo Credits:
Photo #1, #2, #3 & #4: Joanne Weber;
Photo #5: Rachel Plotinsky;
Photo #6 & #7: Joanne Weber.

15 Sniffing

Sniffing is one of the most frequently seen behaviours in dogs. It is used in several different ways. Sniffing is used as a Displacement Behaviour, a Calming Signal, a Negotiation Signal, and, of course, as plain old use of the nose to find stuff.

Humans have a tendency toward using our excellent vision to fill in the details of our world. Our vision is vividly colored; we have good depth perception; and can see fine details. Humans love visual stimulation of all kinds, and actively seek it out.

Dogs, on the other hand, have very different vision from our own. For them, the world of scents and scenting carries far more weight, and provides them with more detailed information than their vision. Dogs have their noses to the ground all the time. Most dogs sniff to do a definite identification of a known friend. If you toss a treat in the grass, the dog doesn't rely on locating it visually, like we do. His nose goes down, and he relies on his nose to find the prize.

Your dog's world is rich with olfactory information. Scenting game to find a meal is a hard-wired behaviour. Catching up on the latest Pee-Mail, finding interesting things to roll in, deciding if you know someone or not: The Nose Knows!

Understanding all that, it is not surprising that dogs use Sniffing in so many different situations, and many use Sniffing as a preferred communication signal.

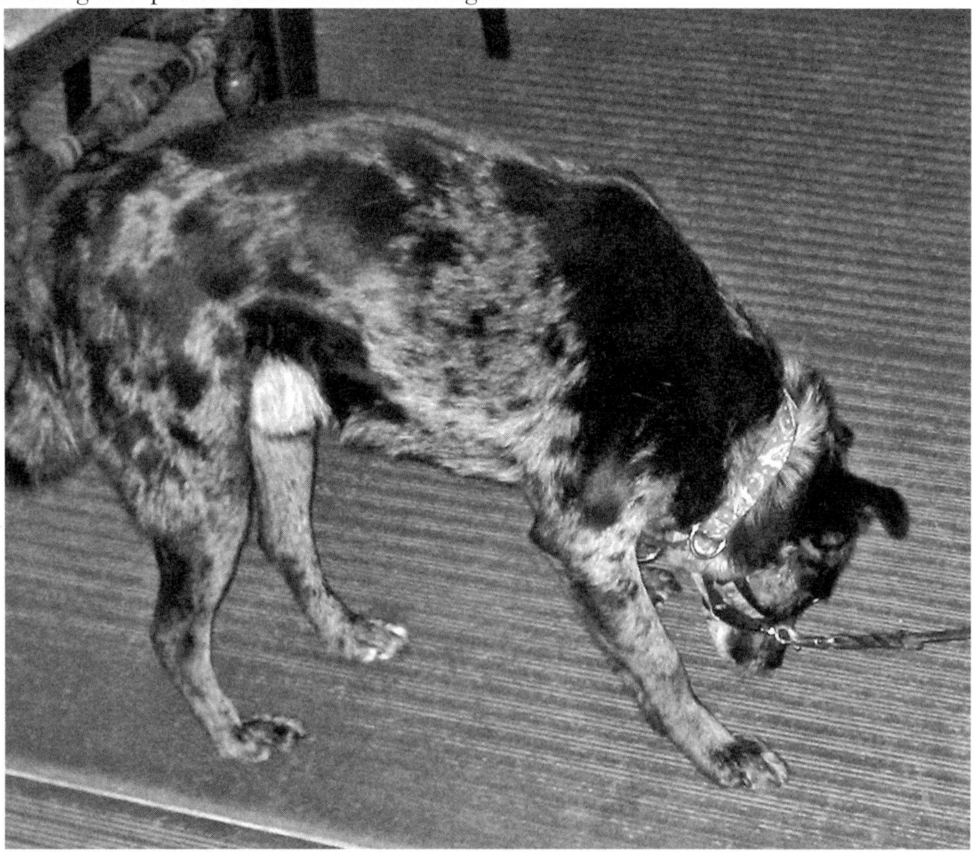

#15.1: Sniffing During Stress

Yup, he's Sniffing, all right. You have seen this photograph already. Unless you know the context, or there are some other obvious signs, it is very difficult to impossible to know if the dog is, indeed, searching for something, smells something of interest, or is using Sniffing as a deliberate communication. In this instance, the dog is stressed.

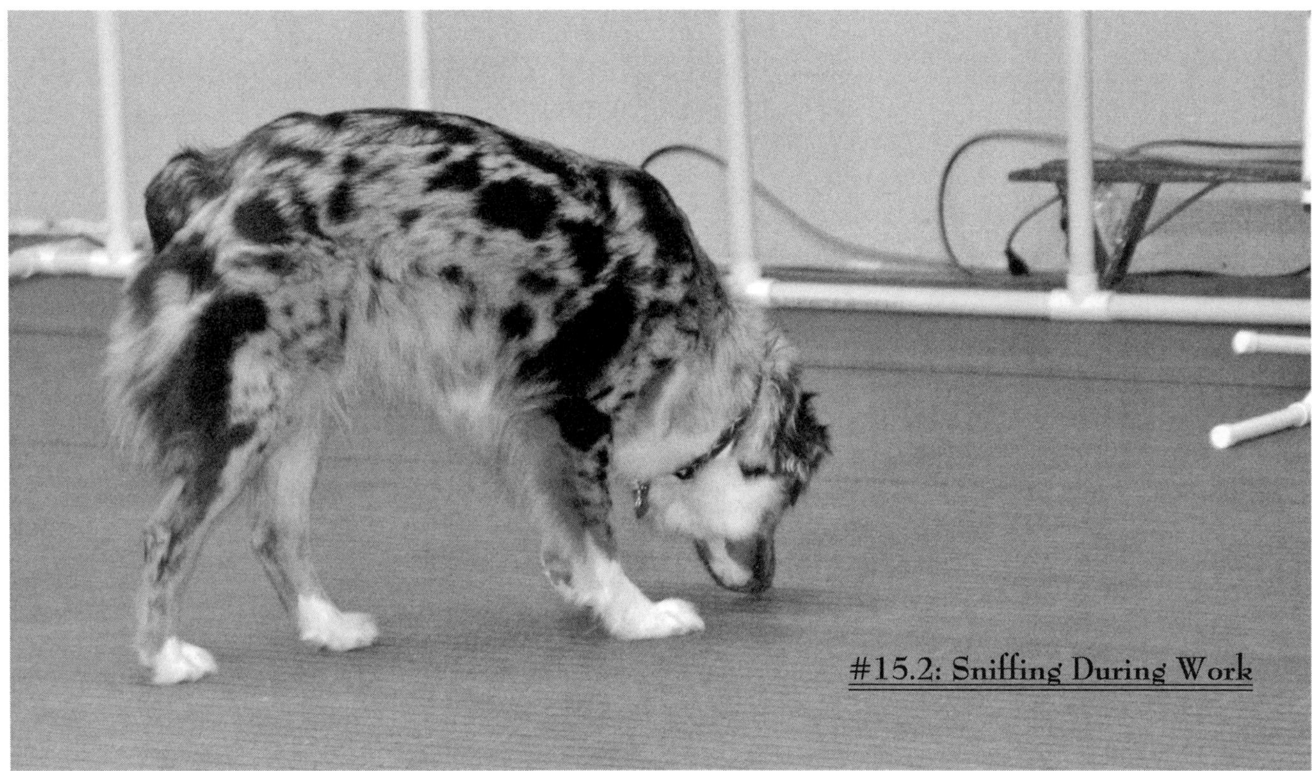

#15.2: Sniffing During Work

This is also a dog who is mildly stressed. Marguerite (handler) and Zoey (canine) were working on stay exercises. Zoey's young age and short attention span were somewhat hindering the progress of the stays. The dog has a very good understanding of the work; the owner has been working these exercises since Zoey was a very young puppy; and the training is very positively-based. The point is, the dog has a good understanding of what has been asked of her, but, when slightly distracted by other activity in the room, Zoey got up from her Down. As Marguerite went to get her, this is the signal that was given.

#15.3: Sniffing as a Calming Signal

Text for this photograph is on the following page.

Text for Photo #15.3: One dog Staring. One dog Sniffing. The Staring dog has her ears up; her tail is up; she is on Alert. The Sniffing dog has her ears drawn back a little bit; her tail is down; her eyes are averted. The Calming Signal says to the Alerting dog: "I see you; I am aware of you; I am not threatening you; Calm Down."

#15.4: Sniffing During Investigation

Golden Retrievers playing near a pond show various emotions. The two adolescents, on the right, move toward a ball that has rolled into the water. They look cautious, but determined to get the ball. The older dog, on the left, is Sniffing. Tail relaxed and at half-mast; ears at normal position; eyes Blinking. Tough call. Because the environment is a rich and varied one, it is entirely possible this dog is just plain old Sniffing in interest. It also possible that he is trying to get closer to the ball and is Negotiating moving closer, into the personal space of the other dogs. This is wise and polite, because this could end up being a Negotiation about a valued object. Because the youngsters do not look bold and confident, I would say that the older dog is just sniffing. He could easily push the cautious youngsters out of the way and take the ball.

#15.5: Chain Sniffing

All righty, then! Three dogs in a play group Sniff. The dog on the far right is scenting. Tail up over her back, ears in normal position, she has found an interesting scent OR she is using Sniffing as a "I am friendly" signal. The middle dog walks by and does a polite Butt Sniff. The Papillon, on the far left, Sniffs, too. The Papillon has her tail up, and her ears at half-mast. Without knowing what had happened just prior to this photograph being taken, and what happens next, the Papillon's reasons for sniffing could take on any one of a number of explanations. If she thinks the social situation is sticky, it could be a Calming Signal. If she wants to Pass By, it could be a Negotiation Signal. And she may have caught a bit of the same interesting scent that the other dog is investigating. A dog's olfactory capabilities are so keen, that she could easily be sniffing the scent of the dog in front of her - a modified Butt Sniff.

#15.6: Puppies Do It Too!

Ivy, the puppy, emulates her Uncle Willie...or, the dogs could be Sniffing because they are in close proximity, a little Negotiation going on.

I am in favor of the first: Willie Sniffs, puppy exhibits allellomimetic behaviour.

Photo #1: Brenda Aloff; Photo #2: Dave Schrader; Photo #3, #4, #5, #6: DeWitt.

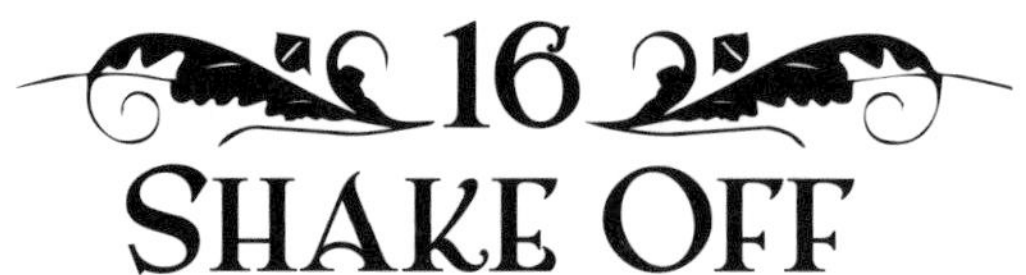

16 Shake Off

Shaking Off is a specific signal dogs use to communicate non-threatening intent.

A Shake Off also indicates that the dog is coming down off of adrenaline. This tells other dogs that the dog is moving into a Thinking or Responding state and out of a Reactive and unpredictable state. This is comforting for other dogs in the area. They want predictable behaviour from others around them, just as we do.

Coming down off of adrenaline is very significant and informative for the handler, too. When you see a dog Shake Off, you know the dog is switching from Hind Brain to Front Brain. Dogs working from their Front Brain are easier to work with and communication can flow readily because the dog is Responding. Dogs in their Hind Brain are just little bundles of Reactivity. Reactive dogs are adrenalized and in fight-or-flight mode.

#16.1: Shake Off

Photo #1, Photo Essay #2: Cherish DeWitt..

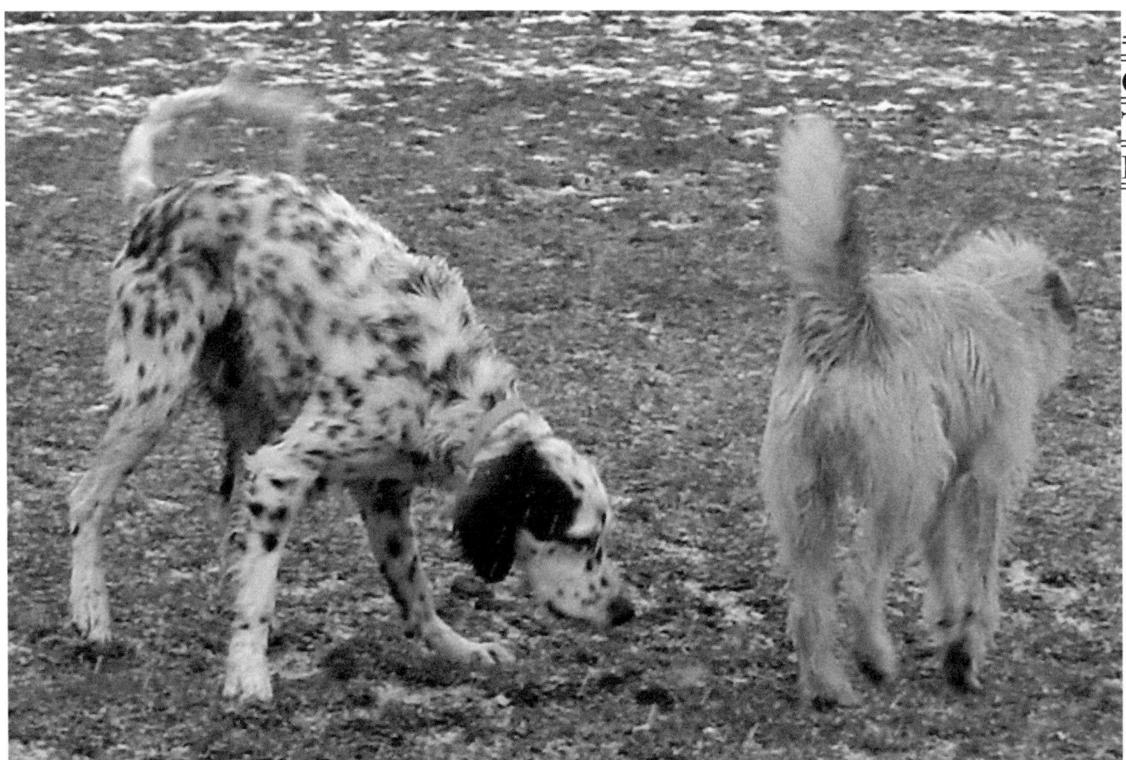

#16.2: Shake Off Between Two Dogs - Photo Essay

Radar, the English Setter, is Sniffing near Olivia, the terrier-mix on the right. It looks like a very polite Butt Sniff, performed at a safe distance. Both dogs are using neutral body language to communicate non-threat to each other. The tails are up and moving, but not forced over the back. Their bodies are relatively relaxed.

These dogs are being very formal and polite with each other. As the Setter moves away, both dogs Shake Off. This is a very common behaviour pattern. Even dogs who know each other well will often Shake Off after sniffing each other. Sometimes dogs will Shake Off after a Pass By or other incidence of close proximity.

17
Scratching

#17.1: Scratching as Displacement

- "funny" ears
- silhouette shows the activity
- orientation of eyes & nose so they are not directed right at whatever is causing concern

The GSD is Scratching because Cherish was taking photos of her. Having a camera pointed at them often makes dogs feel nervous. Sometimes the click of the shutter, approach of the photographer, and the flash going off causes a dog to use negotiation signals. Perhaps most significantly, the eye of the camera is staring and fixed.

#17.2: Scratching as a Calming Signal

- "funny" ears
- orient away from whatever is causing concern

There is a lot going on here! The Golden to the left is correcting the nearby Cattle Dog. The dog to the far right is letting everybody know that she is not involved and intends to stay that way. "Calm Down!" she is saying, as well as, "I am not confrontational." In this case, the Scratching could be interpreted as both a deliberate signal and a displacement behaviour.

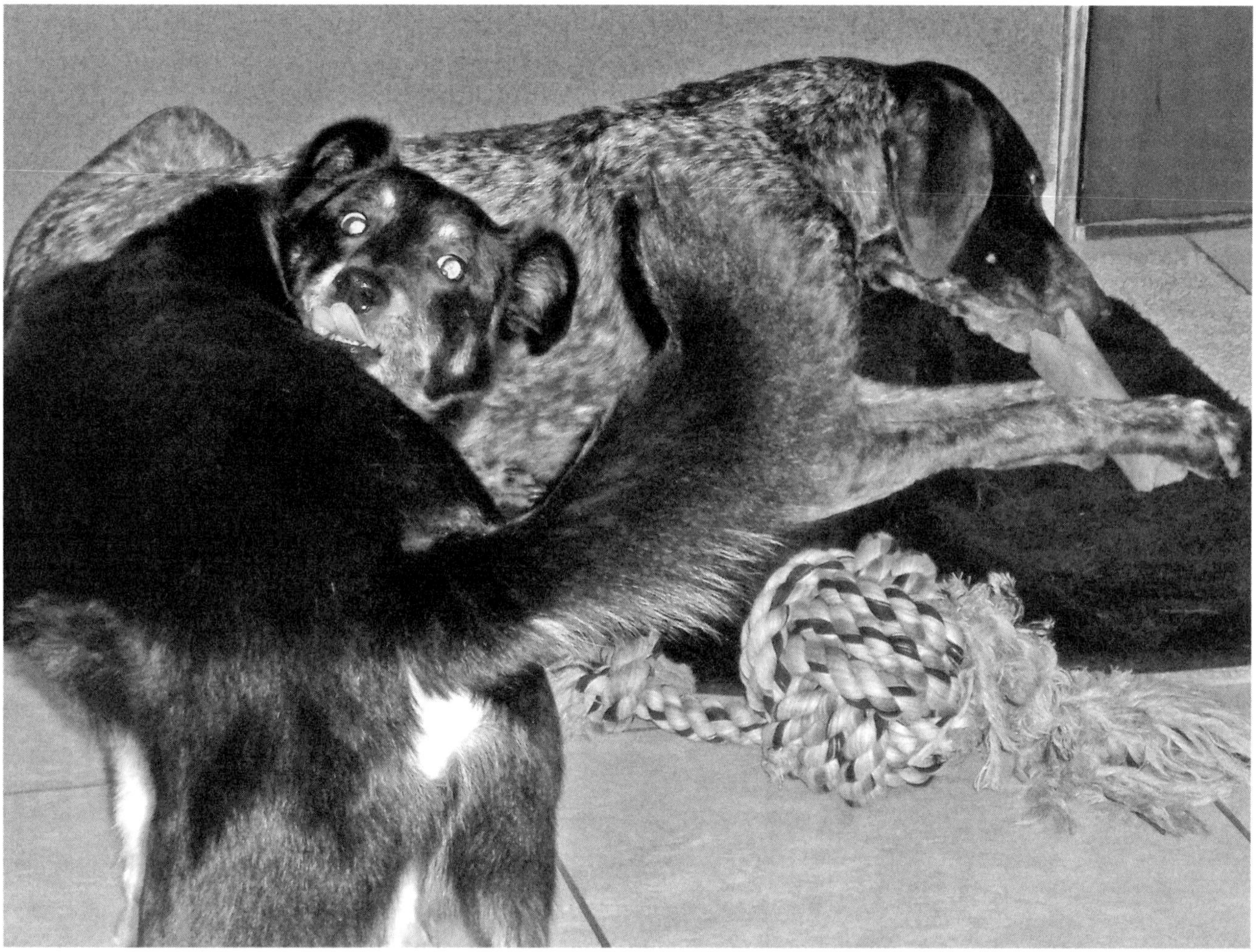

#17.3: Scratching as Appeasement & Negotiation

- Look Away from the dog the message is intended for

This dog is covering all the bases! The German Shorthair has a bone. The approaching dog is using a Look away, a Tongue Flick, and she is getting ready to Scratch with her teeth. All of these Negotiation Signals tell the German Shorthair that this is intended to be a non-threatening approach.

I bet she wants that rope toy that is near the GSP and is working her way politely towards it.

This scene differs from the photo "Scratching as a Calming Signal" because this dog is using signals to approach closer rather than to signal, "I am keeping my distance. I do not want to be involved."

#17.4: Scratching as Non-Threatening Behaviour

- proximity of dogs
- "funny" ears
- Look Away

Scratching, like Shaking Off, is often used when dogs are in close proximity. As the approaching dog gets into the personal space of the other dog, the dog being approached Scratches. This is a signal of Negotiation, and sometimes, Displacement. Either way, it lets the approaching dog know that she has just entered a more sensitive zone of personal space.

You can see that the Papillon gets the message. She has stopped her approach and is standing calmly, using a slight Look Away, waiting for permission to advance further toward the Cattle Dog. Her mouth is open, which is most often an indication of a dog who is using friendly language. Nice language skills!

Photo Credits:
Photo #1,2 & 3: Cherish DeWitt;
Photo #3: Rachel Plotinski;
Photo #4: Cherish DeWitt.

18 YAWNING

Dogs Yawn when they are slightly stressed by something in the environment. It can be something very simple, such as a dog or person passing by a little too closely. Dogs often Yawn when they are feeling like they have to "perform" in some way. Dogs Yawn often when they feel confused or frustrated by the current situation.

Dogs will Yawn when a person or dog places social pressure on them - such as telling by the dog to stay then "staring" at her with the eye of the camera. It is both a stress signal, as in: "You are getting closer," and a Negotiation Signal, as in: "I am allowing you in at this moment."

#18.1: Yawn

#18.2: Yawn

Photo Credits:
Photo #1: Rachel Plotinski;
Photo #2: Cherish DeWitt;
Photo #3: Candy Smith.

#18.3: Stress Yawn with Look Away

- mouth stretched in a Yawn
- ears drawn back
- whiskers flared forward

Doc is Yawning in this picture because I am doing some body work with him. Doc is responding to me rubbing his body all over with my hands by using a Look Away and a Yawn. He is telling me that I am making him uncomfortable, but he is still Negotiating with me.

These "stress Yawns" can look very slightly different depending on the individual and the situation. In general, the dog will draw his ears back and open his mouth very wide. There is not an intentional show of teeth. Sometimes the dog will squint the eyes like the White Shepherd on the previous page. Other times, the eyes will be open and used with a Look Away, as Doc is displaying here. In general, my interpretation is: the wider the eyes during the Yawn, the more stress the dog is feeling.

19
PAW LIFTS

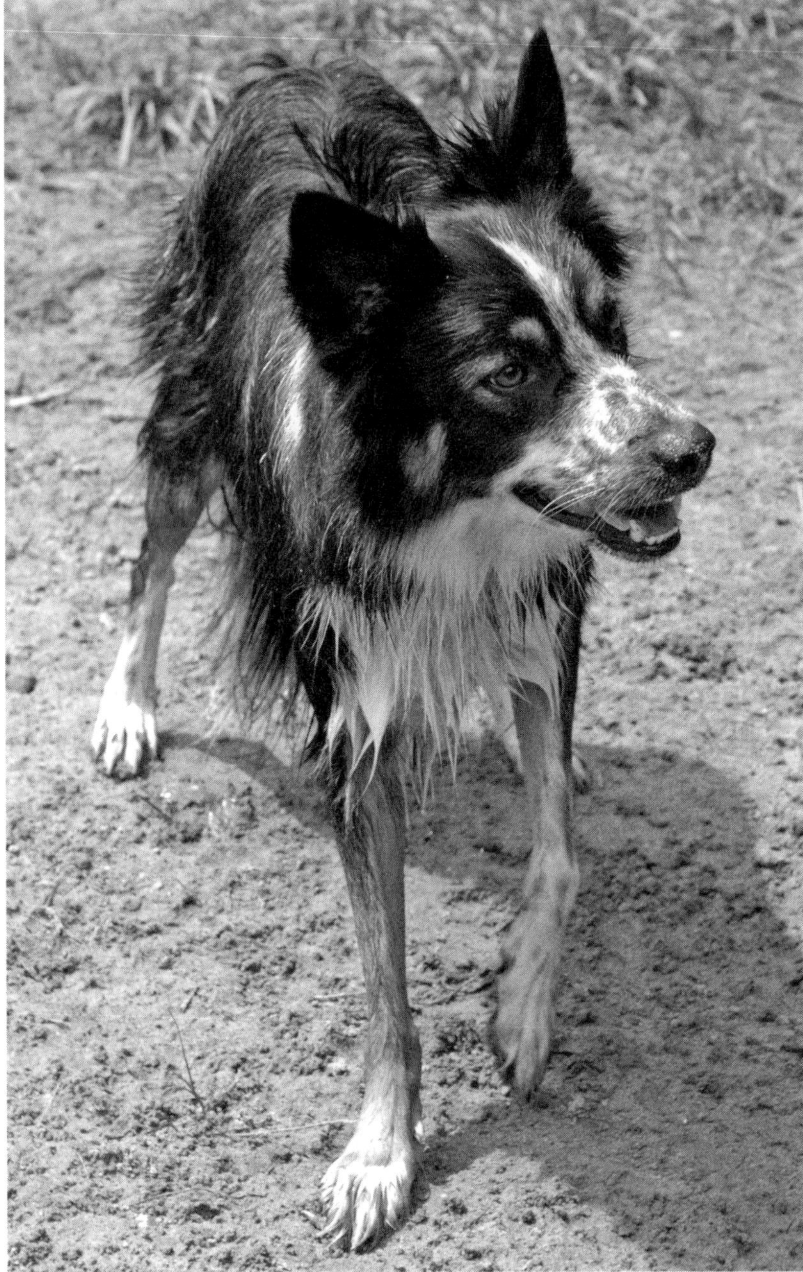

#19.1: Paw Lift - Anticipation

- front paw lifted
- alert, yet relaxed, body posture
- ears up

Paw Lifts are used in many different circumstances. If a dog is curious, she will often lift a paw. When a dog is feeling a little uncertain, she will often lift a paw. When a dog is stalking or "pointing," she will lift a paw.

A paw lift accompanies a moment or two of stillness.

In this photograph, we have a dog who is focused on something - perhaps a toy that the owner will toss.

This is an Anticipatory Paw Lift because the dog is Alert. His ears are up and his eyes are intensely focused on a particular object.

The Paw Lift is a "waiting" gesture. Here the dog is anticipating a pleasant event: What fun thing will the human do next?

#19.2: Paw Lift - Curiosity

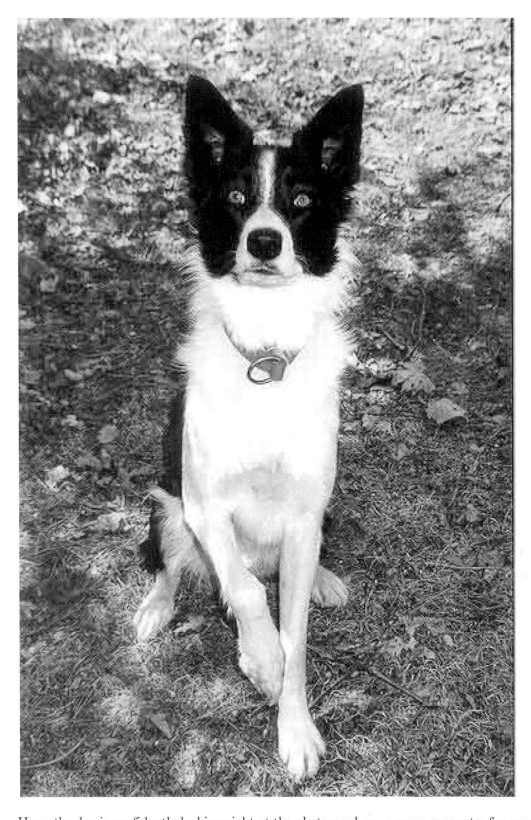

- front paw lifted
- alert, yet relaxed body posture
- ears up

Here, the dog is confidently looking right at the photographer - a scary encounter for many dogs! This dog has her ears up and her paw is lifted in an anticipatory manner. Sometimes dogs do this as they do a curiosity Head Tilt.

"What are you doing?" An attitude of polite interest is demonstrated by this dog's expression.

#19.3: Paw Lift - Curious with a Tinge of Anxious

- front paw lifted
- relaxed body posture
- ears drawn back

This photo was taken in a working clinic environment. Willie's owner is sitting nearby, but the dog is working with me for a moment. He is a very sweet and friendly dog who is letting me know that in many ways.

He is engaging in friendly, blinking direct eye contact. He is one of those dogs who has figured out that human eye contact is friendly and he is showing his trust in humans. This demonstrates how confident he is in his ability to communicate with people. His lips are drawn back and his mouth is partially open. And to top it all off, showing me that he is respectful as well as confident, he has lifted a paw in anticipation of cooperative effort.

He may also be slightly anxious about leaving his mum to come with me, as evidenced by his drawn back ears, as well as the wide-open eyes.

Observation: Dogs become confident in their ability to communicate with humans when they are afforded opportunities to do so with people who are aware that the dog is communicating. Be sure to acknowledge your dog's efforts to communicate with you. Also, you can train your dog to accept some of our "bad" canine language, such as directly staring at and leaning over them.

#19.4: Paw Lift - Submission

- front paw lifted
- backwards oriented body
- ears drawn back
- Look Away

This dog is using a Paw Lift as a submissive gesture. Buster, the Cattle Dog, is by nature shy. He is showing minor discomfort caused by Chris leaning over him, by drawing his ears back and lifting a paw in submission. Some dogs do not like to have anyone (human or canine) leaning over them, creating a "shelf." They find this intimidating.

Buster has his eyes averted in a Look Away and his eyes are Squinty and Blinking. In this Look Away, the nose is oriented away from and slightly down. This is acquiescent and friendly. If the nose is oriented up and the eyes are not following the direction of the nose, it can indicate aggression.

Also note that his body orientation is going backwards. This is another clue to him feeling cautious or submissive. He is not in an extreme emotional state, though, his tail is not tucked or held close to his body. The Paw Lift, drawn-back ears, and Look Away are meant to communicate, "I will not cause a conflict with you. I am allowing you into my personal space."

Observation & Tip: In a dog's native language, being over top of his body is a power play. If a dog puts a foot on another dog's back or shoulder, it is a challenge (unless a dog is testing a bitch for breeding readiness). Dogs will do things like this in play, but that would always be accompanied by specific Play signals. When we bend over a dog and then touch him, it can be construed as a challenge, threat, or "pushy" rude behaviour. This doesn't mean we shouldn't do those things - just the opposite. Using desensitization, train your dog to accept all bizarre human body language. You want your dog well-versed in "human" so he understands your intent. You are merely leaning over him, not challenging or threatening him.

#19.5: Paw Lift - Stalking

- front paw lifted
- forward oriented body posture
- body lowered
- intensity of gaze

Punch is Stalking a small creature in the grass. In this particular moment, she is frozen (still) right before the pounce.

Note the intensity in her gaze. Her ears are forced forward. Her tail is held down in concentration. Notice how short her lips are. Her mouth is held in readiness to do a grab-bite, so, even though her mouth is partially open, this is in preparation for the bite, not because she is feeling relaxed.

(For those who are interested, the big game is a grasshopper.)

Observation: The held-down tail does not always mean the dog is feeling cautious, nervous, or uncertain. It can be held down when the dog is deeply concentrating on something, such as stalking game. The other time you see this is when the dog is fully engaging her brain - figuring out how to complete a task that the trainer has presented her with. You also see this when a dog is concentrating on a self-appointed task, such as when she is consumed by chewing on a bone

Photo Credits: Photo #1, #2, #3 & #4: Joanne Weber; Photo #5: Brenda Aloff.

20 Puppy Licking

Puppy Licking is a submissive gesture. It is a way to get adult dogs to turn off aggression.

Biologically, it is a request by a very young puppy that encourages the adult dog to regurgitate food for the puppy to eat. Remember, feral dogs do not take young puppies on the hunt because they would be in danger and in the way. So, the adult dogs gorge as much food as they can, come back to the den, and vomit food for the puppies. This licking gesture is also used as a communication: as submission, or to appease an authority figure.

You will see dogs use this communication through adulthood. Some dogs use submissive gestures to manipulate an animal of higher rank. Sometimes this does work: the lower-ranking dog succeeds in moving the other dog around, or at least succeeds in turning off the aggression of the higher-ranking dog.

Depending on the personality of the higher-ranking dog, though, this strategy can backfire. The higher ranking animal will often look disgusted and begin to get tense. Instead of heeding this as a warning to move out of personal space, the submissive dog becomes ever more anxious and frantic in licking and groveling. The higher-ranking dog will stand over the sycophant and the lower-ranking dog will lower his body, sometimes to the point of rolling around on the floor, bumping into the legs of the higher-ranking dog. The higher-ranking dog will issue further warning to the sycophant to stop by standing more on tiptoe, leaning over the other dog, and growling. Sometimes this causes the lower-ranking dog to increase his frenzied and uncontrolled behaviour. In the case of a couple of my higher-ranking and confident females, the fact that the groveling dog didn't obey and cease the irritating behaviour is cause for severe correction.

#20.1: Puppy Lick to Adult Dog

- open relaxed jaw on adult dog
- squinty eyes on both dogs
- silhouette, typical lowered body & raised chin

Note the silhouette of this puppy. This is a common posture seen in friendly gestures, when one dog wants to communicate that he poses no threat to the other. This puppy has a lowered body and is reaching up and forward to the animal she is talking to. The drawn back ears and the squinty eyes signify, "Don't harm me."

This adult dog is accepting. You can tell this because his ears are relaxed; he has no body tension; his mouth is open and relaxed; and his eyes are squinting. Most significantly, the adult dog is not moving away or standing over the puppy. He is also not giving the puppy direct eye contact.

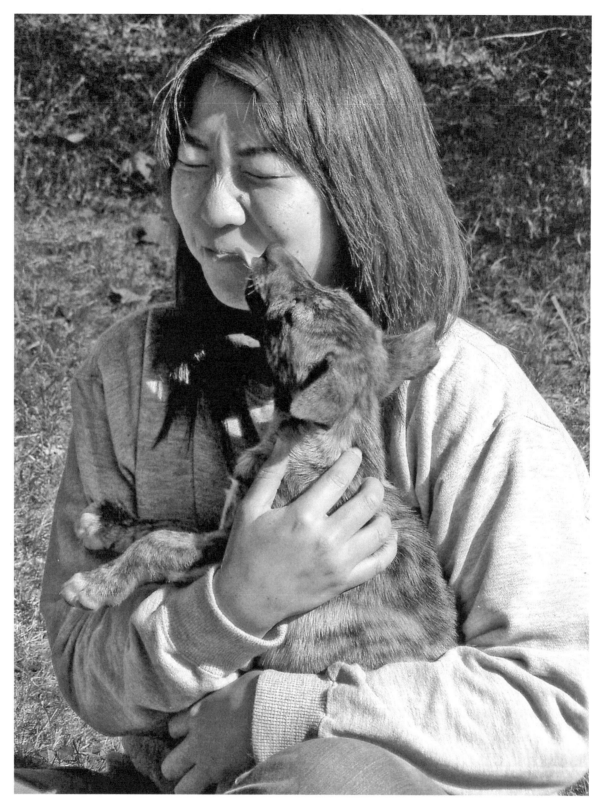

Puppies will lick humans in the same way they will an adult dog. The gesture means the same thing: friendly submission.

#20.2: Puppy Lick to Human by Puppy

- silhouette of puppy is typical: lowered body, raised chin
- floppy, relaxed ears

Adult dogs will use this communication signal just as a puppy will.

Note this dog's silhouette - it is the exact same silhouette as the baby puppy's in Photo #20.1 & #20.2.

Also interesting is the canine reaction to puppy licking as compared to the human reaction.

#20.3: Puppy Lick to Human by Adult Dog

- silhouette of dog: lowered body reaching up with raised chin
- ears drawn back

Dogs tend to orient their nose slightly away from the Licker and open their mouths in acceptance.

Humans tend to squinch their faces in defense of the onslaught of sticky wet tongue. We often turn our faces away and close our eyes and mouths. I wonder what dogs think of that?

#20.4: Puppy Lick to Adult Dog by an Adult Dog: Photo Essay

- ears relaxed & back at half-mast
- soft eyes
- avoidance of direct eye contact
- long lips
- open mouths

This is an encounter between two adult dogs. These dogs do not live together but they do know each other. See the slightly pulled back ears on both dogs? Note the soft eyes, especially on the Licker (the GSD), who also has squinty eyes. The GSD proceeds slowly and carefully - first checking with Willie, the Golden, by just touching Willie's nose with his, keeping a relaxed open mouth.

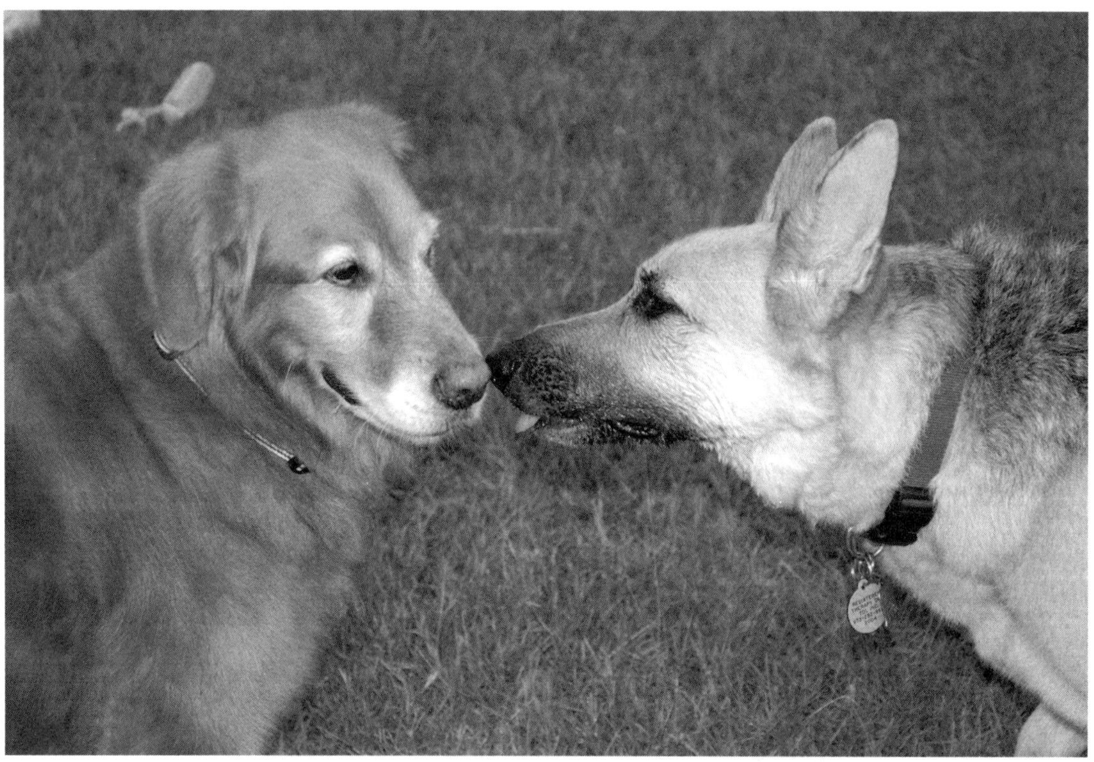

Willie does not move away, and, in fact, shows he will accept this friendly gesture by giving the GSD a Look Away and pulling his ears back just a bit more. Also notice Willie's long lips and his careful avoidance of direct eye contact.

Here, the friendly Puppy Licking gesture is completed by the GSD, and Willie is fully accepting it in the spirit it is meant: an expression of bonding.

Note Willie's open mouth and the relaxed posture of his entire body. And the GSD has lovely manners; he asked permission, never got anxious, groveling or frenetic. He just gave Willie a pleasant and relaxed "hug."

Photo Credits:
Photo #1: Mary Wilmoth;
Photo #2, #3, #4, #5 & #6: Joanne Weber.

21
Calming Signals in a Group Stay

Whenever dogs are near each other, especially if there is some tension between the dogs, there will be a lot of Calming and Negotiation signals passed around.

Left to Right: Sport....Breanna....Maeve....Punch....Dervish

#21.1: Group Dynamics: Photo Essay

- direction dog is looking
- changes in position (over 3 photographs)
- changes in orientation

This photo sequence was taken in my living room.

Sport and Dervish are still intact and are father and son. Breanna and Punch, the two Terrier girls, detest the Shepherd bitch, Maeve. But don't they look happy? It is because at this moment they are. I am totally in control, or as much as one can be with dogs who do not get on together, and all the work I have done to convince them that they don't have to kill each other is, at least for this moment, working. All are maintaining both their Stay and their relaxed attitude.

Maeve is showing very minor stress because of the proximity - her mouth is closed. This could just mean she is concentrating, but she is also poking her nose out just a touch. Sport has his mouth closed and he is not looking in the same direction as the rest of the dogs. This could mean either that he is slightly distracted or using a Look Away. Unless they knew the social dynamics of this group intimately, no one would suspect how much and how easily tension can occur within this group.

#21.2: Calming Signals

- shifting positions
- sniffing, by Sport

In this photo, Dervish changed position without me cueing him to do so. (He moved from a Sit to a Down.) I verbally corrected him, with a mild "Too Bad."

This action caused a bit of a ruckus in my little group. Breanna cheerfully changed position from a Sit to a Down on my "Too Bad" to Dervish. She does this not because she is stressed, but because it is unclear who the No Reward Mark was for. I would have been smarter had I said: "Dervish, too bad."

Sport got up to Sniff, a Calming Signal, meant, perhaps for me; or for the other dogs. Difficult to say, because of my ineptitude and lack of clarity. Regardless, what you can clearly see is that Sport wants the group to stay peaceful, and he is working to promote that emotion.

The tension that was beneath the surface is now showing. I am the immediate cause, but their stress is heightened by the fact that they are already in proximity to each other.

#21.3: Calming Signals

- more dogs shifting positions
- Yawning

Seconds later, as I move toward them to re-place the errant ones, you can see more stress: Dervish is Yawning right at me: "I am a little confused. I want to stay out of trouble."

Sport lies down with his rear quarters tucked tightly under him, indicating some body tension. Sport is also holding his head forward a bit with his nose parallel to the floor and has his lips drawn back, signs of stress and/or appeasement.

Maeve has dropped and put her head on her paws. Her lie down is another Calming Signal, either to me, or the group, very likely to all of us.

Punch is leaving the vicinity because it is getting "hotter."

Breanna has her mouth open (friendly signal), but her tail has dropped a few degrees.

These are all signs of minor stress, and, in this case, those same signs are Negotiation Signals directed at me. Very likely, they are also deliberately directed at any other dog in the vicinity as Calming Signals, as in: "I Am Staying Out Of Trouble: signals.

Breanna is the only one who remains relatively relaxed. She always was the one who figured my mental health was my own problem. Bree is confident in her Stay - that's training. But she also has a tougher mental attitude than the others and is more impervious to stress. That is just her personality.

What you can learn from this is that small changes in your attitude or in the environment can make big differences to dogs. Because dogs are responding sensitively to those changes, they often get in trouble. For all I know, Dervish's initial change from Sit to Down was a Calming Signal to the group. My very minor correction snowballed. This shows how much tension really was inherent for these dogs in this proximity. It also shows how hard all of the dogs were working to keep their surroundings peaceful. What great communication!

Section 3: Neutral & Friendly

Happy, friendly dogs, willing to be approached or to hang out together. Dogs in Lassie mode. This section shows dogs as we best like to picture them!

Many of these dogs are using language that says, "Come on in." Many show neutrality: comfort with their surroundings and themselves. This comfort is, fundamentally, about self-confidence.

When you are reading dogs, remember that the dog does not have to be falling all over HIMSELF (and you) with a wagging tail and wiggling body to show friendliness. In fact, that dog is showing more sycophantic behaviour than friendliness. Dogs who are relaxed and quiet *are* being friendly and *are* very comfortable. Sometimes people look at a dog who is in neutral, so to speak, and think that the dog is bored or unaware of what is going on around him. This could not be less true. Dogs showing neutrality are confident and happy to share their space with others, but are still very aware of who is there and what they are doing.

Dog language has numerous subtleties. Not every signal is a big and dramatic. A dog might, at first glance, look neutral, but have body tension or the slightly lowered head that is indicative of Guarding. Conversely, an unmoving dog is not always Guarding; sometimes he is just relaxing! A lack of tension in the face or tail will tell you that this dog is "just hangin'." Not only are these signs subtle, but, as always, they must be observed in concert with all the other signs the dog is giving you.

Notice, too, how the dogs in this section are not exhibiting signs of tension in their faces or their bodies. Notice how these dogs use neutrality and Looking Away from each other to show that they are not looking for conflict.

Enjoy these relaxed, happy, and comfortable dogs!

Line Drawing: Brenda Aloff

BUTT SNIFF

This is a lovely and appropriate Butt Sniff. Both dogs are participating in a relaxed and self-confident manner. This is the equivalent to a friendly handshake at the cocktail party. Or the familiar grasp of someone you like. Note the distance of the nose from the other dog's butt. (I laugh as I write this. It sounds so ridiculous - whoever thought we'd be discussing the importance of "nose-to-anal face distance?) Both dogs are getting the information they want, but politely. No one is invading anyone else's personal space.

#22.1: Appropriate Butt Sniff

- body posture - dogs mirror each other
- ears, half-mast
- proximity - dogs are keeping polite distance

Butt Sniffs can take on the same variety as handshakes. Ever meet someone who holds your hand too long? Or who, as they shake your hand way too vigorously, keeps moving into your personal space? Or squeezes too tightly? All of those handshakes belong to rude or oblivious people, or people who are playing power games. Well, a Butt Sniff can say all of those things and more.

For a look at Butt Sniffing as a power game and Displacement Behaviour, see the interactions in the "This Is My Territory" Chapter.

#22.2: Butt Sniff, Wide Angle View of Photo #22.1.

I couldn't help showing you some of the human body language involved, too. Look at the lovely relaxed postures of the owners here. The dogs and the handlers mirror each other's relaxed attitude. Nobody brought their issues out for the walk. Everybody is just out for uncomplicated enjoyment of the day.

> *Example: A Butt Sniff Power Game*: My Germans Shepherd Dog, Maeve, is a rescue who came to me with severe human-and dog-aggression. When I first got her to the point where I would allow her to greet people at all, she would go up to them and jam her nose into their crotch and then give a little lift with her nose. How very rude! What she was doing was "taking the mettle" of the person. Did they stand their ground or move away? People who had nerve endings did back away. She loved this little power game, and it was so easy to play. She placed herself in a top dog position with her "handshake." The people she was greeting didn't know what she was doing other than making them physically uncomfortable.

#22.3: Butt Sniff - Borderline Appropriate

- body posture - front dog is confident; rear dog is uncertain
- proximity - how close the nose is to the anal face of the other dog

Not too bad with the social skills. The dog on the left is approaching closely and Butt Sniffing, and this is fantastic, as long as it doesn't continue past two or three more steps. There is still a bit of distance, and the dog on the right, Olivia, a rescue I placed, is a very savvy dog indeed. She is accepting the Cattle Dog's Butt Sniff - you can tell because she is not clamping her tail or looking around in Warning.

The Cattle Dog looks a bit uneasy about this move she is making. See the rounded back? She knows the status of the dog she is sniffing and is being watchful of any signal from Olivia that a boundary has beren over-stepped.

Observation: In dogs, *ignoring* is one way of expressing neutrality, friendliness and acceptance of the actions of another animal.

The GSD (German Shepherd Dog) is clearly uncomfortable with the Butt Sniff that he is getting. You can see that his hindquarters are tucked under, his the top line is rounded, and his tail is held down over his anus. Typically, right after this, a Warning would occur in the form of a staring Look, or perhaps, Stillness. If the dog is reactive, he might suddenly turn and snap. The Labrador is not backing off in this photo. If a dog gives clear signals that he is uncomfortable, the other dog should acknowledge those signals by using another Calming or Negotiation Signal back, or by giving more personal space to the dog who is expressing discomfort.

Observation: Many times, dogs who didn't have adequate opportunities to practice language skills use gestures that are TOO BIG. This probably stems from anxiety or past trauma encountered when greeting other dogs.

#22.4: Intrusive Butt Sniff

- body posture - GSD uncomfortable; Labrador oblivious
- proximity
- GSD: rounded back, tucked hindquarters
- GSD: tail tucked

#22.5: Butt Sniff - Inappropriate. A Photo Essay

- tail tucked on Sniffee
- proximity, invasive

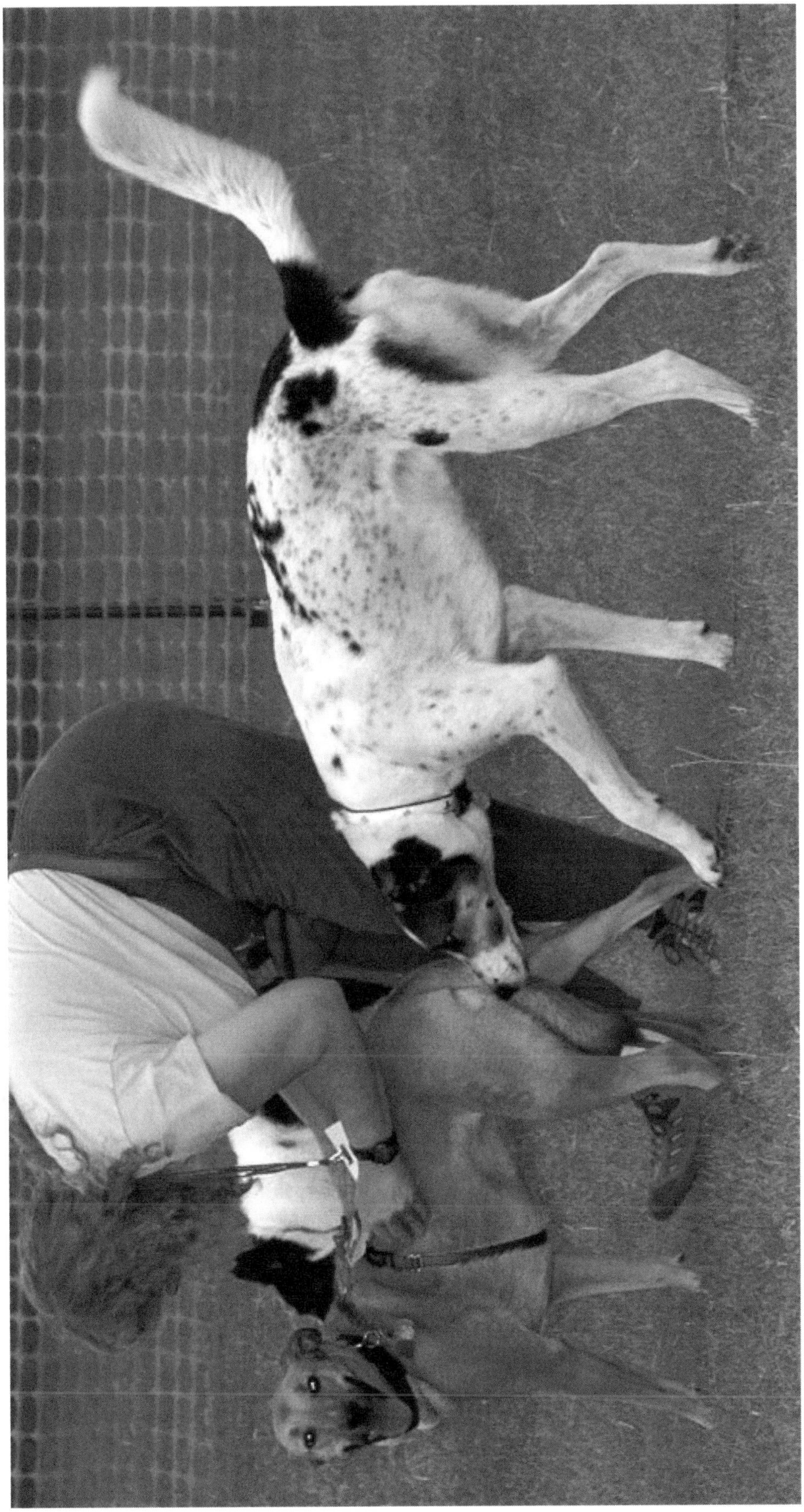

The dog on the right is diving in for an unwanted Butt Sniff. The owner has (unintentionally, I am sure) "trapped" the dog on the left. The dog on the left is turning her head toward the errant Butt Sniffer to ask her to back off, to no avail. Notice the plastered-back ears of the dog on the left and that the direction of her eyes are different than of her nose. Her nose is oriented 90 degrees to her body, but her eyes are looking at the Butt Sniffer. She has tucked her tail: "Enough Already!"

> *Training Tip*: Dogs who have not been well-socialized are often terrified of Butt Sniffs - or resent them mightily. Get your dog around lots of other friendly, appropriate dogs so she understands her own native language.

The dog on the right, correctly figuring that the dog on the left cannot move away, has charged in even further for a proctology-style Butt Sniff. The dog on the left has tucked her tail tighter; you can tell this because she is hunching her back up rounder and has drawn one of her hind legs up further under her body. She has also ceased warning the other dog and has resigned herself to putting up with this - until she can do something about it.

Training Tip: I would protect my dog at Photo #22.5. If another dog makes my dog uncomfortable, I shoo it away. I like it when my dog sees me as part of the solution.

Observation: Some dogs do a proctology exam instead of a Butt Sniff. This is entirely unnecessary and very pushy. This kind of Butt Sniff is like a 'sub-mounting' behaviour. The intent is not friendly. It is a violation of personal space and a display of dominance. I often see dogs who are pushy or insecure use the proctology Butt Sniff.

In Photo #22.6 & Photo #22.7, we have two situations where a dog is paying close attention to some other task, while another dog is allowed to walk up and invade space by their owner. Everybody is handling it just fine, but if the Butt Sniffer persisted, I could easily see the preoccupied dog turning around and snapping: "Hey, I am busy here!"

Unfortunately, when that happens, the dog who snaps is the one everybody criticizes, when it really it is the fault of the other dog who had his nose where it doesn't need to be. Or, more correctly, it is the fault of the owner of the uninvited and intruding dog.

The Dalmatian in Photo #22.6looks like his attitude is a pretty casual, "Hey, there's a butt right in front of me, I guess I'll just give it a little sniff." That's not so bad. This Dal has kept really nice and neutral language: tail and ears at half-mast and legs not braced. The Pariah dog on the right is maintaining her composure, too. Her mouth is open, her ears are at half-mast, and she is very accepting. We can tell this, because although she is certainly aware that the dog behind her has his nose up her bum (see her tail down, to limit access), yet she is pointedly ignoring the other dog. The tail down reminds the "Butt Sniffer" behind her to "be polite, and don't jam your nose too close."

#22.6: Casual Butt Sniff

- proximity
- orientation to the other dog
- ears on the Dalmatian are half-mast
- ears on the Pariah dog are half-mast
- mouth open on the Pariah dog

Training Tip: Some people discourage all Butt Sniffing while others allow their dogs to Sniff too long or too close. Yet others pay no attention and allow their dogs to Sniff everybody, whether appropriate or not. Neither extreme is ideal. Learn to rocognize and encourage "friendly handshakes" and discourage pushy ones. If dogs are on leash, or in a public area, such as a dog show, ideally, both handlers should consent to allowing the dogs to meet, before the dogs get into each other's personal space. Do not allow your dog to be rude and protect your dog from others who are violating personal space without permission.

#22.7: Would-Be Proctology Exam

- proximity
- Rottie is straining forward (the leash is tight)
- Rottie's legs are braced
- Rottie's tail is forced up

The Rottweiler looks like he is just getting started on a proctology exam. The Rottweiler is straining forward against the pull of the leash. If he weren't restrained by the leash, how much closer would he be? The Rottie's tail is forced straight up; that is often a signal of a dog who is thinking about Rank Order. This type of straight up tail is occasionally a signal that the dog wants to play. We can't tell from this small moment in time exactly which it is. What IS clear, though, is that the terrier is preoccupied. The terrier did not solicit the Rottie's approach. The terrier is ignorning the Rottwieler's advances in a mannerly way. The Rottweiler is ignoring the "mood" and is inappropriate for interfering, and is too intense about the Butt Sniff.

The Rottweiler is lucky the Lakeland terrier is being good-humoured about the Butt Sniff. The Lakie has chosen to ignore the Rottie, at least for now! She has remained focused intensely on her mum.

Here are two dogs doing Pass By exercises, where the dogs are walked near each other. The idea with such exercises is that the dog should keep attention on his owner. It takes some practice for that to happen, though! Dogs are naturally curious about each other, but it is up to us to teach our dog that not everything is her business!

The spotted dog doing a Butt Sniff, which the solid-colored dog is handling beautifully. Very confident.

#22.8: Butt Sniff: Acceptance

- proximity
- relaxed & attentive demeanor of dog on the left
- dog on the right is friendly, less intensity, more sideways position (less "mounting" intent)

I wish you could have known the solid-colored dog when Mary, his owner, first brought him to camp. He had been found in a dumpster, and certainly did not get to go to Montessori like the more privileged doggies. He was very poor with his native language, but you can see here that dogs can recover their language with time and effort. Mary has spent years teaching him how to use his language effectively, and here is the proof that Dumpster (that really is his name!) has learned how to speak Dog effectively.

As an aside, notice that all the dogs in Photo #22.8 are avoiding eye contact with each other. Again, this is the hallmark of a peaceful, friendly - or at least neutral - group.

#22.9: Sniffing On Pass By

- dog on the right is Sniffing the ground in response to the Alerting behaviour of the dog on the left

This is another Pass By with the same two dogs. You can see the spotted dog orienting toward Dumpster. The spotted dog has her tail up over her back and is staring at the dog on the right. She has also lowered her head.

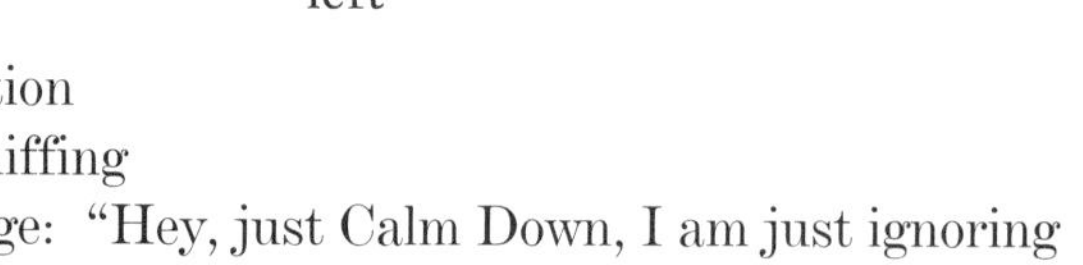

The dog on the right, Dumpster, is using a stunning Negotiation signal to avoid the eye contact - Sniffing. Do not think the sniffing is some sort of coincidence. It is masterful use of the language: "Hey, just Calm Down, I am just ignoring you as I walk by."

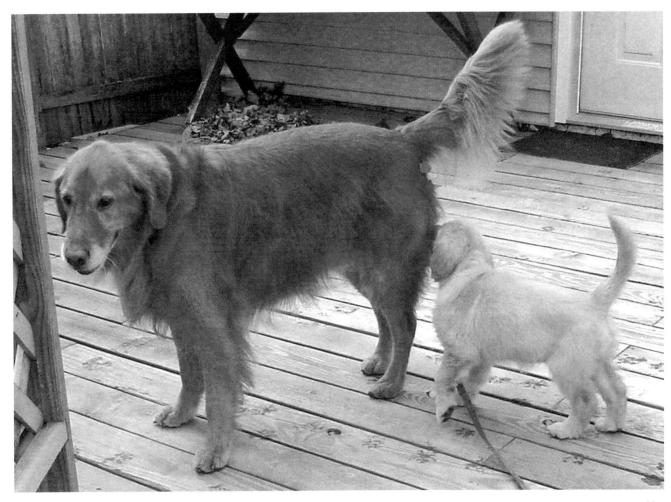

#22.10: Puppy Using Butt Sniff

- relaxed demeanor of adult dog
- orientation of puppy to adult
- puppy is not jamming her nose up into the adults crotch in a pushy manner

Puppies come with Butt Sniffing skills.

Here, tiny Ivy gives her Uncle Willie a very proper Butt Sniff. She even has a paw lifted. The paw lift is frequently used to express, "I Come In Peace."

Willie is very confident and accepts his role in teaching the little one good manners. You can tell this because his ears and tail are half-mast and relaxed. His face is relaxed, with a soft eye and a slightly opened mouth. His legs are not braced. He is not turning around to Warn the puppy, but is using nonchalant body language to tell Ivy that his intentions are friendly.

Getting your puppy around older dogs who have good native language skills ensures a good vocabulary and proper usage of language.

Photo Credits:
Photo #1 & #2: Lonnie Olson;
Photo #3: Cherish DeWitt;
Photo #4, #5 & #6: Joanne Weber;
Photo #7: Lonnie Olson;
Photo #8: Joanne Weber;
Photo #9 & #10: Felicia Banys;
Photo # #11: Joanne Weber.

Inguinal Sniff

The Golden is receiving and accepting an Inguinal Sniff. The Dalmatian is doing a lovely correct and polite sniff. Note the half-mast and gently sweeping tails of both dogs. The ears of both dogs are also at half-mast. Note the arced, sideways approach of the Dalmatian. All the language here reflects beautiful usage.

#23.1: Receiving & Accepting an Inguinal Sniff

- body alignment to each other
- ears, half-mast, mirroring
- lack of body tension
- gently waving tails

A socially perceptive dog will often mirror signals and positions in greeting, as these two dogs do. Notice the similarity in leg and tail positions.

I included the humans here because it is interesting to see how the dogs are focused on each other, and the humans are focused on the dogs. All the humans are relaxed, too.

#23.2: Slight Tension in an Inguinal Sniff

- body alignment to each other
- ears, pulled back slightly, some tension
- Golden has slightly braced legs
- Golden is "standing tall"
- gently waving tails, both dogs

This Golden is receiving and accepting the Inguinal Sniff of the English Setter. Again, see the gently sweeping tails.

Compare, however, these dogs' stances to the ones in Photo #23.1. The two dogs in Photo #23.2 are not quite as comfortable as the dogs in Photo #23.1.

In Photo #23.2, there is a slight bracing of legs in both of these dogs. The Golden has raised her tail just a bit and she has some facial tension. See the fold in the ears: they are half-mast, but ready to come forward. She is also Standing a little Tall, as if she feels she has to show status. This is not unfriendly at all, and the dogs are very appropriate, but there is more tension here.

Dogs who lack confidence or who are not very familiar with each other might show a little tension such as this. Or, if a dog is on her own territory and there is a visitor, which is the case here, the resident dog will often show status to the visitor, just to remind the visitor who has first access to resources in this territory.

Overall, the language usage is great. Both dogs are observing each others' signals and Responding politely. The dogs are not Hind Brain and Reacting out of proportion to the situation. The eyes of the Golden are very soft, and the Setter isn't being rough or pushy.

#23.3: Inguinal Sniff - Puppy to Adult

- body alignment to each other (sideways)
- ears, half-mast, relaxed
- gently waving tails
- relaxed acceptance of older dog
- appropriate, not pushy, behaviour of puppy

This is a puppy doing an Inguinal Sniff on an adult. The adult is receiving and accepting the sniff patiently. What a super-fine educator this puppy has come across!

Note the lowered head, soft eye, and relaxed lips of the adult. You cannot see the whole tail in this photo, but it is apparent that the adult dog's tail is at half mast and, probably, gently waving.

The puppy is displaying some lovely hard-wired language. Her tail is also at half-mast and gently waving. Her approach is appropriately side-on, and she is not rutting or pushing or trying to nurse, but doing a real-live Big Girl Inguinal Sniff.

> *Socialization & Language Skills*: The native language skills that very young puppies come with amaze me. These hard-wired language skills can be damaged. When exposed repeatedly to dogs who pay no attention to language, or who do not mirror back language, or who are reactive, the impressionable puppy's language skills can be eroded.
>
> Luckily for us, dogs are very adaptable. I have watched many of my clients' dogs regain their use of native language with time, patience, and exposure to other normal, well-socialized and confident dogs.

:Photo Credits: Photo #1: Lonnie Olson; Photo #2: Cherish DeWitt; Photo #3: Joanne Weber.

FRIENDLY

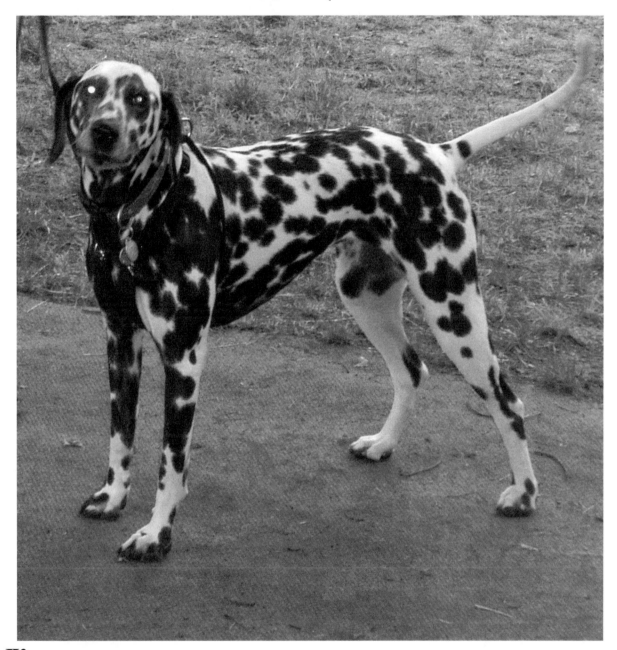

What a lovely expression! The pupils are slightly dilated, but that can be from excitement or expectancy. This dog is standing naturally, just one hind leg bent a bit more than the other. The tail is at half-mast. You can see it gently moving at the tip. There is no facial tension. The ears are resting on the head and a little floppy. She is engaging in direct eye contact while remaining relaxed. The body is relaxed, too. The legs are not braced. The Body Orientation is Neutral: there is no feeling of a Forward or Backward body orientation.

I would pet this dog, but would expect her to move toward me as I did so, eagerly and perhaps quickly. Her lips are relaxed and she is just starting a little "smile."

#24.1: Inviting Body Posture

- tail at half-mast
- ears resting near head
- body not tense, legs not braced
- dog is engaging in direct eye contact and remains relaxed
- lips are relaxed
- neutral body orientation - not forward or backward

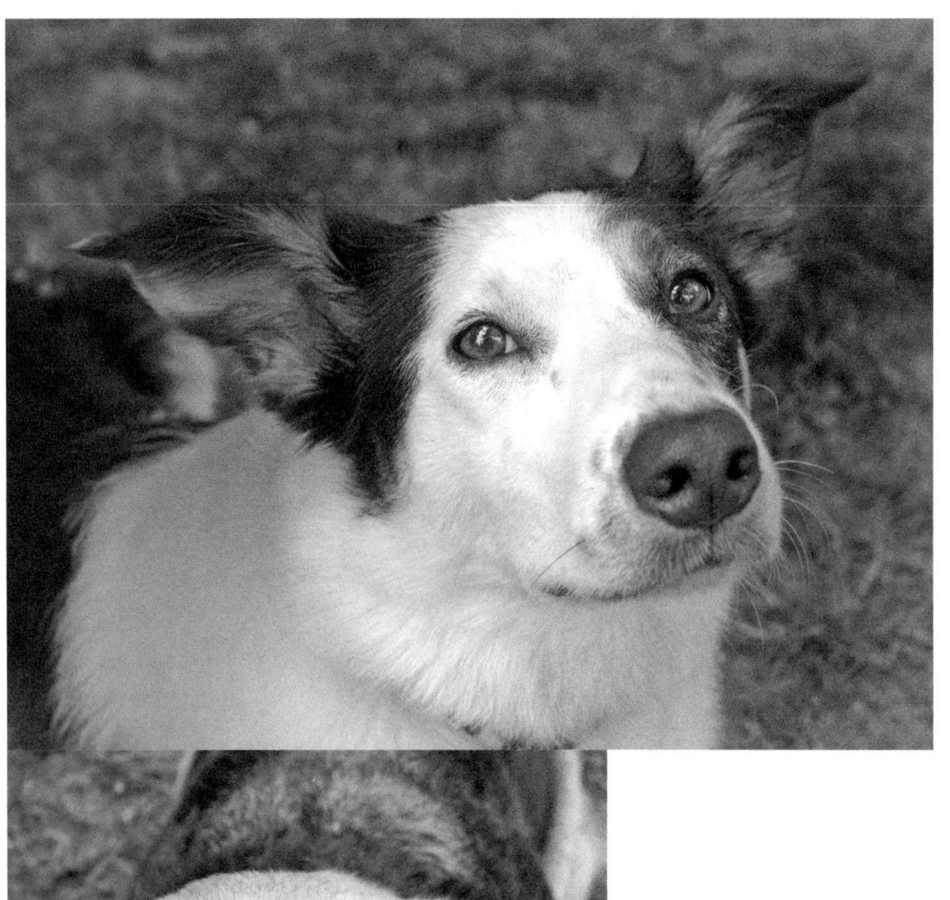

#24.2: "Take Me Home" Eyes

- dog is engaging in direct eye contact and remains relaxed
- lips are relaxed
- ears are not forced into any extreme position

What a darling expression on this Border Collie. Soft and sweet, and the half-mast ears show respect and invitation.

(Below Left)

#24.3: Sweet Faces

(Bottom)

#24.4: Sweet Faces

The Beagle and Fox Terrier both have ears slightly pricked in interest - "What could those humans be up to now?" - and soft

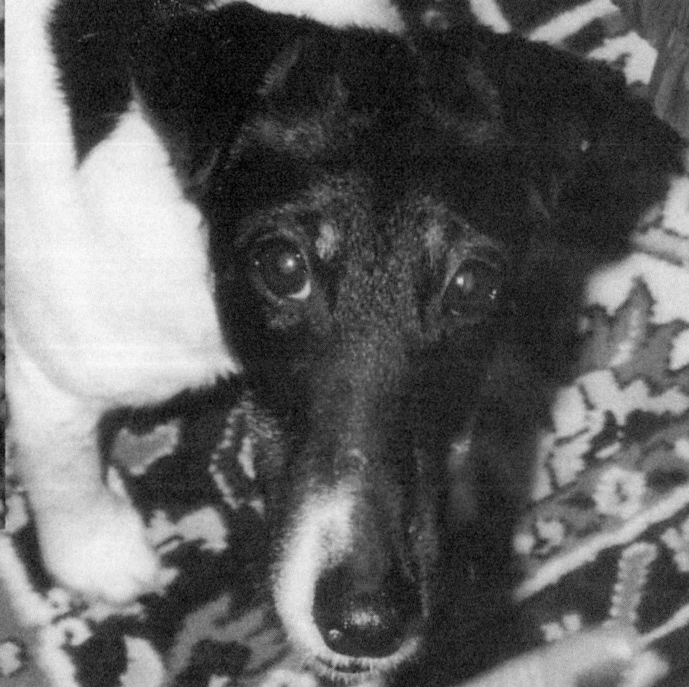

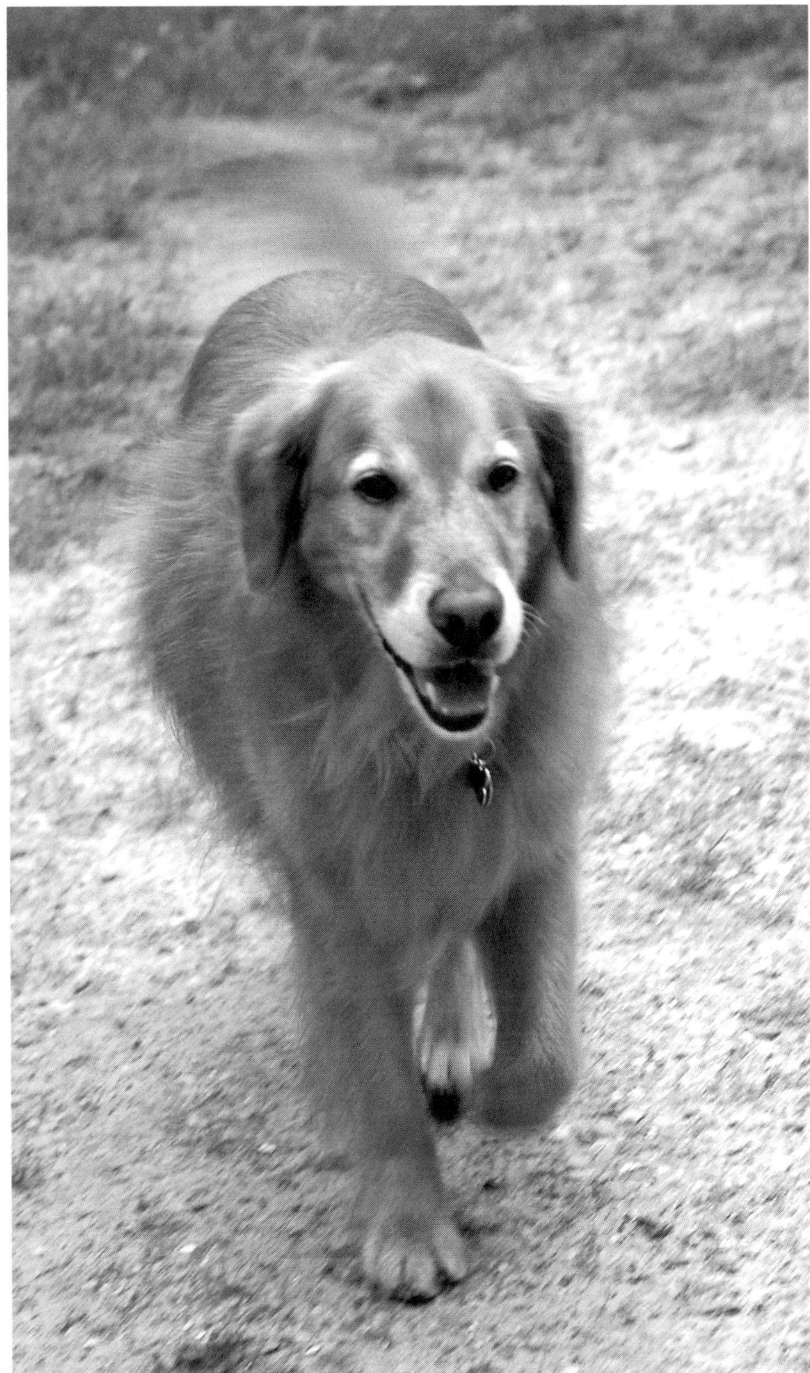

#24.5: Friendly - In Motion

- tail at half-mast
- ears half-mast
- tail gently waving
- mouth open
- eyes soft

Look at the lovely low sweep of this friendly tail. His mouth is partially open; his eyes are not forced open or squinting; his ears and tail are at half-mast. This dog is exuding self-confidence, but not assertiveness. Dogs who are very self-confident are also very self-contained. They do not need to be pushy or assertive to find their place in a group.

#24.6: Lowered Head

#24.7: Lowered Head

- tail at half-mast
- ears half-mast
- slightly lowered head
- relaxed movement

Photo #24.3: The dog to the right has a lovely “I Am Just Staying Out Of Social Trouble” posture. He is just goin’ places. The head is nearly at the same height as the back; the tail and ears are at half-mast.

Note the contrast with the German Shepherd Dog in the background. He is Alerting on the photographer.

Photo #24.4: Here is the same “I Am A Friendly Guy” lowered body posture in a puppy. When I was looking through photos to use for this book, I saw several of this puppy. In EVERY photo, this little guy was using perfect Friendly body language. I just fell in love with him. His owner is a lucky gal.

Note the similar lowered body posture of the adult dogs in the background.

#24.8: Friendly - in a Group

- head in neutral or slightly lowered position
- lack of eye contact

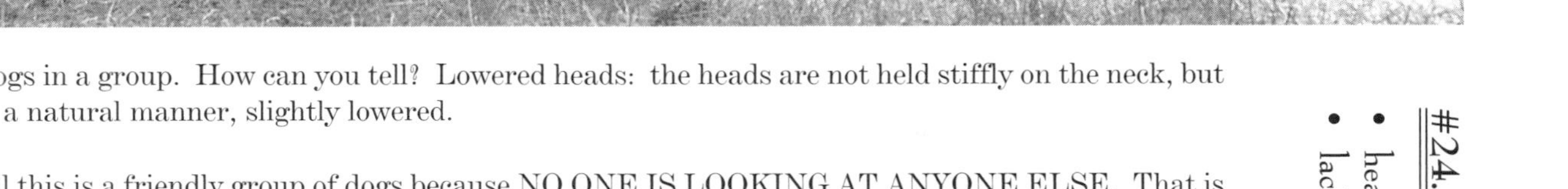

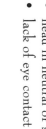

#24.8: Slight Tension

- head held up
- ridge under eye
- ears drawn back in some tension

Friendly dogs in a group. How can you tell? Lowered heads: the heads are not held stiffly on the neck, but are held in a natural manner, slightly lowered.

You can tell this is a friendly group of dogs because NO ONE IS LOOKING AT ANYONE ELSE. That is what really friendly, self-confident and relaxed dogs do in groups - they pretty much ignore each other a great deal of the time. Remember, dogs have super peripheral vision. They can see in a very wide range around their body. If they are looking directly at something, there is a darn good reason for it.

I love the body language of most of the dogs here; they all look like they are comfortable with the proximity of the other dogs.

There is one dog in this picture, though, who does not match this profile. See the close-up to the left, Photo #24.8.

Notice the ridge under the eye? That is a signal of facial tension. He is also holding his head higher than the rest of the dogs.

He has nice blinking eyes and ears slightly drawn back, but he looks a bit tense. It could be the proximity of the dog immediately in front of him, or he might not be used to groups of dogs.

This Spinone puppy is just too dear. As the person bends over him, instead of showing flight or avoidance, he looks right at the approaching person and leans into the hand that is touching him. Just bending over a dog and giving him direct eye contact can cause a submissive response. The puppy does not become overactive and start wiggling around with anxiety because of the "threat" behaviour of the looming human. Instead, he responds with a Puppy Lick. The hood alone could cause some dogs to be very fearful, but this pup is handling the experience with aplomb, self-confidence, and social grace. What lovely examples of native language.

#24.9: "I Am Very Friendly & Respectful, Too" - Photo Essay

- lowered body posture
- Paw Lift
- soft, squinting, blinking eyes
- lowered tail
- squatting rear
- ears drawn back
- eye contact without tension shows trust

Photo Credits:
Photo #1: Jennifer Riess;
Photo #2: Joanne Weber;
Photo #3: Felicia Banys;
Photo #4: Abbey Palmer;
Photo #5: Joanne Weber;
Photo #6:Jenifer Reiss ;
Photo #7:Jennifer Reiss ;
Photo #8: Jennifer Riess;
Photo Essay #9: Joanne Weber.

25
Greeting "I Love You" Stretch

The Greeting Stretch is a posture used only towards someone the dog likes and with whom he is comfortable. There is also a version of this where the dog leans forward and stretches his rear legs out behind him. My dogs use this with me frequently when they approach me or I approach them. Sometimes the "front" stretch, where the dog lowers the elbows, is followed immediately by a "rear" stretch, in which the dog leans forward and drags the rear legs out behind him.

How does this differ from other kinds of similar body postures? In the Greeting Stretch, you do not get the feeling the dog will pounce forward as they do in a Prey Bow. This is not a "Ready-Set-Go" position. In the Greeting Stretch, there is usually not the extreme lowering of the body that you see in a Play Bow; the dog will just go partially down. In the Greeting Stretch, you will also see more relaxed ear carriage, and more squinty eyes.

The best way to tell of course, is the context. The activity level is indicative, too. You will see in these photographs that the dogs have a languid, liquid look about them, rather than the intensely coiled spring look of the Prey Bow or the lively anticipation of the Play Bow.

#25.1: Greeting Stretch

- lowered forequarters
- raised hindquarters
- nose oriented up toward the person the dog is greeting
- elbows remain off the ground (usually)

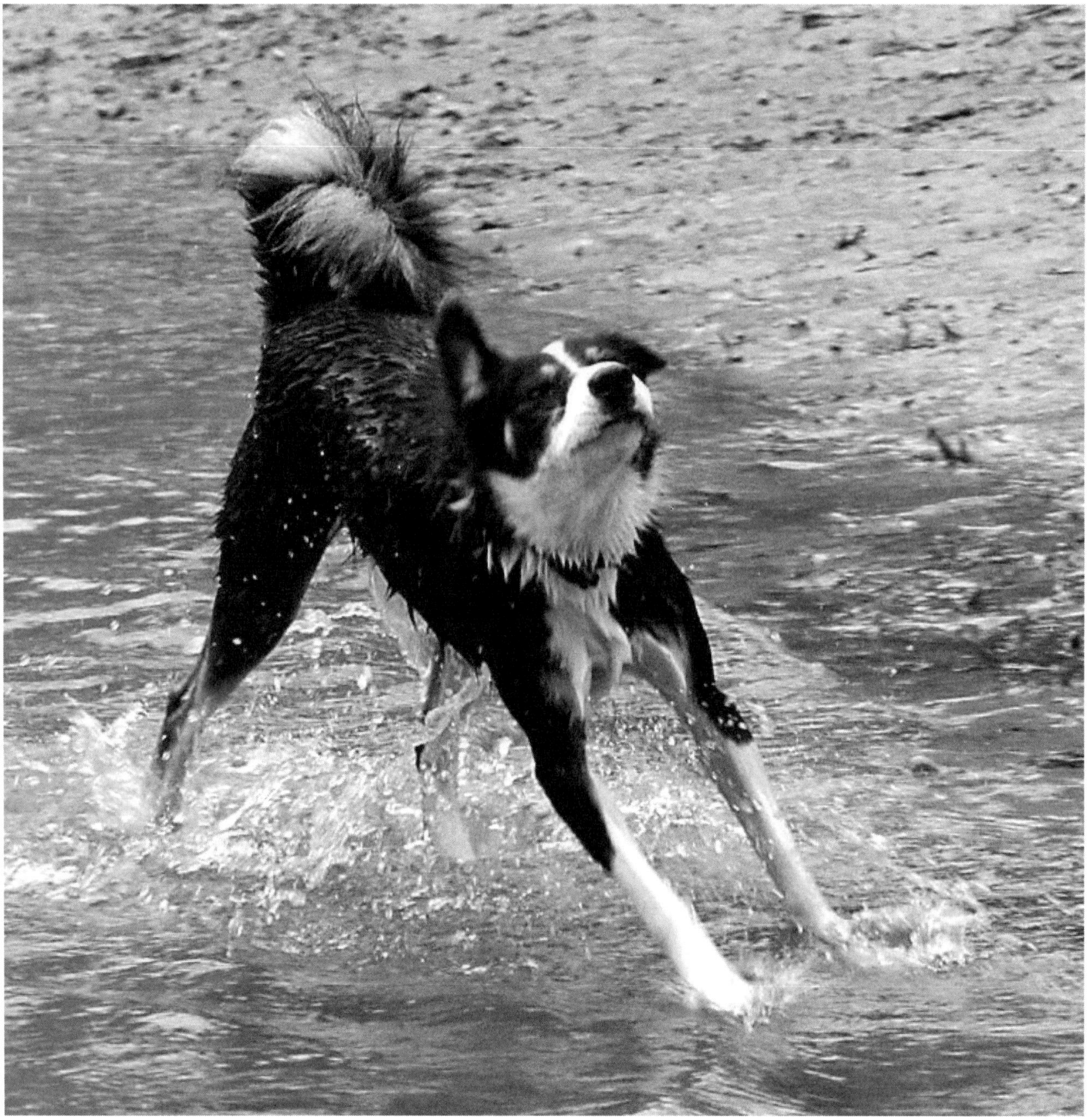

#25.2: Greeting Stretch

When dogs greet me like this, I get all mushy and gooey. It is very flattering to have a dog greet you in this unrestrained, friendly and very respectful manner. This greeting acknowledges your personal space and is a request for the two of you to interact.

The relaxed manner, combined with the body silhouette tell you this is a dog who is happy to be with whomever he is gazing at. The front legs are braced, but this is not a Prey Bow, not enough intensity. The ears are floppy, the tail is up and confident, but not forced or tense.

This is the equivalent of a child offering you a tiny bouquet of "I picked these just for you" flowers.

#25.3: Greeting Stretch

Notice the soft eyes and long lips of this dog as she gazes at her owner.

#25.4: Greeting Stretch - Rear Leg Stretch

As Willie greets his owner, (who luckily happened to have a camera!) he stretches his rear legs out behind him, stretches his tail out and Yawns. His eyes are squinty in friendliness. Sometimes dogs will greet you with a Front Leg Stretch followed by a Rear Leg Stretch.

On rare occasions I have seen dogs use a stretch like this when you are working them and they are a little confused about the task.

Photo Credits:
Photo #1 & #2: Joanne Weber;
Photo #3: Rachel Plotinski;
Photo #4: Joanne Weber.

26 GREETING

#26.1: Dog to Dog Greetings

- paw lift on Setter
- dogs both respecting personal space, no crowding
- ears drawn back
- squinting eyes
- sweeping tails
- relaxed jaws

This positioning demonstrates a prototypical polite, friendly gesture.

The English Setter has drawn back ears, long lips and squinty eyes. Her tail is held at half mast and is sweeping gently back and forth. The Golden also has long relaxed lips, relaxed ear set and sweeping tail.

Note that the dogs are not directly in front of each other but slightly off to the side in a proper and polite arced approach.

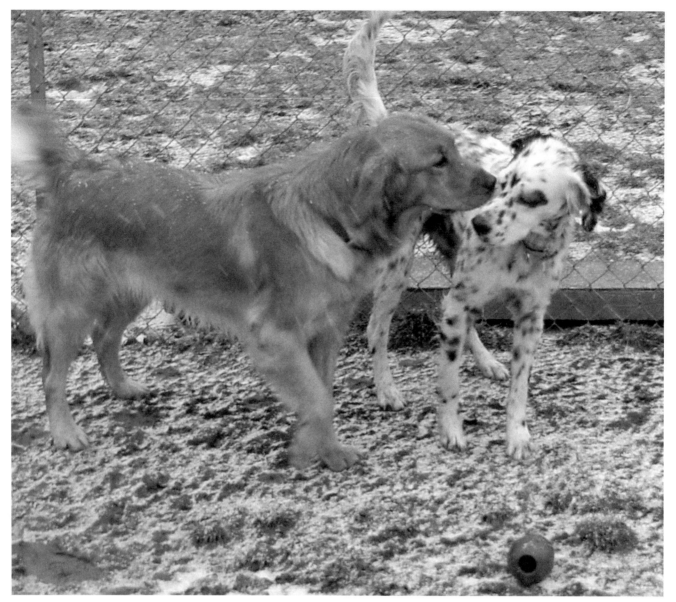

#26.2: Dog to Dog Greetings

- relaxed body posture
- ears half-mast
- squinting eyes
- gently waving tails
- relaxed jaws
- sideways approach

Everything here is appropriate and polite. The dogs are not in "Chicken" or head-on position, but are using a sideways approach. They are not directly staring at each other. Their eyes are soft and blinking. Notice the Paw Lift on the Golden. Ears are half-mast on both dogs. There is a lack of facial and body tension.

All of this language communicates non-threatening intent. Contrast these Greetings with the dogs in the Alerting, Guarding and Warning Chapters.

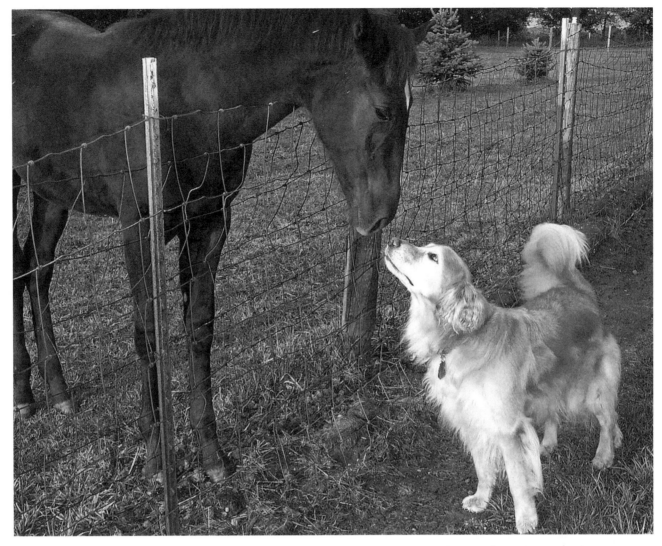

#26.3: Other Species Greeting

- sideways body orientation
- ears half-mast
- eyes soft
- gently waving tail
- no body tension

This canine greeting could not be more polite or correct. There is no improving on this greeting, no matter what species the dog is getting acquainted with. Her body orientation is sideways not the Chicken, "head-on" orientation. Her eyes are soft, her lips are long, her ears and tail are half mast. Her tail is gently waving. There is almost a Paw Lift. The most lovely thing about this greeting is the self-confidence that it displays. I Have Great Coping Skills Even In New Circumstances is evident in every gesture.

The horse is doing pretty well, too, although there is a bit of tension in his muzzle and his lips look a little pursed or shortened. But the ears are off to the side and the eyes remain soft, so the horse will remain peaceful on his part, as well.

The greeting of the pony is friendly; notice the drawn-back ears and the soft, squinty eye.

The dog, however, looks like he is a bit nervous about this: What is this animal? This emotion causes this dog to adopt a Forward body orientation (stance) and raised tail. The dog is not even trying an arced greeting, which would be more appropriate. The dog is staring directly at the pony. He looks like he has decided the best offense is a good defense. This is not to say he is going to attack the pony; he might just tough it out and, if the pony is not reactive, the dog would probably relax a little bit.

#26.4: Other Species Greeting

- "Chicken" or Challenge Position
- forward body orientation
- up "On His Toes"
- tail raised
- direct stare
- body tension
- direct approach

When a dog takes this stance upon meeting someone (person, dog other species), it is not friendly. It is rude or defensive. Usually it means the dog is assertive, or is nervous and therefore "on the muscle." This kind of greeting holds a lot of tension. This dog's body language says, "My next move is Forward." This means that, if the other animal becomes reactive, the dog will MOVE INTO the social pressure, not away from it.

What makes this greeting so unfriendly is the tension in the body posture, the raised tail and direct eye contact. Even more significant than all those, though, is the directly-in-front-of-the-pony, head-on body position - like the dog is playing a game of Chicken. This is confrontational body language. From some of my dogs, this position alone would elicit a correction.

You can surmise what kind of problems this can create. If the other animal moves away, the dog may become predatory and chase. If the other animal moves into this dog and either one becomes reactive, then you have a problem. Both then have to determine whether to give in to the social pressure (move back) or continue to move into the social pressure. If one of the animals becomes reactive, chances are very great that the other animal will follow suit and become reactive also. Animals who are in an extreme emotional state and who are Reactive are not really making decisions using a Thinking process.

Remember, your dog will always try to "talk" to another dog, human, or member of another species as he would a dog, unless he has extensive experience with the other species.

As far as these tiny Papillons are concerned, they might just as well be greeting an alien species.

The dog furthest on the left is doing an Avoidance-style Look Away. Notice her braced front leg, while her hindquarters are tucked under. If she moved, it would be away from the creature on the right.

The other Papillon is hunched down, with a rounded topline, which means she has a lot of tension in her body. She is staring directly at the Big Alien Dog and has adopted a defensive posture: "You Get Out Of My Space." A valiant effort on her part. She may be alarmed, or she may be Resource Guarding the location.

#26.5: Same Species Greeting

Contrast between these dogs:

- body orientation
- ears
- eyes

Although I am sure the two Papillons are not amused, I could not help but laugh at the total unconcern of the big dog. He is obviously approaching in a neutral manner, with just fine body language, though he is pretty much ignoring the signals the two tiny toys are giving. I say this, because he is not making any effort to back up or Look Away in Negotiation.

In spite of all the tension, it does not feel like there will be a horrible confrontation. The small dogs look reactive, but the large dog is not. True, the small dogs are alarmed and the large dog is oblivious, but as long as he, in the next second, heeds the signals the small dogs are giving, it is still a peaceful encounter. Remember, it is also up to the small dogs to read the signals of the large dog, and to think, not just react. Currently, they look a bit overwhelmed by having a large, disembodied "talking head" appear onto their bed.

Photo Credits: Photo #1 & #2: Cherish DeWitt; Photo #3: Maggie Ouillette; Photo #4 & #5: Joanne Weber.

27
Group Look Away

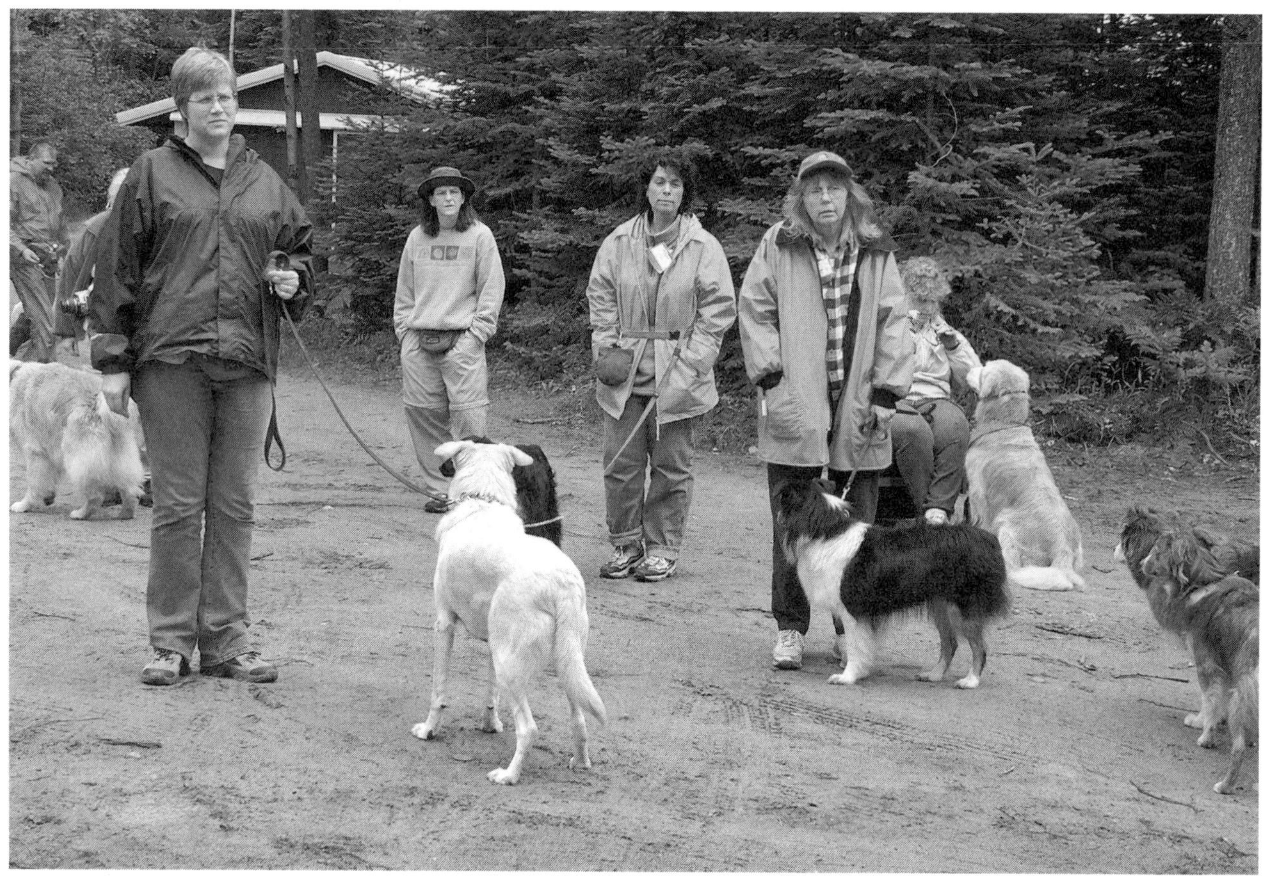

#27.1: Group Look Away

- direction dogs are looking
- body orientation-no dog is facing off or staring at another dog.
- half-mast ears & tails

I just had to open this chapter with another photo that I couldn't bear to crop the humans out of. The humans are obviously all listening to some sort of instruction being given them.

The dogs are all carefully attending also - but in the exact opposite direction of where the humans are. Just makes you wonder, doesn't it? How often was this happening all those times I thought my dog was paying attention to the same directions I was....?

This is a friendly group. How do you know that? *No dog is looking at another dog.* This is not an accident. It is intentional communication on the part of the dogs.

This photograph illustrates an interesting vantage point of looking at two diverse worlds at the same time. There is the physical dimension: One, up above the knees of humans is what we see, and the other, below our waist or knees, is what dogs see. There is also the emotional or mental dimension: What concerns humans often has no relevance for dogs, and the opposite is also true; what dogs find of intense interest is not relevant and often sort of icky (dead stuff, excrement) to humans. Dogs and humans have very different sensory systems and this has an effect on what is salient to each species.

#27.2: Voluntary Look Away

- direction dogs are looking

Friendly again! The dog in the middle is doing a Sit Stay. Without being prompted, all the other dogs are carefully looking somewhere else.

Notice how different human social groups are from canine: humans generally show polite interest in others in a friendly group, while dogs show polite disinterest.

> *Training Tip*: Remember: Eye Contact Rules. If the dog is looking at it he is thinking about it. When you see many examples of it one right after the next, you learn about the importance of orientation and eye contact.

#27.3: Negotiation - Drama in Two Scenes

THE PLAYERS - Dogs left to right are:

Eli, Black Lab, male, castrated
Willie, Golden, male, castrated
Saikou, Border Collie - X, female, spayed
Buster, Cattle Dog, male, castrated
Coyote, Cattle Dog, male, castrated

THE PLAYERS - Humans left to right are:

Heather
Lonnie
Chris

This is a stunning soap opera in two panels.

While the humans are attending to posing themselves and their dogs for a portrait, the dogs are communicating furiously with each other about occupying space together.

On the far left is the Big Drama. Willie, the Golden, is looking at the Black Labrador. The Lab, noting the eye contact, is giving an obvious Negotiation signal: a Tongue Flick. Willie has his ears drawn back, and his body language says: "If I moved, it would not be into your body space." Willie's energy, if you will, is directed inward not outward. His front foot is slightly forward, demarcating a boundary (in this case, a boundary he is saying that he, himself, won't cross, thus reassuring the Lab).

In the middle, Saikou, the Border Collie-X, is doing a Look Away, and it looks as though it is for the benefit of the two Cattle Dogs specifically, or maybe just the activity that is going on with them as Chris encourages them to sit. She could also just be avoiding the Eye of the Camera. Saikou is just showing neutral and friendly signals for everyone present.

On the right there are two Cattle Dogs. Buster, the dark colored one, is a very cautious dog by nature (I know the dog personally). Even so, you can tell he is very concerned about the proximity of the other dogs and humans and the social pressure of "performing" a sit stay amongst them. He is also aware of the Drama going on in the vicinity. His tail is mostly tucked beneath his body, so he is partially sitting on it. This is no accident. Confident dogs don't normally sit on their tails. His ears are back, his lips are drawn back, his front feet are slightly braced. His back is rounded or hunched, another indication confirming the tail thing is not happenstance. He is deriving comfort from his trust in his mum by attending to her to the exclusion of all else.

Last but not least, Coyote, the lighter colored Cattle Dog, is confident. Even though I cannot see his head, his tail is up over his back. I really wish I could see exactly what he is looking at. The interpretation that follows is based on the assumption that the Cattle Dog is indeed staring at the Lab. His field of vision underneath the swing would be unencumbered, and he is most certainly oriented directly toward the Lab. I suspect that he is the real driving force in the Drama to the left: that he is looking directly at the Black Labrador. It appears as though the Coyote's head is slightly lowered, which can indicate a stalking behaviour. If he is, indeed, staring at the Lab from underneath the swing, the Lab could very well feel trapped.
The Lab has Willie directly in front of him, and Coyote, who is telling him to move forward with social pressure.
The Lab's eyes are looking in the direction of the Cattle Dog, which tells us that he is concerned, or at least noticing something in that direction. If he were giving the Golden a Look Away, he would look toward the tree.

Neutral & Friendly:Group Look Away

Chris, on the far right, managed to get both Cattle dogs seated and facing the camera. Notice Buster, the furthest to the right. He managed to get as far away from the other dogs as he could and still meet Chris' requirements. He is Looking Away from the other dogs and his ears are drawn back.

Coyote, the other Cattle Dog, is looking straight at the camera with a happy mouth. Probably pleased that he managed to move some "stock" around.

In the middle, Saikou, the Border Collie-X, feels comfortable enough to turn her back on the Cattle Dogs behind her.

Willie, the Golden, is Looking Away from the Lab, which has allowed the Lab to move forward, away from the eyes of the Cattle Dog. Willie has added a friendly open mouth also. This has given the Lab permission to enter Willie's personal space. Willie stays within his boundary, as promised earlier.

The Lab is now doing a Look Away and using a neutral body position. He is taking a little breather from the social drama that he just skillfully handled.

Really, no matter if I am precisely correct in my microscopic dissection or not, what IS apparent in this photo essay is the main principle: in the group, the dogs are deliberately avoiding eye contact with each other. As soon as the dogs are brought into each other's space, they all begin peace-keeping by using Negotiation Signals. When an incidence of eye contact does occur, an obvious Negotiation signal, the Tongue Flick, is given by the Lab and received and accepted by the Golden.

In Conclusion

I looked through thousands of photographs for this book, and one fact was elucidated thousands of times: in friendly, neutral groups, dogs Look Away from each other. I loved that, because it validated something I already knew from field experience.

When dogs are oriented toward each other there is one of two things going on: the dogs are playing, therefore, they are oriented toward each other, but giving frequent Calming Signals and using breaks in the play to confirm it IS play; or there is some sort of conflict occurring. Dogs are very careful to monitor their orientation and eye contact, if they are allowed to do so AND if their native language remains intact.

Dog language is under constant errosion by us, even though we don't intend it to happen. Much of this happens because we aren't aware that dog language is going on. Dogs aren't just making a lot of random and unconnected actions - much of it is deliberate communication. Humans can cause damage to the dog's native language by correcting dogs at inopportune times. This could occur, for instance, when the dog is trying to use Calming Signals with another dog, and a human interrupts the process.

Training Tip: If your dog does NOT grant the courtesy of avoiding eye contact with other dogs, you should intervene and manufacture a Look Away. Get your dog to look at you, away from the other dogs. This will keep your dog out of trouble AND afford you some control over the other dogs in the vicinity, even though you are not handling them directly. You will still be influencing their behaviour by making your dog appear less threatening.

On the other hand, many dogs do not seem to understand that they can do a Look Away once eye contact has been initiated. Once the eye contact starts it seems as though the dogs are on a tractor beam - pulled toward each other no matter what. All that has to happen to halt this is a Look Away.

Some dogs have been taught by other dogs, who don't have good language skills, that Look Aways or other Negotiation Signals do not work. Sometimes this happens because dogs do not get opportunities to practice language with other dogs who are good native speakers. Often it occurs because dogs do not get opportunities to practice their native language with other dogs much at all.

Take note of how a dog is oriented. Which direction is the nose pointing? Is the nose pointing the same direction as the eyes are looking? The direction a dog is directly looking or directly not looking is a very good clue about what she is thinking about right this second. Armed with this clue, you can be in a better position to stop trouble before it begins. You will also develop a much greater understanding of your dear friend through your observations. Through such observations great communication and a better relationship with your dog is possible.

As I am always so involved with dogs and their point of view, I was struck over and over again by the two different worlds that were coexisting - one right above the other one. We recognize those worlds as dog trainers, but it is easy to forget how different those two worlds are.

As dog trainers we are constantly the advocate of the dog and so are more concerned with them and are often watching them more closely than we do the people. We do watch the people, but through the eyes of how we think the dog is responding or reacting to that person. Because of a dog trainer's experience level, it is easy to forget the level at which the novice handler understands dogs. At some point, with the trainer who has been training ten years and more, it becomes difficult to identify with the novice in many ways. Not that we do not try, it is just that our paradigm has changed so much with experience that it becomes impossible to "feel" the way we did at one time about certain situations.

Photo credits: Photo #1: Felicia Banys; Photo #2: Joanne Weber; Photo Essay #3: Joanne Weber.

28
Pass By

A Pass By occurs when dogs pass by each other in opposite directions, in close proximity, as if they are passing on a sidewalk. Sometimes humans are involved and sometimes just dogs. How the dogs pass each other determines whether the encounter will be friendly, neutral, or confrontational.

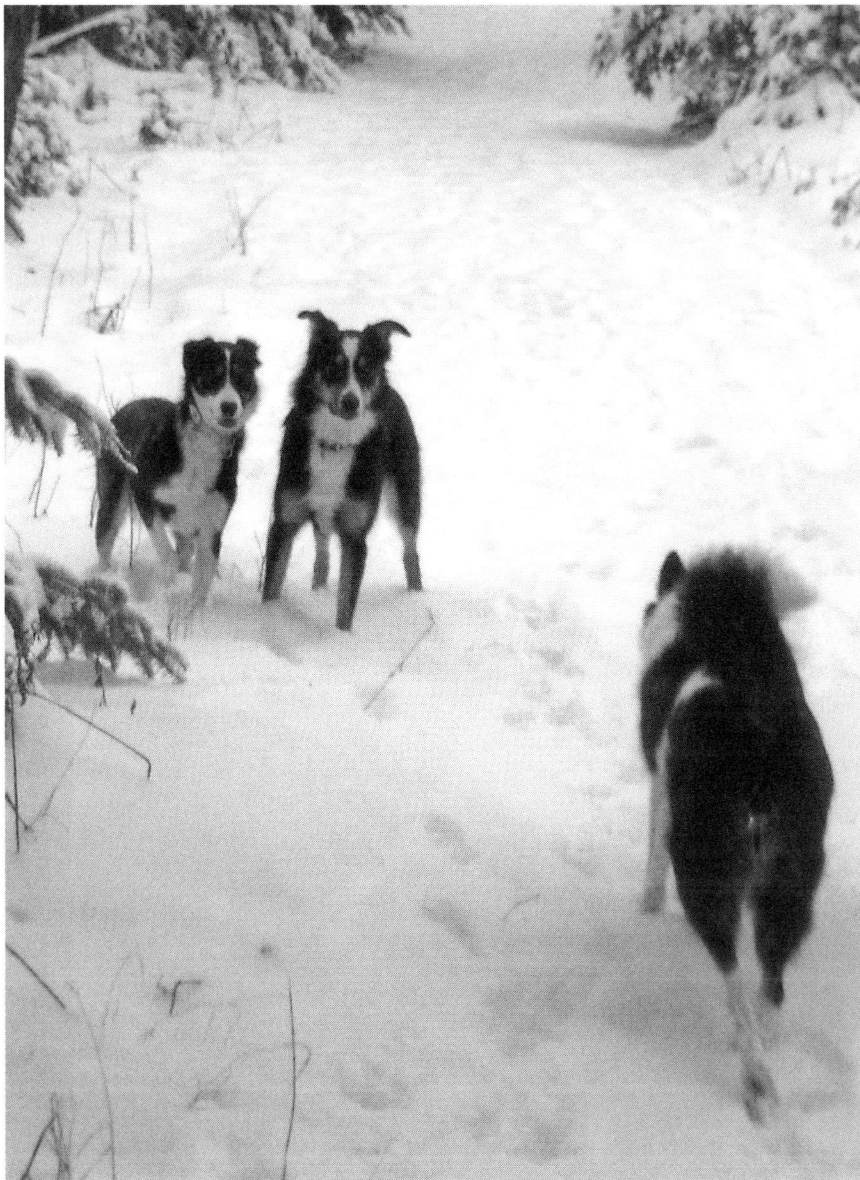

#28.1: Indirect Approach

- orientation of nose and eyes
- body postures
- paw lift
- ears

One dog passes peacefully by two dogs. The two dogs are Alerting, but not making any move to block the path of the oncoming dog. The dog on the right is keeping far to the right so she is not in a direct line or Head On Collision formation, which equals Conflict.

The dog on the far left is doing a Paw Lift. The dog in the middle has ears at half-mast. Neither of the two dogs on the left have their tails over their backs, nor are they on tip-toe and leaning forward into the oncoming dog's space; they are conceding space to the oncoming dog - allowing her passage.

It is interesting to see how dogs off-leash Pass By each other in opposite directions in close proximity, as if they were passing on a sidewalk. Notice how no dog is lunging at any other, and how they politely mind their own business. Aware, but calm, not reactive.

Training Tip: I teach my students a particular way to Pass By another dog, encouraging the dog to arc and do a Look Away to promote peaceful Pass Bys. Doing this also teaches people the importance of paying attention to eye contact between dogs.

Here two dogs do a lovely Pass By. You can tell there will be no conflict because the dogs are Looking Away from each other and arcing to avoid encroaching on each other's personal space. In this case, the dogs are attached to humans, and each dog is looking at her own human. It is interesting to note that this Look Away would be quite similar even if the dogs had nothing in particular to focus on. The only difference might be that the dog on the left might not have it's nose lifted so high. Both dogs look confident and neither dog's leash is tight; they are trusting their owners to make decisions.

#28.2: Look Away

- orientation of nose and eyes is arced away from each other

#28.3: Neutral Pass By

- orientation of nose and eyes is neutral

Another peaceful Pass By. Both dogs are avoiding direct eye contact with each other. This is the hallmark of the peaceful Pass By. Both dogs have open, relaxed mouths. The Doberman has a lowered head, the "I'm Just Minding My Own Business" posture.

#28.4: Dog "too" Interested - Photo Essay

- Dalmatian is oriented towards other dog

Kaddi, the dog on the right; is doing the Pass By without looking directly at the Dalmatian. The Dalmatian is looking at the other dog, not giving direct eye contact, but still orienting towards Kaddi. The Dal, by looking at the other dog, is showing that he has some concerns (he may be worried or just interested - we cannot be sure) but he is avoiding conflict by keeping his gaze surreptitious.

If a dog is looking at it, remember, he is thinking about it.

Here, the Dalmatian does a Butt Sniff. (Kaddi, the dog on the right is handling the situation very well.) She has pulled her ears down and has an "open mouth" to show "I want no trouble." She is not turning to Warn the Dalmatian out of her personal space.

The item of note is that t*he Dalmatian told us in the previous photo that something like this was going to happen.* He showed "too much" interest in Kaddi by looking at her. These subtle signs are the ones humans tend to miss.

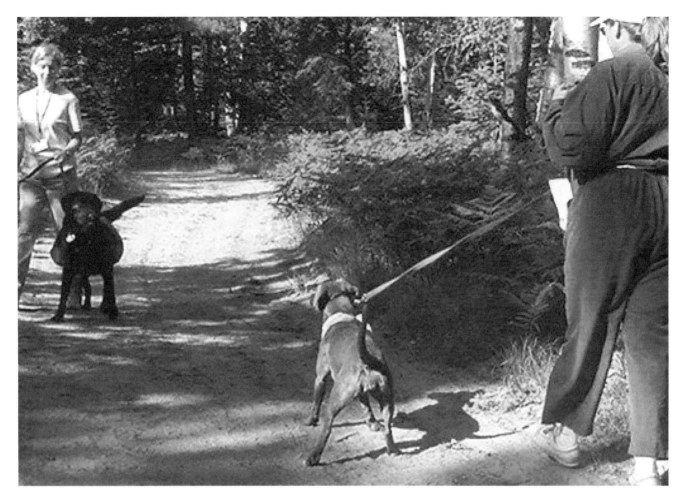

#28.5: Alerting Pass By

- dogs oriented towards each other
- tails up
- body posture is forward

These two dogs are Alerting on each other. The Pass By may be end up friendly or it may end in conflict. One thing you can see is that it will not be a neutral or a peaceful Pass By. You can tell this because the dogs are looking intently and directly at each other. Both dogs have "ditched" their owners (evidenced by the tight leashes). This means the owner is no longer in immediate control over the dog and the dog has ceased to include the owner in the decision making process.

This situation does not mean that there absolutely will be conflict, but it sure does increase the probability. At the very least it is evidence that the dog is operating out of his Hind Brain and not his Front Brain.

I detest these kinds of Pass Bys. The chances that there will be trouble have gone up.

> *Training Tip*: Where the dog's eyes go, so goes the brain. Back away from the other dog and get your dog's eyes ON YOU to avoid possible conflict.

#28.6: Sniffing on Pass By

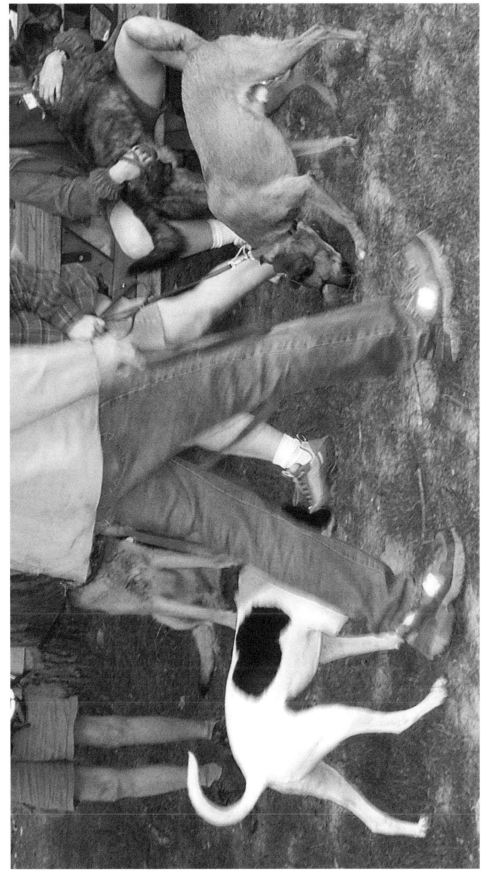

The spotted dog is oriented toward the dog on the right, who is responding with a lovely Negotiation Signal: Sniffing. Such a signal can prevent aggressive or reactive behaviour by the Staring or Alerting dog.

The signal is given during a Pass By the handlers are "forcing." Such forced Pass Bys are commonplace when you are a dog.

The dog on the right says: "I am not invading your space. I wish to Pass By." He is negotiating his way through "airspace" the spotted dog is claiming as hers. She has indicated this by staring at and orienting toward the dog on the right. She is, by this action, placing social pressure on the other dog.

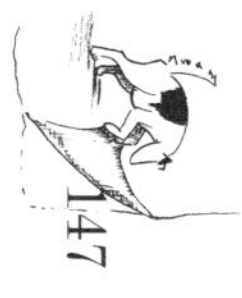

#28.7: Friendly Interest on Pass By

Kaddi, on the left, gives a brief glance to the dog Passing By. This glance is indirect and not aimed at the other dog's eyes. The dog on the right is doing a great job of staying focused on the handler. Both dogs have friendly body language. The dog on the right has a half-mast, sweeping tail. Kaddi, on the left has a tail that is confident, but not "on the muscle" and over her back. Her tail is not forced up and over her back, nor is the tail held down. Her ears are relaxed and her eyes are softly shaped. All of these factors keep the encounter friendly. Kaddi looks interested in a friendly way in the Labrador.

In this larger view of the scene, you can see many interesting things going on. Of all the many dogs in the photo, none of the dogs are looking at any other dogs, demonstrating a lovely peaceful group Look Away.

The exception is the two dogs on the far right who are oriented directly towards the Pass By dogs and handlers. As it turns out, those two dogs are Kaddi's house mates.

#28.8: Reactive Pass By - Photo Essay

Here is a Pass By that is “person-to-person:” the dogs are buffered from each other by the handlers being next to each other. Therefore, the dogs are “split up” by their handlers.

The dog on the right looks relaxed and confident. Her ears are relaxed and floppy, her tail is up, but not forced. She has her nose turned toward her handler, and can easily see the other dog from this vantage point.

The Shepherd on the left has a lowered body posture. He is either worried or Guarding. Perhaps both. What you can see is that his body is lowered, with a rounded top line, and his head is carried very low.

Here is the first dog-to-dog Pass By.

The Shepherd is using a Tongue Flick to show discomfort. He is orienting toward whatever is causing his concern. You cannot tell yet if it is the other dog, her handler, or just the proximity of both of them.

He is not using a friendly Look Away, but is looking toward the Passer-By. His head is up, his ears are up and his tail is on it's way up. Clearly, the Shepherd is uncomfortable with the others Passing By. There is facial tension; his skin looks stretched tightly over his skull. You can see ridges around his eyes.

The clue that the Shepherd is not being particularly acquiescent lies in the direction of the eyes: a Tongue Flick that is not paired with a Look Away, and the upright body posture. He is not using friendly signals to encourage approach by the others. There is tension on the leash, which indicates he is Moving Into Pressure. This is just one more sign that he is moving out of a Thinking, Responding state and into a Reactive state.

Now the handlers turn, and re-approach from the opposite direction.

Kaddi, on the left is using neutral, friendly body language and is showing her trust in her handler. She is also very confident and is not showing intimidation. Her ears are relaxed, her eye is soft and her tail is up, but not forced over her back. Her whiskers are not flared forward. Her mouth is closed, though, which tells you that she is aware of the Shepherd's proximity and discomfort. It is the only sign that she is not totally relaxed.

The Shepherd, an adolescent, is continuing to show his concern. See the lowered hind quarters? Also, his attention is all directed toward the dog on the left. Even though we are looking at the dog from the rear, you can see the ears and the tilt of the head. His front legs are braced. He has transferred his weight to his rear legs to ready himself for action. See the right rear leg? You can feel his tension.

Learn to identify body language from a "behind the dog" perspective; it is often the view point the handler is viewing from.

Kaddi leans away and turns to face the Shepherd as he barges into her personal space.

See the Tongue Flick again? He is transferring weight to his hind quarters to move forward even further into Kaddi's space. The Shepherd's owner is handling this very calmly, which is good. She has the leash short enough to prevent the Shepherd from moving closer to Kaddi, and she is working to get his attention onto her.

Even so, the dogs are now looking straight at each other. Not good.

The whites around Kaddi's eyes become visible as she orients toward the rude intruder.

Now both dogs become more reactive as the Shepherd attempts to move ever closer. Both dogs are locked on eye contact. Kaddi is telling the Shepherd she is planning on Standing Her Ground. She is refusing to be intimidated.

If you look closely you can see the ridges around Kaddi's eyes and mouth as she tenses her jaw.

Kaddi has lowered her head and is not Staring, but still has her nose oriented toward the Shepherd. She is telling him she is not going to start a conflict, but she will finish a conflict if it is brought to her.   Kaddi is actively working at keeping the peace, which is helping to calm the Shepherd a bit. At least he is not continuing to escalate his behaviour. This is also due to his owner's intervention, as she calmly encourages him to come around to her and by not becoming over-reactive herself. Kaddi's handler also is encouraging Kaddi to come away from the Shepherd at the same time, to alleviate the tension between the two dogs.

Here it is easiest to read the intent of the Shepherd, not so much by looking at the Shepherd, but by looking at Kaddi's body language. Kaddi, on the right is obviously uncomfortable with the Shepherd's language and proximity. She sees that the Shepherd is still looking very intent and is not giving any Make Nice signals to soften his approach. Kaddi has lowered her head, ears and tail. She is moving in closer to her mum (Moving Into Pressure is a sign of stress) to get a little more space between her and the Shepherd. It is significant, though, that she is not moving behind her mum. She is not going to be pushed around!

The Shepherd is continuing to stand tall and upright and is Staring straight at Kaddi. Kaddi is looking indirectly at the Shepherd. She doesn't want to turn her back to him and is trying to stay out of trouble, but is not throwing in the towel quite yet either.

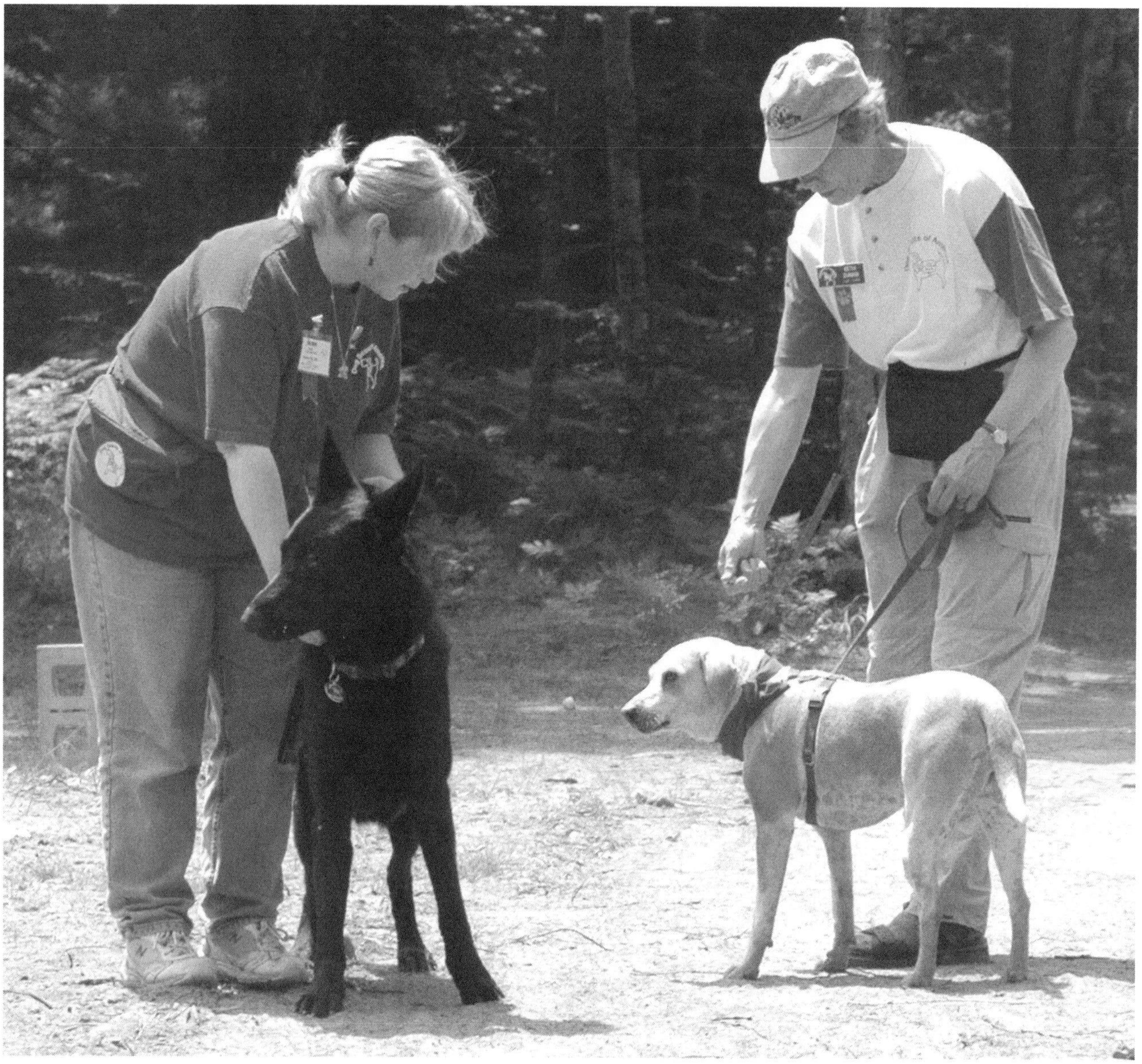

The Shepherd's owner helps him to succeed by insisting that he use a Look Away.

You can see how much better that makes Kaddi feel. She is quite relieved - her ears have come up a bit, and she is not squashed up against her owner quite so closely. Her eyes and jaw still show remnants of the tension. Beth, Kaddi's owner, is encouraging Kaddi to come around to face her.

The Shepherd looks pretty relieved, too. His body language is much softer, his ears are more relaxed, and he is content to let his owner take charge. He is squinting his eyes and is Switching to Front Brain, where he can listen to his handler.

Photo Credits:
Photo #1: Lonnie Olson;
Photo #2, #3, #4, #5 & #6: Joanne Weber;
Photo #7: Felicia Banys;
Photo Essay #8: Joanne Weber.

Section 4: Space Invaders

Dogs are extremely aware of personal space. In this section, you will get to see some dogs who are confidently and quietly handling a Space Invasion and others who are totally Hind Brain and reactive.

Canine aggression is about Space Invasion. A huge amount of dog talk, both friendly and not, is about personal space: "Yes, we can share this space, go ahead and approach;" "You can be near me, but don't touch me;" "Get away from me now!" Threats to a possession are also a frequent cause of aggression, but this is really the same message: "Get away from my stuff!" Territoriality reveals an extended sense of "me" and "mine." Even status-related aggression is ultimately about who will control this space and the things in it.

Photo by: Brenda Aloff

Dogs communicate about space and the things in it all the time, and, if they feel these are threatened, their communications can vary from Guarding and Warnings to outright aggression. Body tension, Stillness, and how the dog is using eye contact are indicators of what may happen in the next second if the Warning he gives is not heeded. It is important to remember that there are two (or more) dogs involved in these discussions: how the *other* dog responds is often critical in determining how aggressive the communication will get. This is especially true of dogs who are sophisticated users of language; they will give good, clear Warnings when threatened with space invasions and will typically use aggression as a last resort when their Warnings are ignored.

Of course, not all dogs are so savvy, and many dogs who are "dog aggressive" truncate or omit the appropriate Warnings, going directly to the aggressive display when they (mis)perceive a threat to even a very extended territory.

An appropriate canine response to invasion is, of course, about degree, just as it is for people. If you touch my sunburned shoulder and I say, "Ouch, please don't do that again," it is socially acceptable, and good communication! If you touch my sunburned shoulder and I pull out a knife and stab you, it is inappropriate in the extreme. Dogs, too, can overreact or skip the Warnings that would keep them out of trouble. Just be aware, however, that many canine Warnings appear very subtle and quick to us (though not to other dogs!), especially until we learn to recognize them. Therefore, do not assume that there were no Warnings given until you are very confident that you can recognize them.

For safety's sake, as well as just to understand dog communication better, watching for the earlier, subtler signs of Warning and Guarding is critical. We all want to catch the communication at these stages, before it segues into full-blown aggression. This transition can happen *extremely* rapidly. Learning to see the Warnings requires a lot of practice, and a good sense of exactly what to look for.

One thing that can help is to look at the reaction of the *other* dog who is approaching and receiving the communication about whether it is permissible to proceed further. If your dog, for example, is consistently avoiding another dog, look closely at that dog to see what message he is sending about his body space or possessions. (For a good example of this, see the Chapter *Rylie and Emma.*)

Let's return to the "sunburned shoulder" model: you touch my sunburned shoulder and I ask you politely to stop. If you persist over my protests and continue to touch me even harder, at some point I will probably get nastier about it. Justifiably so! Well-spoken dogs use the same sort of escalation. They will subtly and politely Warn. If the other dog does not respect the warning and continues to invade space, the invaded dog must choose between having no boundary and making the boundary clear to the uneducated/rude invader. It is not only up to the dog giving the Warning about Space Invasion: the other dog must receive the message and acknowledge it. Puppies raised in multiple-dog households (of three or more normal dogs) get opportunities to practice manners frequently. They learn how to Negotiate personal space and how to respect the boundaries that other dogs have. They learn how to give and receive Warnings without panic and without undue escalation.

Dogs have individual needs for personal space. Some have big "bubbles" and some have almost none. Context and current stress levels affect a dog's sensitivity to her boundaries, too. Your adult dog, for example, may be very comfortable with letting your puppy crawl all over her at home where she feels safe, but unwilling to allow this at the vet's office where she is more anxious.

People have a very different sense of canine space than do the dogs themselves. It is considered acceptable by many owners to allow their dog to invade another's personal space. For instance, they allow their dog to run right up into another dog's face, or mob a person and jump up on them. People think that this means their dog is being "friendly," but most dogs (well, perhaps, except for Labs) would consider this sort of approach rude. Typically, humans will not see the subtle Warnings the invaded dog gives. Then, when she finally escalates her protests, everyone blames the dog who asked for a little room, instead of recognizing that their own dog was horribly intrusive.

In the world of Well-Spoken Dogs, approaches are sideways, not head-on in "Chicken" position. Dogs who are savvy do not rush up into another dog's personal space and immediately put their feet or nose on that dog. You check with that other dog BEFORE invading personal space and use Negotiation signals to do so. You wait for an invitation to invade space.

It is imperative to note that many behaviours associated with Aggression overlap considerably with Predation behaviours. Alerting is an excellent example. In a predation sequence, the dog will Scan, then, when he finds something of interest, he will Alert (begin to look intensely at prey). This same sequence is evident when a dog is Looking For Trouble around other dogs.

In a Predatory sequence, the dog becomes calmer and more focused, moves slower and then, when the moment is right, explodes into action. During this entire Predation sequence, though, the dog has a calm and purposeful aura about him.

If the target is not a prey object, but another dog, and the conflict has to do with status, there is often an almost identical sequence. Frequently you will see both dogs engaging in the same behaviour: Scanning, Mutual Alerting, Mutual Targeting, and then slow movement followed by explosive action.

A dog defending himself or protecting his space is not quite so predictable, but you will still typically see some of the same elements, such as Alerting and sudden reaction.

Stillness is a crucial behaviour to look for because it almost always predicts some sort of Guarding or Warning. This is not the relaxed lack of activity you might see in a neutral or friendly dog, but a riveted Stillness that is tense and focused.

A dog uncomfortable with the environment or individuals in it will usually display slow movement, then explosive reactivity if there is a slight change in the environment, even though that change is not threatening. The dog is, in a sense, paranoid and overreacting because he does not have the skill set needed to cope with his current context. Again, practice with recognizing these signals is key. Learning to distinguish relaxation from Stillness from this "paranoid" slowness can take some time, but the end results will be very worthwhile!

29 AGGRESSION

By the time it looks like this, aggression is very easy to identify. The GSD (German Shepherd Dog), on the right, would be on Saikou if not restrained by the leash and collar. The display is to drive the other dog away, and to warn that further aggression will be forthcoming. Once physical contact is made, the intent changes somewhat - now the object is to "win." By win, I mean: to retain possession of whatever the resource being contested is - be it a piece of food dropped on the ground or a location.

These dogs are at a dog camp. In this case some treats were dropped on the ground accidentally. The GSD, away from home, probably even more stressed by the volume and proximity of dogs and people at camp, is laboring under a chemical overload. His body was just waiting for that straw that breaks the camel's back. The Border Collie-mix wanders by; perhaps she eyed the treats and told the GSD to step away. That would have been accomplished with a look and a little stare. Perhaps she was just wandering by and caught the eye of the GSD in the course of looking around normally, or perhaps she didn't look at him at all. Either way, it triggered the GSD into a reaction.

#29.1: Full Display of Aggression

- body orientation forward
- mouth open
- lips C-shaped
- teeth bared
- braced legs

The Border-Collie-mix on the left has laid down as a Calming Signal. She has lowered her body, tucked her tail close to her body and drawn her ears back and down closely to her head. She is still looking at the GSD, but in an effort to soften this, she is squinting her eyes. She has her body sideways to the Shepherd. In short, she is doing all she can to appear non-confrontational and appease the Shepherd.

In this photograph we are observing the stage in the bar fight where the aggressor breaks the neck of the liquor bottle off on the pool table and lunges for his victim. How far do you get reasoning with a person in that frame of mind?

But, just for a moment, let's look at our human bar fight. Did the aggressor, (let's call him Bill) for no reason, jump off his bar stool and choose a random victim? Excluding some form of mental illness, no. Perhaps Hal, the other guy, ogled the wrong gal. Maybe he bumped Bill, violating his personal space and spilled Bill's drink. Perhaps Bill was under a lot of other pressures, and, poor Hal who merely made a stupid social gaff or is seriously clumsy had his actions misconstrued by Bill. Perhaps Hal did something intentionally or maybe he was just socially inept. In Bill's mind, his own extreme reaction made sense on some level. One thing is certain: once everybody goes Hind-Brain, things quickly go downhill.

I am certainly not saying people and dogs are the same. What I want to do is to provide a helpful mental exercise for understanding that dogs have a full and varied emotional life. They Resource Guard valuable items just as humans do. Dogs get caught up in circumstances and go Hind Brain just as humans do.

Different dogs have different triggers; that is, they find different resources important. Context has everything to do with it. My Smooth Fox Terrier, Breanna, who never played with toys, would instantly grab a random toy as soon as a new puppy came into the house so she could play power games (possession games) to let the puppy know "I control resources here!" Bree would entice the puppy to approach the toy by playing with the toy in the puppy's proximity. When the pup bounced over to try to take the moving object, Breanna would warn, subtly and briefly. This would be followed by a lunge at the pup and a Correction Bite (open mouth "hit") and/or a Roll and Pin. This would startle the puppy and be very impressive without hurting the puppy in the least. The lesson, quick, terrifying and performed with high drama, had a lasting effect on the puppy. Very seldom did it have to be performed twice.

Dogs will also "unload" on each other, just because the other dog happened to be standing nearby. When the chemicals in the system become overwhelming, the dog wishes to release the stress. As in humans, if the animal is under more stress that day, the triggers will be more sensitive.

Remember, the GSD is not a Bad Dog, she has just found herself in a situation and got emotional. Happens to people all the time...

#29.2: Good Social Skills

- Look Away
- Anchor on owner
- squinting eyes
- down or half-mast ears & tails (except Basenji)
- rounded back on Basenji

I include this "larger" view so you can see the interesting behaviour of the dogs in the background. These dogs are practicing their most excellent social skills. The Basenji is looking to its owner for guidance, as are the Lab and the Golden on the right. They are using their owners as an Emotional Anchor. The little dog facing you in the middle is doing a deliberate Look Away. Also notice this dog's distinctive squint: I Am Non-Threatening. These dogs are not just coincidentally oriented away from this scene. They are hyper-aware of it.

As an aside: Lonnie is helping the owner. Even though I have blurred the foreground, you can see the relaxed expression on her face. She looks in-charge and calm, which goes a long way toward diffusing the situation. The handlers in the background are doing the same thing: remaining still and calm, which is of great service to their dogs.

This is a rescued Border Collie puppy at 5 weeks of age. Aggression expressions are hard-wired and occur very young. Note the classical defensive posture, and the mix of "I am a little guy, don't hurt me" and "Get away or I will kill you" signals. The body is lowered. You can see his tail is tucked; it is not held over the back in a "I am gonna kick your butt" position. His eyes are wide and staring. His pupils are dilated. His paw is lifted. His body is rigid and Backward. The darling puppy teeth are displayed for your viewing pleasure.

In short, this puppy is in his tiny Hind Brain, fully adrenalized and not thinking at all. He is Reacting defensively. If you reach for him, he will bite you in a frenzied manner.

#29.3: Defensive Display in 5-week-old puppy

- body orientation backward
- eyes wide
- staring
- pupil dilated
- lips long
- teeth bared
- braced legs
- paw lift

This picture may, at first glance, look less dramatic than the previous photographs in this chapter. But prior to those dramatic displays, something this subtle was the very likely precursor. Subtle to us, perhaps, but the dogs are all very aware of what is going on here.

Three dogs in this picture are using Negotiation signals to convey peaceful intent. One dog is targeting a victim. Another dog is making a note of the tension.

#29.4: Targeting - the Beginning of a Stalk

- body orientation forward
- staring
- paw lift
- tail over back
- ears forward
- stillness
- reactions of other dogs nearby

The dog on the right with tail up, ears up, body Forward is the dog doing the Targeting. Note the Paw Lift. In this instance it is not a Paw Lift of supplication, but of predation. In essence, the dog is Pointing (a precursor to stalking) the victim. The victim, the Border Collie-mix, knows she is being targeted and is doing her best to remind the Targeter that she is a dog, not a prey object - and a peaceful dog, at that.

This photograph captures that tense moment: The Calm Before the Storm. The next thing that did happen was that the Targeting dog lunged for the Border Collie-mix.

Look how ALL the dogs are responding to the Targeting dog. They all know that something bad is going down. All of them are using some kind of Calming Signal - in this case three of the dogs are Sniffing. Willie, the Golden in the foreground has taken note of what is happening. Notice how he has his body sideways to the Targeting dog, and his tail is down.

Targeting, in short, is the Choosing of a Victim, whether it be a dog or a tennis ball. Alerting slightly precedes the Targeting. How can you tell if a dog is Alerting and Targeting? If a dog looks at anything for more than a count of 2 or 3, he is Alerting. This is often accompanied by bringing the ears forward and an increase in intensity. If the dog is not Blinking, or he has continued to orient toward and Stare, he has moved into Targeting: the victim has been chosen.

Training Tip: This is the Alert & Target body language to notice. If you were training, the Alerting or Targeting dog needs to be reminded to Check In with you before making any rash decisions. Catch the behaviour at this stage and avoid dealing with it at the stage you saw in Photo #29.1!

Paradigm Reminder: People seem to constantly forget that dogs are dogs. They think that the things that are important to people are important to dogs. This is not even close to the mark in many situations. Your dog may not always get on with other dogs. This is a fact.

Aggressive displays surprise and horrify us. How could my dog act that way? That other dog was doing nothing! This may not always be true. Remember, there is a Grand Drama happening far below our eye level (dogs are quite short!). Many times we are embarrassed by our dogs behaviour and this prevents us from being effective with the dog. You can be unpleasantly surprised by your dog's behaviour, but once you learn to Read your dog, you can cut down on these instances. Instead of being surprised, you can be effective. You will increase desired behaviour because you will be educated and aware enough to reinforce good social judgment.

Keep in mind that the other dog might have been like Hal, in the bar fight, behaving in a subtly provoking or just plain-old inept way. Or maybe your dog was the Hal.

People often have their dogs in a restricted physical situation or under a lot of social pressure without having prepared the dog for it. Realistically, these kinds of situations are unavoidable. Your dog will frequently be placed in these situations, and you with her. Teach your dog to keep Two Eyes On You. This will help keep her out of trouble! When you learn to Read dogs well, you are going to find yourself in fewer hair-raising situations because you will be communicating better with your own dog, as well as being able to recognize dogs who are socially inept which might mean trouble.

When aggression occurs, it is a physiological process. Recognition of the processes of the neuro-transmitter system help you to make sense out of emotionally charged events. At the same time, take this as training information: If your dog is having trouble with Impulse Control (over-reacting) and is having trouble handling stress, it is up to you to guide your dog's behaviour to burn new neural pathways. This includes teaching your dog to cope with stress, and providing him direction so he can learn to channel all those wild body chemicals that send him into his Hind-brain into calm and focused attention on you.

Yikes! Okay, I'm off the soapbox. Thanks for your tolerance!

For this book I chose not to search out endless dramatic photos of full-blown aggressive displays. (They occur explosively and I am usually in the thick of them and always without a camera.) While fascinating in a horrific sort of a way, full displays are easy to spot. You probably don't need practice identifying those displays!

The language elements that I see my clients missing are the subtle precursors to Reactive behaviour. Intention behaviours are the really important behaviours to identify. The juncture at which you are able to modify behaviour occurs BEFORE the reactive behaviour explodes into action: it is that moment before the dog goes entirely Hind Brain.

Photo Credits:
Photo #1& #2: Joanne Weber;
Photo #3: Candy Smith;
Photo #4: Joanne Weber.

30
Alerting & Targeting

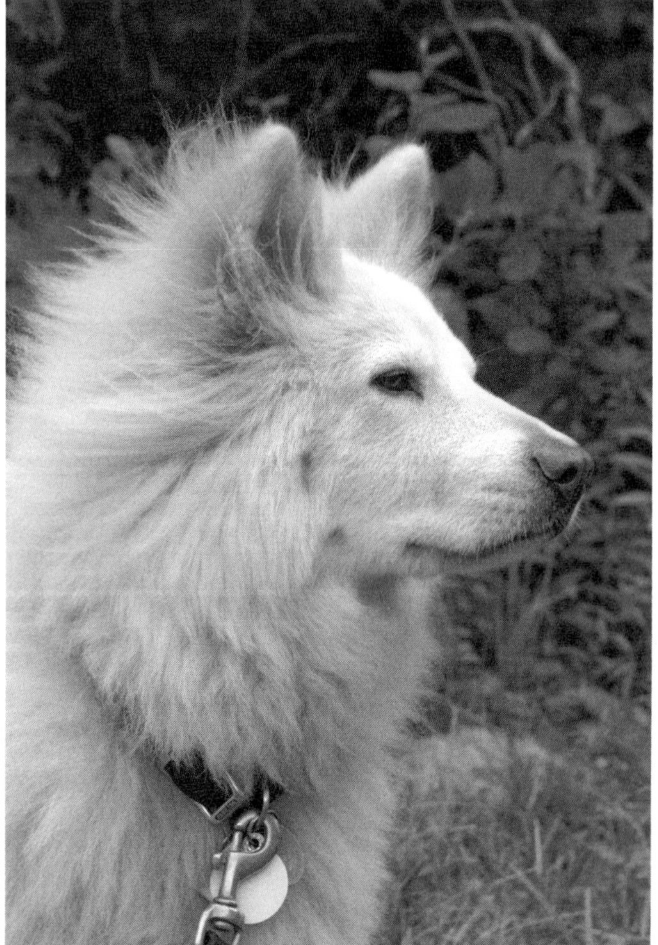

#30.1: Scanning

- ears up
- eyes, ears and nose all oriented the same direction
- dog turns head from left to right, Scanning

These photographs depict a dog that is Scanning. Scanning always occurs just before a dog Alerts.

This dog is looking around and checking the environment. If he finds something of interest he will then Alert on it.

Scanning is a typical behaviour for dogs. If your dog is not looking at you, chances are she is Scanning.

Scanning is not necessarily a bad thing, but it is a precursor to reactive behaviour.

Scanning can be predatory in nature. Since each dog varies in how much predation he exhibits, Scanning may not mean much in some dogs, whereas in others it means the dog is just Looking For Trouble all the time. Scanning can also be done in defense, rather than predation.

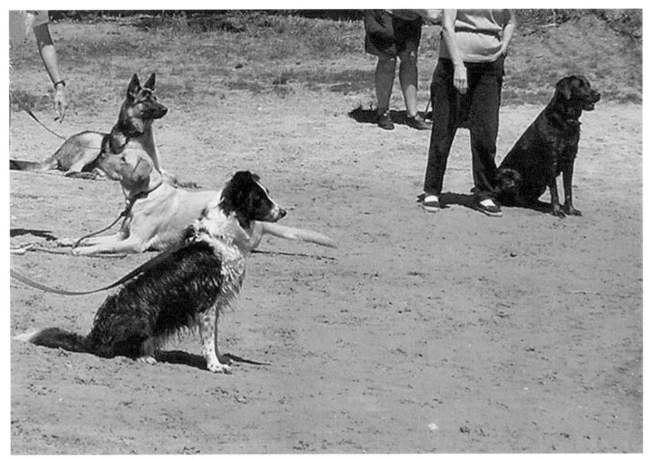

A group of dogs focus intently. Three are On Alert, even though they have retained their sit or down position. Two of the dogs have closed mouths, and the Black Labrador has an open mouth. I use this as a guage as to how "far into" the Alert the dog is and how close it is to Targeting and "action." Closed mouth means that the dog is getting more serious about action. Note the Forward feel of the bodies; if the dogs got up, which direction would they move? Their ears are forced into a forward position. Their eyes are looking where the noses are pointing.

#30.2: Alerting While Still

- intensity - a forward "feel"
- eyes are wide open, staring and fixed on target
- whole group mirroring Alert

#30.3: Alerting In Motion

- intensity
- mirroring

Two dogs Alert on something to their left. Note the forward ears and eyes looking where their noses point.

Even though this Shepherd's face is in heavy shadow, and he is in motion, his Alerting posture is evident. Ears forced forward, eyes intently focused, he is checking out the photographer. Is she dangerous? Is she safe? Do I know her? Is she tasty? Will she throw a ball?

The lolling tongue tells us the dog isn't too serious yet: this is a first check. The dog has been actively Scanning, and has just honed in on an item of interest. His eyes are not yet forced into a rounded shape.

I can feel the dog beginning to pull on the leash. If the dog is going to become Reactive, it will be in the next few seconds, as he gets closer to his Target. Then, the lunge at the Target will already be in the bag.

I love the contrast in this photograph. Note the neutral and relaxed body posture of the dogs behind the Shepherd. This photograph nicely highlights the difference in the silhouette of the Neutral vs. the Alerting dog.

#30.4: Alerting

- intensity
- ears up
- forward body orientation
- eyes & ears directed toward Target
- difference in body language to that of the other dogs

#30.5: Target

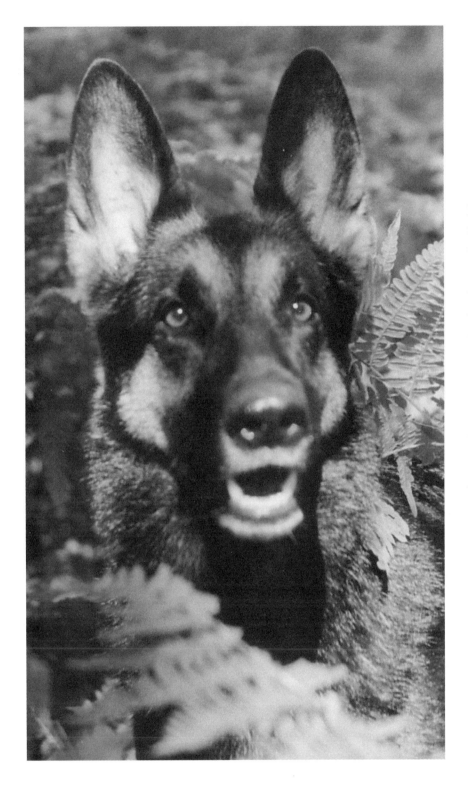

- intensity
- eyes are wide open, staring and fixed on target

Maeve is just past showing the interest of Alerting. She is Targeting. Her victim has been chosen. Focused intently, ears up, she is Still at this moment but her body language says, "When I get up I will Move Forward." The eyes are still of a normal, not forced shape, but they are held open and are rounded in shape, not squinting or relaxed. The closer to round, rather than oval or triangular, the eyes are held, the more excited the dog is.

Maeve's mouth is partially open, which indicates that the jaw is not held in tension as with a tightly closed mouth.

The open mouth tells you that the dog is concentrating intensely on something, but is not yet reactive.

(In this case,Maeve is looking at a tennis ball - read: prey object - that I am holding so Joanne can take this lovely portrait. Maeve is anticipating the toss of the ball.)

Behaviour Tip: Alerting can be a dog's way of communicating to those nearby, "Hey, there is something of note here." It is how pack members communicate to each other that a hunting opportunity is available.

Alerting can also be an indication that your dog may be moving into her Hind Brain. This means Alerting is a precursor to Reactive behaviour and is certainly present as a precursor to a full-blown display of aggression.

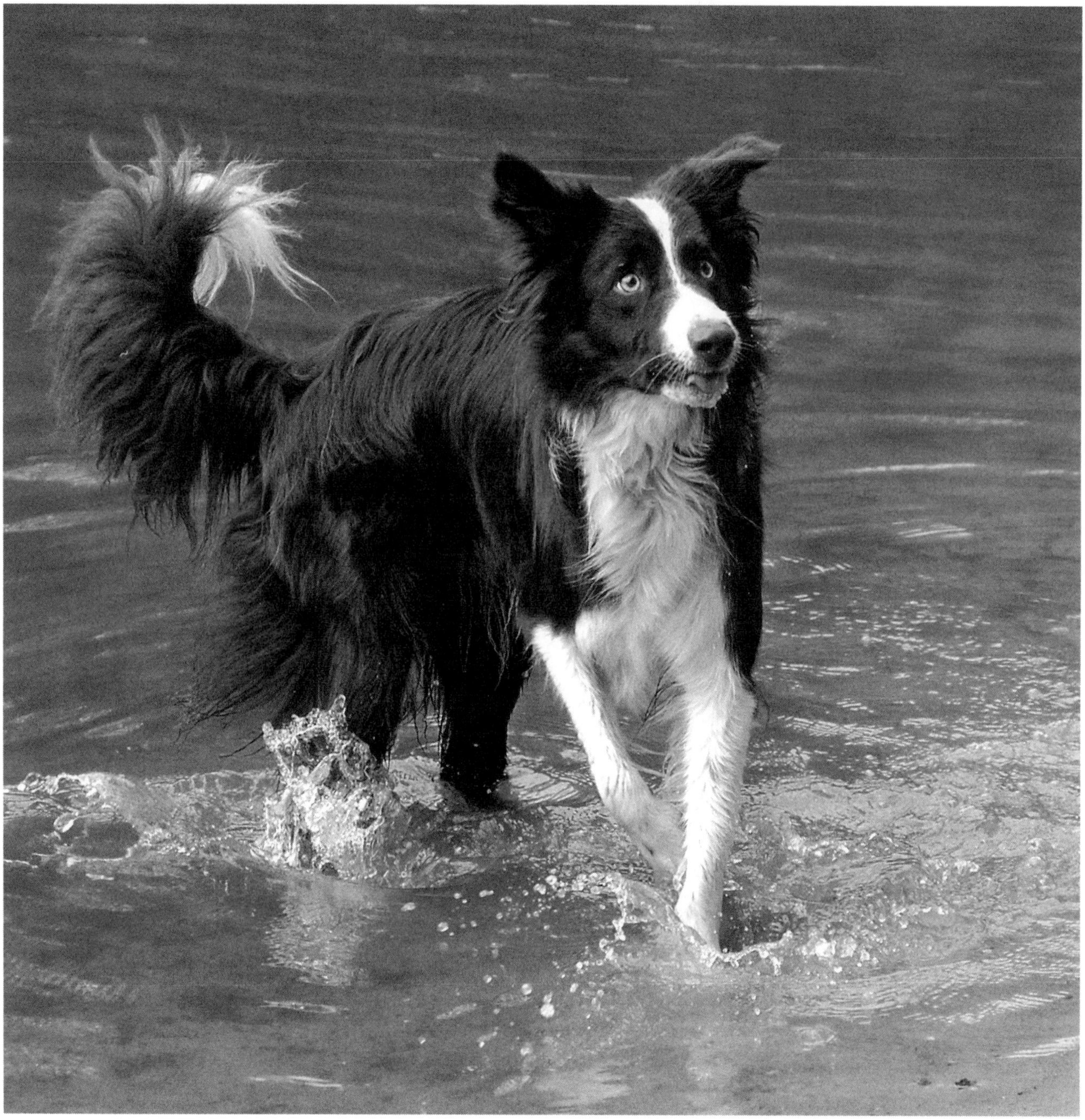

This Border Collie is past Scanning. He is past Alerting. His victim has been chosen, he is Targeting. He exhibits intense concentration. We see the body held expectantly. The Paw Lift is a modified Stalk - the dog is Pointing at his target. In this case it is a prey object (a toy). His tail is not over his back, but is held in tension out behind him, his mouth is very slightly open, and you can see the foam from hypersalivation - excitement. His eyes are held wide and he is Staring.

When dogs are Alerting, you get the "feel" that it is the Calm Before the Storm. The dog is held In Tension and is waiting for the moment to move forward toward whatever is holding his interest.

#30.6: Targeting

- body held in tension & expectantly
- salivation
- pointing posture
- wide open eyes
- forward body orientation

Training Tip: This is your training moment. When your dog is ahead of you, Scanning and beginning to Alert, this is the point in time when the dog is beginning to make decisions that leave you out. Getting and keeping your dog's attention NOW can prevent him from lunging and practicing other undesirable behaviours. Prevention of Scanning at all in those dogs who exhibit risky behaviour is even better.

I am not saying that this dog will next attack the photographer. I am saying that the dog is not checking in with his owner, and his body language says that he is not intending to check in right now, but is instead going to handle this situation as he sees fit.

The dog in the foreground has Alerted and is Targeting. I don't know if it is on the Golden, or what the Golden is doing, or what the Golden "has." Either way, if the Chow were off leash, where would he be? Right in the Golden's body space. If that happens, and the Golden is frightened by that, or thinks it is rude, there could be an altercation.

How can you tell the dog is Alerting, even though you are looking from behind? Ears are forced forward and body orientation is forward. A front paw is lifted, as if the dog is Pointing at the target. The Chow's head is lowered. This is a Stalking position. How can we tell the lifted paw is not in appeasement? The lowered head with forward ears tells you this.

#30.7: Targeting

- body orientation
- ears forward
- head slightly lowered
- tail up
- "pointing" at target

#30.8: Targeting vs. Look Away

- body orientation of the dog on the left is toward
- contrast with the dog on the right in body tension
- dog on the left has tail held stiffly
- dog on the left has short lips

Kaddi, the dog on the right, is deliberately Looking Away and keeping her ears and tail at half-mast. Very lovely non-threatening Negotiation signals.

The dog on the left has made Kaddi her Target. Her ears are held forward, her tail is coming up and her body is oriented toward Kaddi. What labels this as Targeting, rather than just looking, is the intensity and the facial tension that accompanies the orientation of the eyes and nose. The dog is still blinking, but you can see how tight her lips are, and how her lips are getting "shorter." It is also indisputable that the dog has made her leash tight, meaning she has, for all practical purposes, excluded the handler from the decision-making process. You can see that the handler is making an attempt to get the dog's attention back on her, but the dog is actively resisting those efforts.

Notice that the dog on the left is clearly ignoring Kaddi's Negotiation signals. This is one more reason that this is categorized as a Target. If this dog were not restricted by a leash, what do you surmise would happen? Do you think the dog would approach politely and carefully? Probably not. This dog is an showing intention to rush in, rudely. If Kaddi took exception to this you would have the beginning of a dog fight.

If a dog is giving Negotiation signals, she is expecting a signal back, as a reassurance about intention and to ascertain that the signal sent was received. That kind of exchange is not occurring here.

> *Training Tip*: You should not panic when you see your dog Alerting. You darned well better make note of it. It is a signal telling you the dog is very interested in something. It could be curiosity or it could be targeting a prey object. Either way, you are beginning to be left out of the dog's decision-making.
>
> If you take note of the context, and check what the dog is Alerting at, then you can make good training decisions.
>
> If my dog Alerts, I then expect her to check in with me. If she doesn't, I remind her to do so. This is a learned behaviour, and it does take some time and effort to teach it! Many repetitions! Well worth the effort!

For Further thought and observation:

The "Eye" can be thought of as divided into three basic sub-categories:
(For more discussion regarding the "Eye" see Section 5 *Predation.)*

- The Scan (or Shopping) is observable as the dog actively and purposefully "scanning" the environment. This behaviour could arise out of "Looking For Trouble" (on the muscle, status-related or Guarding) or predation (hunting) or defense (fearful). The Scanning dog can be moving forward or standing still. Her head will move from side-to-side. This side-to-side motion may be very slight, using only the eyes (in which case you only see the eyebrows moving if you are behind the dog). Or the side-to-side motion may include a head swing.
- The Alert, which is indicated by a quickening of the dog's interest. The dog's head may raise or lower, her ears may come forward, her tail may raise or lower. The dog may quicken her gait, or make a slight pause and then continue on.
- The Target, in which the victim has been chosen and the dog has yet to take action, but is getting ready to approach the victim. That approach may be pursuit, as in predation, or rushing in on another dog or person.

When Scanning, the eyes are still blinking and moving. In the Alert and the Target, the eyes will cease moving and the blinking will slow down and then stop. As the dog Alerts, her ears will be forced forward and the intensity of the focus increases through the Target, and until the dog takes action. The Alert and Target may both involve Stillness. Think of the Scan as "Ready," the Alert as "Set" and the Target as "I am going...Now!"

A point of interest in observing animal behaviour is when you see a Behaviour Change, *pay attention*! If the dog is walking along with her head up and suddenly lowers her head, she is reflecting that she has just "thought a different thought." Different thoughts can be precursors to an emotional and, therefore, a behavioural, change.

Photo Credits:
Photo #1, #2, #3, #4: Joanne Weber;
Photo #5: Jennifer Riess;
Photo #6, #7, #8 & #9: Joanne Weber.

31 Correction

#31.1: Correction

- Differing Body Silhouettes
- Who is in Stillness vs. who is in Motion

The English Setter is Correcting the Golden. The Golden accepts the correction and uses appeasement behaviour.

Though the Golden is blurry because she is in motion, you can still tell by her silhouette that her tail is tucked, one paw is raised, and her body is lowered to the ground. The Correcting animal is standing still and the Supplicating animal is in motion at this point. When the Golden finally holds still, the Setter will know that the Correction has been understood.

The lips of the English Setter are confident lips - C-shaped and brought forward rather than elongated. This bespeaks of the confidence of the Setter; he is certain of the outcome. The English Setter has his ears forced backwards, and his tail is held low and tensely; even the curve up at the end looks rigid. His tail could also be held stiffly over his back, which would indicate a more intense emotion. The Setter's nose is raised, and the top line of his muzzle is wrinkled, as he bares his teeth.

I like this photo because the Setter depicts a very typical stance. I think that most of us think that the dog is going to have everything forced Forward (ears forward, tail over the back, on tip-toe) when they are the aggressor. This is not always true. It depends on what kind of message the dog is intending to send.

The Sheltie on the left is correcting the other dog, who is both taking it and also keeping the peace by moving out of the area, though still giving back a little glance of his own.

The Sheltie, on the left, has a history of resource guarding food. His house-mate has walked by a treat that is on the floor.

#31.2: Dog Corrects House-Mate

- facial tension
- dilated pupils
- defensive stance
- teeth bared
- stillness
- ears drawn slightly back
- long lips indicate defensive state

The Sheltie on the left has drawn back ears, extreme facial tension, a wrinkled nose and bared teeth. This dog has elongated lips (compare to the English Setter, in Photo #31.1). Notice also how the Sheltie has a more defensive attitude than the Setter in Photo #31.1, indicated by the lowered body and longer lips of the Sheltie. Long lips combined with the snarl and facial tension indicate a lack of confidence and defensiveness. (A dog that is confident and "on offense" will have short, "C-shaped" lips. Look also at the position of his head, which is lowered.

The dog in the foreground has his nose partially oriented toward the aggressor. He is either giving back a little glance of his own, or he is just keeping an eye on the aggressor. This Sheltie has a slightly lowered-from-normal head position. He has also drawn his ears back and is not confronting the "guarder." His acquiescence isn't occurring on nearly the scale as that of the Golden in Photo #31.1.

Defensive dogs can be more unpredictable when pushed. The confident dog will do something assertive. But the dog who is lacking confidence is much more difficult to gauge; he may fold or he may explode.

Here, the same dog corrects his owner in exactly the manner he corrected the dog. The owner was feeding him treats and then gave him the "all gone" signal. There are extenuating circumstances: you cannot see the whole context in this photo. Her other dog is just at her feet. So, although the dog on her lap would usually not growl at her over food, he has an added stressor: the other dog in close proximity.

#31.3: Dog Corrects Owner

- facial tension
- teeth bared
- stillness
- ears drawn slightly back

This is a dog who (obviously) has problematic behaviours. This dog is not just misbehaving: he displays slightly abnormal behaviour patterns. Dogs like this often have communication problems; that is, they don't "think" before they "talk." Dogs with abnormal behaviour need special kinds of help and training: patience at the right times and excellent management and boundaries.

Comment: People get really reactive when they see a dog show teeth. I am not saying I am thrilled, but it is one way that a dog expresses itself. Using the language the dog gives us as information to train is the smart way to train. Getting emotional just gets in the way of effective training.

#31.4: Dog Cuddles with House Mate

- facial & body relaxation
- eyes

Here is the same Sheltie, shown here in Companionship with the dog he was correcting in Photograph #31.2.

The emotion here is clear, too. He is comfortable in this context with this dog. He cuddles with his owner, too, when he is not resource guarding.

The merled dog is a treat, with a lovely sense of himself and his ability to handle his house-mate.

#31.5: Engagement

- contrast in body posture
- approach
- orientation and position towards each other

The Cattle Dog approaches the Golden with a playful posture. Notice the "held in" energy of the Cattle Dog. She has her ears drawn back, lips long and tail wagging. She is working hard to engage the Golden. She has politely "arced" her approach; that is why she is off to the side and not directly making eye contact.

The Cattle Dog is using an extreme version of a Play Bow. Most often when dogs are using this kind of Play Bow, it is done swiftly and in an almost frantic manner. The dog will run up, slam to the ground in this Extreme Play Bow position, writhe around underneath the other dog's nose, and then tear off madly, running in circles with the "butt on fire." (Refer to Photo #42.10, "Butt's On Fire," in the *Pursuit* Chapter)

Though the approach of the Cattle Dog is generally appropriate, her gestures are very "big." They are typical of a dog who is socially inept, indicating she is either anxious or oblivious. Dogs are inept for a lot of reasons: lack of opportunities to learn dog language; anxiety because of past experience; lack of experiences; or a lack of self-confidence. Such "big" gestures can provoke a correction from other dogs if they are bothered by the intensity. There also are differences amongst the kind of play you see in groups of dogs. For instance, (and please take these next statements as generalzations): a lot of Shepherds like to body slam; Terriers like to wrestle; and Bor-

der Collies like to eye, stalk and chase. Some play elements are "hard-wired," but dogs also learn play gestures and other play language from the dogs they play with.

The Golden has her tail held way up and forced over her back; her ears are drawn slightly back and are in a forced position; and her lips long. You will see this posture just before a correction and a similar posture, on occasion, (minus the facial tension) just before a Play Bow. Let's take a closer look to see if more can be determined.

The Golden is standing up, but not over the Cattle Dog. She is STILL. *Stillness always precedes something notable* - it can be the explosion of a correction or the invitation of a Play Bow. Read the Signal Clusters to determine which it is. Her chin is drawn in and slightly up, indicating tension in the neck and jaw. Her legs are braced. There is some facial tension. See the ridge below her eyes? All of these indicators show plenty of tension in the Golden, more than would usually accompany play. The Stillness, in conjunction with tension, indicates a Warning. The general impression is that the Golden is *not* going to kick ass and take names immediately; the situation might even settle down and be okay. Either there is something in the manner of the Cattle Dog that this Golden does not like, or the Golden wishes to pull a little rank before commencing with play.

The back of the Golden is straight, and the back of the Cattle Dog is slightly rounded. This is significant, as it adds to the general impression that the Golden is in charge and the Cattle Dog will abide by the rules set by the Golden.

The Golden may just be put off by the intensity of the Extreme Play Bow. Many dogs are. This intensity may make it look to the other dog as if the invitation is tinged with anxiety. The frantic-ness may signal play that is rougher than the other dog likes. Perhaps the Golden doesn't want to play at all. The Extreme Play Bow tends to accompany fanatic insistence on play. This is too intense for some social situations, and if the dog using it is not socially sensitive, it can really cause problems.

I could easily visualize the Golden holding this Stillness for two or three more seconds, then attempting to disengage in one of a number of ways. The Cattle Dog acknowledges the Stillness and just tears off and plays by herself. She might even approach the Golden again to see if the Golden really means it. The Golden might begin to relax and then use a Negotiation signal, like Sniffing, to disengage from the Cattle Dog. If the Golden were to simply move away, which is unlikely, the Cattle Dog would barrel into the Golden's body space in an attempt to convince the Golden to interact.

This is a Moment of Decision: that moment where a Change of Emotional State is going to occur that could go in any one of several directions. How it goes depends on how savvy the dogs are.

The following Text is for Photo #31.6: Correction..

Here is the correction from the above encounter. Sorry about the blurriness of the photo, but the speed with which the dogs moved is incredible.

You can see how wide the eyes are on the Cattle Dog (notice the whites of her eyes), and also how pulled back her ears are. Her back is very rounded as she pulls her hindquarters far under her body (startle or fetal position).

The Golden has her ears drawn back and you can see the facial tension in the ridges under the eyes. Unlike the Cattle Dog, the Golden has not lowered her body at all.

Text for this photograph is on the previous page.

#31.6: Correction

- Golden standing over
- Cattle Dog down on the ground

#31.7: Apology

- Contrast in body postures

This is an interesting photograph. This is the same Cattle Dog, seen in Photo #31.5 & #31.6, interacting with a different Golden Retriever. You can see again the "too big-ness" of the gesture.

The Cattle Dog is displaying the lowered body posture, drawn-back lips, lowered ears, and lowered tail of "I'm sorry." Note also the squinty, blinking eyes. Although the dog is in motion, you can still see the exaggerated lift of the right front paw: supplication. As I have mentioned before, anxious animals have a marked tendency to Move Into Pressure, a clear indication that this dog is anxious.

Although the dog has an apologetic countenance, she is moving into the Golden's space in such a pushy way. Why is she doing this? Uncertain dogs often ask to interact in this apologetic, yet pushy manner. Remember, dogs will try to manipulate their environment at best they can; some will use assertive behaviour and others feel acquiescent behaviour is more profitable.

The apology/request to play of the Cattle Dog is peppered with anxiety, which is creating much more tension in the interaction than is necessary. The anxiety is causing the message to be exaggerated. In the company of some dogs (like my Shepherd bitch), this over-done gesture would garner her another correction.

The Golden has her tail held up. Her ears are holding some tension and so is her face. See the ridges right below the eyes? Notice that the shape of the Golden's eyes is pretty soft. She is tolerating the Cattle Dog. She is using a Look Away to signal, "Go away, I don't want any conflict." She also doesn't look that interested in Playing. Mostly the Golden wishes the Cattle Dog would go be bizarre somewhere else.

#31.8: Uppity Youngster

#31.8: Uppity Youngster

- Contrast in body postures
- "Up on the toes" silhouette of the puppy
- tail forced over puppy's back
- raised head of puppy
- ear position of puppy is "forced"
- body tension in puppy

- wide open eyes of the puppy
- closed mouths on both dogs, very tense, short lips on the puppy
- lowered head and Guarding posture of English Setter
- forward orientation of the Setter

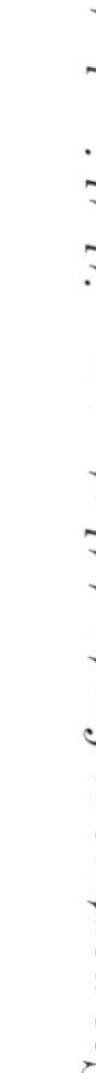

See next page for text that goes with this photograph.

Text for Photo #31.8: Uppity Youngster.

Although at first glance it may appear that the puppy has the upper hand, do not be fooled.

The English Setter approaches with squinty eyes and a half-mast tail and ears. The Setter is using many Negotiation signals. This approach does have an element of "set-up" to it, though. There is the head-on orientation of the approach and the closed mouth, accompanied by a lowered head which says: "Puppy, your uppity little attitude on my approach is rude. Show me respect and allow me to sniff you with an acquiescent attitude, or move out of my path to show social awareness." Either of these actions on the part of the puppy would be correct.

The puppy doesn't give way. Instead, she receives the approach with a disrespectful attitude. Her silhouette says, "I'm kickin' ass and takin' names! You don't get to push me around. I am Super Puppy!"

With her head-on orientation and tail over her back, she sends a message of confrontation to the adult dog. Notice, the puppy is Warning: her nose is oriented slightly *away from* the English Setter, but her wide and staring eyes are *directly on the other dog.* This kind of direct stare combined with a ever-so-slight Look away is definitely Warning behaviour. I associate this particular combination with the dog who is not quite confident enough or sure enough of the outcome to use a direct stare. The puppy has a closed tense mouth; the lips on the Setter are longer and more relaxed, showing confidence.

The English Setter is using a softened approach. Her eye is not forced wide and staring. She is, in essence, giving the puppy a chance to back down. The puppy is not taking advantage of this chance.

You can tell that the Setter is not acquiescing to the puppy, because she is holding a head-on position and is not lowering herself to the ground, but advancing forward into the puppy's space. She is also not using a Look Away, and the neck is long, with the head pushed forward and down. She is looking at the puppy.

This is a condensed version of two dogs playing a game of Chicken.

Text for Photo #31.9: Correction

When the puppy does not return any Negotiation signals, the Setter lunges into action: "Puppies should be more polite!"

She rolls the puppy over and stays in the puppy's space.

The Setter has made the ultimate invasion into body space - a Correction. Corrections of this type often consist of a growl and a lunge, accompanied by an open mouth bite.

The puppy, who is outclassed and knows it, says "Uncle." She has allowed herself to be tumbled over and tucks her tail and all of her legs close into her body into a fetal position. She keeps her nose oriented towards the Setter, though. Her eyes are squinty, now!

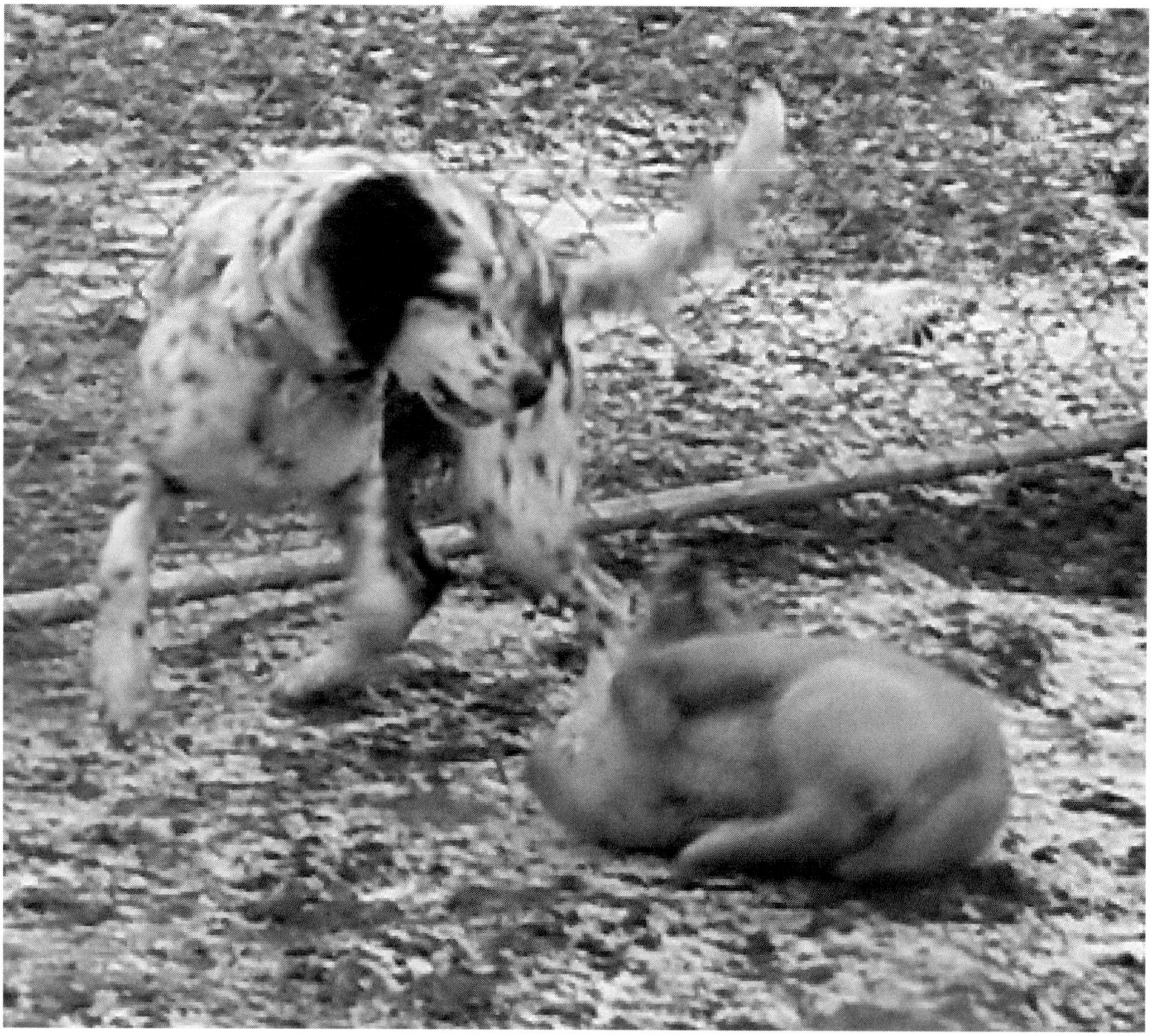

#31.9: Correction

- puppy is in fetal position
- English Setter is over puppy
- puppy is holding still
- Setter is in motion

In Dog World, wimpy victories invite the corrected animal back to challenge again. Definitive Victories are really the only ones that count. The Correcting Dog, to be effective, must persist until the Correctee displays total acquiescence. That is what is happening here. The Setter is making the puppy good and uncomfortable, not just for a second, but for at least a few seconds, long enough to drive the point home. "Are you sure you got The Message?"

After this, it is common to see the Victor Standing Over the other dog for a few seconds to make sure the Correctee is being obedient, and does not try to get up until the Correcter moves away, giving permission to get up.

The most important observation about this Correction is that it is filled with High Drama, but nobody gets hurt.

#31.10: Reconciliation (Kiss & Make Up)

See next page for text that goes with this photograph.

#31.10: Reconciliation (Kiss & Make Up)

- puppy has head lifted in apology
- Setter has a paw lift
- both dogs have squinty eyes
- both dogs have ears back
- dogs are closely mirroring each other's body positions
- puppy has a rounded back

Text for Photo #31.10: Reconciliation (Kiss & Make Up)

The Setter allows the puppy to get up and retreat. Then she approaches the puppy again.

This time, the reception is much improved. The Setter uses a gently waving tail and a Paw Lift as she approaches the puppy: "See, I will show you respect and be polite, if you are polite and show respect to me."

The Setter extends her head and neck into the puppy's personal space, but is not pushing her whole body in. She sets a good example of language for the puppy. The point has been made: "We are Kissing & Making Up, just don't forget your lesson!" The puppy is accepting this politely: "Yes, I remember."

The puppy mirrors the gently wagging tail and reaches up toward the Setter with her nose. Her eyes are squinty, and her ears are drawn slightly back to show respect.

Mirroring (copying a body position) shows affinity with another. This rule crosses species.

The puppy is apologizing to the Setter, who is encouraging the reconciliation. The Setter is showing the puppy a Paw Lift. Both dogs have squinty eyes and long lips.

Good lesson!

> *Comment*: Lest you feel too sorry for this puppy, she absolutely deserved this correction. Puppies, like small children, should show respect for older members of their species. Allowing puppies to think they are Invincible leads to many errors in judgment as the puppy grows up. Boundaries are very important for puppies to learn. Boundaries teach the puppy Social Rules of Dog Etiquette, just as they do for humans. *Clear Boundaries are essential for friendly group relationships.* This adult dog was an excellent teacher.

Photo Credits:
Photo #1: Cherish DeWitt;
Photo #2, #3, #4: Courtesy of Theresa Jacobus;
Photo #5, #6, #7, #8, #9, #10: Cherish DeWitt.

WARNING

Warnings are rampant in dog language. Most of them are so quick and subtle that the majority of people don't even know they occur. I am extremely sensitive to Warning Looks because I have Terriers, who have a marked tendency to go from Zero-to-Sixty in milliseconds. They give one quick Warning, then they act on it. Also, I work with so many aggressive dogs that if I weren't observant of micro-behaviours and very careful I would be bitten more frequently.

Many dogs will Warn, then wait to see if it gets the response from the other dog (or person) that they wanted. If the response doesn't meet expectations, they won't necessarily back it up with real action. Other dogs are not kidding and do not give empty threats: it really is a One And Only chance to change one's behaviour - immediately - or else there is a swift consequence.

Whenever you see a Warning look, it is wise to assume the worst: that the dog is not just using an idle threat and intends to back it up with action.

Warning Looks are always accompanied by Stillness or Freezing. Both describe the total immobility that comes with extreme body tension. Both may be so sudden that it is difficult to detect when you are first learning to look for it, but it is there. Both may last a fraction of a second, or be prolonged and quite obvious. After much field experience, if I feel sudden body tension of any kind, I assume that the dog is Warning me. If you are standing behind or beside the dog, he will often not move his head, but just his eyes to give you The Look. In my own clinical notes, I differentiate between the two by using "Stillness" to indicate deliberate intent (response)- a Real Warning that the dog might follow up with a growl, snap or bite. I use "Freezing" to describe fearful reaction. A fearful reaction might also be followed up by a growl, snap or bite, but the function the behaviour is serving for the dog is definitely different, even though the result is the same! For more discussion, see Table 1, in Chapter 33: Guarding.

Dogs warn other dogs about personal space infractions all the time. Dogs will administer the exact same warning to a person.

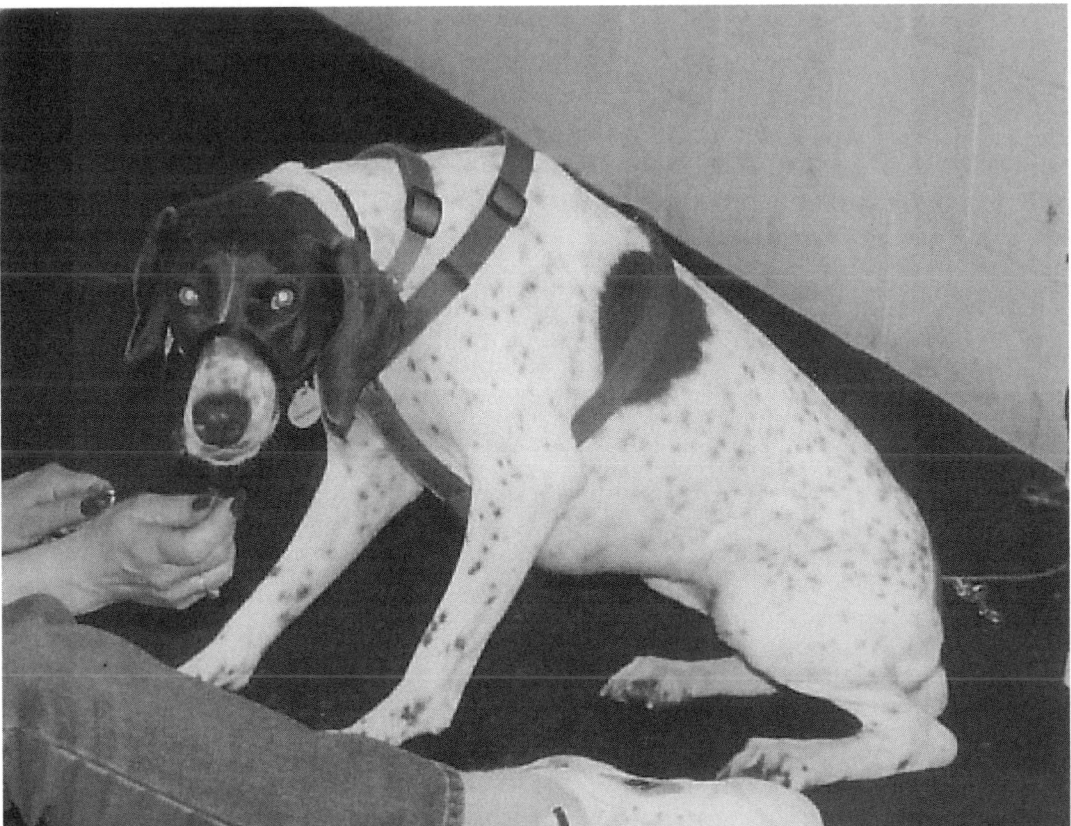

#32.1: Stop Your Approach

- head lowered
- direct stare
- braced legs
- tucked tail
- closed, tight mouth

This dog is at a Clinic and is Warning me not to continue my approach. The head is lowered, the eye contact is direct and the dog's mouth is closed. This dog is also fearful, with a tail that is tucked and front legs braced in tension.

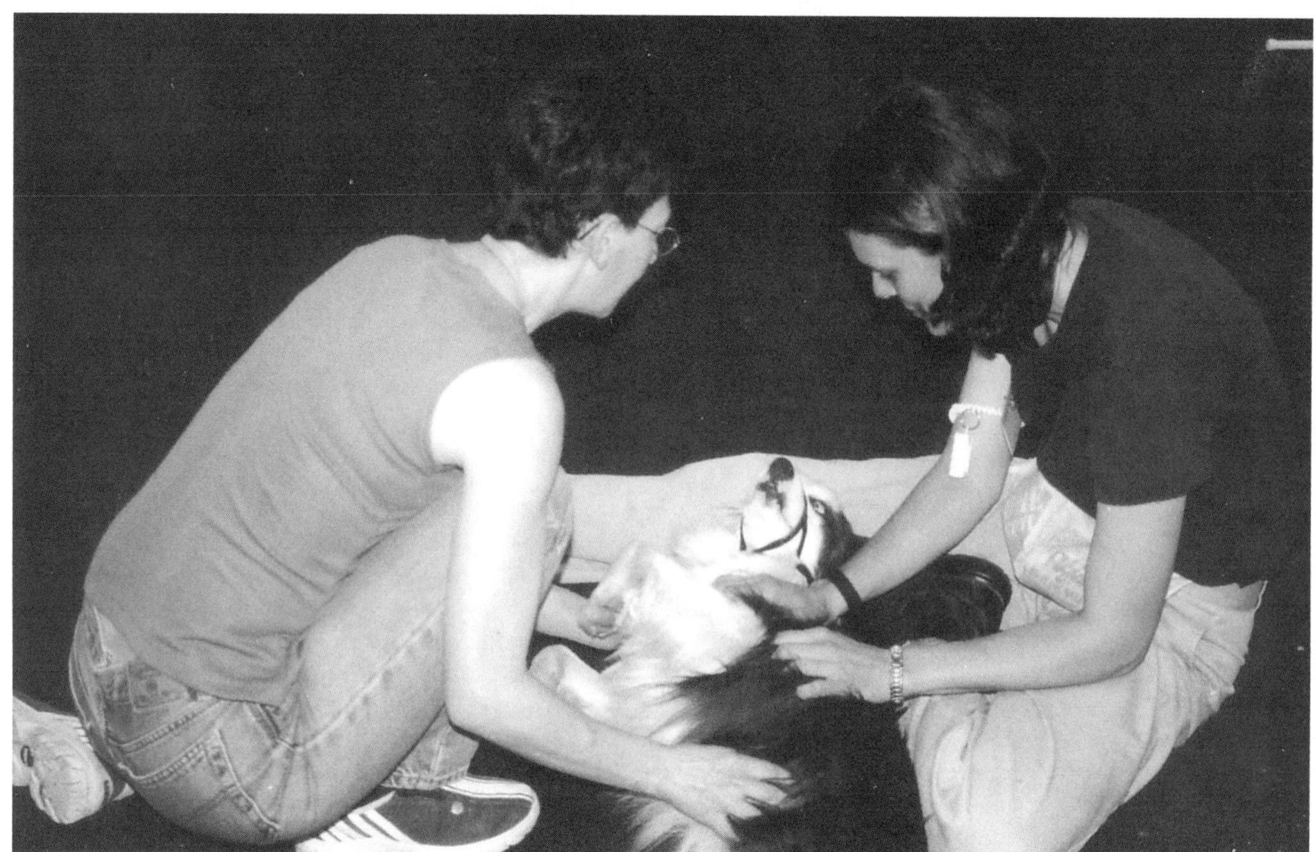

#32.2: Warning from a "Submissive" Position

- direct stare
- nose pointing same direction as the eyes
- wide open eyes
- rigid body

Don't let the "submissive" position of this dog fool you. She is Warning me out of her space.

This Aussie is feeling very defensive. Her nose is oriented toward my approach and she is giving me direct eye contact without blinking. The rigidity in the limbs can be seen in her front legs. She is telling me in no uncertain terms to move away. I am intruding into her personal space and she is darned uncomfortable about it.

This photograph was taken at a clinic. The owner is doing a super job by keeping her hands calmly on her dog and not being reactive. I am using TTouch (Linda Tellington-Jones body work method) along with the owner to teach the dog that different human approaches and touches are not threatening. The dog is very tense, but has just begun to tone her warning down a bit in response to her owner's calm attitude. Just prior to this photograph, the dog's head was raised toward me. I am looking at the dog, but not with a staring eye, I am blinking and keep giving the dog Look Aways to reassure her.

Training Tip: Heeding this kind of language is the secret to avoiding bites from dogs with whom you are working. Learn the circumstances under which Warnings are given. This will help you pinpoint problem areas and discomfort levels. Once triggers are identified, you can apply a behaviour modification protocol to make the dog both safer and more comfortable.

#32.3: Warning Look

- extremely lowered head
- direct stare
- closed tense mouth
- down tail
- forced back ears
- eyes wide open

The Border Collie-mix on the right is Warning the GSD. The reasons can be myriad: she doesn't want the dog next to her owner. There are treats nearby. She just doesn't want to be in such close proximity. Whatever the reason, it is valid to her, and she is letting the Shepherd know that she wants him to move away.

The Paw Lift is interesting. It could indicate a bit of uncertainty about the outcome on the part of the BC, a slight lack of confidence that she can move the GSD away effectively. Her tail is lowered, too, which backs this interpretation up. Her nose is oriented slightly away from, with eyes directly Staring At, the GSD: Classic Guarding behaviour. When I watched my World Class Resource Guarders who were really confident, they did not use a paw lift. They gave a quick Warning Look, then lunged into the side of the offending dog, snapping and snarling. Then they would move back, walk a step or two away and Shake Off.

The Shepherd's response is very interesting. His response tells me he is not taking the Border Collie-mix very seriously. He is giving her a soft look, with half-mast ears, and has remained seated. He is telling her he doesn't want any trouble, and is not feeling threatened enough to move out of the way.

#32.4: Play Warning - Photo Essay

- direct stare
- wide open eyes
- relaxed ears
- tail up & gently sweeping
- head & neck are up

This Warning Look tells Karli, wearing the coat, that Saiko intends to retain ownership of the toy. However, the up but relaxed and moving tail tells her that it is not meant to be taken very seriously. Saiko's ears are also up but relaxed and not held tensely. Most significantly Saiko's head and neck are not extremely lowered.

The ancient BC, Karli, (who was resident elder when Saiko was a puppy) reads it correctly: This is a Warning, but not a serious one, and "I can push the envelope."

#32.5: Concern about Possession

- orientation of dogs' noses
- compare the direction of dogs' eye contact to the orientation of it's nose

The dog on the right is concerned because the approaching dog is looking at the toy. You can tell this because Zeta, the dark-colored dog, is looking at Mecca. Zeta's up ears signal that the dog is not feeling like she needs to guard the toy. The long lips and held back ears of the approaching dog are friendly signals. Mecca's mouth is ever so slightly open. Those signals cool down the interaction, so it will not become volatile.

#32.6: Mine

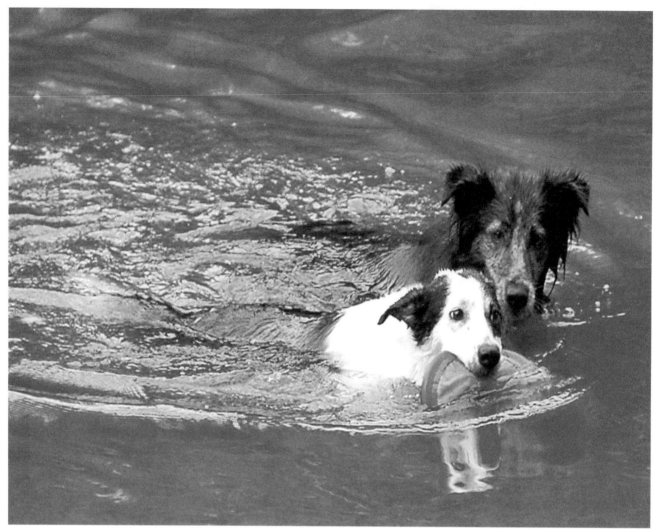

- orientation of dogs' noses
- compare the direction of dogs' eye contact with the orientation of it's nose

The dogs have exchanged the toy. The eyes of Mecca, on the left, are directed towards Zeta. However, Mecca intends to retain the toy, so she has her nose turned away from the other dog to keep the item as far from Zeta as possible.

These dogs are exchanging the toy back and forth, but the play has an intense look about it. I would be watching these dogs to see if the interaction got any more intense and, if it did, I would initiate and enforce a play break so the adrenaline levels could go down (which will cause judgment levels to improve). Remember, the average Border Collie or Sheltie can get more intense in play and have it still be harmless; in a similar context I would have to intervene with my Terriers.

Observation: Watch for the direction a dog directs her eye contact. If a dog is Looking At It, she is Thinking About It. Just as telling, what is a dog deliberately Looking Away From? How much body tension is evident? If you are alert to that signal alone, you will be much farther along in predicting what a dog will do next.

#32.7: Back Out of My Bubble

- Stillness
- braced front legs & up ears show some body tension
- closed mouth
- ridge by lips

This is not just a Look Away on the part of the Sheltie. There is a little edge to this Look Away.

The closed mouth and the slight ridge by the lips, along with the Stillness and down tail, tell you that the Sheltie is telling the Terrier that he is taking too much liberty with personal space.

The next move by the Sheltie will be a glance of direct eye contact as a stronger message to the Westie.

The Westie doesn't look worried and is coming in gently, with a confident, but friendly, manner and an appropriate sideways approach. It would be better if the Westie acknowledged the Sheltie's discomfort with a Negotiation Signal, or backed off a bit.

#32.8: Mine - and I Intend to Keep It That Way - Photo Essay

- direction of eyes
- nose (& valued object) turned away

The dog on the left has her eyes directed towards the dog on the right. She is rightfully concerned, because the dog on the right has his eye on the bumper.

Warning looks are all about possession - either of a tangible object or personal space.

Here, the up ears and the intensity of the gaze of the dog on the right is an Alerting look. He is telling the other dog that he wants to possess the bumper.

The dog on the left keeps her nose turned away from the other dog. She intends to retain possession and by turning her nose away makes this clear. If she wanted to share the toy and play with the other dog she would turn his nose towards the other dog to initiate a game of tug or keep-away.

The ears of the dog who has the bumper stay down.

After the brief Warning in the previous photo, the dog on the right gives it up. The Warning worked. The dog on the right Shakes Off and the dog on the left retains possession of the bumper.

The dog on the left gets the message of the Shake Off and relaxes also. Notice how the eyes are no longer directed toward the other dog and are squinty.

Another peaceful solution to possession.

Beautiful language skills on the part of both dogs.

#32.9: Mild Invading Personal Space Warning

- looks directly at Labrador
- nose slightly different direction than eyes
- ears slightly back
- Stillness
- mouth closed

Willie, the Golden, Warns the young male Labrador. His Warning Look, with the nose tipped slightly away from the Lab, while looking directly at him and with a lowered tail say: "Do not continue to move into my bubble, young man."

The Lab lowers his head, draws his ears back and has a low, sweeping tail. This is still a tense moment. The Lab is being a little cheeky by maintaining eye contact as he moves through and out of Willie's space.

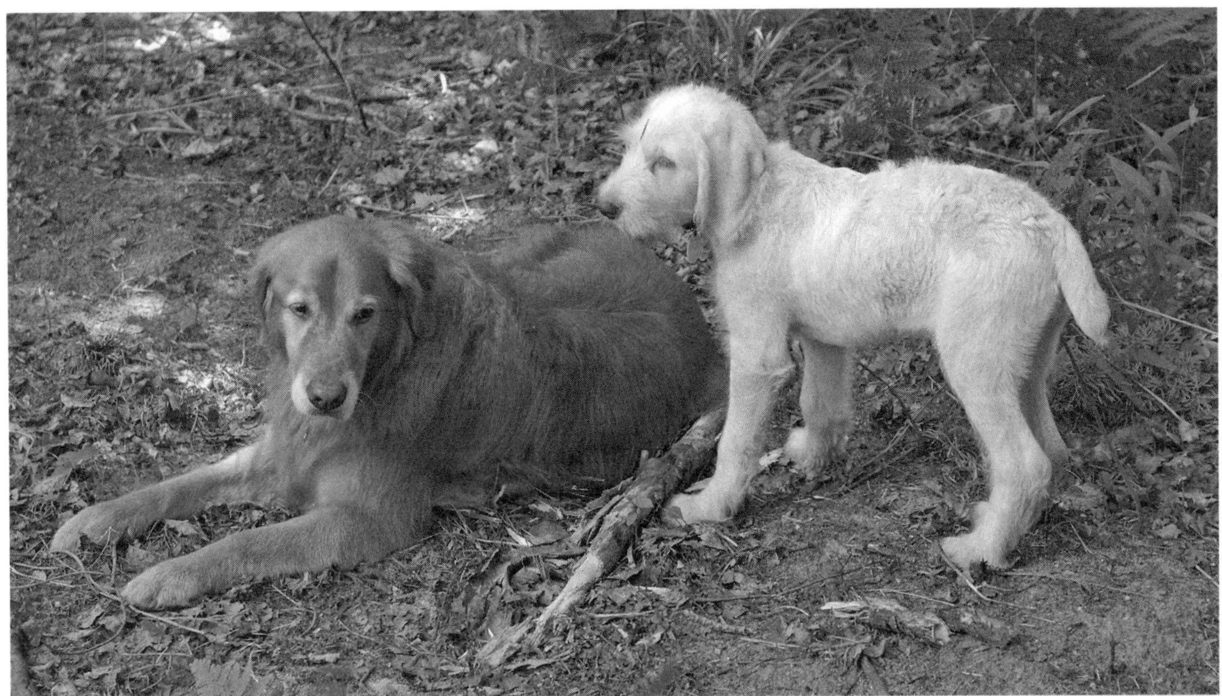

#32.10: Subtle Warning - Photo Essay

- looks toward puppy, but avoids direct eye contact
- ears slightly back
- Stillness
- mouth closed

Willie, the adult Golden, warns the approaching Spinone puppy she is about to commit a personal space infraction. The puppy is wonderful - she gives the Golden a Look Away and pulls her whole body backwards, away from the Golden. Willie responds by returning the Look Away, allowing the puppy to stay near and chat. What a beautiful and appropriate exchange. See how subtle it is? The time taken for the entire exchange is less than five seconds and could be over in as few as three seconds.

In the top photo, Willie orients his nose slightly towards the puppy and gives her a pointed look. Skillfully, Willie keeps it non-threatening by not looking directly into the puppy's eyes and staring. There is just a head turn and brief Stillness to communicate the Warning message to the pup. What a master communicator: get a firm message across, but without risking defensive behaviour from the approaching dog.

Once the message has been delivered and received, there is no lingering emotion. It's over.

#32.11: Gentle Warning

- Looks at puppy, but avoids direct eye contact
- ears slightly back
- mouth closed

Willie, the Golden, gives Zasu a gentle Warning. He uses a nose turn and Look Toward the Terrier. The young Terrier sees it and holds her ears back in appeasement.

Notice the way Willie is holding his ears: forced back. This is often part of a Warning Look.

This is interesting because both dogs are using held-back ears to communicate. Looking at the context and the combination of signals is how you learn to read the dog. Willie's ears are held back and his nose is *lowered*, the Terrier's ears are held back and her nose is *raised* in the typical, "I am appeasing you" signal. She looks as if she is about to begin Puppy Licking.

Photo Credits:
Photo #3 through #11: Joanne Weber

33 GUARDING

One step up from Warning is Guarding. Guarding has everything to do with establishing ownership. Ownership is about Possession. There is a lot of overlap between Warning and Guarding Signals, and they are so interconnected that it is difficult to separate the two of them. In this chapter, however, I placed the photographs that, on my "Read," were a step up in intensity from the Warning photographs.

In the Book Of Canine Law, one important law is that of Possession.

Possession, to a dog, means: What Is In My Immediate Space Is MINE. Dogs have great respect for this law. It is observed by "well-spoken" dogs, that is, dogs who are skilled at their native language and understand group dynamics.

Showing possession of objects or locations is used to determine or clarify status. And yet, you will see many examples of a higher status dog allowing a lower status animal to retain possession of an item.

Possession includes all tangible items: the ground you are standing on, the bed you are lying on, the human who is standing next to you.

Doggie possession rules do not always parallel ours. Take this common example: Dog #1 will make nice with a human who is not theirs, and take some treats from the human. When that human's own dog approaches, Dog #1 warns the other dog off. Sometimes this is done with a subtle look, sometimes with a quiet growl and sometimes with a lunge and correction bite. The subtle looks are often not even noticed by the humans. The more obvious stuff tends to cause humans to over-react and then be puzzled about what occurred. This happens because we humans have a different sense of "possession." We differentiate: *This* dog is Mine, *that* dog is just a Visitor. But the dogs are staking their territory quite differently. They are much more In The Moment. Whoever is Possessing *at that second* is in charge. (see Chapter 35 *Rylie & Emma* for an example.)

This brings us to another Canine Law: What You Have Is Yours - *unless* someone else can intimidate you out of it.

Dogs don't always follow these rules - but there are certainly patterns of behaviour that can be established amongst individual dogs. Until you know the dog well, don't be surprised when she switches definitions of Possession Laws according to context and current stress levels.

#33.1: Guarding & Confident

- ears forward
- Stillness
- direct stare
- lowered head

Saiko, the Border Collie-mix on the left, is telling Abby, on the right, in no uncertain terms, to move away from the cool water toys. Saiko's owner is also sitting on the lawn chair, which in many dogs intensifies the urge to guard. Owners often have toys and food in a bait bag, and are, themselves, considered to be the most valued resource!

Saiko's owner is intent on helping the student's dog, so she is unaware that Saiko is telling Abby to do just the opposite of what the people are urging her to do.

Saiko's lowered head and tensely forward ears, combined with a direct stare say: "Move Away Right Now." Because of her breed, the guarding looks very "stalky." It is the "up" ears that cause this Guarding to have the "stalking" overtones. She is trying to use a 'Strong Eye' as if the other dog were a sheep.

The Border Collie on the left is ready to go chase that frisbee. The Border Collie-mix, on the right, is Guarding. The direct stare of the dog on the right, and the Stillness, say: "I am Guarding." The valuable item could be the frisbee or the human, perhaps both.

#33.2: Guarding

- Stillness
- direct stare

The Border Collie on the left is ignoring the warning of the other dog, she is so intent on her prey object. Also, there is a human between her and the other dog, who serves as a buffer, reducing the impact of the warning quite a bit.

The human doesn't seem aware of the possibility of social conflict. She and the Border Collie are intent on their fun game.

Note: I interpreted this photograph without any background information, as I did the majority of photographs in this book. I wanted to have the same disadvantage that you, the reader, would have. When I first looked at this photograph, I was immediately struck by the nonchalant response by the dog on the left: there is no caution or acknowledgement of the Warning directed at her. This struck me as incongruous. But, I figure most dogs understand their Native Language better than we do, therefore, there was something about this context that made the Border Collie on the left feel safe enough to disregard what I saw as a strong message. In talking to the photographer later, I discovered that the human is owner of both dogs, and the dogs are housemates. This accounts for the lackadaisical attitude of the Border Collie on the left. She has experience with the other dog, so knows she can ignore such a message. Mystery solved!

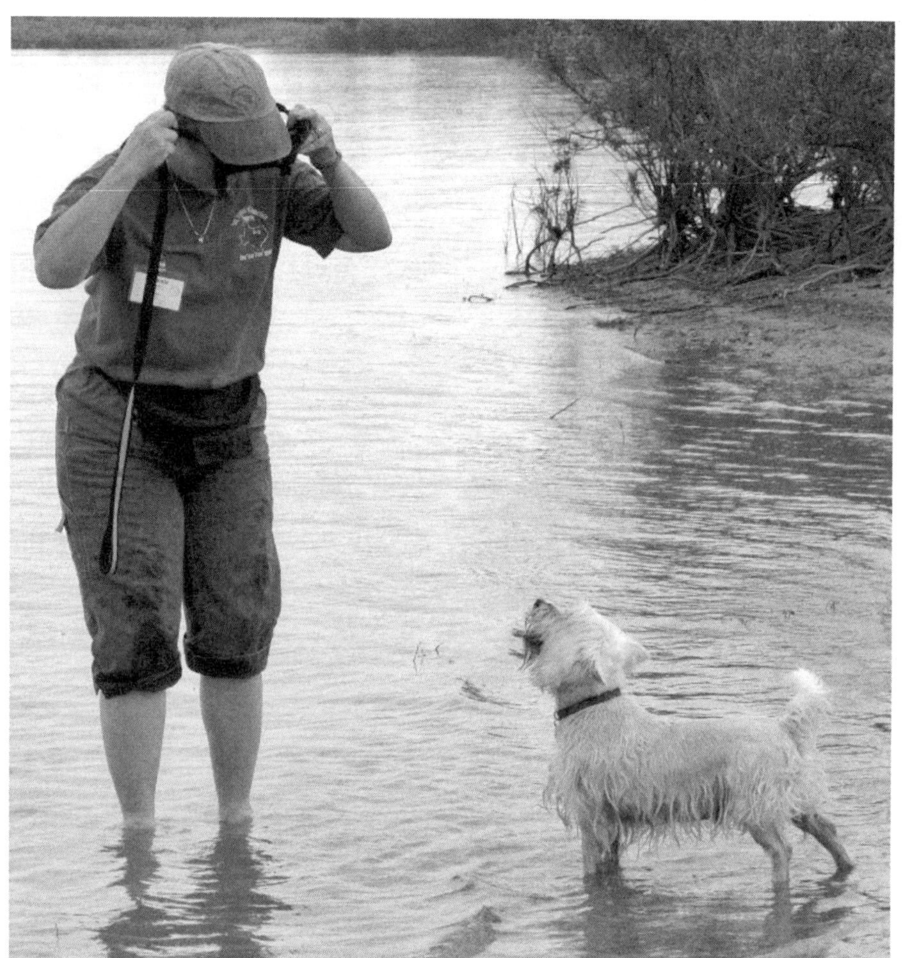

#33.3: My Owner - Scene 1

- tail up & wagging in interaction
- Happy, open mouth
- orientation toward owner
- body energy forward

Another little drama! The Westie is clearly having a very important and intense conversation with his mum.

#33.3: My Owner - Scene 2

- tail up
- Stillness
- direct stare
- lowered head & ears
- orientation change - toward Aussie

And along comes an Aussie. Unlike Miss Muffet and the spider, however, the Aussie is not about to drive the terrier away from HIS resource.

Because of beautiful language skills displayed by both dogs, a conflict is avoided.

The Westie's tail up over his back tells us he's pretty certain that the outcome will be in his favour. The lowered head and drawn back ears, with a direct orientation (if we were looking from the side or front, the direct stare would be evident) toward the Aussie say clearly: "Move Along, You. This is my property."

The Aussie is responding in a lovely manner: open mouth, ears drawn back, head lowered in acquiescence, as he does as the Westie requests - moves away immediately.

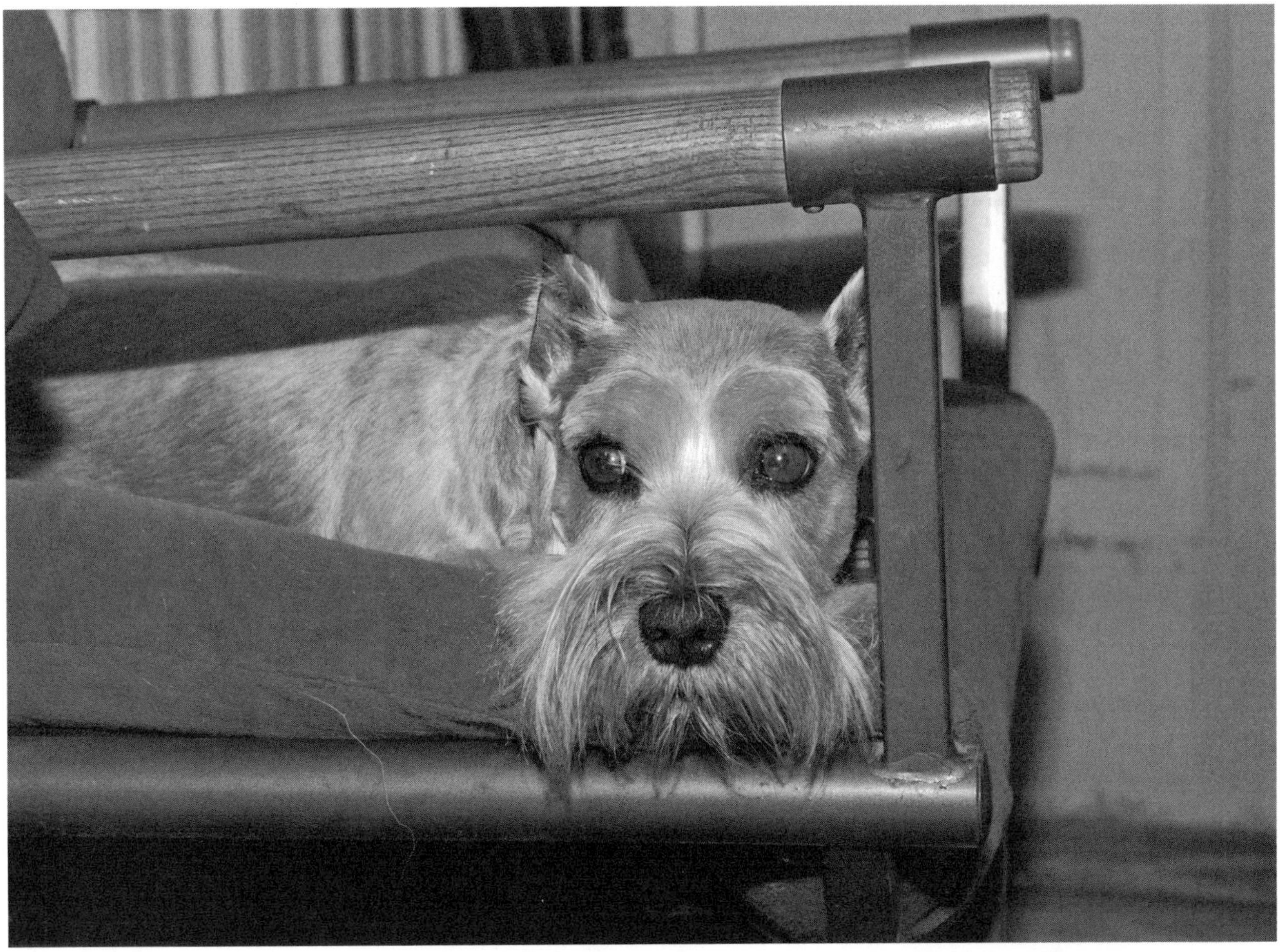

#33.4: Alert

- ears forward
- stillness
- eyes very wide open

Although this dog is lying down on the chair, he does not have a relaxed pose. His eyes are very wide, to the extent the whites are showing. His ears are held forward. There is a Stillness and intensity about his bearing that tells you this dog is Guarding either a specific location (This Chair Is Mine) or his personal space. It is probable that another dog (or person) is walking by.

Training Tip: I assume, when I am handling a dog, that *any* Sudden Stillness indicates a Warning from the dog to me.

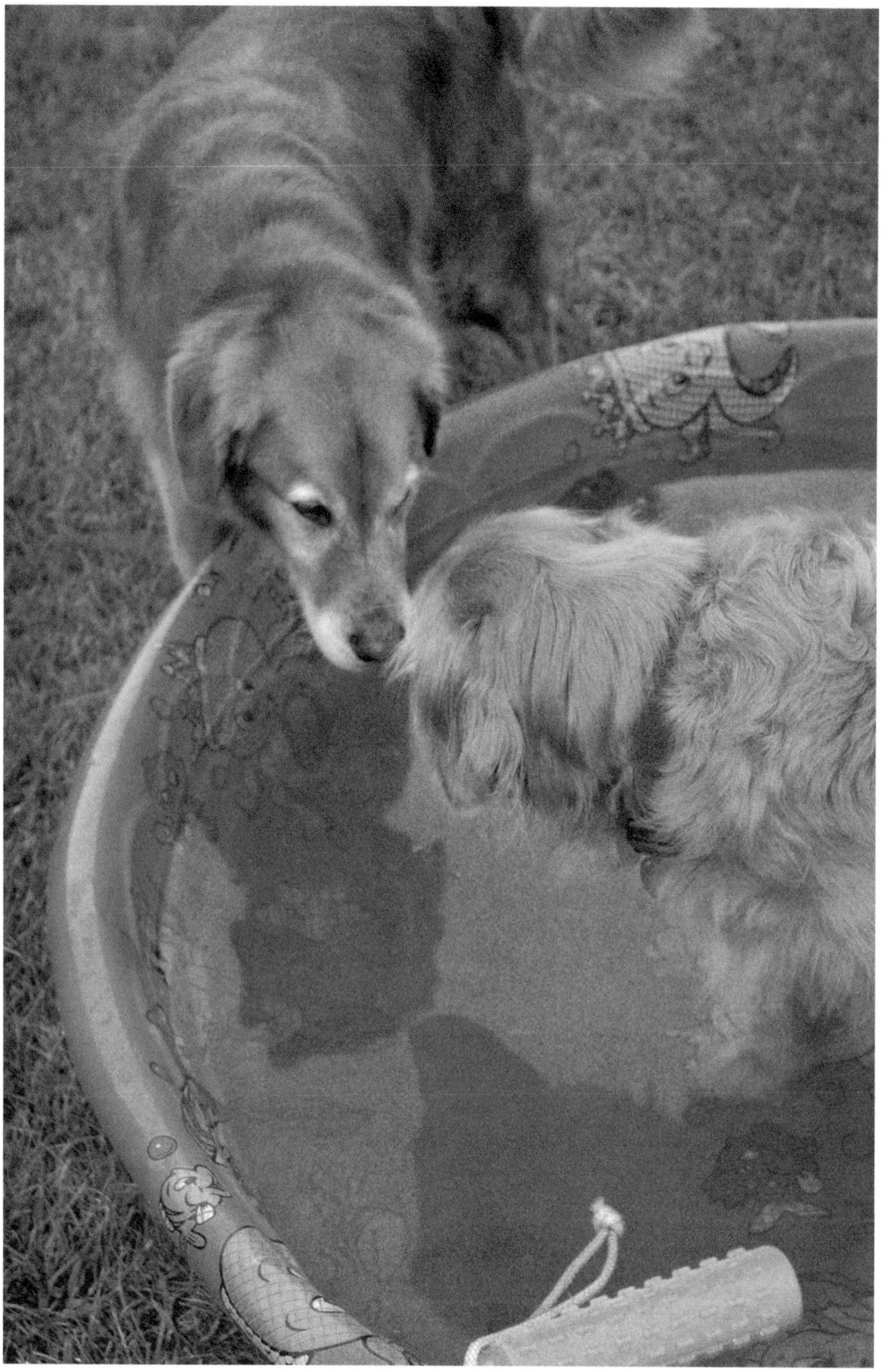

#33.5: Rear View of Guarding Posture

- lowered head of the dog on the right
- Stillness

I love this photograph of a subtle example of Guarding.

Even though one cannot see very much of the Golden on the right, one can easily observe the lowered head and the Stillness that goes along with resource guarding. This is an example of Guarding from the rear - the perspective from which dog handlers are most often viewing. It is useful to be able to identify At Risk Behaviour from different angles.

The Golden on the right is looking very directly at the Golden on the left. It is easy to see the resource - the bumper floating in the baby pool.

Willie, the Golden on the left, does not appear to be very alarmed, but he is using Negotiation Signals. Since he is in a situation that could turn into conflict, he has pulled his ears back in deference and is squinting. The next correct move would be a Look Away, and then Moving Away to avoid conflict. Offhand, I would say Willie is not very concerned about the threat from the dog on the right.

Note: The dog on the left is a male and the dog on the right is a female. Guarding behaviour crosses sexual boundaries.

> *Pay Attention*: Resource Guarding is a behaviour that crosses all boundaries. It can cross species, and be directed at another dog or a person or even a cat. It crosses sexual boundaries also - you are no longer dealing with the relative predictability of male-to-male or female-to-female aggression and posturing. Many dogs stop at posturing and Warning with Resource Guarding, others have no inhibition about backing up their threat.

The most distinguishing characteristics of Guarding are the lowered head, staring "hard" eye, and body tension. These same characteristics are a common thread in the dog's Native Language, and the lowered head is used as part of a variety of communications.

Table 1: So Just How do you distinguish Guarding from Deference? Ask yourself these questions:

Where is the dog's nose oriented?	Is the nose oriented in the same direction the eyes are? In one kind of Guarding posture, the dog looks up at you with a hard, staring eye, and his nose and head are lowered: the dog will look up out of the tops of his eyes, and there will be white showing around the eye. When the nose is oriented one direction and the eyes another, Guarding is a definite possibility. The other possibility is worried about
Where are the dog's eyes directed?	When Guarding the dog will look at the Target. In Deference the dog will often Look Away from the Target. (The Target being defined as who the dog is communicating with at the time.)
Are the pupils dilated?	Dilated pupils are the physiological response to an adrenaline dump. The adrenaline dump can be caused by any one of a number of reasons: excitement, stress, fear, anger.
Is the dog Blinking or Not Blinking?	Blinking is friendly and acquiescent. Not Blinking is a Staring eye - indicating confrontation and threat. A "hard" eye is a Not Blinking, Intensely Staring eye.
Is the dog still?	Stillness is the Calm Before the Storm. Sometimes dogs pause just before or after using a Play Bow or a Prey Bow. Stillness, which is a deliberate response, or Freezing, which is a fearful reaction, are both ways that the dog is still. Following Stillness or Freezing, when the dog does move, *it is often explosive in nature*. In addition if the Stillness is not preceded by a Negotiation Signal, it usually means conflict.

Observation: A lowered head with staring and body tension = Warning/Guarding. A lowered head with averted eyes can be submissive or defensive behaviour, or a bizarre combination of the two. You must look at the context, and often take a read on both dogs to interpret.

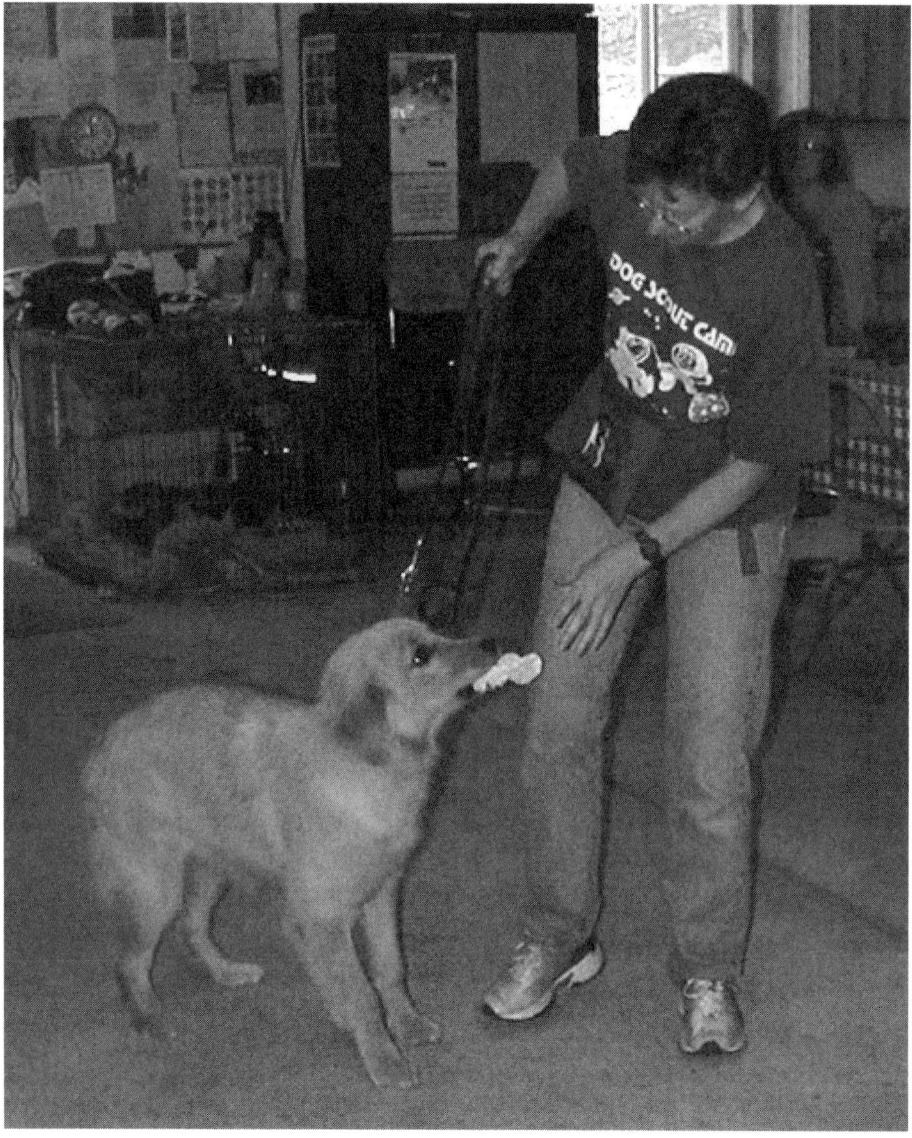

#33.6: Typical Guarding

- stillness
- eyes very wide open
- direct stare
- rounded back
- tail clamped and slightly tucked

This puppy, during a Leave It exercise, has confiscated the item. Her rounded topline, braced front feet and lowered ears and tail tell you that she is feeling defensive. Her direct stare and the tension in her jaw say, "Mine, mine, all mine."

She understands by my body language that I want the item, and she is young and senses my authority. On the other hand, she has decided OR is compelled by instinct to try to retain the item. Her body language tells you that she really isn't very certain about the outcome, so she is displaying a defensive posture.

Dogs who are Resource Guarding, especially from humans, often present with this particular type of ambivalence. The abnormal dog really cannot get a grip on himself, therefore, YOU will have to make the move to prevent him from becoming defensive.

Photo Credits: Photo #1, #2, Photo Essay #3, #4, #5, #6 & #7: Joanne Weber

34
Guarding Among Friends

In this photo, notice the lowered and forward body posture of the Papillon. She is Guarding. The Shepherd is acknowledging this. She is keeping her eyes averted from the little terror, and is holding her ears drawn back. The Papillon is turning her nose slightly toward the Shepherd, and is also directing her eye contact in that direction. The Papillon is not just reaching downward towards the plate to eat, but is hovering over the plate, taking up as much space as she can.

#34.1: Guarding among Friends

- braced legs
- body tension in both dogs
- drawn back ears of the shepherd
- orientation of the Papillon's nose
- direction of eyes on the Papillon
- Shepherd is doing a subtle Look Away, carefully avoiding the Papillon's sideways stare

#34.2: Peaceful Resolution

Now all the food is gone, the Papillon is much more relaxed. At least now you can determine she was Guarding the food itself and not the empty plate or the location... Now she is just reaching down toward the plate in a casual manner. The Shepherd has moved away and given the Papillon more room. You can see the change in the Shepherd's face as well: her ears are not forced back and the forehead looks broader and less tense. The Shepherd was definitely more tense in the preceeding photograph...but she did not leave the scene entirely! Instead, she compromised by orienting herself away from the Papillon, so she could stay and eat while radiating, "I am not a threat!"

#34.3: Companionship

- relaxed and trusting contact
- proximity

Just because you "have words" doesn't mean you will not curl up and enjoy each other's companionship! People try to anthropomorphize dogs too much. They think that just because the dogs will curl up together and look so dear that they will never harm each other. This is simply not so. It is a gross generalization. Behaviour is very contextual. The dog's behaviour will be based on the minute-to-minute situation.

Photo Credits:
Photo #1, #2 & #3: Cherish DeWitt.

35
RYLIE & EMMA

#35.1: Rylie Mobs Lori: Friendly

- friendly ears drawn back
- tail drawn down
- sideways approach

#35.2: Puppy Licking

In this photo sequence Lori interacts with two dogs. The Am Staff is her dog, Emma. Rylie, the Border Collie, is my dog. We were just hanging around in the kennel, chatting and letting the dogs run around. Rylie and Emma are both very friendly dogs and get on well with other dogs. Both girls love people.

Since Lori didn't repel her, Rylie moves right into Lori's lap and gives her the Puppy Licking Treatment.

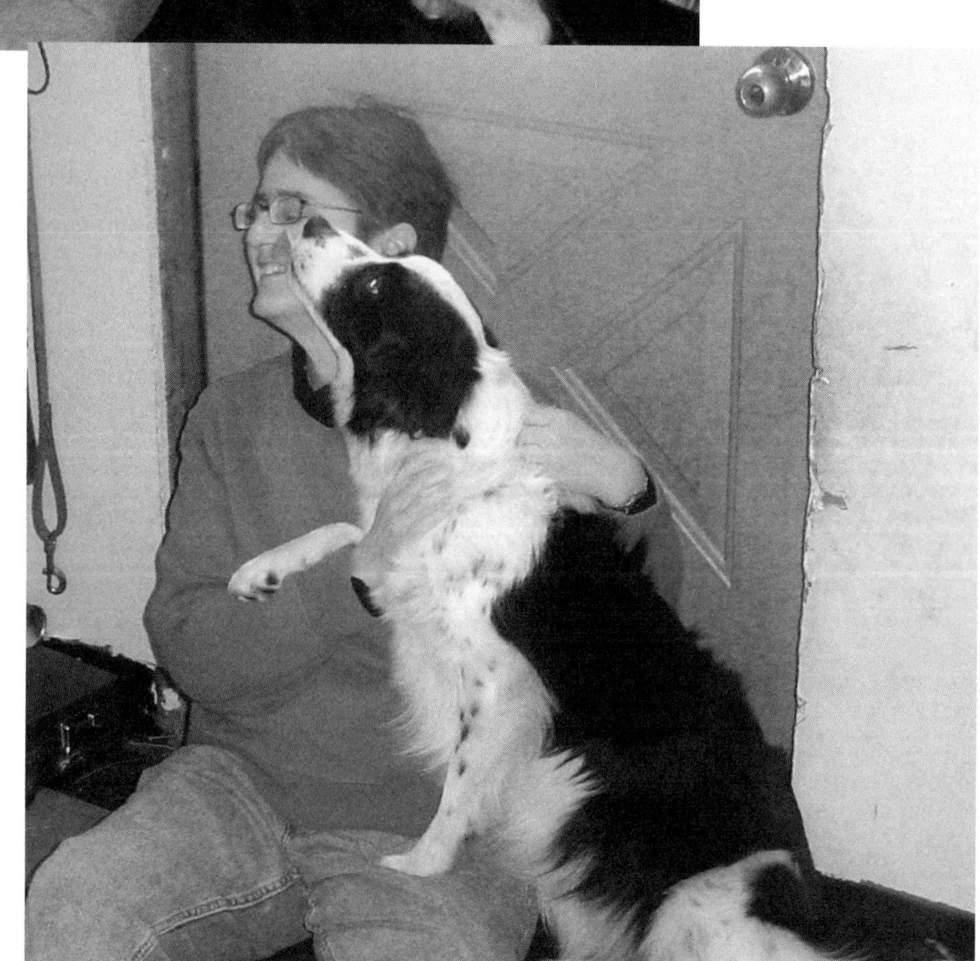

#35.3: Rylie Guarding Lori

- wide open, hard, staring eye
- stillness
- closed, tight mouth

Emma sees someone with her mum, and starts wandering back and forth in front of Lori. That is Emma's back and tail in the foreground.

You can see what Rylie thinks of Emma's actions. Rylie has moved in. She is guarding "her" person (who is not really hers!). Rylie is staring directly at Emma. Rylie has a hard, wide-open and staring eye.

You don't have to see Emma's face to know that Emma is aware of Rylie's stare - see her lowered tail and rounded topline? She also has her head held down.

Lori cannot see the evil Rylie's face, so she is still being nice to her!

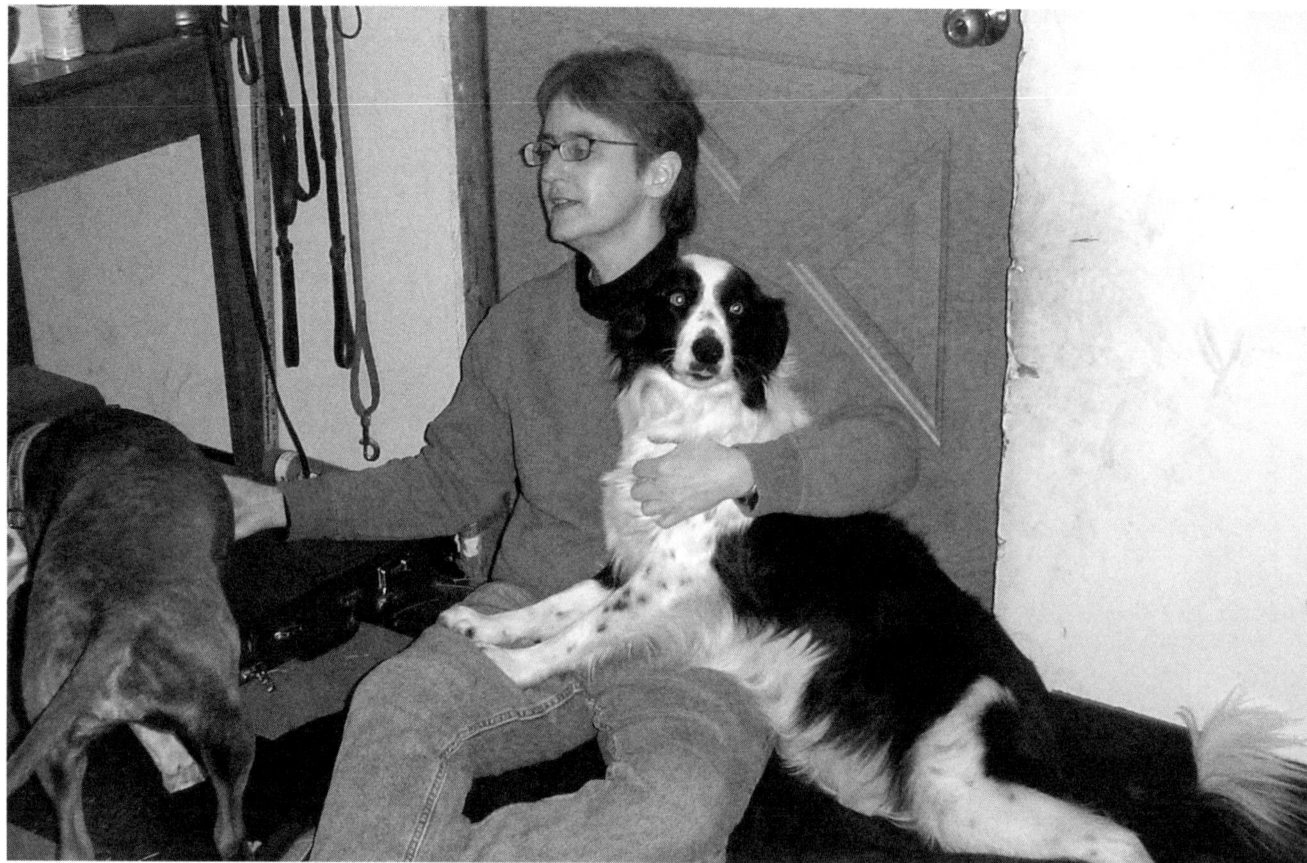

Lori turns her attention to Emma, who is pacing back and forth in front of her and Rylie in mild agitation. Note Emma's Look Away and lowered head, as well as her body orientation, which is *away* from Rylie.

Rylie sees me watching her; I have walked up behind the photographer. Rylie immediately softens her eye and tips her nose up towards me in a "friendly" way. She knows I have noticed her guarding behaviour, so she is appeasing me: "Ha ha, Mom! Just kidding!"

This keeps the peace momentarily, until...

Rylie's Body Language in the photograph above:

#35.4: Rylie Gets "Caught": Apology

- eyes still wide, but softened
- Tongue Flick
- nose tipped up

Emma's Body Language in the photograph above:

#35.4: Emma: I Am No Threat

- Look Away
- lowered head
- half-mast tail
- body curved away from Rylie

...Emma, because her mum has encouraged her, finally gets brave enough to come over to Lori's lap, even though Rylie keeps telling her to stay away. That is why Emma was doing all the pacing. She is in conflict about what she wants to do (get near her mum) and what the other dog is telling her to do (stay away, mine, mine, mine).

Rylie gives Emma a hard eye and a low growl - "This lap is mine, mine, mine." Emma acquiesces - she does a Look Away and flattens her ears back in apology to the Border Collie.

See the intensity on Rylie's face? And there are ridges around Rylie's eye and jaw. She has a lot of facial tension, the skin on her head looks as if it is very tightly stretched across her skull.

You can see Rylie thinks it's an easy win though. She has Emma pegged well as a dog who will back down. Rylie hasn't even bothered to get up out of a lying down position, and there isn't a lot of tension in her body.

#35.5: Rylie: This lap is Mine, all mine

- hard, wide open eye
- direct eye contact & stare

#35.5: Emma: Let me Go, Mum, this dog is mean!

- Look Away
- body orientation "away from"
- flattened ears

> *Observation*: One sign of facial tension is when the dog's skin looks like it is tightly stretched on the dog's skull.

I finally tell Rylie, "Enough." Now Rylie gives me the "Oops, got caught!" expression. Rylie leaves Lori's lap to come over and apologize to me. Emma is avoiding the entire situation, she has her ears flattened and she is Looking Away in Avoidance.

This sequence shows excellent communication resulting in no horrible fight or serious physical confrontation. I am not trying to pass judgment about whether this is desired or undesired behaviours in this photo sequence. It is simply dog behaviour. Dogs guard stuff all the time.

My own bitches seem to be particularly fond of staking a claim to someone and then keeping that person's own dogs away from them. I have a whole houseful of girls like that. I would guess this is due to two factors: I tend to choose a certain personality type - a strong, drive-y dog - and the younger dogs learn the behaviour from my older dogs. I am not fond of the guarding behaviour and can easily stop it.

What you should know is that this is very common and normal dog behaviour. Dogs play possession games constantly, and they are practicing for situations just like this. When there is conflict, someone must back down or there must be compromise to have a peaceful resolution. In this case it was Emma who gave way, so there was nothing exchanged other than looks.

#35.6: Rylie Apologizes to Me

- flattened ears
- slightly open mouth
- soft eye

#35.6: Emma Reluctantly Stays

- Look Away
- flattened ears
- body somewhat stiff & feet planted

This Drama, which came along at an opportune time, when we were collecting photographs for this book, intrigued both Lori and I. Therefore, we both had a lot to say about it!

Brenda's Training Tips: Interrupt and stop Guarding behaviours frequently. This serves several purposes: It alters the behaviours and attention before the dog becomes reactive. It also tells the dog that you really "own" everything and will decide who gets what.

If your dog begins Guarding something, and you do not interfere in some way (what you do depends on the dog), your dog will take ignoring as tacit approval for the current behaviour and will often escalate the Guarding behaviour.

In this particular photo sequence, we decided we needed some more photos for the "Companionship" section. We thought it would be nice to show Lori and a couple of dogs piled together. Because Emma and Rylie are dog-friendly and were available, I was bustling around getting a position for the photographer, etc. You can see that the dogs changed the photo session! What was most interesting here, for me, was Rylie noticing that I saw her behaviour, and, because I didn't interrupt her emphatically enough, continued with her little Guarding Frenzy. Because Rylie never takes her Guarding beyond a growl and a snap, I get a little lax in my reaction. After you have had some really nasty characters (I have had the pleasure of several Guarders) and you know that a particular dog is harmless, one does tend to not be as panicky about that animal. This was my error in this case. But it made for a great photo essay!

Lori's Training Tips: I was a typical human here, absorbed in my own agenda! We were trying to get photos of Puppy Licking and Companionship, and I knew that both Emma and Rylie were avid Puppy Lickers. I did not anticipate that Rylie would Guard me from my own Emma, and, worse, did not see it while it was happening. I was all too focused on getting Emma to come over and give me Puppy Licks, and basically ignored all of her Avoidance body language. Poor Emma!

She saw Rylie was Guarding and acted on that; I did not. It is okay to ask a dog to do something she is uncomfortable doing, but you need to be aware of the dog's discomfort and the reason for it. Trying to attend to your agenda and your dog's needs at the same time can be overwhelming sometimes! Even as you are taking care of your own plan, pay attention to what your dog tells you!

It is easy to miss quick dog signals, especially when your attention is on another part of the task (e.g., getting the dogs set up for a photo). Have someone take lots of pictures or videos while you are working your dog. You will see all sorts of communication you missed at the time. This photo sequence was a big eye-opener for me!

Photo Credits:
All Photo's in this Chapter by Cherish DeWitt.

36

This Is My Territory!

Lori and Alicia are dog-sitting Larko, a young Malinois. He is a five-month-old castrated male. In the household there are four resident dogs - Emma, an AmStaff, spayed female, two years old; Cora, a Corgi-mix, spayed female, six years old; Amanda, a Shepherd-mix, spayed female, six years old; and Data, a Cattle Dog/Border Collie-mix, castrated male, five years old.

The girls all think the new boy is just fine, but Data, Mr. Control Freak, is very upset at the disruption of the household. This particular play involves three of the resident dogs and the new kid on the block.

#36.1: Unrest In The Household - Data & Larko

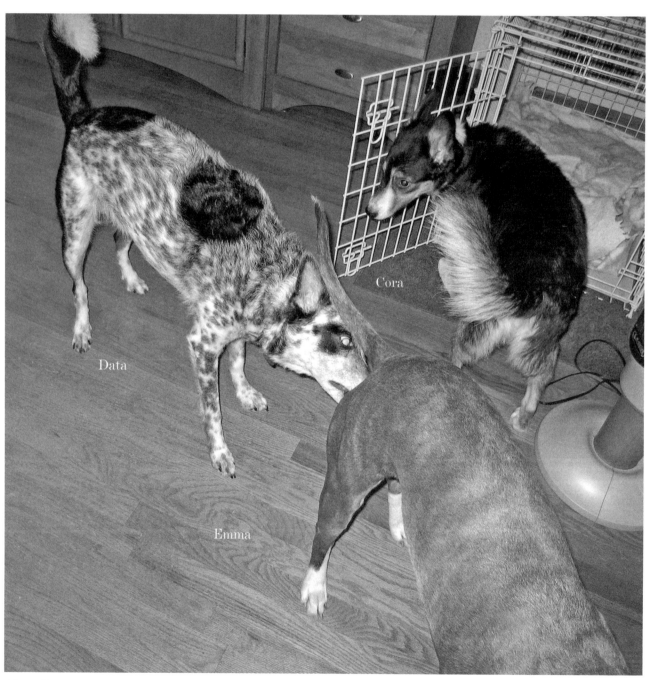

First, Data runs around sniffing the two resident girls, Emma, in this photograph; then Cora, in the next photograph.

Data sniffs because he is using the Sniffing as a displacement behaviour to alleviate anxiety. The Sniffing is also intended to send a signal to the Interloper - "These are my girls."

Anecdote: If Data were one of my terrier boys, he would just urinate on the girls to claim possession and be done with it, but Data observes the rules of the house-broken dog. Butt Sniffing is also a default behaviour for Data, observed many times by Lori and me. When Data becomes anxious, if there is a butt nearby to sniff, he takes advantage of it. Evidently, this can include any butts he had access to while herding! Once while we were working in a small pen with the sheep, and when he got very close to the sheep, he started Butt Sniffing them, because he didn't seem to know what else to do, much to our merriment.

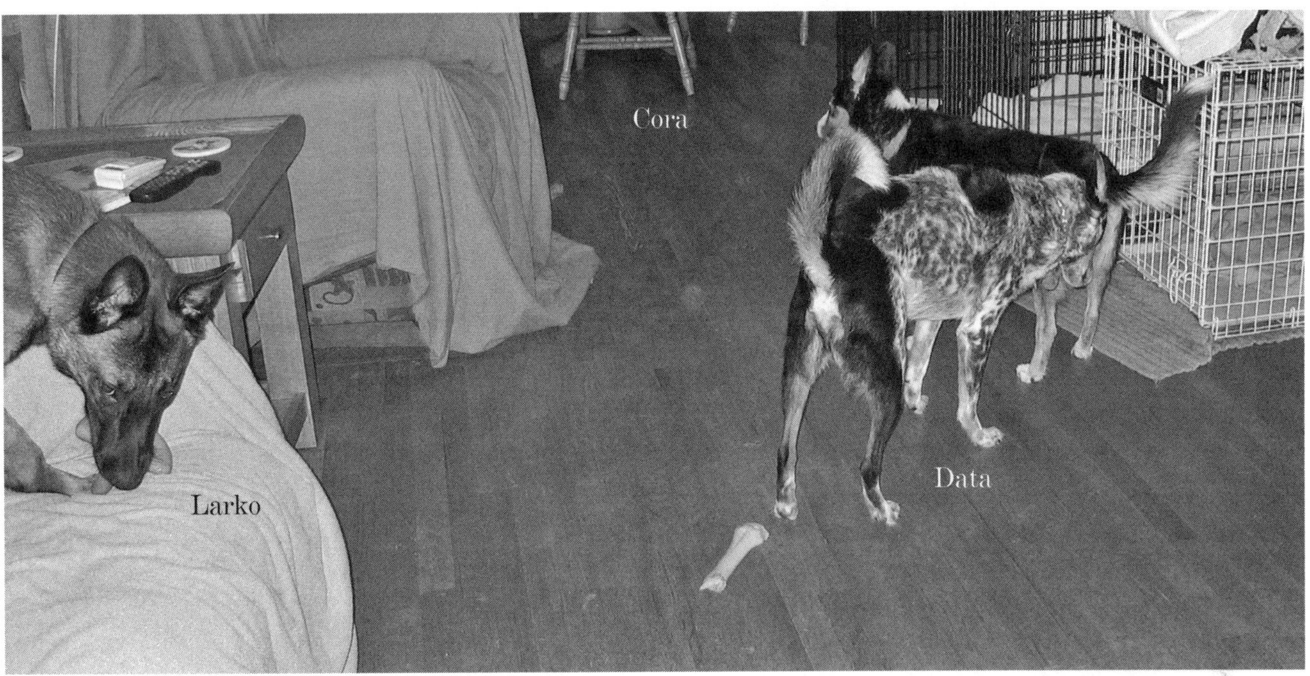

Most interesting is Larko markedly ignoring all of Data's possessive, chest-beating behaviour. The young Malinois remains on the sofa chewing on a toy. His ignoring is a signal. Larko is working at keeping the peace, rather than challenging Data. Larko can easily see Data, because of the range of a dog's vision, but he carefully keeps his nose oriented away from Data and does not stare. Larko communicates tolerance and acceptance of the senior, resident male, as would be in accordance with his age-group. At nine months old this acceptance might not be so accepting...

The following text goes with the top photograph on the next page.
After Data is done Butt Sniffing all the girls, and Larko feels safe, he gets off the sofa to play with Emma. (see the photograph on the next page.) Immediately Data runs over to Butt Sniff Larko, and not all that politely. He is doing more of a proctology exam than a courteous handshake-type Butt Sniff. Larko puts up with it very nicely though; after all, he is young and the new kid. So he puts up with it with no protest.

Notice how wide open Data's eyes are. This speaks of his inner emotional state, which is anxious and agitated.

Text for this photograph is on the preceeding page.

Larko gets back up on the sofa to play with the toy. Emma comes over to see if he would like a playmate.

Emma's approach is very friendly. Her lips are long and relaxed and slightly parted in a "happy face." Her ears are drawn back and her body orientation is "contained." Larko accepts her approach by remaining calm and not even looking at Emma. This invites Emma to continue her approach.

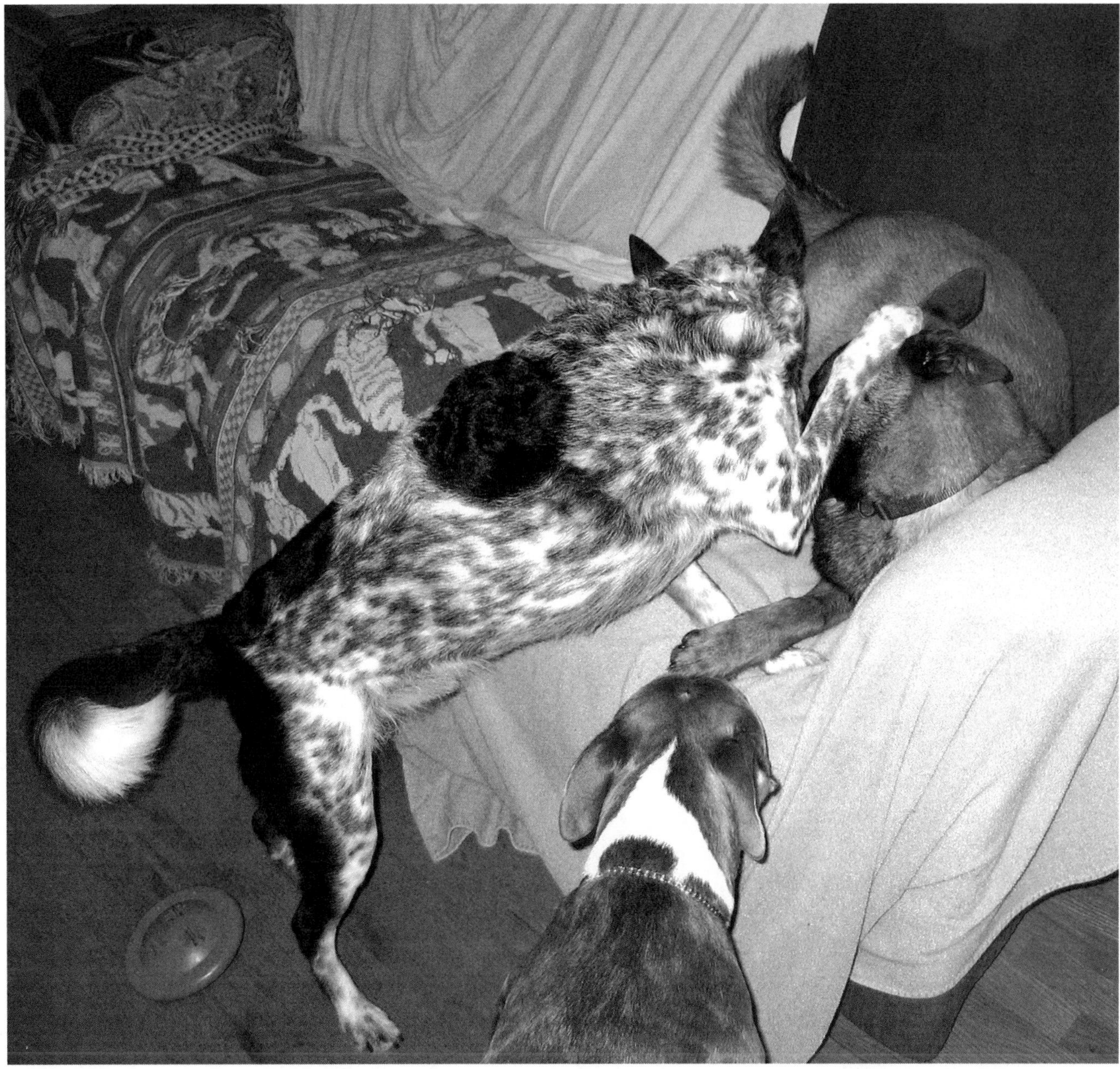

Immediately, Data has to run over to interfere. He doesn't want Emma to interact with the new dog, so he gets in Larko's personal space. Data places his foot on Larko's head and administers a Correction to Larko, by grabbing Larko's entire muzzle into his mouth. Emma watches the drama, ears down.

The dog who tells us a lot about this Little Drama is the dog who is conspicuously absent. Remember I told you there were four resident dogs? Amanda, who is very socially sensitive, but friendly, left the room as soon as Data began with his Butt Sniffing behaviour.

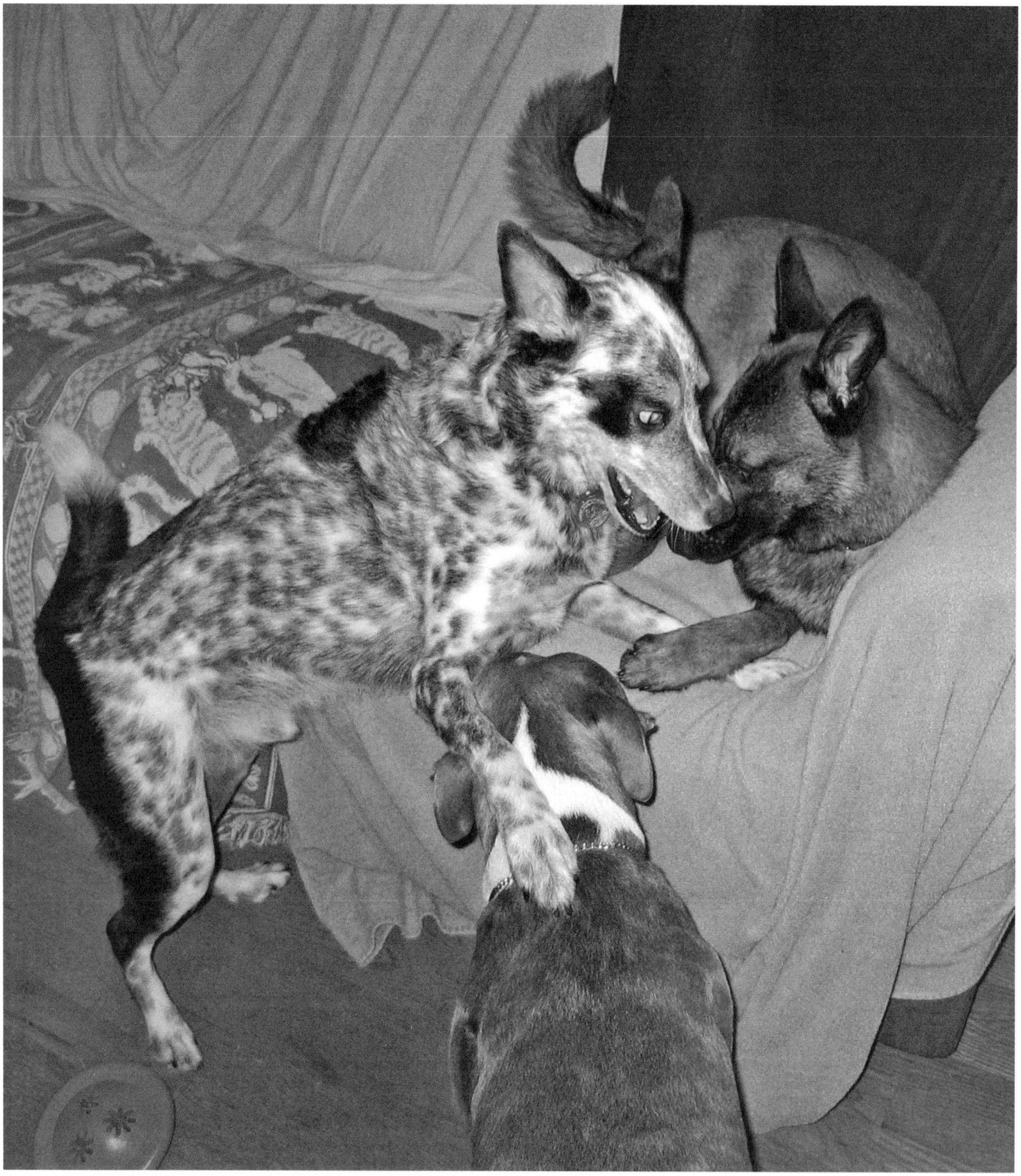

As Data's mouth administers a correction-hold-bite to Larko's nose, simultaneously his front paw is placed directly on Emma's shoulders, asserting himself over her.

Larko, the young, polite dog gives Data a Look Away: "I am trying to stay out of trouble." Data pushes the issue and climbs up on top of Larko, discounting Larko's communications.

Larko has decided Data is not all that powerful, so he distracts himself by beginning to play with Emma, who is still nearby. Notice that Data blows by all of Larko's communications, and just keeps pushing. Larko may feel that because communicating with this Data guy isn't working, perhaps pretending Data is not there will work.

Data is, in Lori's words, "An Alpha-Wannabe." His lack of self-confidence is what is causing this persistence. Data feels his territory has been violated by this young male, and wants to make certain Larko understands the hierarchy. Larko is giving every possible signal to indicate, "I am no threat," yet Data keeps pushing and pushing.

Data, like many dogs, is a member of the Fun Police. This is a trait that is seen in dogs who follow a certain type of personality profile: they are control freaks want to be in charge of motion. Yet there is another, underlying element - status. Anxiety, a need to be in control, and an intrinsic drive to gain status are combined in a bizarre way in some dogs. The lack of confidence and presence of anxiety means that the personality profile of this kind of dog just isn't "Leader" material, and other dogs know it, yet he feels the need to keep trying.

Data continues to get between Emma and Larko. He finally bullies Larko off the sofa. Larko lies down to keep the situation calm, and Data has to do another intrusive sniff to Larko's genital area.

As soon as Data leaves, Emma comes back to play with Larko. She has been waiting patiently for Data to tire of his game so she could come back and interact with Larko.

Data Alerts & Targets on Larko who is having fun with Emma. Larko is FORBIDDEN to have fun. So Data Must Interfere. The Fun Police strike again!

Data gets between the two dogs, Splitting Up. He administers another correction-hold-bite to Larko. Larko gets up and leaves. You can see the very hard eye on Data in the bottom photograph.

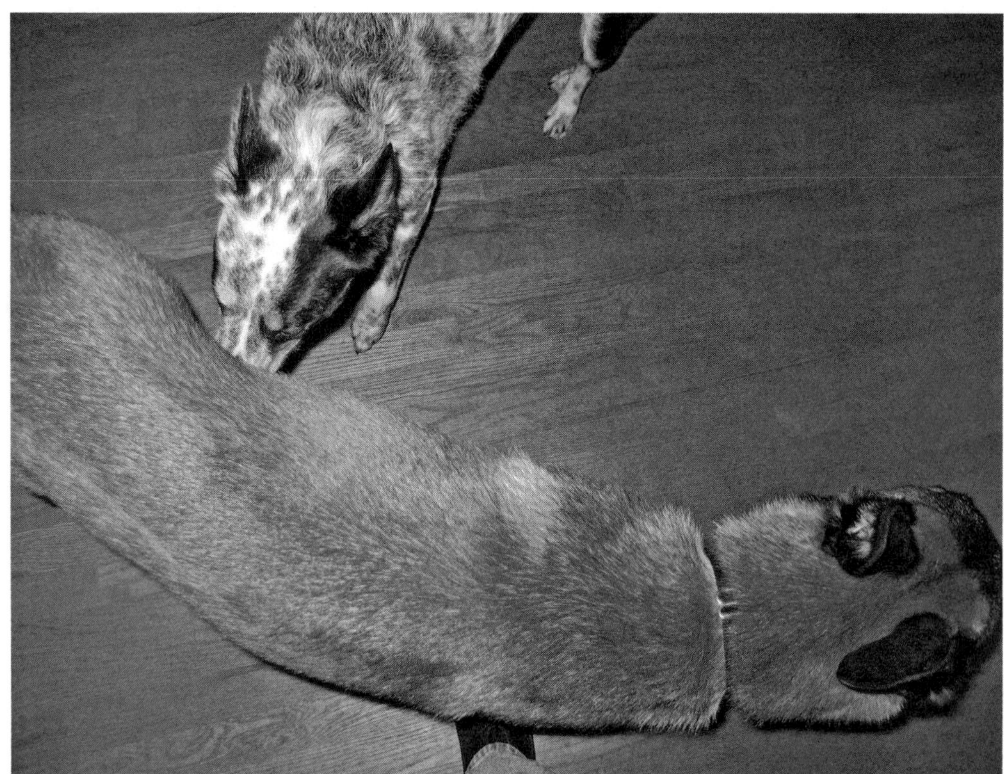

Data cannot just let Larko leave peacefully however. Data has to follow and do yet another Sniff. This time it is an Inguinal Sniff. Data is being pushy, rude and intrusive. Because Larko is young and has good impulse control with dogs, he is putting up with all of it. Impressive is how Larko never panics or becomes reactive, even with all the tension.

Here, everybody is minding their own business except Guess Who...Data is staring Larko down. Larko is showing deference to Data with a slightly lowered body posture, ears and tail half-mast, and an open mouth. Larko is also showing more stress, with a rounded topline, braced front legs and a Spatulate Tongue.

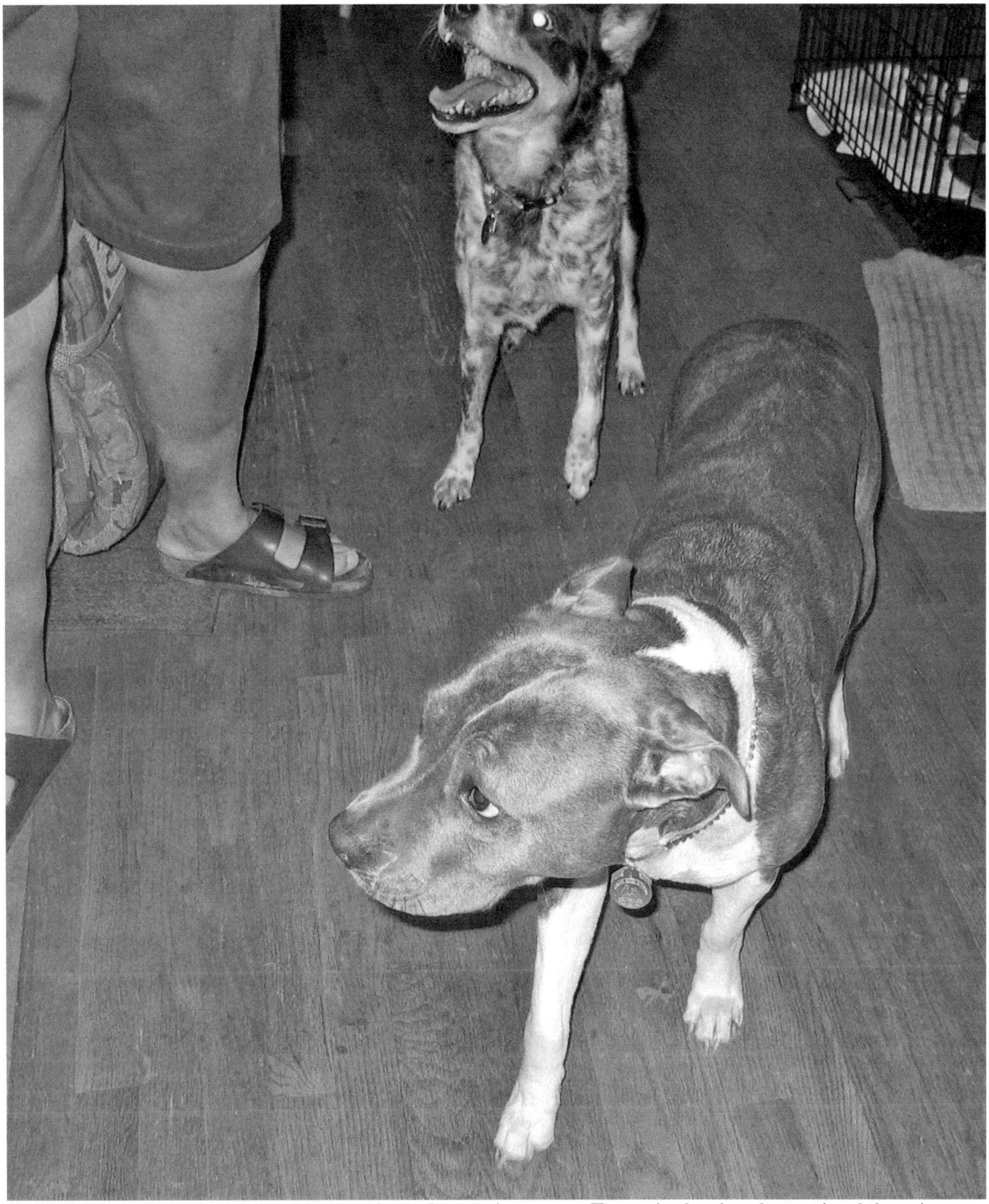

In both this photograph and the photograph on the previous page, Emma is showing the strain of these interactions, even though she is not the Target. Dogs are extremely sensitive to what is going on socially, and this is a socially tense situation, for sure.

Data looks up at Alicia with a big happy mouth and a deferential Paw Lift. He is feeling smug because he has succeeded in pushing the puppy around. Even so, those dilated pupils tell you he is in the grip of strong emotions: excitement and anxiety.

Next, Larko seeks some relief by coming over to see Alicia. Of course, Data has to come over to see if he can interfere. He administers yet another Butt Sniff to Larko. Larko looks down, but feels a bit safer - Alicia has him. Do not think the look on Data's face is a happy, playful one. He is Targeting on the Maliniois. See how Data's legs look stiff and braced? If Data moved, it would be to pounce forward onto the puppy. So his posture is, in fact, a threat: "I am going to jump on you."

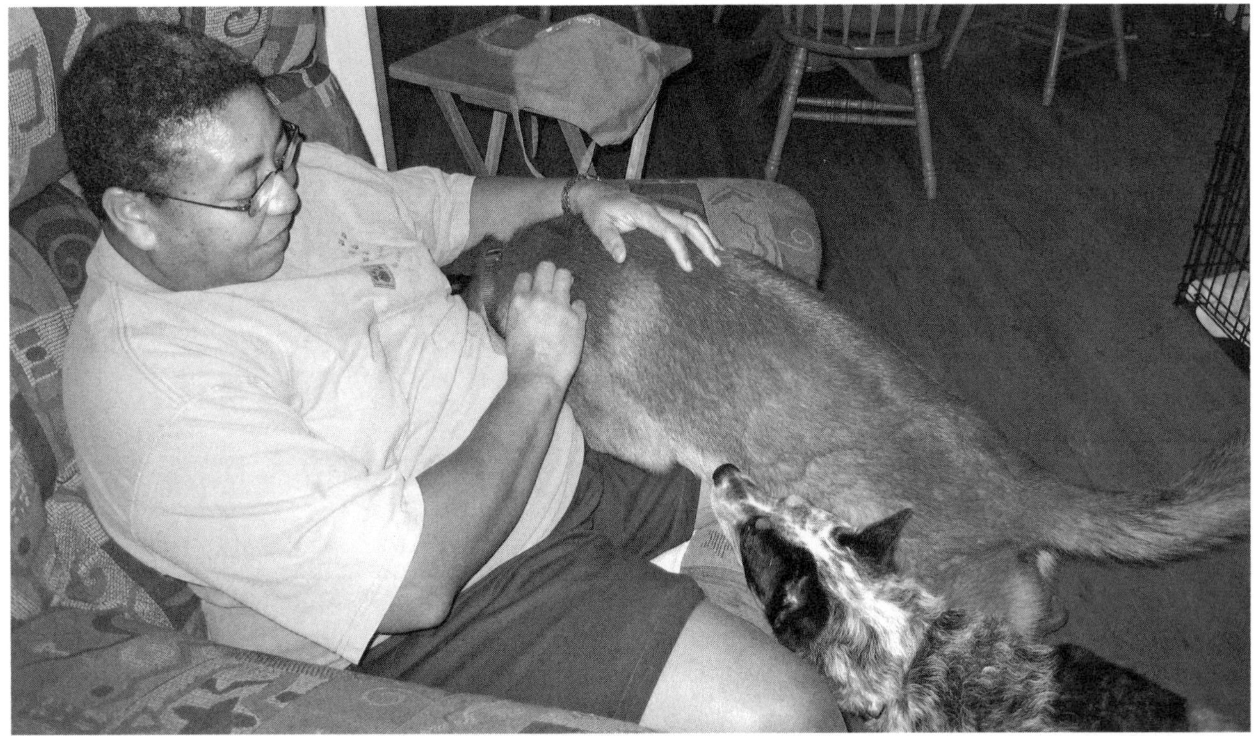

Data continues to move into Larko's personal space. In defense, Larko hides his head under Alicia's arm. Larko is protesting having to move away from Alicia, a port in the storm. Avoidance is another emotion Larko is expressing. Stress and feeling overwhemed by the situation is causing him to Move Into Pressure, hiding his face. No matter what kind of language Larko tries, Data continues to move in. Larko surrenders to the social pressure and leaves.

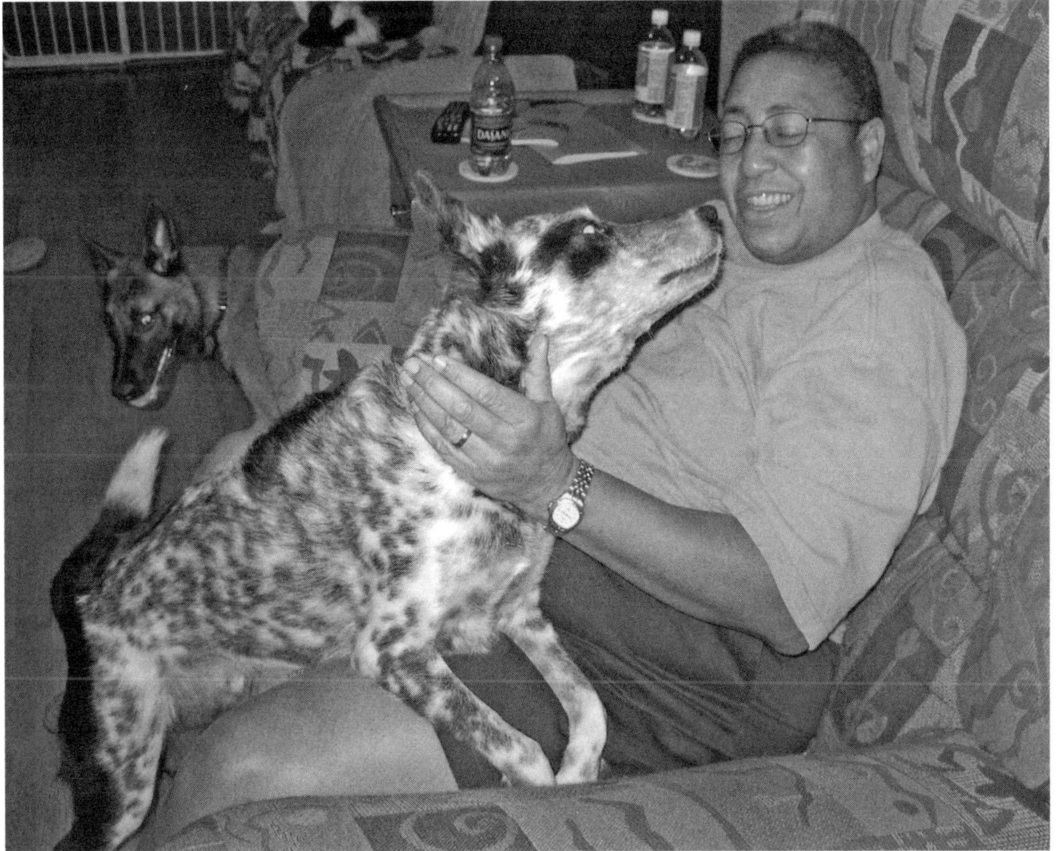

Data climbs on to Alicia. Although expressions of affection are gratifying to people, the dog also uses this kind of language to claim possession. So, although this looks flattering and affectionate, it is not. It is a declaration of possession. In this circumstance, the dog's body language will usually be active, merging into frantic. The dog will be fervently pushing into the person's space. When your dog is showing calm, contented affection, the movement will be slower and softer.

Alicia attempts to push Data from her lap. Data is Moving Into Pressure, a common behaviour in stressed or anxious animals. As Alicia pushes Data away, instead of acknowledging this politely, Data pushes back into the pressure of Alicia's arms and "clings" to her with his paws and body.

In the bottom photograph, you can see how dilated Data's pupils are, as well as other signs of stress: the body tension, the extremely flattened ears, and long, drawn-back lips. His whiskers are "flared" forward.

This is not a game for him. He is insecure and threatened by Larko, even though Larko is doing nothing except putting up with Data's social ineptitude.

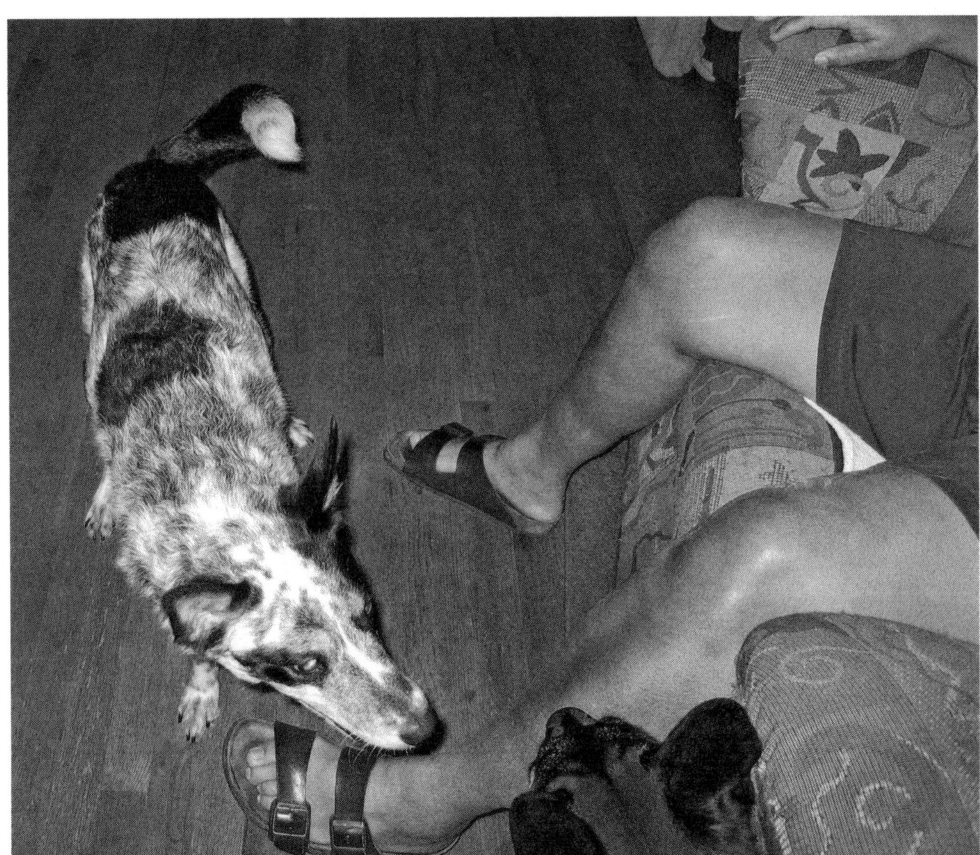

Larko approaches Alicia, and Data gets down and gives Larko a Warning Look: ears up, tail coming up, and hard direct eye contact.

Larko decides to chance an approach, ignoring Data's warning. It doesn't matter whether Larko has appropriate behaviour, or not. Data keeps bothering him anyway. So why not push the envelope a bit to see where the boundaries really lie? Besides, Data has not given the puppy an effective, terrifying correction - he just keeps nagging at the puppy.

Larko looks worried. He keeps his tail and ears down and crawls onto Alicia again. Data continues to stare at Larko. Look at Emma: she is like a canary in the mine shaft. Her ears are down, and she is expressing the social tension that exists between the two boys.

Again Larko hides his head, and again Data Sniffs Larko.

This kind of Sniffing is intrusive, not friendly.

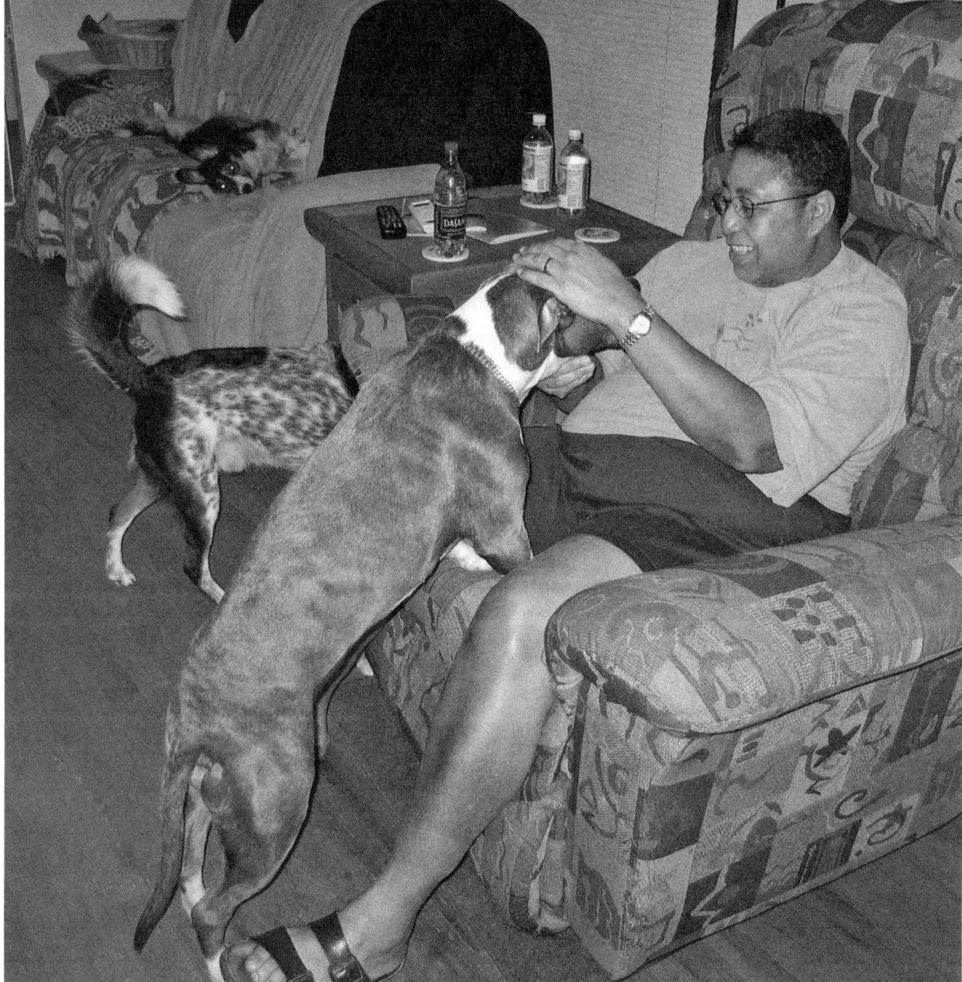

The boys move off and Emma comes over to Alicia for a little comfort. Too much tension! Data hovers in the background, ready to interfere. He is cannot bear to let anyone do anything outside his authority.

Notice which dog is Alpha in this pack: Cora. She has stayed out of all the ridiculous piddling affairs of the underlings, up on the sofa, relaxed and confident.

Meanwhile, Data crawls up onto Alicia and Emma, crowding in and totally disregarding anyone's personal space.

Data's anxiety is conspicuous in both his actions and his appearance. He has increased respiration; he is panting. His drawn-back lips, the ridges around his lips and eyes, and his drawn-back ears all reveal his extreme discomfort.

He cannot believe that an interloper has been brought in and will not leave!

Data then warns Emma off, with direct eye contact and by placing his face and body right in between Emma and Alicia. Emma backs off slightly, and Data wins. He gets fully between Emma and Alicia. This is dog language for "Mine, mine, mine. You get away."

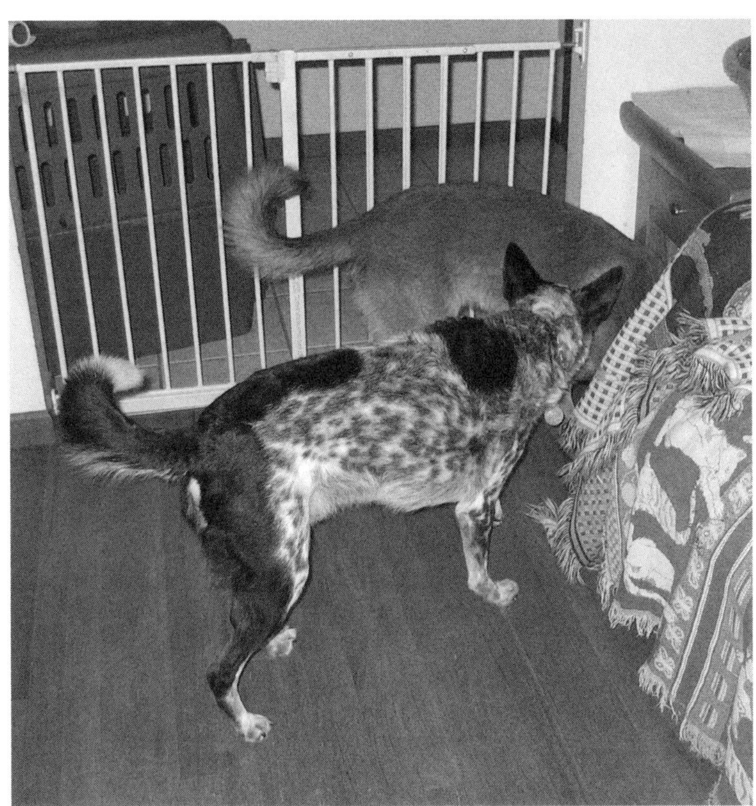

Alicia ejects the two annoying dogs. Data has to run over and bother Larko some more. Data Stalks Larko, indicated by the lowered head and neck, Stillness and Staring.

In the photograph below, Emma sneaks back over to Alicia. She doesn't even want to interact with the boys anymore because they are just causing too much strain. No fun to be had there!

Data Warns Larko away from Alicia and Emma again. Larko doesn't leave, but does acquiesce by using a Look Away with drawn-back ears. See how Larko's body orientation is going backwards?

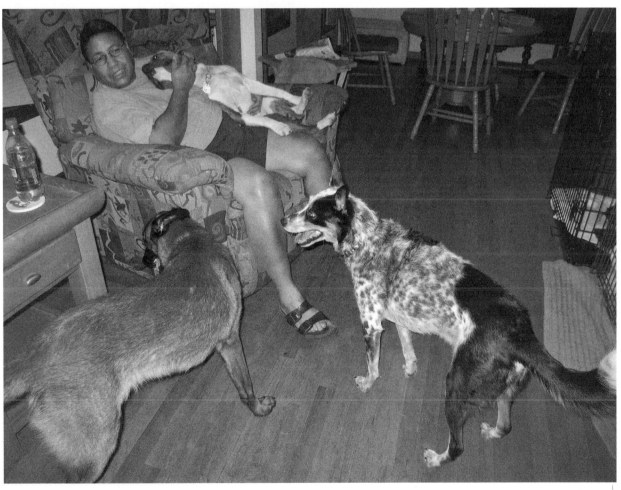

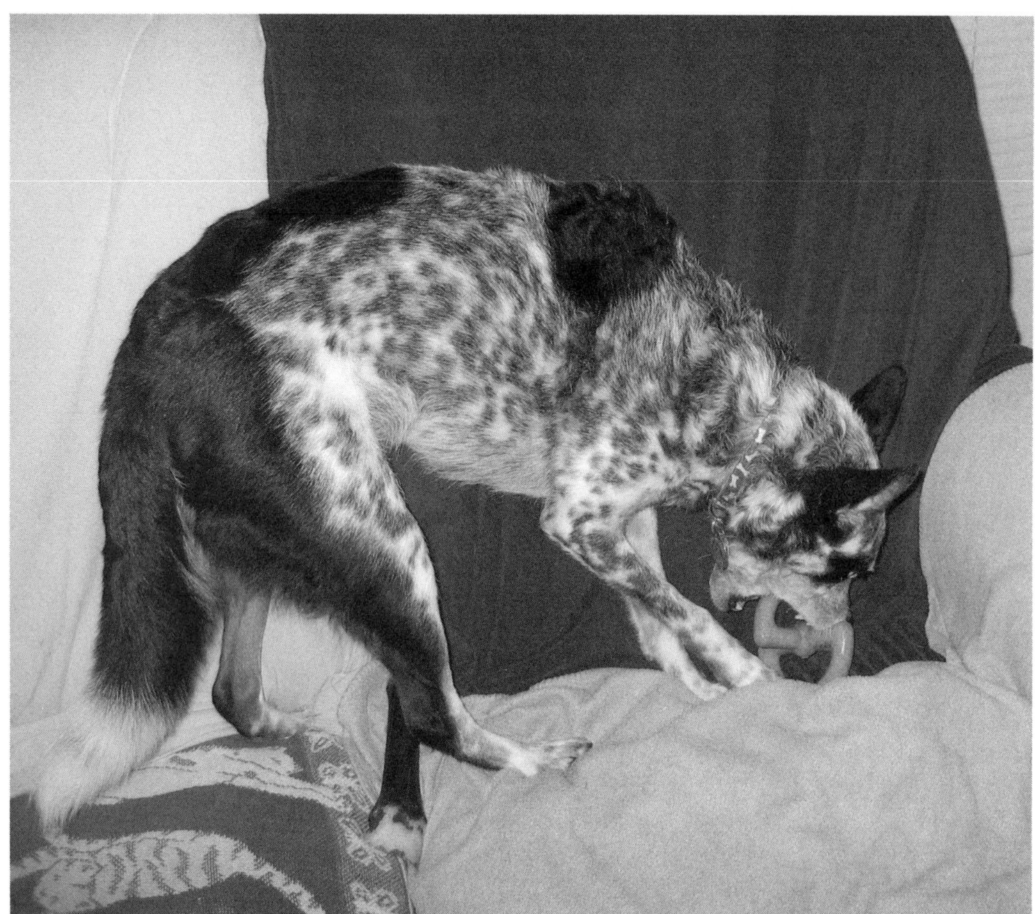

Data then gets up on the sofa and steals the toy that Larko originally had, just to show how very cool he is.

Larko approaches Cora to socialize with her. Clearly, she is a safe port, since handles all social situations with elegance and dispatch, with no ambiguity. She is confident nobody will be bothering her! Data leaves her alone. Larko takes advantage of this.

In the photograph to the left, Data uses another Warning Look. There are tension ridges visible around Data's eyes.

In the photograph to the right, you can see who this Look is for. Larko is walking by.

As Larko walks by, Data turns around to move the toy further from the edge of the sofa - and Larko. Data keeps an eye and an ear on Larko, and curls protectively around the toy.

Background Notes:

A couple of days before this, immediately after Larko arrived Cora corrected him. Upon meeting Cora, Larko was mouthy and got in Cora's space, in the way of obnoxious adolescents searching for boundaries. Cora's response to rude puppies is to give a loud vocal correction, get right in the offender's face, and show lots of teeth. The puppy always responds with deference... and then the scary, but otherwise harmless, correction is over forever. Puppies always respect Cora after that, and she is comfortable with them. Cora's response to Larko in this sequence can be contrasted with Data's response to Larko. Since Cora is confident and got Larko's respect right away, she is unconcerned with his presence, and can get desired behaviour from him with a polite request; such as a quick Look. Data, however, remains insecure, and continually and ineffectually nags at Larko, getting minor compliance for his demands but never getting the real respect that Larko gives Cora.

Brenda's Training Tip: Do not ineffectually nag your dog! If you are trying to get a response or a behavior on cue, and well-executed positive methods are not working, consider using a "Cora-style correction" rather than a "Data nag." I do not mean growling and getting in the dog's face, but to emulate the timing of Cora. A quick and effective correction is the only kind of correction worth making.

Punishers have a temporary effect. Before you ever administer a correction that utilizes punishment of any kind, a good working knowledge of learning theory is imperative. *Tailoring the correction (punisher) to the dog is mandatory*. The only reason to use a punisher ever is to "get your foot in the door" in order to manufacture desired behaviour that you can reinforce. *Reinforcement is The Power in training.* It goes without saying the punishment should be designed to startle, distract and gain the attention of the dog; never to hurt the dog physically. Again: the punisher needs to be CAREFULLY TAILORED to the individual dog. In addition, your timing has to be spot-on, that is, stupendously good!

Lori's Training Tip: I wanted to get a photo record of Data's anxiety-ridden, control-freakish behaviour, so I let him persist much longer than I normally would. Typically, I would interrupt by about the second photo (the first rude Butt Sniff). Interrupting him and taking charge actually relieves his anxiety. He wants to know that he does not have to control the situation, that, instead, I control it for him. I think that he feels protected by this, inasmuch as his anxiety is partly based in fear of what those "uncontrolled hooligans" might do to him. Obviously, my taking charge relieves the anxiety he causes the other dogs as well. The sort of behaviour Data is demonstrating here could easily lead to a dog fight.

Habitual, early interruption of his anxious rude behavior and keeping his attention on me has allowed me to take him into the obedience ring and get titles on him. I can now get him to stop these ridiculous displays in a microsecond and get back to work (he is a very fine working dog). What you see in this sequence is as bad as it gets with him these days. Once upon a time, he would have violently exploded at another dog 100 feet away, and a strange male puppy in the house would have been unthinkable. While his underlying anxiety remains, his behaviour has been shaped so that he now looks to me for direction as soon as I offer it, instead of trying to aggressively control everything in sight.

Section 5: Predation

Canine body language developed to facilitate what dogs do together, and nothing better exemplifies what dogs do together than hunting. Dogs are scavengers and social predators. As a species, they are very successful because they are opportunistic about meals and will eat pretty much anything. They are happy to eat offal, kills made by others, and trash. They will also work together to fashion larger meals out of prey animals that are too large to kill alone. Dogs are happy to hunt in a pack, and much of their language centers on the cooperative activity of the hunt.

A predatory sequence follows a chronological series of steps. Steps may be omitted, truncated, or exaggerated, depending on the details of a particular hunt, but the typical predatory sequence is as follows:

- Eye (subdivided into: Scan & Scent (Air or Ground); Alert; Target)
- Stalk
- Chase
- Bite
- Kill
- Dissect

(Note: See the Space Invaders Section for photographs of Alerting and Targeting. These two behaviours occur in predatory sequences as well as during Warning and Guarding. Choosing the victim is choosing the victim! That is, the intent of the dog indicating these precursers is to select a victim, regardless of the differing outcome: killing prey or showing possessiveness. See also Chapter 40, Prey Bow for discussion on the predatory sequence.)

For my own uses, I separate the "Eye" into three distinct stages, which I name for my students. First, the dog will Scan the environment. The dog, whether walking or standing still, will swing his head, looking around. He may lower his head. He may also air scent. When talking to my students, I refer to this Scanning as "looking for trouble" or "window shopping."

The next phase is the Alert. This is the "Hey! Here's something interesting!" stage. The dog will lift his head and bring his ears forward. His pace, if moving, may either quicken slightly or slow down. His body tension will increase.

The Target phase occurs when the dog has Chosen his Victim. The dog deliberately Fixes On the victim: he orients towards and stares at the intended prey object.

This Target phase may last for a count of two or three, or the Alert & Target phases may meld into one another so quickly that they are observed as one and the same. For instance, the dog may Alert and, within a second, Target and Lunge towards the prey object. Even when occurring rapidly and seamlessly, these are separate behaviours. The dog's state of arousal gets ever higher at each level.

Specific Predatory Behaviours occur in the obvious hunting behaviour sequences, as well as many behaviours associated with "innocent" canine activities such as play, herding, and retrieving:

- Typical predatory behaviours include: chasing; stalking; some kinds of competition-for-resources-type fighting (from tug-of-war to resource guarding); killing; grab bites to the top of the neck; hold bites in the jugular area; grabbing and holding or shaking; sniffing; rolling in things; specific kinds of eye contact (the typical "eyes on, brain off" of the Border Collie); bites to the legs from the rear; carrying things; gathering and driving behaviours; alerting and targeting (choosing the victim).
- Herding behaviours include: chasing; nipping; curiosity-type bites; circling; gathering; driving.
- Retrieving behaviours include: taking objects; carrying objects; chase games with objects; chewing; grab bites and hold bites.

All of these behaviours vary by age and developmental stages and by breed (herding behaviours are more pronounced and frequent in Herding breed dogs; for example). All are predatory behaviours.

Dogs exhibit the above listed behaviours to prey objects, of course. Dogs also exhibit these behaviours to non-prey objects, including other dogs and people, as well as family members. Whether the behaviour is exhibited and to whom it is directed is highly dependant on context. These behaviours all arise from original predatory behaviours and have prey drive as the motivating force.

Predatory behaviour, then, includes a wide variety of behaviours, many of which are practiced in play. Some of these behaviours are very social in nature in that they are communications to conspecifics to encourage cooperation or decrease competition (some social interaction around the kill, for example, discourages competition). Play is rehearsal for living. Thus you see many Prey behaviours during Play. (See also the Play Section for examples of this.)

Predatory behaviours involve great intensity and produce tremendous chemical changes in the dog. It is not unusual to see dogs who reach a certain intensity level during play or other activities "drift" into predatory behaviours or display predation in ways that humans find inappropriate. The thing to remember is that dogs are, indeed, dogs! They are not moral creatures, and do not think that killing cats, for instance, is "wrong." Some dogs get so fired up during play that they begin to treat other dogs as prey. Unless the other dog is adept at reminding everyone that this is Play by using Calming Signals, some very bad stuff can go down!

Some dogs aren't very predatory. We see these dogs in calendar photographs: the Golden Retriever with a bird on his head or the King Charles Cavalier Spaniel curled up with a hamster. These dogs may limit their predation to balls and frisbees. I had a little Sheltie-Terrier mix years ago who, one day, did not come when I called her. I could hear her barking madly in the distance. I ran to the barn, to find her surrounded by a group of stalking cats. On closer investigation, I discovered four baby swallows who had fallen out of their nest. My dog was curled around them protectively, licking them. She was happy to chase a ball but never harmed kittens, birds, or even "pocket pets." Had any of my Smooth Fox Terriers been on hand in those days, this scenario would have been gruesome - a killing field.

Some dogs are predacious, but not big on killing. They have truncated prey sequences. My friend's Border Collie chased a rabbit to a nest of young rabbits. When the rabbit stopped at the nest, the dog nuzzled them and gently licked them - until his Dachshund "sister" came over to investigate and promptly grabbed the baby rabbits and broke their necks.

Then there are the dogs who are on the alert for, and actively seek out, every opportunity to be a predator. Dogs of this temperament will "test" each encounter for Prey Potential. Take my own sweet Breanna, for instance. Breanna is the most predatory dog I have ever had. Some dogs hunt to live, others, like Breanna, live to hunt. Once Breanna chooses a victim, you have to kill her to stop her (or remove her from the area, carefully, so she did not redirect onto you). The other animal's behaviour however, plays a part in whether it is chosen or not.

Breanna allows the other animal to present itself, then takes that presentation at face value. Thus, if she meets up with one of those cats who has been raised with dogs, and who uses dog greeting postures and is unafraid, she is happy to treat the cat politely, as long as the cat holds up his end of the bargain. If an animal behaves in a frightened way or becames defensive, she treats that animal as Prey or Competition. (No one competes with Breanna, as far as she is concerned.)

One day she was standing in the living room bay window, looking outside. Her metronome tail caught the attention of Philip, our black house cat. Phil was washing his face, then glanced at Bree's gently swaying bottom, and got a gleam in his eyes. He reached out and bit Breanna right on the upper thigh. Before I could even get out of the chair, Breanna had that cat by the throat, on his back, and was standing over him. This all took place without so much as a peep by either party. There was no sound except for the thud of Phil hitting the floor. Philip, a cool customer, remained non-reactive. He didn't become defensive, he didn't struggle, he just lay very still. In other words, he didn't act like a Prey animal. Breanna held him there for about five seconds, then she turned around and continued looking out the bay window. Philip sat up and continued washing. I was able to resume breathing. Philip, by his calm behaviour, kept the correction a harmless correction, instead of turning the situation into a Prey sequence.

When I talked to ethologists at Wolf Park, they discussed how wolves look for signs of "prey-worthiness" in other animals. Wolves administer something specifically labelled a "curiosity bite." If wolves find an animal that isn't moving, they will approach it, look it over, and eventually bite it to see if it moves. If it does, then it has passed the Prey Test, and giving chase is the typical response. A curiosity bite is one strategy that domestic dogs use to get another animal to act like prey. If the animal responds in a non-reactive manner - well, okay, then, maybe it's not prey. In herding, when a dog uses an open-mouth bite or a grab-bite on the stock to move it, this is a version of the curiosity bite: "Move, you! Then I can give Chase!"

Data lives in a house with cats. Data is an Australian Cattle Dog/Border Collie-mix who is exactly what you would expect from that cross: he displays herding drive. Each of the cats interacts with him with one of the typical cat temperaments. Hera, for example, is fearful, and Data treats her as a cow (Prey) substitute, pushing into her personal space. This pushing into personal space is a precursor to a curiosity bite. When Hera runs, Data willingly gives chase. Lucy, on the other hand, genuinely likes the dogs, and is non-reactive with them. Data constantly tries to get her to be the prey object by rolling her, another version of a curiosity bite, but Lucy just purrs and rubs against him, so he walks away, disgusted and disappointed. When the predation Trigger is not activated, the sequence can be truncated by the other party.

The Trigger can also come from another predator. Emma, a sweet tempered American Staffordshire Terrier who lives with Data, is, by herself, never predatory with the cats. But when she sees Data take chase after Hera, she eagerly joins in. (This is why their house is full of cat trees and baby gates!) Dogs respond very strongly to the predatory signals of other dogs: "Let's hunt together!" is a primeval communication.

Prey behaviour requires certain Triggers to be activated. If another animal activates these Triggers, you get a predatory response. The fact that the behaviour of the prey animal is often critical in the prey sequence is one of the reasons that Predatory behaviour is so difficult to control. You have to be able to control two (or more) sets of reactions. It takes two to tango and the reaction of the other participant - neutral and non-reactive, defensive, or fearful - largely determines the outcome.

This phenomenon is how Play becomes something else: Play that escalates into Predation. Or, as this is sometimes categorized, Predatory Drift.

When I first got Maeve, she had a long rap sheet, including disabling bites that hospitalized other dogs. Her behaviour around other dogs was not social; it was either status-related or reeked of predation. I introduced her to my male Smooth Fox Terrier, Dervish, and did some work with them around the house for a couple of weeks, until Maeve was non-reactive around him. Then I took them outside in a larger area to interact. Dervish imme-

diately began to run around in a fast, exhilarated manner, ready to play. Maeve took up the Chase in Play, but I could see that, after one trip around the yard, this was becoming something else for her. Her body got more streamlined as she moved faster but closer to the ground. Her ears were pricked forward as far as they would go, and her tail was held level with her back. Her head lowered, and she fixed an intense gaze on Dervish. He felt it, too, and started glancing behind him. Just as I was feeling the first flutters of "Oh no, here's another fine mess you've gotten yourself into," Dervish screeched to a halt and immediately placed his nose on the ground, Sniffing conscientiously. The effect on Maeve was instantaneous and amazing. Her head rose, her gaze softened, her body lifted, and her gait slowed. She loped up to Dervish. They both Sniffed for a moment, then she Play Bowed to him and invited him to Chase her.

Similarly, you might see Work that escalates into Predation.

Just the other night I was working Rylie with Utility Go-Outs. After about three of them, she was getting increasingly intense. I could tell this because she was getting "Stalky" looking as I was giving her the hand signal. And she was getting "sticky" about sitting. Instead of sitting, she was crouching in a stationary stalk. These are sure signs she was going Lizard Brain (becoming Reactive - reflexive - instead of Responsive -cognitive, - hanging up the phone) on me! Running often shifts her into Prey Drive, particularly when I am involved because I am associated with Herding and Agility (which is just weird herding as far as she is concerned). As I bent over to give her a hand signal, she caught the motion of my hand and jumped out of her stalky crouch toward me, bumping my hand with her teeth (an Open Mouth Correction-type bite), just as she would use to move recalcitrant sheep, then raced forward to do a precise and lovely Go-Out. This is a great example of displaced predatory behaviour. The Triggers were present for predatory behaviour (prior associations and motion, as well as the frustration of waiting for the signal), so I got predatory behaviour. Displaced, inappropriate, but understandable and not abnormal.

Do not think of predatory behaviour as bad. Dogs develop their exquisite teamwork by hunting together. Engaging in predatory behaviour as part of a team with your dog builds your relationship. (Just make sure you don't present yourself as the prey!) That is why working with your dog and playing with your dog improves your relationship: you become a team in the way that speaks most clearly to your dog. Agility, for example, appeals to dogs' predatory (and herding) instincts. Doing agility together makes for a well-oiled team whose members communicate with the slightest of non-verbal signals – just as dogs do in the hunt! This is the way that is most natural for dogs to communicate.

Throwing a tennis ball or frisbee speaks to your dog on a very primal level. When you are engaged in this activity, you are, for that time, a hunting partner and you are both sharing the same goal – something that, from the dog's point of view, doesn't happen often enough.

Another great activity to build teamwork is Tracking. This is a very "binding" hunting experience you can share with your dog. Using Tracking (footstep style such as is used for AKC and Schutzhund tests) as an activity you share with your dog places you "in" the hunting partnership very effectively. Mixing air and ground scent, as for Search & Rescue work is also a fun, binding tracking activity.

Competition Obedience work, if trained to take advantage of predatory behaviours, can also serve as a "pack hunting" experience. The retrieves are blatantly predatory-type activities, as is the scent work in Utility. You can, with a little imagination, use the other exercises as well. For instance, I teach heeling to my dogs as a sort of precise chasing or herding game, done at a slow speed. The heel work is also intermingled with a lot of prey games, balancing precision and intensity.

39 Excitement

#39.1: Excitement

- ears forced out to the side
- relaxed body in motion
- intensity

I call these "airplane ears." Often, when a dog is really pleasantly excited about something you will see the ears held forward in such a way that they drape off the head in this amusing manner. What makes this Excitement vs. Target, is the lack of body tension and the prevalence of a more playful and curious attitude, rather than the dead seriousness that Targeting can take on. However, it might quickly slide into Targeting!

#39.2: Excitement

- jaunty tail
- ears forced into that little "curiosity fold"
- intensity

Everything about this dog says, "I have found something GREAT!" The tail is held jauntily over the back, the ears are forced back into the same configuration you might see in the dog who is Play Bowing. The lips are drawn back also, and curved up slightly. Looks like Willie is smiling, doesn't it?

Dogs who display Excitement quickly attract the attention of other dogs. Excitement is light-hearted, but can be a precursor as it can quickly become predatory behaviour, and have a more "serious" feel to it.

Photo Credits: Photo #1 & #.2: Joanne Weber

PREY BOW

A Play Bow is used to initiate, verify, or remind about play. It helps both the sender and the recipients keep the peace. A Prey Bow, which looks somewhat similar, has a very different purpose. The Prey Bow is a "Ready" position: a winding of the spring before the launch toward the victim.

A Prey Bow also serves as a communication to other dogs that the victim has been chosen and that the hunt has changed from stealth mode to action mode.

Remember that a predatory sequence follows a chronological series of steps. Steps may be omitted, truncated, or exaggerated, depending on the details of a particular hunt.

The "Eye" has three distinct stages. First, the dog will Scan the environment, shopping. The next phase is the Alert. This is the "Hey! Here's something interesting!" stage. The Target phase occurs when the dog deliberately Fixes On the victim.

This Target phase may last for a count of two or three, or the Alert & Target phases may meld into one another so quickly that they are observed as one and the same. For instance, the dog may Alert and, within a second, Target and Lunge towards the prey object. Even when occurring rapidly and seamlessly, these are separate behaviours. The dog's state of arousal gets ever higher at each level.

If the dog goes into the Prey Bow, it will happen soon after the Target. You will see the dog bounce down into the Prey Bow: the winding up before the Lunge. A dog does not always Prey Bow during the prey sequence. I associate the Prey Bow with minor frustration. The dog may be behind a fence or on leash or watching a person getting ready to throw a frisbee - the dog is highly aroused but unable to act immediately. Wolves also use the Prey Bow, which is sometimes followed by a curiosity bite to get a prey object to move. In this case, perhaps the wolves' frustration involves a victim that is not moving as anticipated or other uncertainty about the prey. The Prey Bow may be an anticipatory behaviour or a displacement behaviour. It is reasonable to assume that canines use the Prey Bow to communicate that hunting opportunities are immediately available, or that testing for Prey Potential is in process. Our dog may be telling us to let go of that leash or throw that frisbee. Let the hunt begin!

Dogs may also use a version of a Prey Bow when playing with other dogs. In this case, the Prey Bow would be preceded by Signals that indicate the dog is, in fact, playing and not treating the playmate as real prey to kill and dissect.

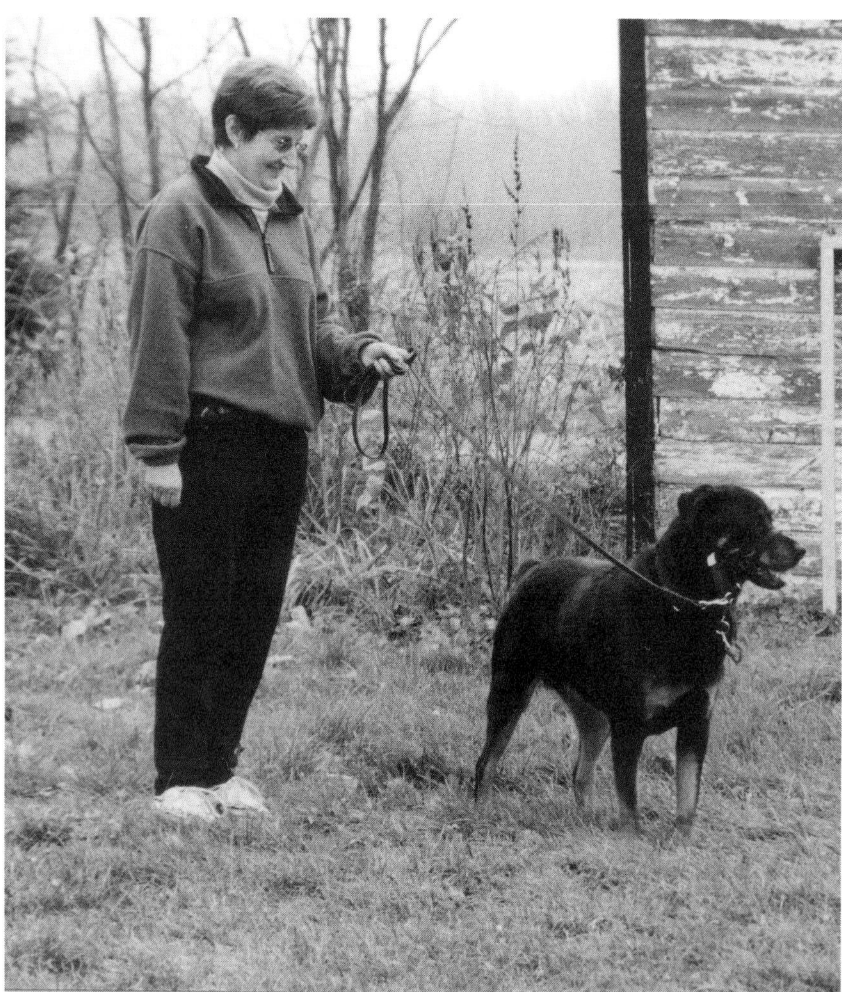

#40.1: Alert & Target

- body orientation is forward
- tail is up
- dog is staring - attention is Fixed On object for a count of 2 or 3 without wavering
- body tension

Here, you see the Alert melding into the Target. Misty, the Rottweiler, is Targeting one of my cats. (My student, Marylu, would typically have interrupted Misty well before this point in order to get the dog's attention back on her. I asked her to let Misty go through the full sequence so I could to get it on film.)

#40.2: Prey Bow

- body orientation is backward, but set to spring forward
- tail is up
- head is up
- dog is staring - attention is Fixed On object
- front of body is lowered
- front legs are braced
- body tension

Misty is in a lovely Prey Bow. Next would come the Lunge and Chase.

#40.3: Target and Truncated Prey Bow

- eyes are fixed on object
- ears are up
- front legs are braced
- body is ready to move
- tail is in Rudder position
- happy expression

Here is a Target melding into a Prey Bow. This is a commonly observed type of pre-Prey Bow, if you will. It is not nearly as extreme as that of the Rottweiler in the preceeding photographs.

This dog's tail is moving into Rudder Position which will stabilize her when she moves. Her ears are forward, she is Fixed On the prey object, her front legs are braced, and she gives a feeling of getting ready to move after the frisbee. The happy open mouth exhibits the joy that dogs have when hunting. No matter that a frisbee is being substituted for a rabbit here - it's all prey drive to the dog!

Training Tip: If your dog looks at any one thing for more than a count of 1...2, you should interrupt that behaviour and ask the dog to orient back to you. I call this "Checking In:" having the dog check in with you by looking at you. This interrupts the prey sequence and lowers arousal. It promotes your dog including you in the decision-making loop. Checking In can also prevent aggression and reassure other dogs nearby who might take offense at the fixed stare of a Targeting dog.

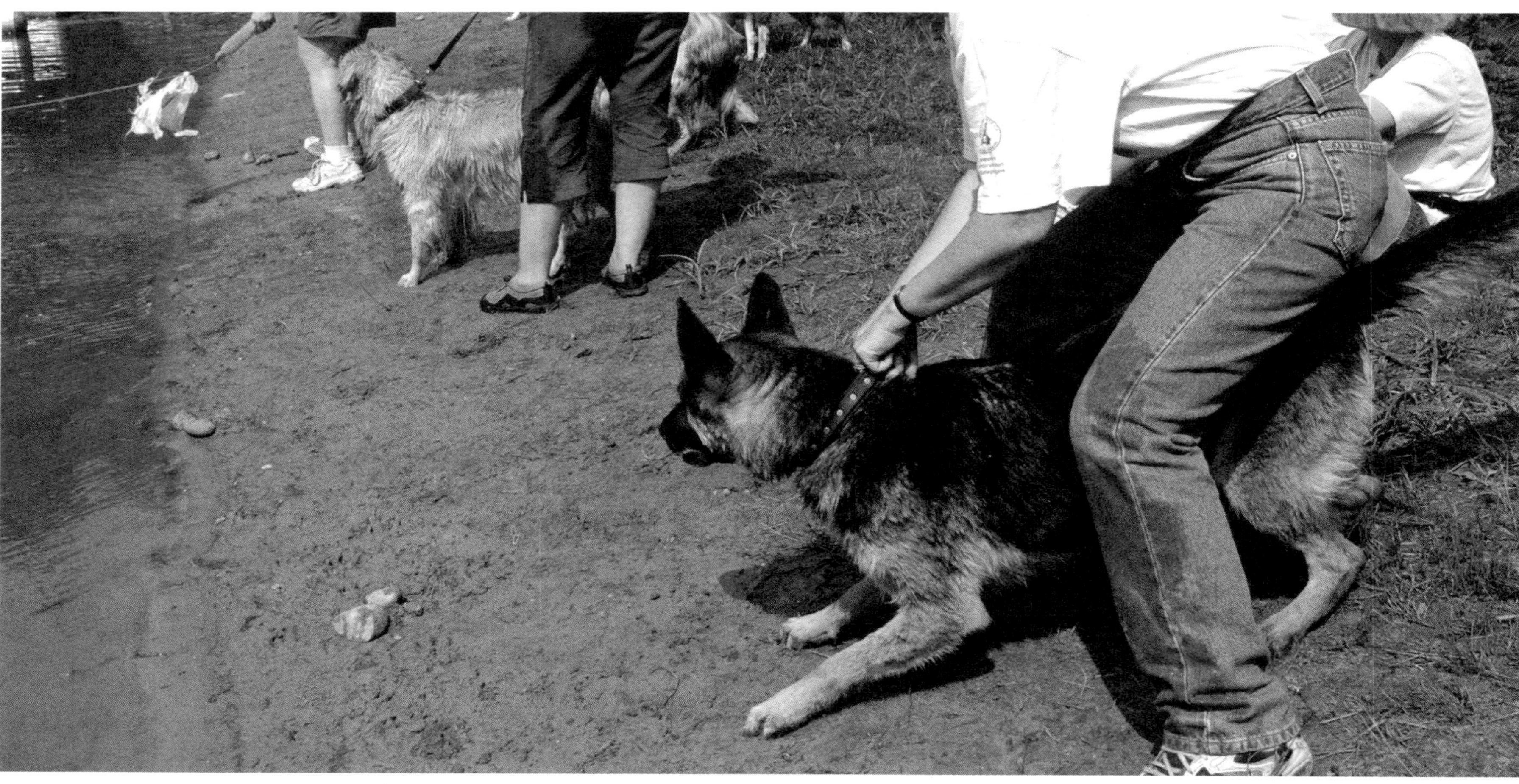

#40.4: Prey Bow

- ears are forced forward
- front legs are braced
- elbows are up
- rear legs are poised to spring
- extreme body tension
- eyes Fixed On object
- toes "digging in"

This German Shepherd is keenly focused on the prey object (the bumper). His owner is thwarting him from immediately getting it, so he goes into a Prey Bow to prepare himself to launch after it. As soon as she releases him, the chase is on!

#40.5: Lunge

- ears are forced forward
- eyes are Fixed On object
- tail is in Rudder Position
- movement entirely directed toward prey object

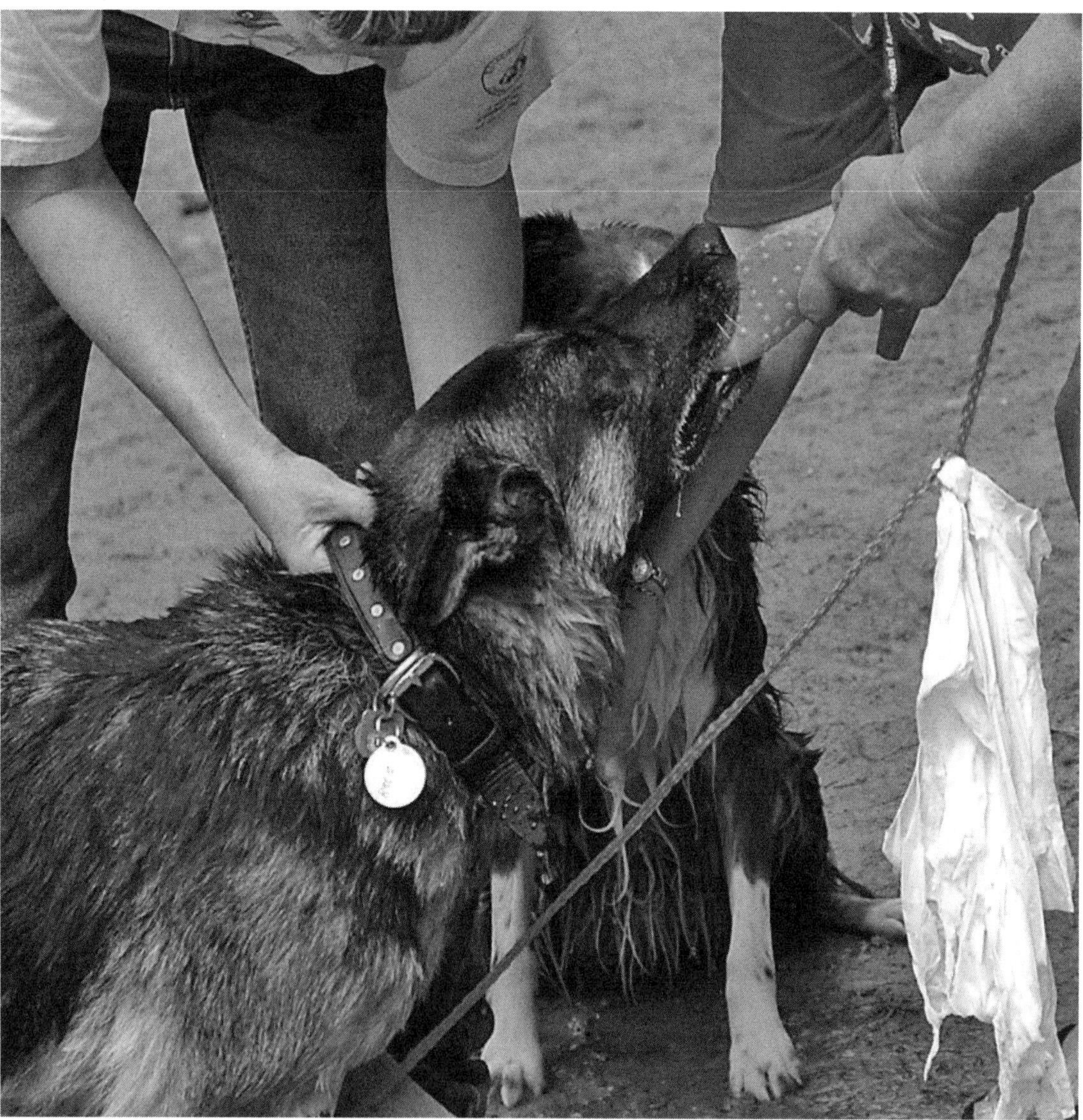

#40.6: Hold Bite

- ears are down and held close to the head
- eyes are narrowed

The Hold (Kill) Bite is displayed here. This dog is still in the grip of his intense emotional state: prey drive. You can see his partially closed eyes, his laid-back ears and his "death grip" on the bumper. If you touched this dog, his body would feel like a rock. If you tried to force his jaws open, you would be amazed at his strength (and at the futility of your actions). Often during the "death grip," the dog's eyes are closed or nearly so, and if the dog opens the lids up, his eyes may be rolled back into his head. Very eerie.

Do not be surprised if you are dealing with a dog in this state and observe extreme behaviour, such as: if the dog does let go of the object, he may snap at or bite at anything else moving near his head.

In not letting go of the bumper, this dog is not being willfully disobedient, per se. He is still in the throes of the rush of the hunt, and the accompanying adrenaline surge, and possession is an intrinsic part of that. You can overcome this tendency with a lot of training. But, without this training, pulling on the object will keep the dog profoundly in prey drive. Why? If the dog had a gazelle by the jugular, he would continue to hold (eventually hanging on with a vise grip but otherwise going limp like a dead weight) until the victim stopped moving. This is how a dog strangles his victim. As long as the victim moves, the hold must continue, so pulling on the dog's toy only causes him to secure his grip.

#40.7: Hold Bite

- ears are down and held close to the head
- eyes are narrowed
- dog is becoming a dead weight
- jaw is clenched, but otherwise he has a relaxed face

Note how similar this dog's face looks to that of a happy and relaxed dog. If you took the clenched jaws out of the picture, the rest of the dog's facial features display bliss. The Bite is an enormous release for a dog and obviously feels good.

Photo Credits:
Photo #1 & #2: Brenda Aloff   Photo #3, #4, #5, #6 & #7: Joanne Weber

41 STALKING

Stalking dogs are mesmerizing. The intensity that is held in such controlled movements fascinates. Stalking dogs are in a predatory state of mind. What the dog does after the Stalk, of course, is very individual. When my fox terrier, Breanna, was Stalking, death was imminent. She was never kidding around. Many dogs use Stalking behaviours in play. Behaviours which look like Stalking are also prevalent during Warning and Guarding.

Remember the Predatory Sequence? Eye-Stalk-Chase-Bite-Kill-Dissect? The Eye portion of this sequence can be split into three phases: the Scanning phase, where the dog is "looking for action;" the Alerting phase, where the dog has located something of interest; and the Targeting phase, where the victim has been chosen and the dog is Fixed on it.

Stalking, like the Eye portion of the prey sequence, also has a number of components. After the victim has been chosen, the dog may do one or more of the following:

- Point: the dog becomes totally Still and focuses intently. This is usually associated with a head-up, tail-up posture, and accompanied by a Paw Lift. Pointing will, typically, only occur at the beginning of a Stalk. Many dogs do not Point at all.
- Move Up Stalk: the dog moves with a measured, very deliberate pace. Each foot will be slowly and ever so carefully placed. The body is low to the ground, the head will be lowered. Some dogs will be almost crawling along the ground.
- Still Stalk: the dog becomes totally Still, in a head-down, tail-down, ears-up posture, with the body lowered to the extent that sometimes the belly is brushing the ground.

Once Stalking, the dog may oscillate from Moving to Stillness several times, until he is close enough to take a run at the prey or pounce on it.

It is fascinating to watch the dog's mouth: it can be either open or closed. In the "less serious" or earlier phase of the Stalk, the mouth is often open. As the dog nears the prey, the mouth will close, then may open again toward the end of the Stalk in anticipation of grabbing the prey.

The more intense, serious, or later phase of the Stalk, the lower the tail. A higher tail indicates playfulness or an earlier phase of the Stalk.

The Point is a more upright Stalking position. That is, the head of the dog is not lowered in the typical Border Collie style of Stalking. The paw is lifted, the head is up, the tail is up as the dog becomes totally laser-beam focused and almost unnaturally Still.

The Upland Game dog is bred to locate and Point the game, hold the Point while the hunter shoots, and then retrieve the game. So dogs such as German Short-Hairs, Wire-Haired Pointing Griffons and Brittany Spaniels have been selected for not just the Point, itself, but also the prolonged Stillness and truncated Pounce.

But wait, there's more! See photograph #41.2 for the Stalk after the Point.

#41.1: Point

- head up
- tail up
- ears up
- perfectly still
- Paw Lift

#41.2: Move up Stalk after the Point

- tail up
- ears up
- moving
- head down

After the brief Point - "Ooooh! What is that?" - this dog moves toward the prey object. My bet is it's a bumper or other water toy, or perhaps a canine playmate.

This dog shows predatory interest by assuming The Classic Still Stalking posture: head lowered, tail down, ears up, and Stillness. This photograph was taken at a dog camp, so the prey is most likely a water toy, not an elk.

Some Stalking dogs have an open mouth and some have a closed mouth. The closed mouth would be in the more "serious" or later stages of the Stalk, usually just before initiating pursuit after the prey.

#41.3: Still Stalk

- tail down
- ears up
- still

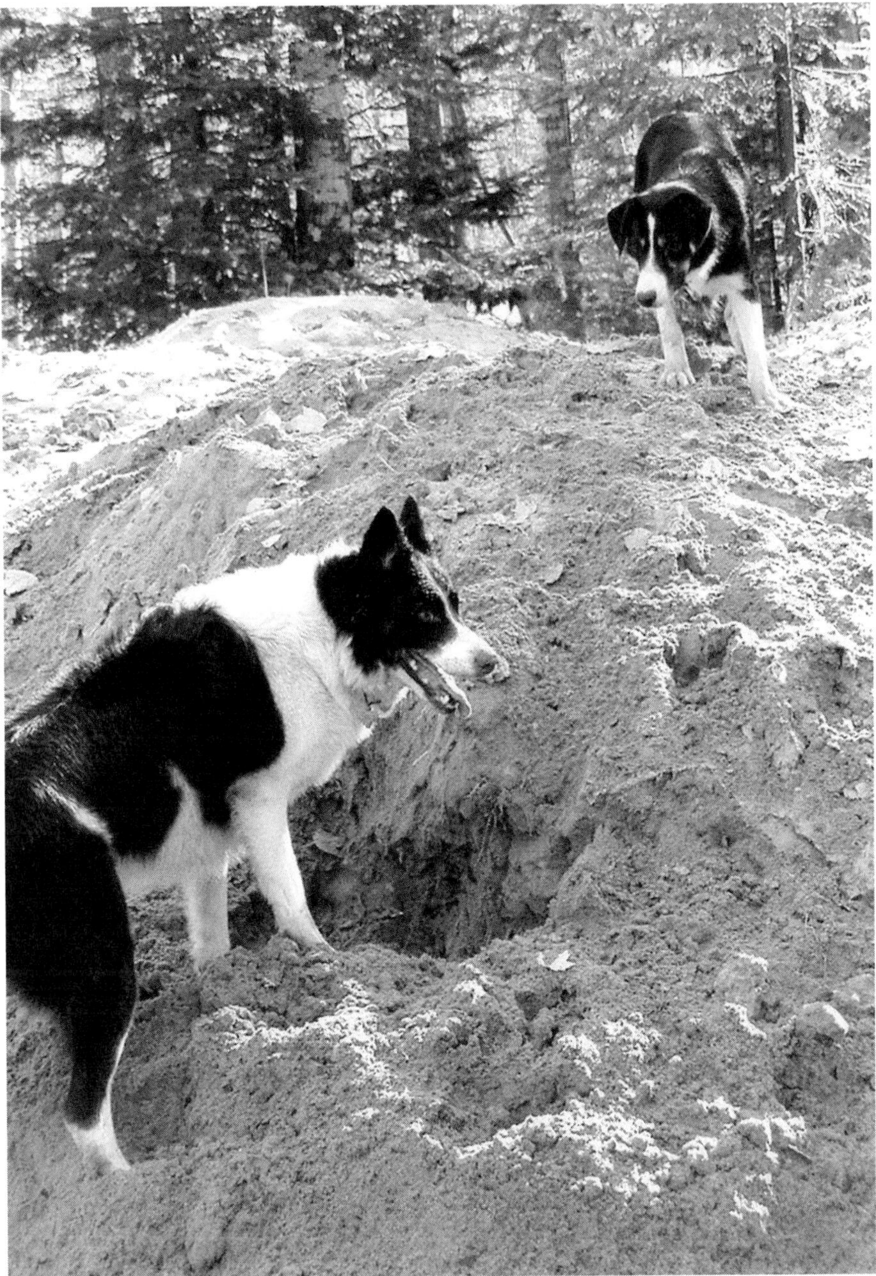

#41.4: Still Stalk During Play

- tail down
- ears up
- still
- head down

The dog to the right is Stalking the dog to the left during Play. The dog to the right has the lowered-head, tail-down, ears-up silhouette of the typical Stalking dog. Her eyes are fixed on her "prey." Her closed mouth indicates that this dog is ready for the Pounce.

Do not think that the Border Collie, to the left, is unaware. She is inviting Play by using a neutral position-with her ears at half-mast, a Look Away, and her mouth is open.

You can tell this will be Play because of the Negotiation Signals that are being used by the "victim." The victim dog is relaxed and at ease, not nervous and frightened. She is not using conflict-oriented language, nor is she using submissive or appeasing language.

In other words, you can tell it is Play by taking the information given by the "victim" rather than focusing solely on the "predator."

#41.5: Walk Up Stalk

- tail half-mast
- ears up
- moving
- head down
- mouth open

The "Walk Up" phase of the Stalk. Here the dog is either getting ready to enter or has just terminated a Still Stalk.

#41.6: While Stalking, Pause & Point

- tail down
- ears up
- still
- head down

Punch has paused during a Moving Stalk and is Pointing. Her posture is interesting, reminiscent of a Point because of the Paw Lift. But the rest of her says, “I am Stalking.” Her head is lowered, her body is lowered, her tail is down, and her mouth is open. In about two seconds, she pounces on the grasshopper victim.

The Paw Lift, typically associated with a Point, is occasionally seen when dogs go between the Moving and Still Stalk.

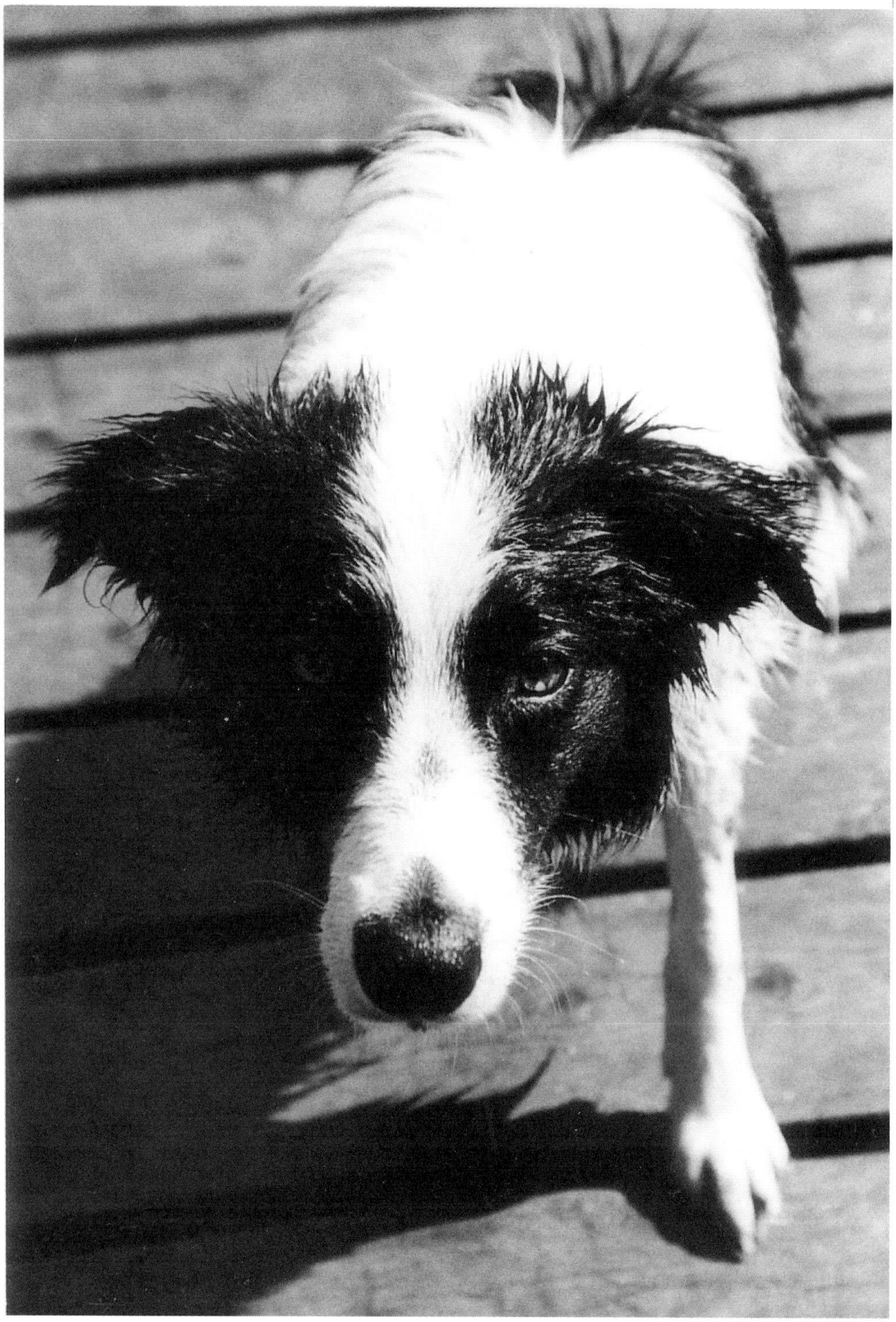

#41.7: Eye

- tail down
- ears up
- still
- head down
- crouched sitting posture

It's the Border Collie "Eye."

Rylie takes this "Eye" stuff very seriously. She Eyes everything, including the camera.

The intensity of her gaze, her "on alert" ears, and the Stillness are all typical of the Stalking dog. When Stalking, the dog's universe narrows to encompass only the prey, to the exclusion of all else.

#41.8: Moving Stalk

- tail up
- ears up
- moving
- head lowered

This dog is Stalking her owner. Gotta love those Border Collies! They just put that Herding behaviour everywhere. Her tail is up, indicating that she is feeling more "playful" than predatory.

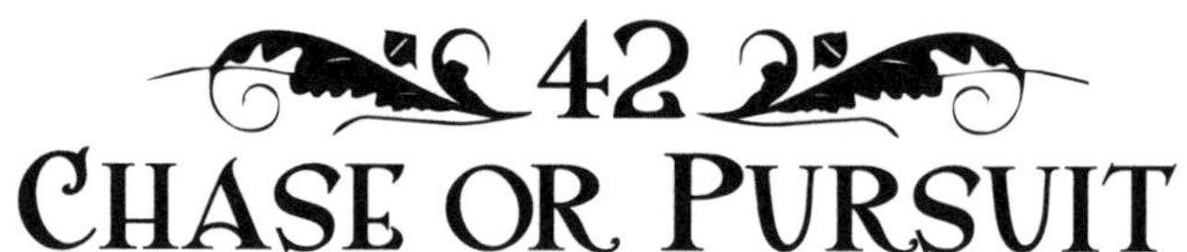

42 Chase or Pursuit

The following photographs all have in common the intensity that a dog puts into pursuing a prey object. In this case, the dogs are lure coursing. The prey object here is a rag. But this same intensity is there any time the dog chases prey.

The lowered head and intense, fixed gaze are typical of the dog in pursuit. The ears will be, for the most part, forced forward. The dog's tail may be tucked, curled, to the side or over the back, in any position that it is most useful as a rudder to help balance the dog when he is turning at high speeds.

Just as when you are engaged in a physically and mentally demanding task, the world narrows, excluding everything that does not directly pertain to the end goal: capture of the prey.

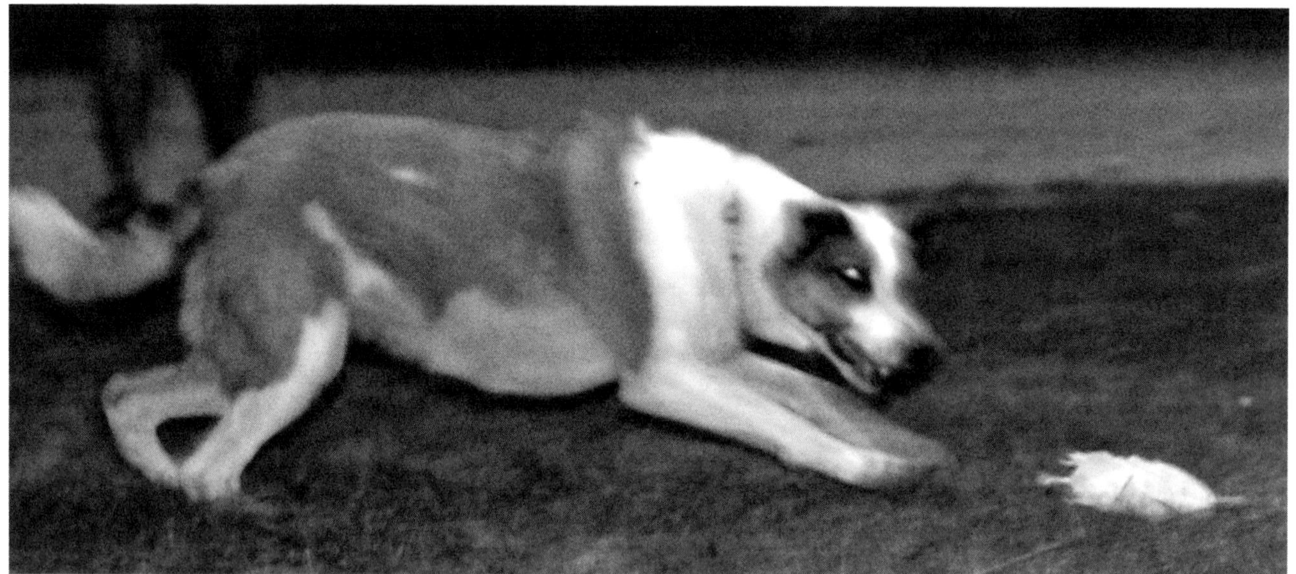

#42.1: Pursuit

- extreme physical effort
- pupil dilation
- fixed intensity on prey

About Behaviour: Some dogs come with good judgment about what is and what is not a prey object. Many do not. I don't depend on a dog having good judgment until it is proven to me. Guilty until proven Innocent in this context keeps other animals, dogs, children and joggers safe. It is important to notice when your dog is this intense. It can mean a nasty surprise for you to discover your neighbor's cat is a prey object. Some dogs just like the chase and seem a bit puzzled once they catch up to whatever they were chasing. Some dogs are socially sensitive and heed the warnings of the animal as they come upon it. For example, if a cat hisses, the dog stops. Other dogs blow right by any warnings and will kill or maim the animal once they contact it. We shouldn't be surprised by this. Dogs are historically and genetically social predators and scavengers. Don't be surprised when your dog rolls in excrement, licks bloody meat wrappers with joy and loots the trash, either.

#42.2: Pursuit

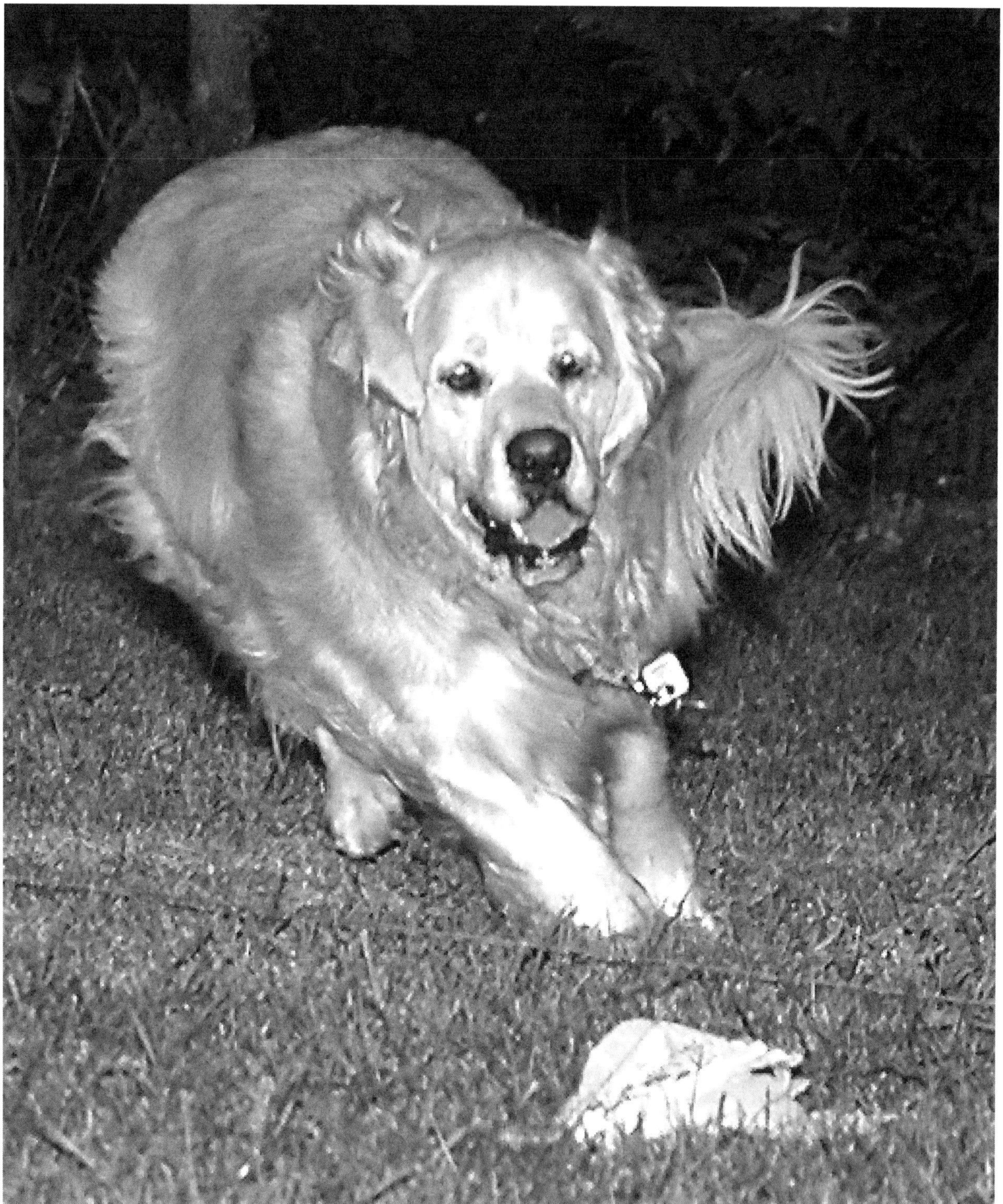

#42.3: Pursuit

Even this mild mannered looking Golden gets right with the program!

#42.4: Pursuit

#42.5: Pursuit

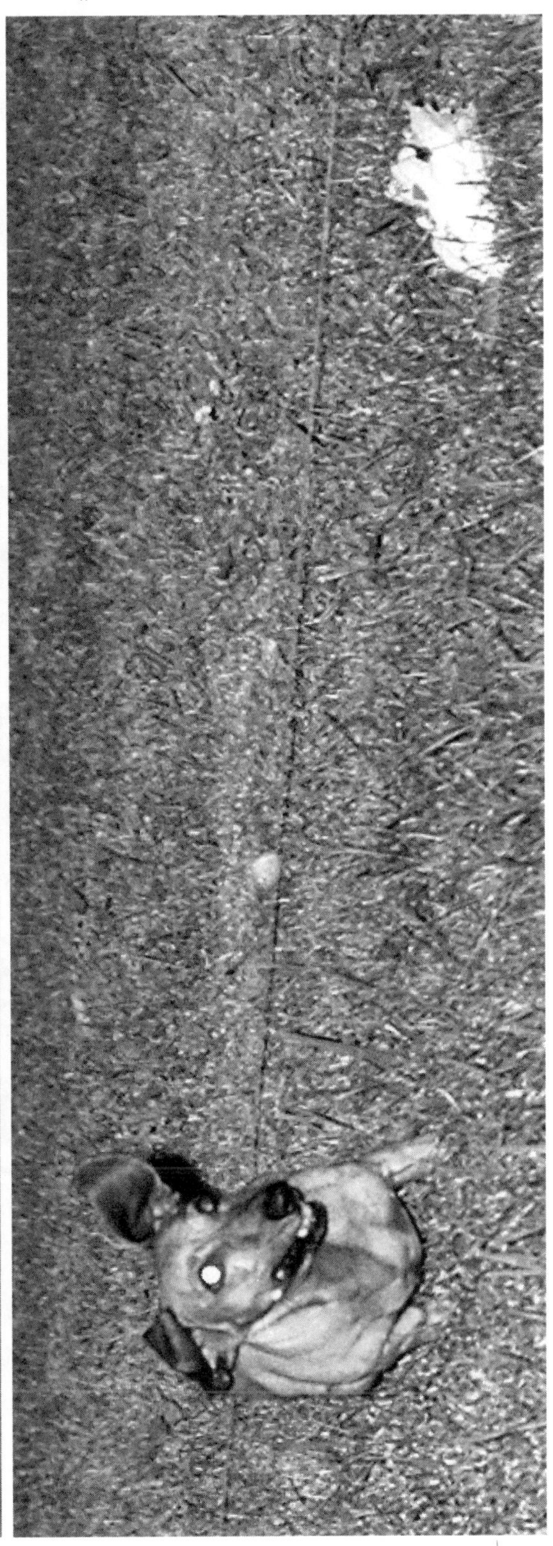

#42.6: Pursuit

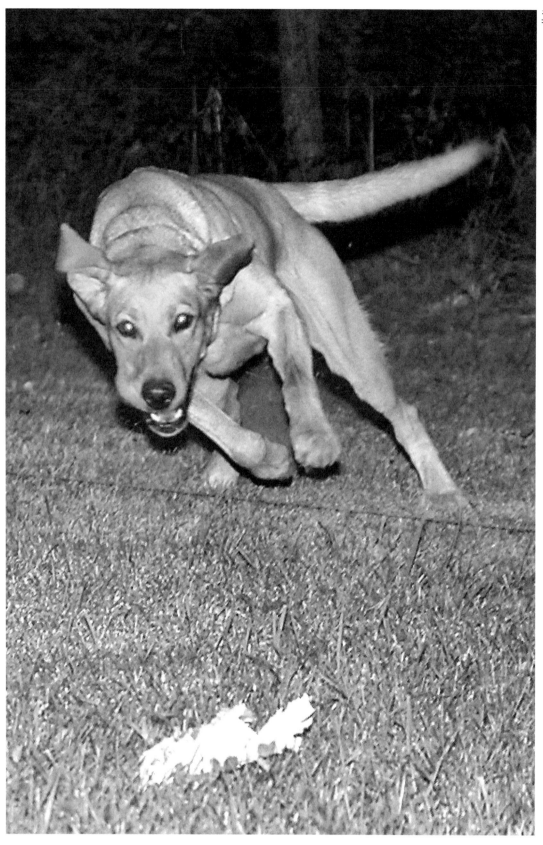

The *intensity* with which these dogs are chasing is typical of an animal in prey drive.

#42.7: Pursuit

These dogs are moving at great speed. This makes these pictures blurry, but also gives you good practice. Often the silhouette of the dogs body is all you need to tell the story.

Training Tip: When a dog is this involved it will be very difficult if not impossible to interrupt the behaviour.

To prevent tragedies, such as your dog harming someone or another animal or running into the side of a car, it is essential that you practice good management. Be aware of what your dog's triggers are and make sure your dog is safe from himself.

#42.8: Contact

Contact! There is an expression change as the dog uses the Grab Bite. The mouth closes on the prey. The eyes come up as the dog enters the Real World again.

Notice how dilated the pupils are - lots of wild eyes! The dilated pupil is a physiological reaction to the adrenaline dump(s) the dog is getting.

#42.9: Pursuit

#42.10: Butt's On Fire

Compare this dog (photograph to the left) to the other dogs in this Chapter who are in the pursuit or chase phase of prey drive.

The dog in the photo to the left is just running for the fun of running. Good ol' "butt's on fire" kind of a run. Can you see the difference? The dogs in prey drive have a lowered, closer to the ground, flattening of the body and lowering of the head and neck. The dog to the left has thrown his head up in the air and and has tucked his hindquarters underneath himself..

#42.11: Pack Run

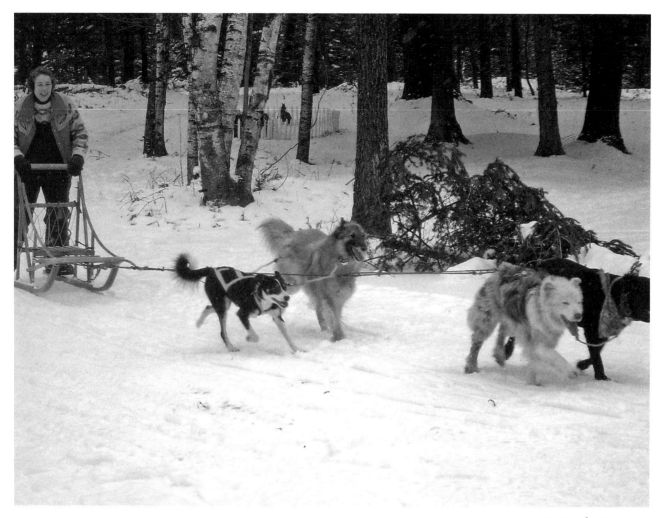

Dogs running together at a task. Again you can see the difference in the body language. The intensity is way down; the dogs have mouths open in a variety of "grins." The heads are lowered, but the dogs are using a ground covering trot rather than an all-out, no-holds-barred dead run of the dog in pursuit of prey. The ears are held at half-mast, as are the tails.

Also note how the dogs are very closely mirroring each other's postions. They are not an exact replica of each other, but are clearly in concert with each other, exhibiting a lot of the same language and body positions: ears, tails, open mouths; the dogs are very close in appearance.

Photo Credits:
Photo #1, #2, #3: Joanne Weber;
Photo #4: Ginger Bross;
Photo #5, #6, #7, #8, #9: Joanne Weber;
Photo #10: Rachel Plotinsky;
Photo #11: Joanne Weber.

Section 6: Play

Play is practice for living. When dogs Play they will use all of the same body language that would be used for status battles, reproduction and hunting.

As dog owners, our biggest concern with Play is that it can escalate unexpectedly into a dog fight before our very eyes. In this section, you will get to sample a variety of situations: dogs who know each other well and dogs who are meeting for the first time. There is a chapter on "Play Gone Wrong," where the Play does escalate into conflict.

When you are watching dogs Play, look for those Calming and Negotiation Signals - the way dogs keep reassuring themselves that the Play is Play and is not turning into something else. Another indicator is the intensity level of the dogs involved.

As they Play, dogs should heed each others signals and they should be willing to trade roles.

As dogs go through different social development periods, Play serves different functions. When dogs are small it is all about social interaction. As they go through adolescence, practice for social status becomes more important. As adults, some dogs still enjoy Play and others are uninterested. There are, as always, some constants across the species and some variables according to the individual.

Line Drawing by Brenda Aloff.

43
Dogs at Play

#43.1: Cooperation

- squinty eyes vs. wide eyes
- direction of eye contact
- ear positions
- proximity
- position of head and neck

#43.2: Warning

The dogs above are playing. There is no direct eye contact. Both dogs have squinty eyes. They are also Mirroring each other. Mirroring is a communication of comfort with and in sync with each other. By contrast, in the photograph below there is a Warning.

The dog on the right is giving direct eye contact to the dog on the left. The Border Collie-mix has her eyes held wide open. The shape of her eyes is rounded and you can see white around the iris. She also has her ears forced way back, especially her left ear. The dog on the left is accepting the Warning. His ears are held half-mast and his eyes are squinty. He is not particularly worried, just accepting the communication. His tail is still held up jauntily, not forced over his back in a Challenge position. The mouths of the dogs in the photograph above are relaxed and they are holding onto the items lightly. In the bottom photograph, the dog in possession of the item has her mouth clamped tightly onto the bumper; you can see the tension in her lips and jaws if you look closely.

Observation: Squinty eyes mean acquiescence or a spirit of active cooperation: "I got your message." They are a friendly signal!

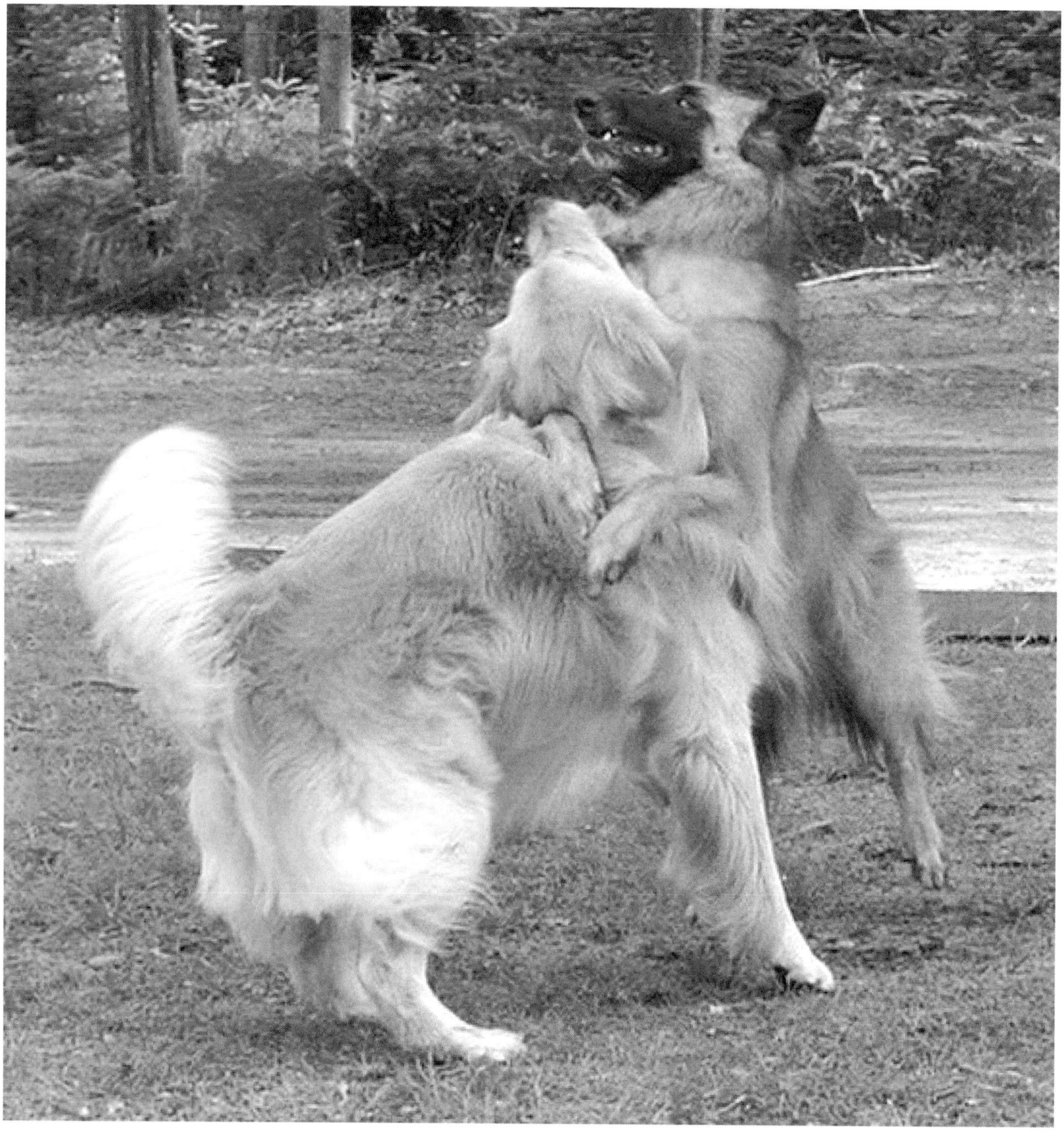

These dogs are playing without reservation.

There is a distinct lack of body tension in both dogs. Both dogs are touching and are electing to remain in each other's body space.

There is no direct eye contact in this entire photo essay, excepting one photo. This instance of eye contact is fleeting.

The ears are at half-mast. Both dogs have gently waving tails.

#43.3: Friendly Play Sequence - Photo Essay

- absence of eye contact
- proximity
- lack of tension
- relaxed lips
- half-mast ears

Look at the mouth on the Terv. This is the Happy Mouth look - the lips are long and the mouth is open. No teeth are menacingly exposed

The Golden is using a great tactic: going underneath for a Jugular or Leg Bite. This is a predatory maneuver.

Even though the Golden is using a Fiercesome Face, it is almost laughable. When you see a real dog fight there is absolutely nothing humourous about the facial expression. It is deadly serious. These dogs have a "goofy" look about them. Their floppy ears and relaxed tail sets help you identify their lack of body tension.

Their feet are not planted or braced. Notice the Paw Lift on the Golden.

Even though the lips of the Golden are C- shaped and the canines are visible, and his eyes are rounded and there is some white around the iris, this is still play. The lack of body tension is the key.

The lack of intensity and the constant movement, with no Warnings being given shows that the dogs are in concert about playing. The dogs are quite comfortable with each other and are confident in their ability to communicate with each other. This explains the lack of tension.

The Golden delivers a "fearsome bite" to the Terv.

Text for this photograph is on the following page.

Text for photograph on preceeding page: Then the two dogs move apart and re-initiate play. In a real dog fight, this moving away from each other would never happen. Once the dogs are locked in combat, the only time they move away is to get a better hold on the other dog. It doesn't look anything like the "play dance" above.

When these dogs re-initiate play there is a moment of orientation towards each other. During this moment these dogs Mirror each other, with gently waving tails, half-mast ears and almost identical body postures, right down to a Paw Lift in motion.

#43.4: Invitation to Play from Alpha Adult to Puppy

- absence of eye contact
- proximity
- relaxed lips
- floppy, relaxed ears
- adult taking submissive position

This is Breanna, an adult, taking a "submissive" role, in order to encourage Fletcher to play. Adult dogs will invite play from puppies using a "vulnerable" body posture. This allows the polite puppy access to come into personal space.

Photo Credits:
Photo #1, #2, & Photo Essay #3: Joanne Weber;
Photo #4: Brenda Aloff.

44
PLAY BITING

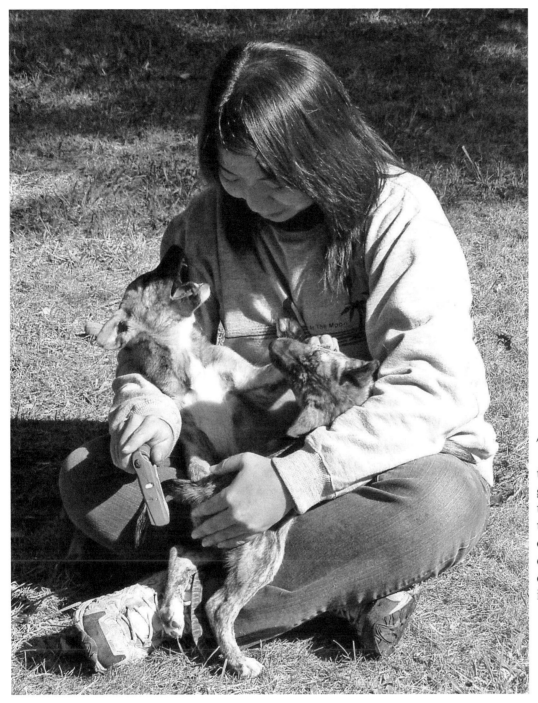

#44.1: Play Biting Humans

- squinty eyes
- floppy ears

The puppies use the same body language and bite on the human just as they do with each other. This is a common theme in dogs communicating with humans.

You can tell this is play biting because the puppies have loose, floppy ears and relaxed facial expressions. The open mouth of the puppy on the left allows the tongue to hang partially out, and has the same meaning as a "happy, laughing" face. Even though the pup's mouth is open and she has her teeth out, her lips are not wrinkled on the top of the nose as they would be if the puppy were being aggressive.

This is very typical puppy play where the dogs roll around, mock fighting like Tweedle-Dee and Tweedle-Dum and mouthing each other all over. They will chew on each other's ears and face endlessly, with an occasional verbalization.

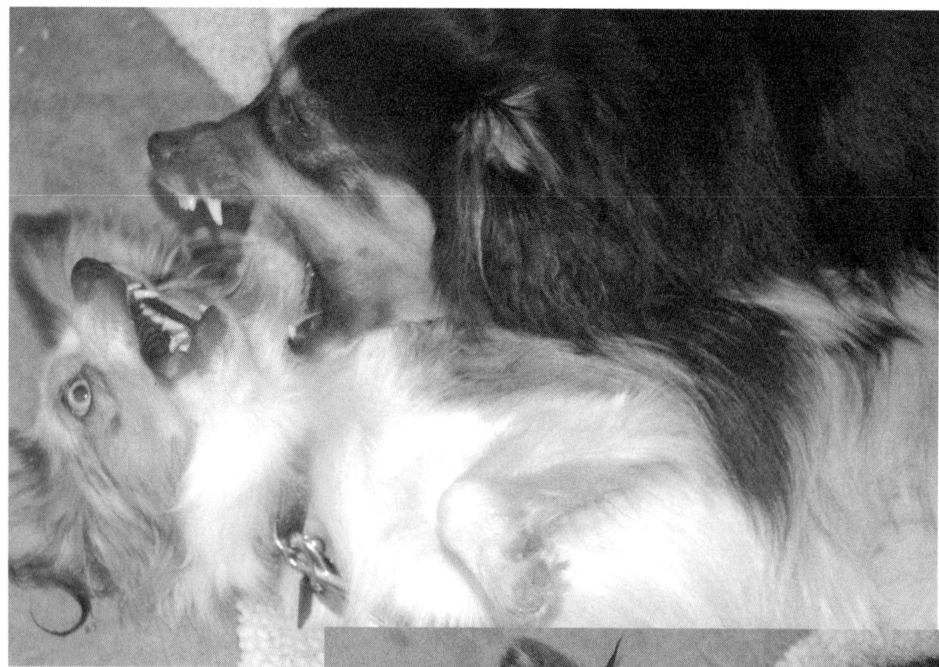

#44.2: Play Biting - Photo Essay # 1

- direction of eye contact
- ears are "floppy"
- lack of tension

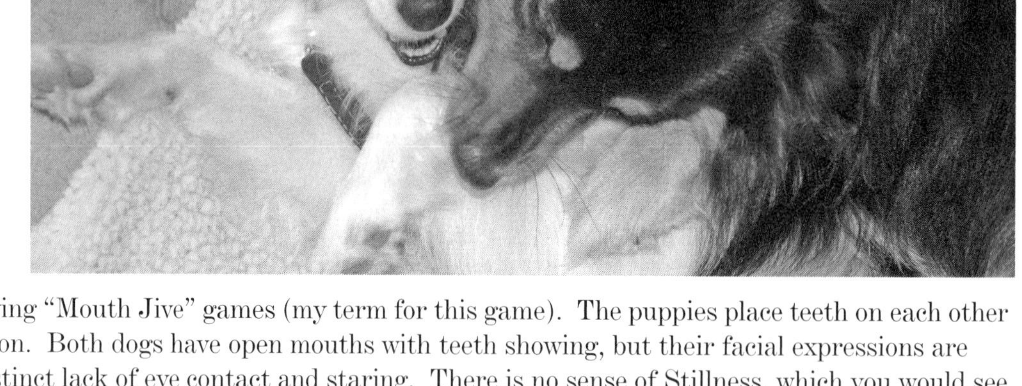

These puppies are playing "Mouth Jive" games (my term for this game). The puppies place teeth on each other with great bite inhibition. Both dogs have open mouths with teeth showing, but their facial expressions are relaxed. Notice the distinct lack of eye contact and staring. There is no sense of Stillness, which you would see if there were Warning signals being passed around.

The pupils are slightly dilated with excitement, but a wide margin of the iris is still visible.

I am always struck by how "silly" the facial expressions of playing dogs are. Their teeth look all "ferocious" while they lack the Staring, Stillness and tension of dogs in conflict.

While the dog in the top photograph has a slightly fierce expression at times (see the wrinkled nose in the first photo), you can ascertain that this is play by looking at the relaxed manner of the dog on the bottom. Since he is not taking the situation seriously, I wouldn't either.

The gentle grasping of the neck, in the area of the jugular vein, is typical of wrestling, playing dogs. Again, notice how relatively unconcerned and relaxed the expressions of both dogs are. These playing dogs lack the intensity and the feeling of purpose of fighting dogs. Fighting dogs look - and are - very goal-oriented.

What fun! Both dogs are using an inhibited bite. Even though they have their mouths and teeth on each other, neither dog looks alarmed. Compare these photographs to some of the dogs in the *Stress*, *Guarding* and *Warning* Chapters. There is great contrast between how tense those dogs look and how easygoing and affable these dogs are, even though this play is intense.

Training Tip: If you are not sure if your new puppy is being too aggressive in its play, look at how the *other dog* is reacting. If the other dog is relaxed and returning the play, all is OK. Otherwise, intervene. If a group of more than two are playing, watch for discomfort in any members of the group that are selected for Prey Roles. Monitor the group also for Fun Police types, that *continuously* patrol and split up the play, inappropriately. Be able to identify the socially appropriate dog who is splitting up the play for a legitimate reason, to prevent a dog fight, too. Another way to identify appropriate play is to watch for role changing. Neither one of these play sequences shown are long enough to show this, but you can refer to Chapter 46: *Play Sequence: Role Change*, to see an example of this.

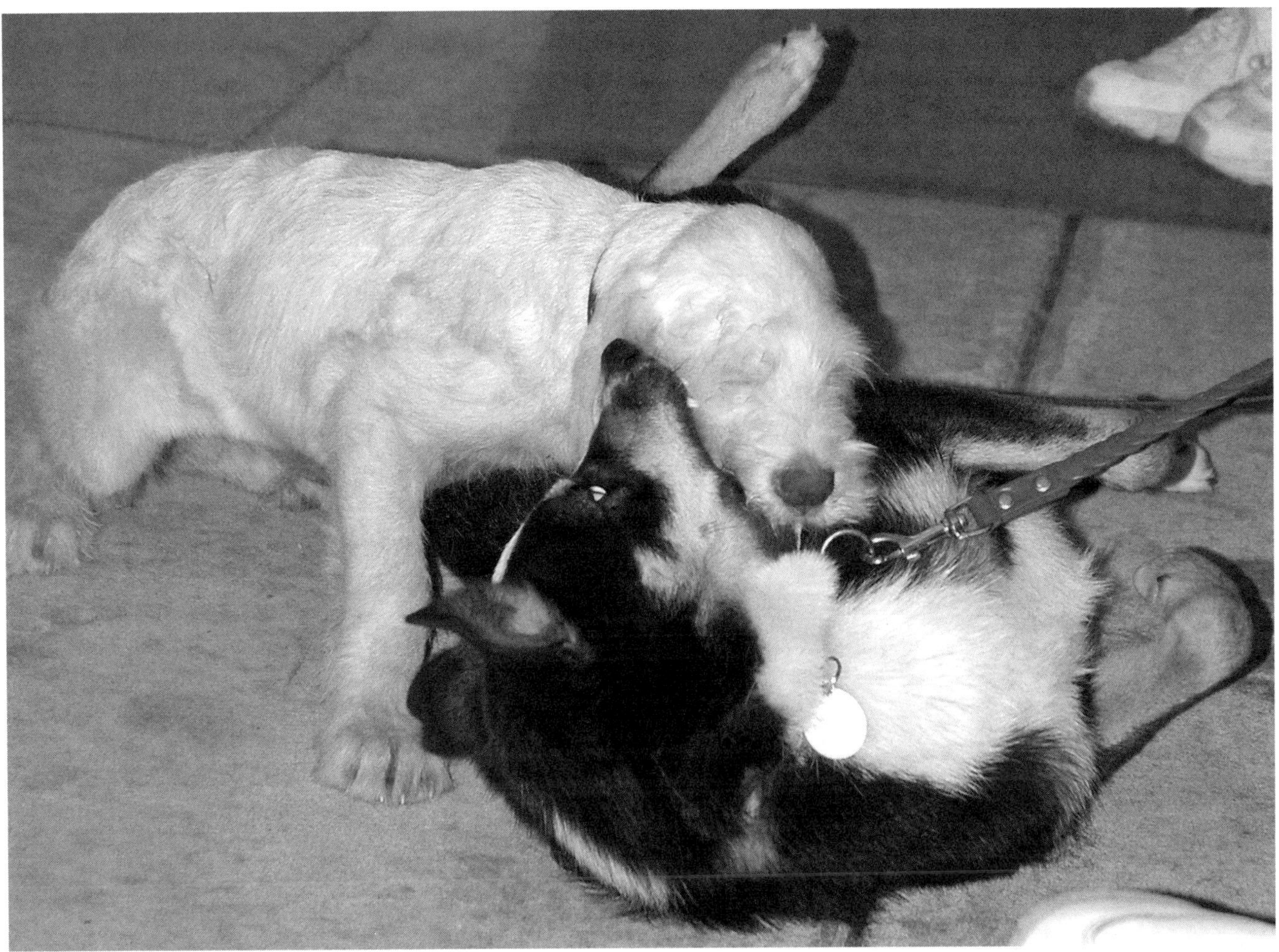

#44.3: Play Biting - Photo Essay #2

- squinty eyes vs. wide eyes
- direction of eye contact
- "floppy" relaxed ears

Here again is the neck-biting play commonly seen in wrestling dogs. When dogs play for extended periods, look for a Change of Roles - that is, the dog on the top will take a turn being the underdog from time to time.

The Spinone puppy has his eyes closed. He is so relaxed looking that if you took the other dog out of the picture, he almost looks as if he is resting!

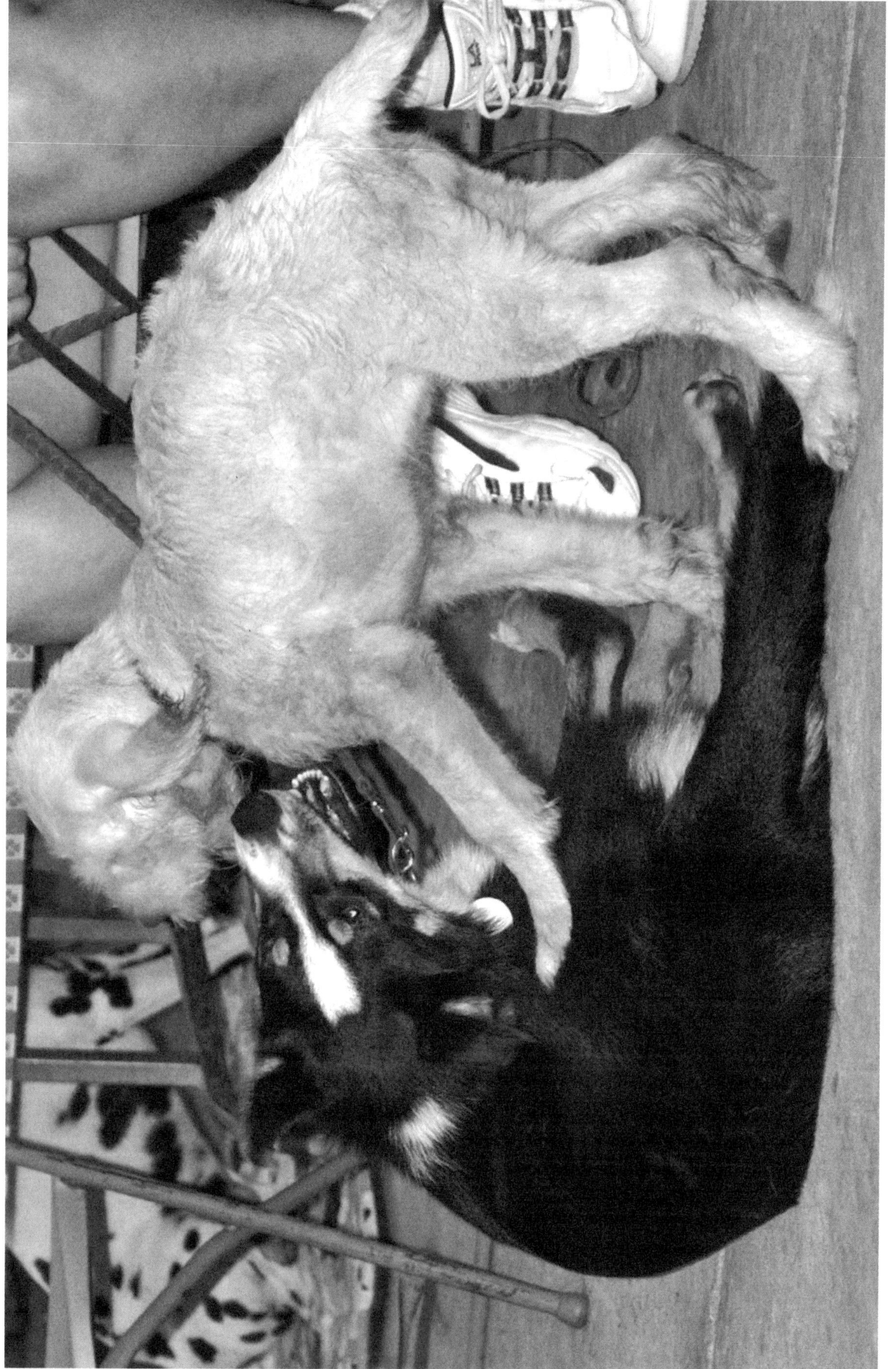

The faces of these dogs do not have ridges of tension, and they are very lighthearted and comfortable in each others space. Even though the dogs are "biting" each other, there are no Warning Looks or direct eye contact. The lips are not tense or curled. There are no up-over-the-back tails, with tense short movements, which indicates tension and the "pulling rank" of status-related aggression. These puppies have half-mast, relaxed tails.

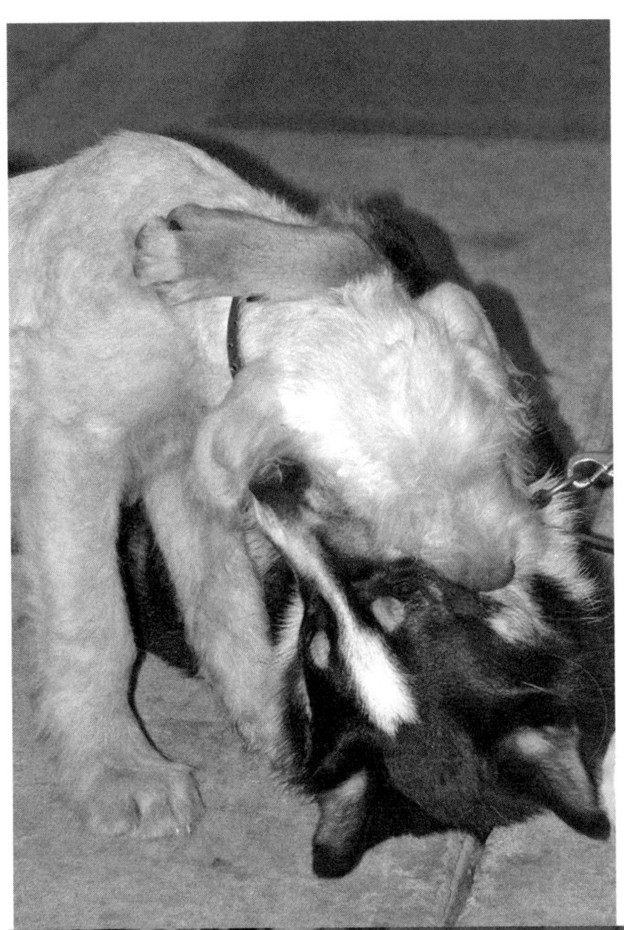

The half mast, floppy ears and the relaxed tails tell you that these dogs are playing.

When you check for facial tension, there is, surprisingly for the amount of contact and action going on, none.

Play Biting is hard-wired behaviour. An overwhelming majority of puppies and dogs use an inhibited bite in play.

Although Play Biting is normal behaviour, it is not necessarily desirable behaviour when directed towards humans. Play Biting is obnoxious if the puppy persists past another dog's or a human's attempts to stop the behaviour. Allowing Play Biting to humans sends a puppy the wrong message. Allowing puppies to harass dogs who will not "stand up for themselves" and who feel overwhelmed by the puppy sends yet another wrong message.

Photo Essay: Joanne Weber

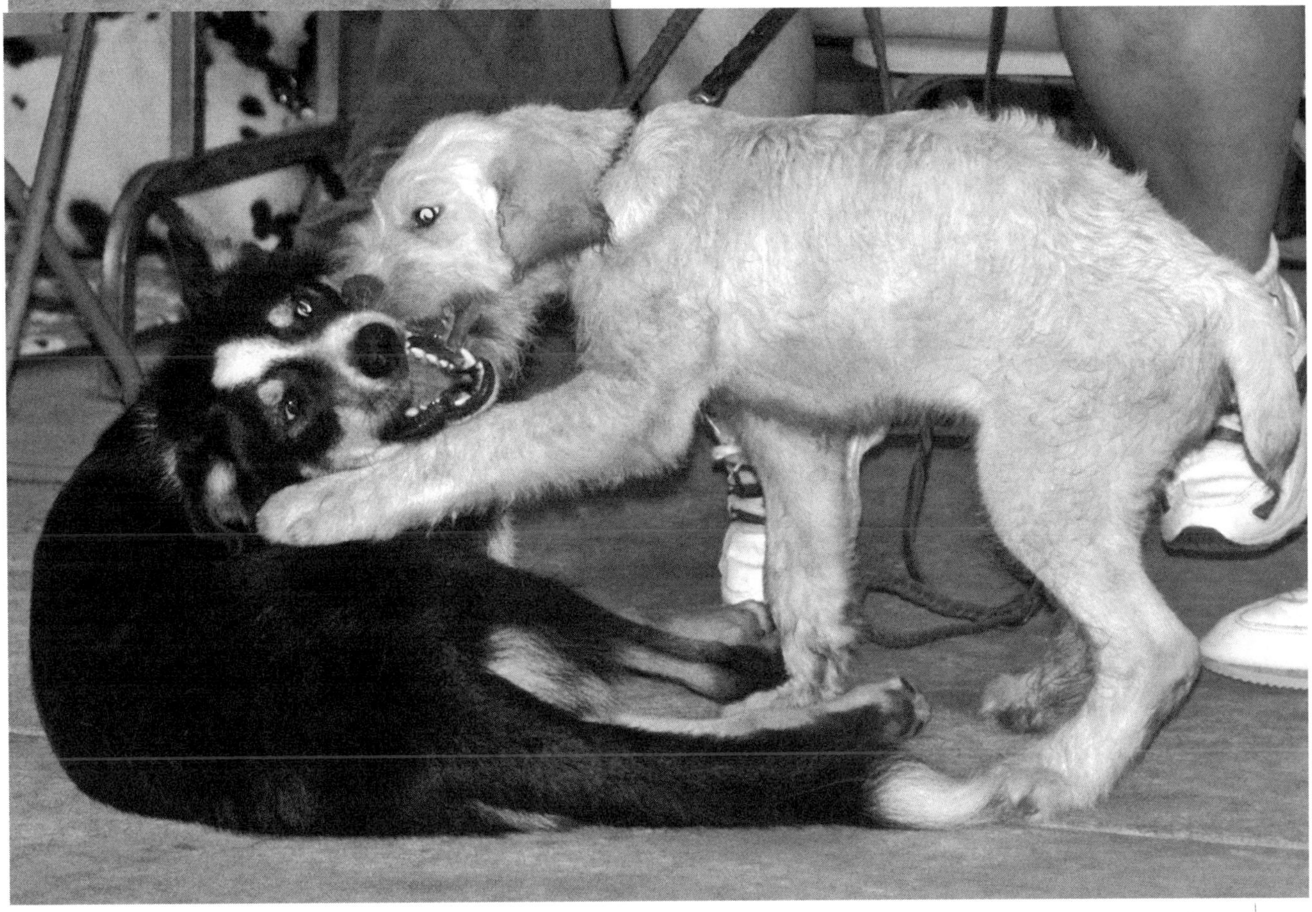

45 Play Bow

This chapter has some of the cutest poses you will ever see. All of us love to see our dogs Play Bow. It is such a joyful expression. Other dogs like to see a Play Bow, too, because it is a signal that means, "I am not confronting you, I am friendly. Let's Party!"

Play Bows are often used to initiate play as well as to interrupt play as it becomes intense. The Play Bow is a reminder to other dogs: "Remember, we are playing! This is not for real!"

#45.1: Play Bow

- rear up
- elbows touching or very near the ground
- direction of eye contact follows nose orientation
- ears up, alert
- lowered or down tail
- mouth partially open, lips relaxed

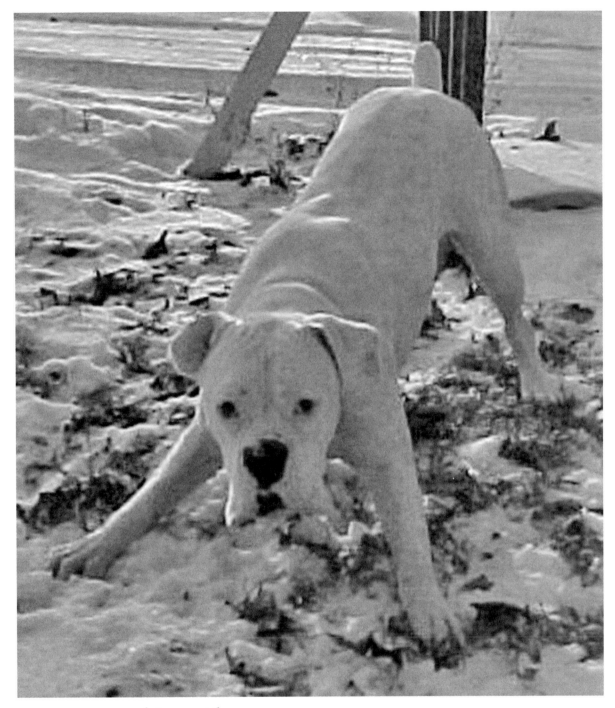

#45.2: Prey Bow Used During Play

- rear up, ears up
- elbows touching or very near the ground
- tail up
- mouth closed

This is more of a Prey bow. Note the “up” tail: this indicates a slightly different intent or mood. It signals more an intent to “pounce” rather than “I am playing.”

Compare this photograph of a Prey Bow used during Play to the Classic Play Bows on the following pages.

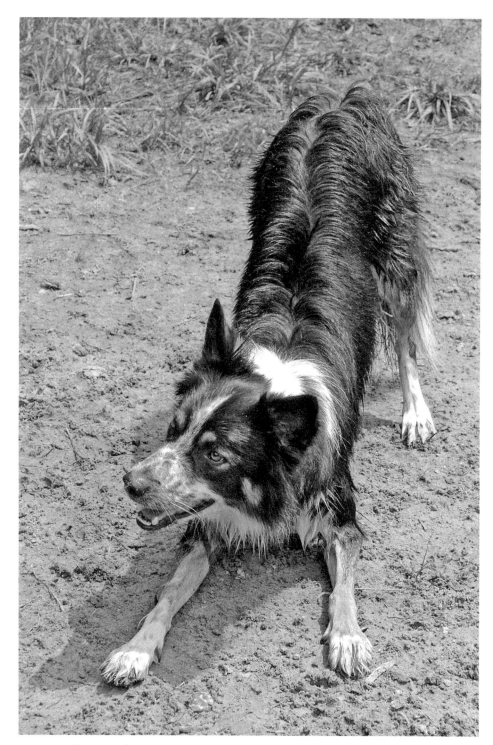

#45.3: Classic Play Bows

- silhouette
- down tail
- alert ears
- eyes & nose directed toward the one the dog is communicating with
- long lips, relaxed lips (on both) open mouth (Border Collie, this page)

#45.4: Play Bow as "Calm Down"

- difference in silhouettes between challenging dogs & Play Bowing dog
- tail wagging & at half-mast on Play Bowing dog
- Play Bow used to Split Up

The two dogs to the left are involved in some sort of interaction. It could be play or it could be a minor status challenge. What is obvious is that these two dogs are in direct eye contact with each other. The dog in the foreground has her tail right up over her back. She is confident of the outcome and feels she has the situation well in hand.

The Golden is using a Play Bow as a Splitting Up gesture. The Play Bow is used here as a very specific communication: to stop conflict between the other two dogs. Look at how different the Golden's facial expression is. Her mouth is open and her lips are long.

I have seen a Play Bow used in this manner by my Terrier bitch, Breanna. The most notable time probably saved the life of one of my male Terriers, and most certainly prevented vet bills. I was in the kitchen and Breanna was with me. For no apparent reason I felt the hairs rise on the back of my neck and the sudden tension in the air. I turned around and looked into the living room and could see Sherman and Sport, two of my Terrier boys standing nose-to-nose. There was no mistaking the intent of the direct eye contact and the extreme body tension, the tails held high over their backs and their tightly closed mouths. Those boys were getting ready to rumble. I knew any movement I made would probably send them for each others throats, but I had to try. Just as I was opening my mouth in a feeble attempt to delay disaster, Breanna leaped to her feet and ran right between the two boys. She did a huge and dramatic Play Bow. Then, the most amazing thing happened. I could feel the fairy dust sprinkling down around all of us. Those boys broke eye contact, both of them Looked away, Shook, and walked away. Breanna came roaring back into the kitchen and sat down and looked at me. I found I was able to draw breath again and finished the dishes - right after I distributed cookies to everyone, but especially to Bree!

It is truly amazing how effectively savvy dogs communicate. Crystal clear, Quick and Beautiful. We could take a hint!

#45.5: Play Bow Used in Play Possession Game - Photo Essay

Pit Bull on the left:
- tail is up
- airplane ears
- Play Bow used to invade space safely

The Cattle Dog has a rope bone and is determined to retain possession. He is Guarding his toy. Notice the tail up over his back and the lowered head that is so indicative of Guarding or Warning behaviour. Instead of the typical up, alert ears, the Pit Bull has Airplane ears of excitement.

The Pit Bull Play Bows. You can tell this is not serious because the Cattle Dog has allowed the Pit Bull to come right up into his personal space. If he were truly serious about Guarding the bone, the Pit Bull would never have gotten a chance to get this close before the Cattle Dog made good on his threat.

The Pit Bull is very careful to let the Cattle Dog know that she is playing and not confrontational. The Play Bow precedes her jumping on the Cattle Dog in Play. Even though the Cattle Dog is still retaining possession of the bone, notice how relaxed his grip is; he is holding onto the rope toy; but does not have his teeth clenched onto it for dear life. The ears of both dogs are held back as they wrestle for "play possession."

The Play Bow helped to keep everyone relaxed and happy. The Pit Bull used the Play Bow to invade the other dog's personal space, and it let the Cattle Dog know that she was just "Playing" for the possession of the toy.

Photo #1: Joanne Weber;
Photo #2: Rachel Plotinski;
2 Photos #3: Joanne Weber;
Photo #3 & Photo Essay #4: Rachel Plotinski;
Photo #5: Cherish DeWitt.

46
Play Sequence: Role Changes

As you look through this play sequence, what will be noteworthy is that the dogs change roles. Dogs often play one of two kinds of games: Possession games, where a toy, object, or location becomes the focus of the play "conflict," or Predator/Prey games. In either case, a sign of good play is that the dogs change roles. This is nicely demonstrated in this sequence.

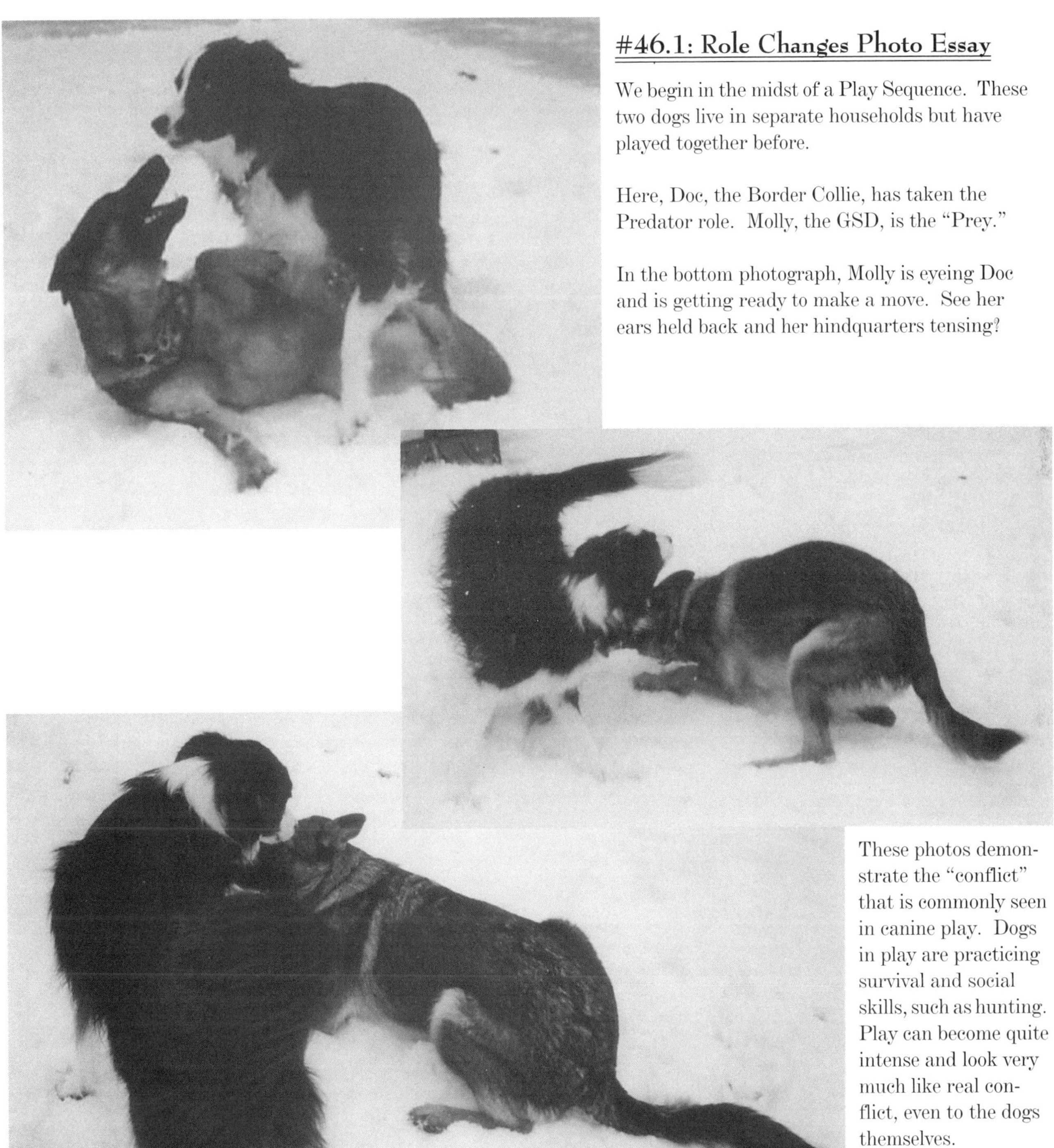

#46.1: Role Changes Photo Essay

We begin in the midst of a Play Sequence. These two dogs live in separate households but have played together before.

Here, Doc, the Border Collie, has taken the Predator role. Molly, the GSD, is the "Prey."

In the bottom photograph, Molly is eyeing Doc and is getting ready to make a move. See her ears held back and her hindquarters tensing?

These photos demonstrate the "conflict" that is commonly seen in canine play. Dogs in play are practicing survival and social skills, such as hunting. Play can become quite intense and look very much like real conflict, even to the dogs themselves.

After the intense "conflict," these dogs Break. "Conflict" in play will be constantly interrupted by less intense behaviour, as we see here, so that the participants can reassure each other that this is still Play and not real predation or aggression. Breaks also allow adrenaline levels to go down.

Molly uses a Sit as a Negotiation Signal. See the Look Away Doc is giving back to her in acknowledgment of the Sit? Both dogs also have half-mast tails and half-mast ears.

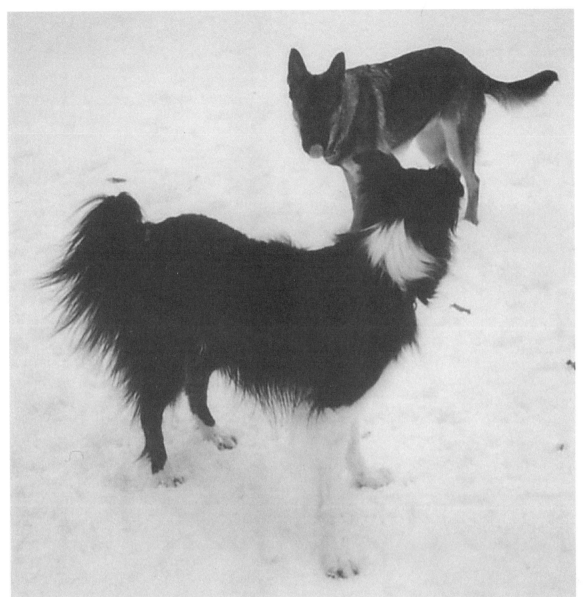

Okay, now the dogs are getting ready to kick the intensity up a notch! This is the moment when the dogs decide, for this round, who is the Prey and who is the Predator. Molly gives Doc a Tongue Flick. She has also lowered her head a bit and is gathering up her hindquarters.

Molly lies down as the voluntary Prey and Doc charges in, in Predator mode.

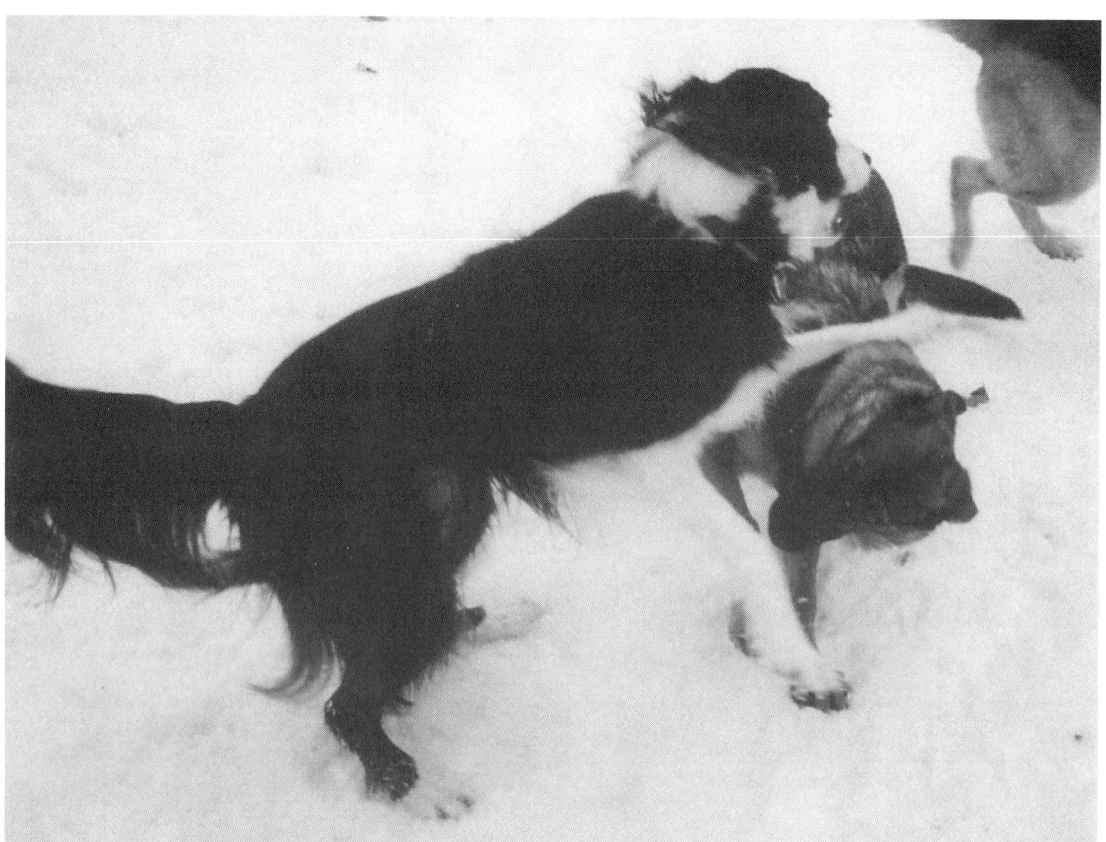

Molly gets close to the ground to handle Doc's onslaught.

Molly allows herself to be rolled, and Doc makes a fiercesome face.

Sometimes you cannot tell how serious things are by looking at the "attacking" dog. Instead, look at the dog who is the "Prey." If the "Prey" dog is looking frightened or uneasy and is giving signals that are being ignored by the "Predator" dog, then you have problems.

Molly looks unconcerned here, so we know that this is still innocent fun. The play has not morphed into something else.

In the midst of this intense “conflict,” note that Doc is not staring at Molly, who is on the bottom. The deliberate lack of eye contact keeps the encounter playful.

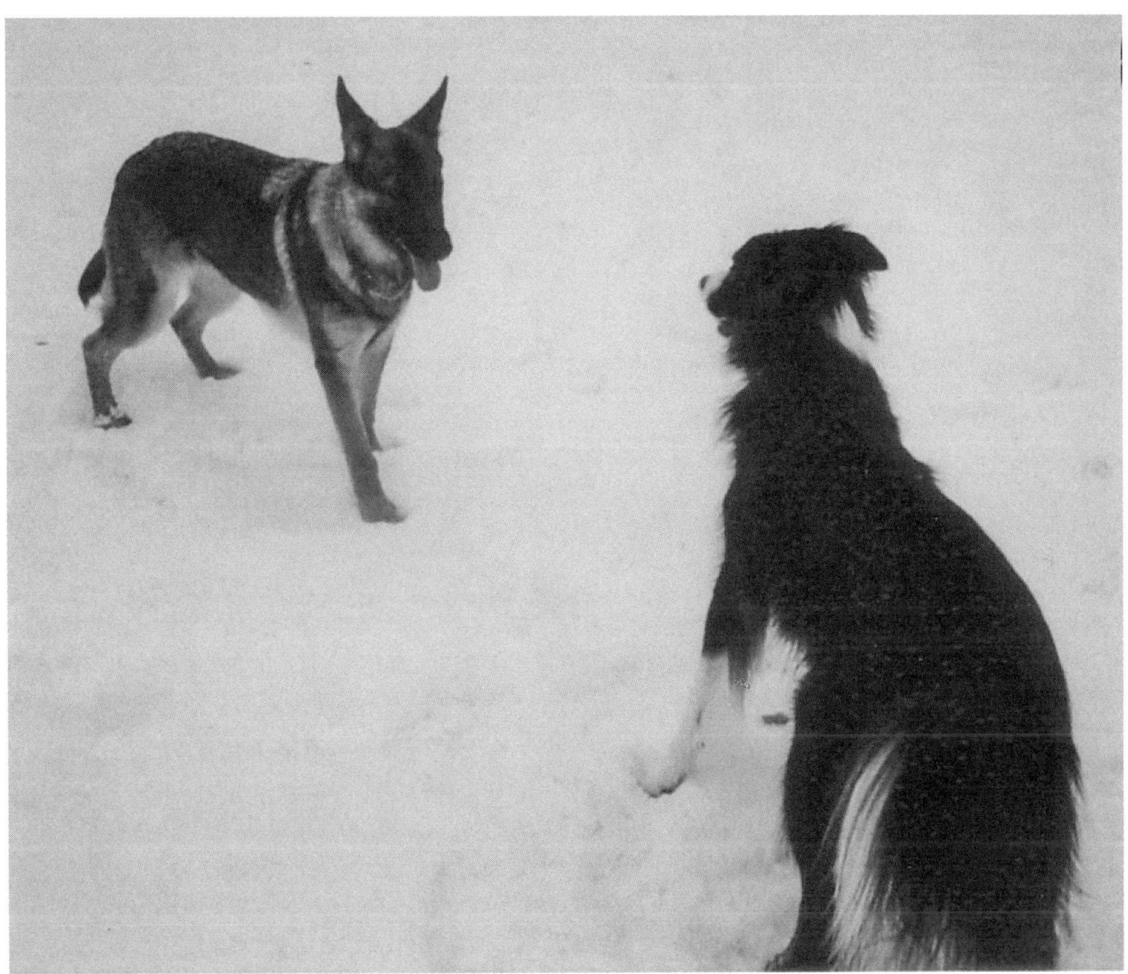

Another break. Again, the moment of decision: who gets to be the Chaser and who is Chased?

Doc gives a brief Look Away and Molly will now become the Predator. The dogs change roles.

Molly begins with the chase.

Doc interrupts with a Play Bow. Molly is poised for his attack...

...and another "conflict" ensues. This time, Doc is the Predator.

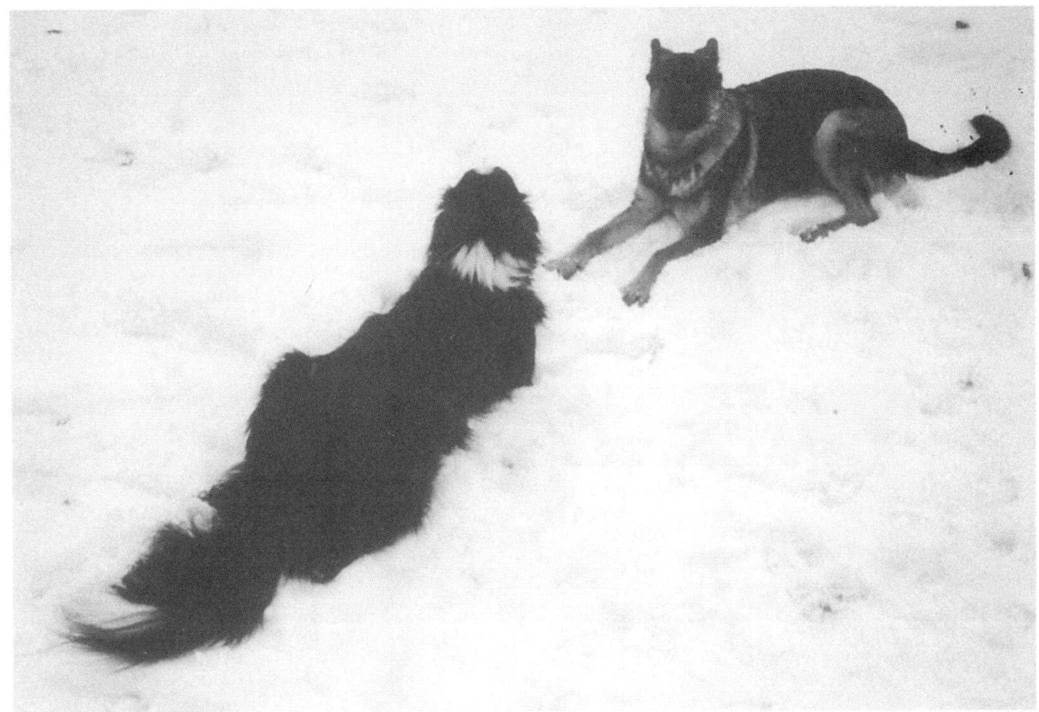

After a brief wrestling match, there is another Break. The dogs offer each other Look Aways.

And another Role Change. When the dogs spring up from the Break, Molly gets to be the Predator. Doc, as Prey, obligingly runs off so Molly can chase.

Photo Essay by Candy Smith.

47
Play Sequence: Prey-Predator

The dogs in this photo sequence are at a camp. They do not know each other well. Typically, in a new, friendly group, dogs will exhibit a congenial curiosity about each other, though many will show some caution as well. What identifies a group as "friendly" is that there are a lot of Negotiation Signals being tossed around and, most importantly, that these signals are acknowledged by the other dogs. For instance, if a dog were intimidated by one of the others and began to lick her lips and Look Away, the other dogs should return a Negotiation signal and, ideally, back off by turning away from the intimidated dog and leaving the immediate area.

This sequence is of a group of friendly dogs, some of whom engage in rambunctious play. Other dogs in the group decide the play is too intense, and choose not to participate. Very early on, all the dogs clearly communicate their intentions to play or not, and all of these signals are respected. This communication continues throughout, and so the group remains amicable.

Keep in mind as you look at these photos that this is an abbreviated Play Sequence. These photos show approximately two minutes of action. I chose this sequence because it illustrates a typical Prey-Predator Role Playing game.

In a Play Sequence that is "complete," you would get to see Conflict-Break cycles as well as Role Changes between the dogs. To see this, refer to the other Chapters in this Section.

#47.1: Prey-Predator Play Sequence - Photo Essay

In the photograph above, to the right is a cluster of dogs. They are displaying numerous Negotiation Signals. There is some sniffing, a paw lift, ears at half-mast, and no extreme tail positions (forced up over the back or tucked). We especially know this is friendly so far because *no dog is looking directly at any other.*

To the left are two dogs who are hanging back from the larger group. The Westie is Sniffing - it may be (and most likely is) a displacement signal, or he may just be finding something interesting to sniff. The black dog is watching the group from afar. Though you cannot see his face, you can see that his ears are pulled back and his topline is a bit rounded. This indicates some uncertainty and caution.

Frequently, in such groups, there are dogs who are very sensitive to the intensity of play. You often spot these dogs on the periphery of play using Negotiation signals - just prior to joining the play, just after leaving the play, or when they are not interested in engaging in play at all.

Here, two of the dogs who were in the original cluster are starting to engage in rowdy play. The Sheltie in the foreground is using a variety of Negotiation Signals: a Look Away, Lip Licking, and half-mast ears and tail. This Sheltie does not appear to be nervous; she is just stating calmly that she has no interest in being rowdy, either in play or conflict.

In a playgroup it is common for dogs, both those who are playing and those on the sidelines, to constantly use Negotiation Signals to emphasize that this is Play and Not Conflict. This happens throughout the entire interaction, not just at the beginning. Failure to use or to heed these signals is what can turn play instantly into a fight. Fortunately, in this group, the dogs are good communicators, and the play stays fun.

These dogs are the ones who will engage in the boisterous play. They are in the midst of deciding who is Predator and who is Prey. Or, if you like, who chases and who gets chased.

The Light Dog on the right is moving in and pretending to be the Predator. The Dark Tan Dog on the left is using a Look Away and half-mast ears as Negotiation Signals. She is just waiting to see what happens and then will choose a role. Unlike the dog on the right, she is a "follower" not a "decider."

The Rottie is looking at the approaching "Predator." She, too, is a "decider." See her slightly rounded topline and lowered head? She has her hind legs braced and is getting ready to be the Prey (the one chased). This lowered head and Stillness, as always, precede some sort of explosive action.

The two "deciders" are looking directly at each other with lowered heads. The "follower" watches the major players and will take on an auxiliary role. Her head is up as she watches the Rottie to see when the Rottie will move. She will not make the decision to start the action herself, though she will gleefully join in when one of the "deciders" acts.

Who moves first and in what direction reflects who is Prey and who is the Predator.

The Light Dog circles around the front of the Rottie, thereby cutting off all avenues of escape. The Rottie moves, and Tally Ho! The Chase Is On!

You can see that the Decider role is ongoing: the Light Dog and the Rottie are still looking to each other for direction and information, not at the Dark Tan Dog.

Many play sequences contain the same aspects as an actual prey sequence. The Dark Tan Dog is focused on the Rottie - but not on her face. She is aiming at her rear quarters. In your mind, replace the Rottweiler with a gazelle. When canines (dogs or wolves) are hunting, they use a precise strategy. They choose a victim via a process that ethologists call "Shopping." Once the victim is Targeted, the chase will begin. If everyone in the pack went for the same part of the victim, all they would do is get in each other's way. Instead, the hunt is tightly choreographed. In each pack there is usually one dog who aims for the throat. That dog goes for the jugular vein to do a hold bite, cutting off blood and oxygen to the brain. Think of this animal as the Header; a sort of Quarterback, who controls the direction of the prey, therefore having the most influence on the hunt itself.
Then there will be a few who work at hamstringing the victim. The Header and the Hamstring-ers will pull the prey taut between them. This leaves the job of evisceration to the other members. These roles are decided upon instantly, and probably become habitually taken by the same members of an ongoing pack.

With all this talk of killing and prey sequences, why aren't all these dogs dying already? Because they are constantly communicating to each other that this is Play, not Conflict. How can you tell? Despite the intensity of their attention and motion, they look pretty carefree and even goofy. The Rottie has an open mouth and her tongue is hanging out the side. Nobody takes you seriously when your tongue is hanging out the side of your mouth (not even another dog!). You cannot see it in this picture, but I would bet you that the dogs are all Blinking. It is one of the subtlest signals for people to recognize, but dogs really take note of whether there is blinking going on. Even though you cannot see the blinking here, you can see evidence of it: the eyes of these dogs have a relaxed look with no ridges evident, rather than being wide open with the whites showing, or hard-looking. Even though they constantly look at each other for information, no one prolongs a stare.

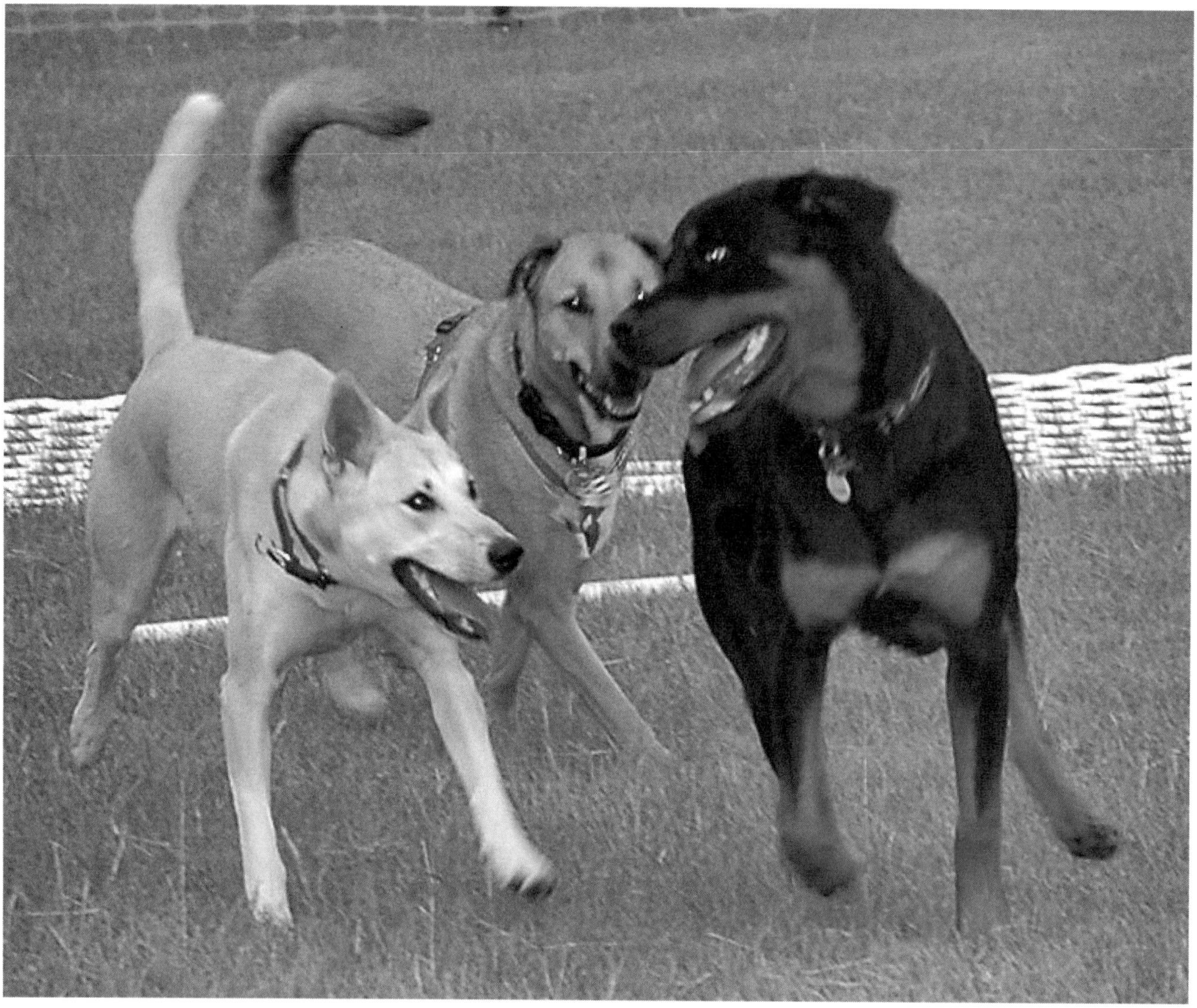

What a super photo! Here the Victim is still keeping an eye on her primary pursuer. The Header has the classic lowered head and close-to-the-ground posture of the canine predator. She is moving in for the grab-and-hold bite.

The Hamstringer is still following, looking for her chance to seize the Prey from the rear.

All the dogs still display the happy open mouth, long lips, and lolling tongues of the relaxed dog, even while the intensity continues to build. Their pupils remain normal. Their tails are wagging and, even though they are held up over the dog's backs, the tails are not held in a tense way.

Here we go for the "kill!" The Header has made her move for the grab bite, but has been evaded by the clever "victim," who wheels off to her left.

The follower dog is still having a great time bringing up the rear and waiting to see what will happen next.

In the group of people, notice the Sheltie who earlier decided to opt out of the rowdy canine group. Her wishes were respected, and she was left alone. Good dogs!

Also, from a dog's eye view, you can tell who, of the people, are watching the intense play unfolding before them. We can tell so much so easily about human body language - even people's feet tell a story. All these human feet in the background look relaxed; not poised for flight.

Tip: In a larger group, our attention is naturally drawn to the roughhousing dogs, where all the intense action is. In most groups of dogs, some will choose to engage in the rowdy, body-slamming, running, chasing, biting kind of play. In my puppy classes, I call this group of dogs "The Graffiti Painters." These dogs are the rugby players. They are out there to Party!

Other dogs will choose to watch the rowdies from a distance. These dogs may join in by running around on the periphery of the play. Or they may choose not to participate at all, but wander round the area deliberately ignoring the rowdies. These latter dogs would prefer to be reading a book or sipping on an iced tea. I call all these dogs "The Chess Players."

Really savvy dogs are able to adapt themselves to the playing style of the other dog(s) they are interacting with.

A soft dog will never become A Graffiti Painter. But the rowdy dog who plays roughly with another Graffiti Painter can learn to "dial down" and play gently with a Chess Player. You see adult dogs do this sort of shifting of postures all the time with young pups.

It is a common error to assume that all dogs like to play. Those who do enjoy play do not all have the same style of playing. Some dogs prefer chase and bump games. Others prefer wrestling. Many like to do Mouth Jive games with lots of pretend biting, but little other movement. Yet others like tug-of-war and other possession games. But for some dogs, just walking around quietly and companionably with another dog is a good interaction. Do not be concerned if your dog does not prefer playing with other dogs, as long as he remains non-reactive and neutral in group situations.

Photo Essay by: Joanne Weber.

48
PLAY SEQUENCE: CONFLICT & BREAK

In a peaceful play group, dogs repeatedly cycle through periods of "Conflict" and periods of "Break." When the dogs are in the Conflict stage, they actively and intensively chase each other and there is a lot of physical contact, such as biting, body slamming, and wrestling. Even in Conflict, though, you will see the occasional Calming Signal or a Negotiation of Passage through personal space. This is how the Conflict phase remains Play instead of erupting into real conflict.

In the Break stage, the dogs take a "break" from the intensity and physical contact. This Break is essential for keeping the play peaceful. It allows adrenaline levels to go down and for everyone to check in with Calming Signals: "We're all just here to have fun, right?" Just because there is a Break in the play, however, does not mean that there is nothing of note happening. Often during the Break, as seen in Chapter 46 *Role Changes*, there will be a Role Change where a new "victim" is chosen for prey (chase) games. There may be communications about status, Calming Signals given, Negotiation Signals given, acknowledgment of another dog entering the group, or a host of other "discussions" that set the dogs up to either start playing again or separate peacefully.

In any given play session, not all of the dogs necessarily have the same agenda. By "agenda," I don't mean a premeditated plan. What each dog does bring to the play session is a reflection of his personality, how he thinks, and what he "wants to get out of" this set of interactions.

When some dogs play, they are there for the joy of the social interaction. Other dogs act as if they have to prove their status non-stop. Some are merely using the other dogs as a prey or herding object, and are not interested in social interaction, per se. These motives can all be occurring simultaneously within the group, as each dog extracts from the "play" what he needs.

#48.1: Conflict & Break Play Sequence - Photo Essay

#1: In the back you can see Mostly White Sheltie chasing Spotted Dog.

Play is largely a rehearsal of hunting behaviors. With dogs, this includes typical predatory behaviours, such as chasing and biting, but also includes herding behaviours (driving, gathering). Curiously, too, playing dogs voluntarily take on the role of prey. Ideally, dogs will change roles often between predator and prey. This is an indicator of a peaceful play session. Some dogs, though, tend to seek out either the predator or the prey role.

The dogs in this photo essay are all house mates. This photo essay starts in the midst of a play sequence. The dogs have been turned loose together in a large area.

#2: Here, another dog joins the group as Spotted Dog stops, faces Mostly White Sheltie and uses a Look Away to Negotiate entering space. Dark Herding Dog, on the right, circles around in a herding "outrun."

#3: Everyone respects Spotted Dog's request. Mostly White Sheltie and the dog wearing the Bandanna, far right, do not actively stop Spotted Dog from entering; they "ignore." This neutrality gives Spotted Dog permission to enter the area.

This is an example of a Break. This Break may have been initiated because of the arrival of the new dog or because Spotted Dog wanted to lower the intensity level of the chase.

#4: Seconds later, the dogs enter into a New Conflict. The two herding dogs on the left, Mostly White Sheltie and Border Collie, are on the fringes. This fringe behaviour is typical of many herding dogs - they come with a hard-wired "work at a distance from the stock" repertoire. This is typical Gathering behaviour. In any group of dogs, individuals will take on a role or task according to their natural inclination. Some dogs dive in and Head the prey, some move in from the rear to Hamstring the prey and others will Gather or Drive the prey for the Header dog. Don't think, though, that your Terrier would not have a "Gathering" personality; non-herding dogs also exhibit these behaviors, which are, after all, all roles in the predatory dance.

#5: There is "Conflict" in the top middle. The Header dogs are converging on the "victim." The Gathering dogs are on the fringe, waiting to come in when the "prey" is down.

Mostly White Sheltie and Border Collie are on the fringe, and so is Spotted Dog who was the previous "victim." (Role Change!)

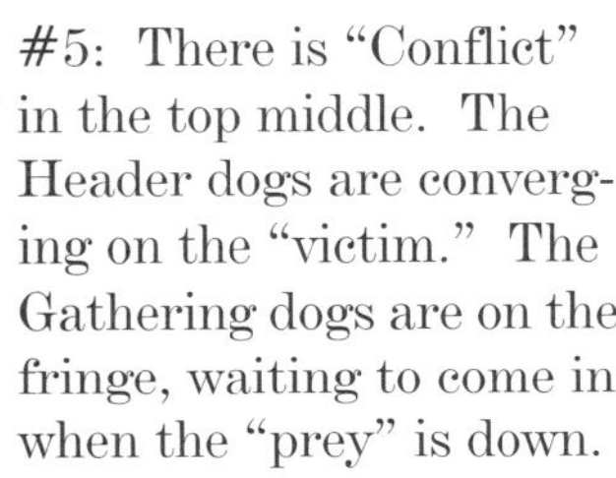

#6: Border Collie stands and barks at the dogs in Conflict. You can see one of the other fringe dogs - Spotted Dog - in the back.

#7: The Gathering dogs remain on the fringe of the intense action between the two dogs on the far left. As you go through this sequence, you will notice that these two dogs on the left are often involved in their own private game. This is another example of the different agendas the dogs bring to the play: subgroups of dogs involved in their own private parties.

Border Collie isn't looking at the big action anymore. He has turned away from a little mini-drama occurring right behind him. Spotted Dog is telling Mostly White Sheltie that he is not a sheep! The intensity kicks up a notch, just for a moment, as Spotted Dog protests being a sheep substitute: "This is getting just too irritating!"

#8: There is a marked lessening in the dogs' intensity. Spotted Dog has temporarily foiled Mostly White Sheltie. As Dark Herding Dog comes up to investigate, Border Collie responds to the commotion that was just behind him, barking at Mostly White Sheltie and telling her that he, Border Collie, is also not a sheep.

The two dogs that were in the main conflict are still engaged in some mild wrestling.

#9: Mostly White Sheltie has moved away for a moment, and the two dogs on the left take a physical Break from each other although they remain engaged. Border Collie leaves for a Break, and Spotted Dog moves in closer.

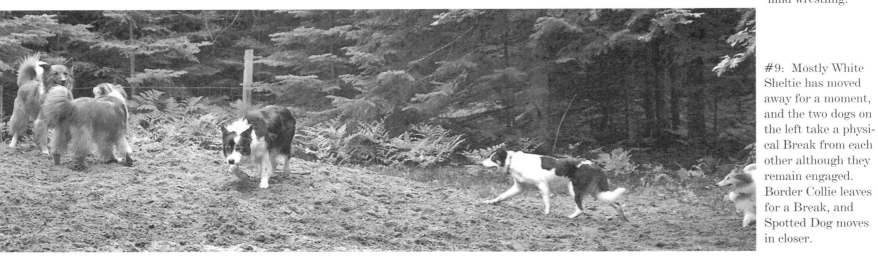

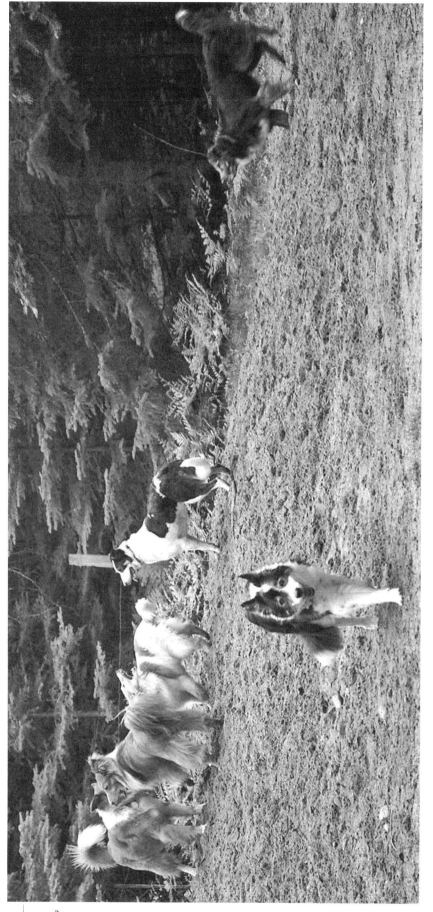

#10: The two dogs on the left give each other a Look Away. Mostly White Sheltie moves toward the main "Conflict" and tells Spotted Dog to stay back. Bossy! Spotted Dog acknowledges this signal with a Look Away and half-mast tail. What a nice dog! She also shows her neutrality with an open mouth.

Border Collie, in the foreground, leaves the action for a Break - or because he has found something else to interest him. He does not like the chaos. You can tell because he is never in the thick of it, and often goes near only to bark at everyone to tell them, "Stop It. Stand Still."

Dark Herding Dog enters stage right, carrying a fantastic find - a stick.

#11: Without leaving each other's presence, all the dogs take a Break. You can see the early signs of this Break in the preceding four photos where the dogs are voluntarily lowering the intensity level of their "Conflicts." This is lovely: everybody maintains position, but pointedly "lets down" and relaxes for a few seconds.

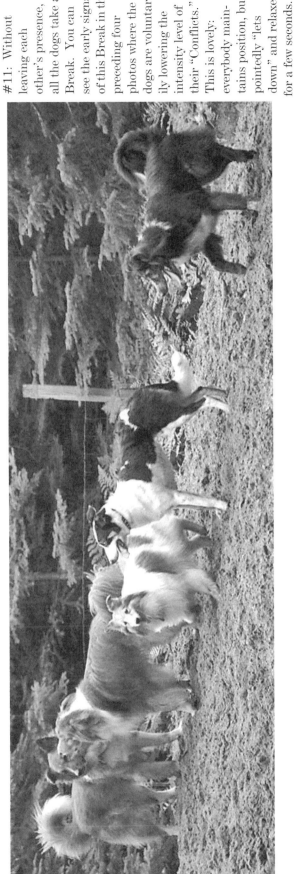

#12 - Below: One of the Gathering dogs, Dark Herding Dog, initiates Chase again.

Mostly White Sheltie remains still as Spotted Dog moves into her personal space in a neutral way, sideways to the Sheltie. Both dogs have half-mast ears and open mouths. The two dogs on the left are still standing face to face in Conflict position (still at their own private party), but the dog on the far left, Bandanna Dog, is using a pronounced Look Away. It is a confident, "You can come in" Negotiation Signal, and she is very relaxed. Her tail remains over her back - confident. Her mouth is open in friendliness and Negotiation.

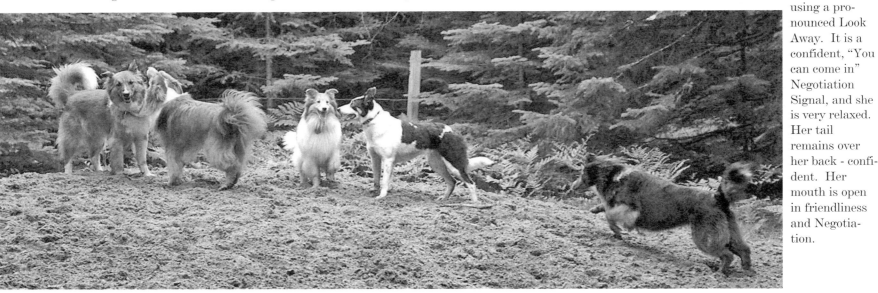

#13: The "prey" has been chosen: Bandanna Dog.

Everyone in the immediate group gives chase. While the other dogs target the chosen victim, Mostly White Sheltie goes off on her own little mission - after Spotted Dog again!

What is fascinating about this photograph is that it looks like one group of dogs chasing, but it is really two groups of dogs, with one dog who is a member of both groups. Spotted Dog is a willing member of the chasing group and an unsuspecting sheep substitute in the other group. This is an example of a subgroup within a larger play group, the subgroup having a different agenda. The subgroup members may switch back and forth from their own, personal agenda back to the agenda of the larger group.

#14: Two of the dogs are still chasing one dog, and Mostly White Sheltie is still in pursuit of Spotted Dog, ignoring the majority-chosen victim.

Three of the dogs are playing one game while Mostly White Sheltie is playing her own little game.

#15: Mostly White Sheltie moves in on the group-chosen victim for a moment. Opportunistic little fellows are dogs! The fringe dogs, meanwhile, hold to the fringe. Border Collie comes back into the play, entering on the right. And our initiating dog, Dark Herding Dog, who tends to like to circle the group, enters from the left, barking.

#16: Bandanna Dog, the victim just one moment ago, quickly changes roles to her probable real life personality: a calm, confident leader-type. The prior playmates "pack up," and acknowledge the intruder on the left.

Dark Herding Dog, on the left, opens her mouth and wags her tail in greeting. Bandanna Dog keeps it neutral with half-mast ears and slightly lowered tail.

Mostly White Sheltie, though, does not turn her attention to the new dog and is instead, again, pretending Spotted Dog is a recalcitrant sheep. Spotted Dog pretends the Sheltie doesn't exist.

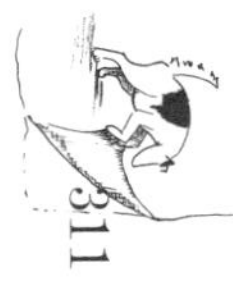

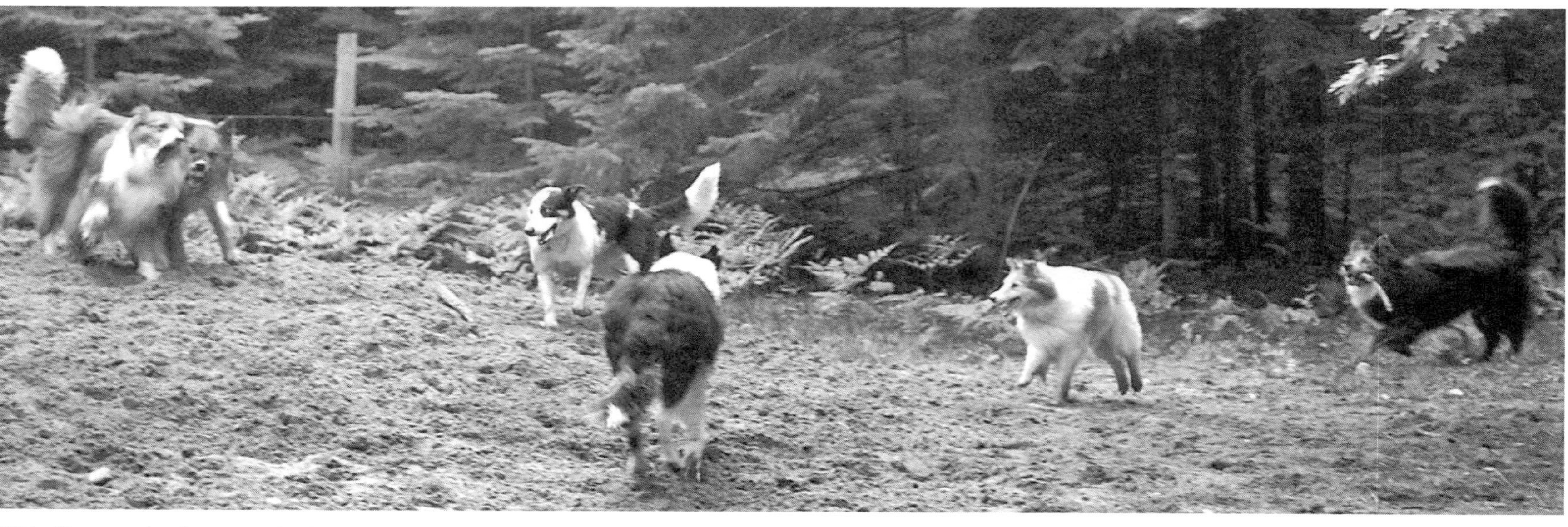

#17: Former play is resumed. The two dogs who like their Own Party go back to their "Conflict" and the fringe dogs hang on the outer edges. Dark Herding Dog has decided to carry a stick around with her. This is common behaviour in dogs: carrying objects whenever they feel a little excited.

Mostly White Sheltie continues to Target Spotted Dog, who continues to ignore the Sheltie.

Border Collie joins back up and all the dogs converge on the location of the victim and the main "Conflict."

#18: Still moving towards each other, into an ever tightening area...

You have to give Mostly White Sheltie credit for persistence. She doggedly follows on Spotted Dog's footsteps.

#19: When Bandanna Dog races off again, as the voluntary prey, the other dogs happily give Chase. Even Mostly White Sheltie gives up on the Spotted-Dog-as-sheep-victim for a moment and joins in the fun. Border Collie Stalks in the rear. He has the appearance and some of the movement typical to an older dog. Perhaps this is why he takes more frequent breaks and why he does not get in the middle of the main conflicts thereby risking physical jostling. My guess is, that he has always played in a similar manner, albeit with less caution as a younger dog: staying to the edges of this sensitivity to social pressure and proximity is common in certain lines of Border Collies.

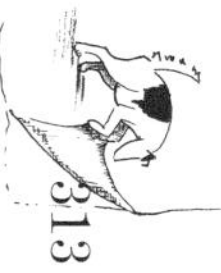

#20: The chase goes on....

#21: ...and on.

#22: A slight Break in the chase ensues. Mostly White Sheltie, to the right, resumes harmlessly harassing Spotted Dog.

Bandanna Dog takes advantage of the break to Butt Sniff the other main Header dog. This serves as a bonding and/or status-related gesture.

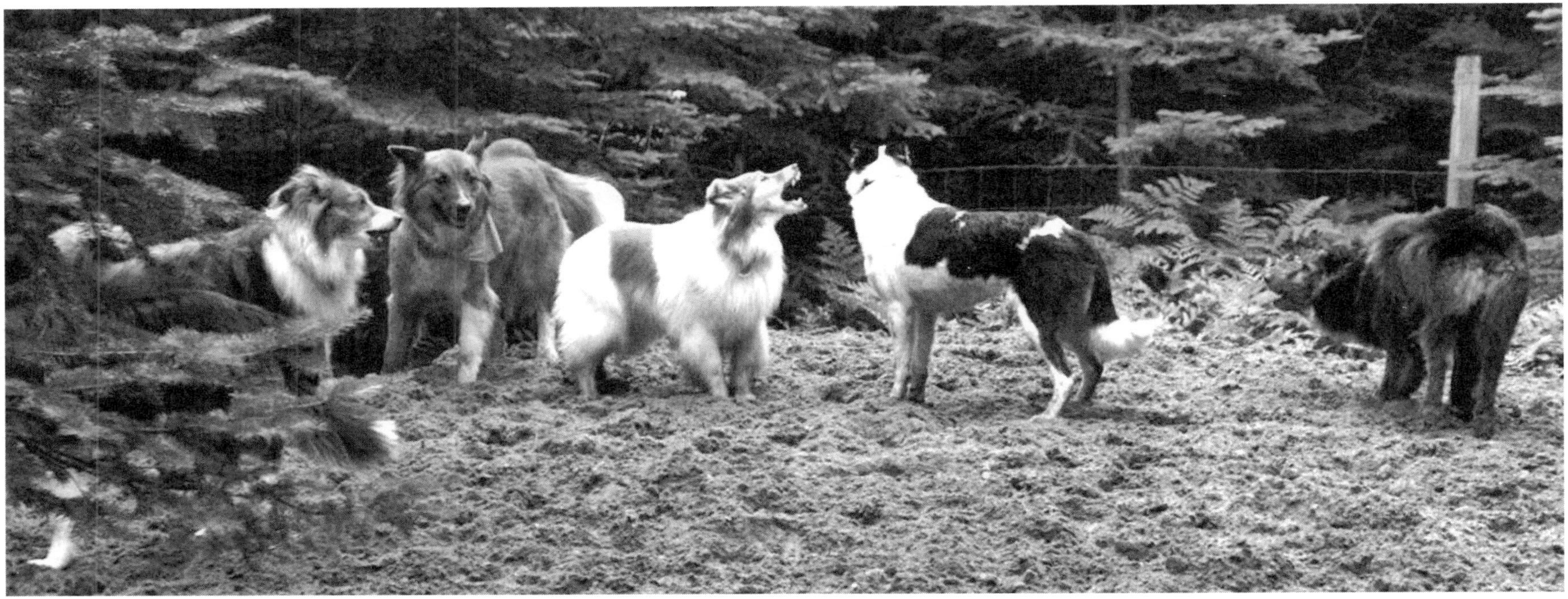

#23: Mostly White Sheltie "heads" Spotted Dog and barks in her face. Spotted Dog holds her ground, her body orientation slightly "backwards," and uses down tail, pulled back and almost flattened ears with a Look Away to maintain neutrality.

Behind Spotted Dog, Dark Herding Dog is ready to "hamstring" or help contain Spotted Dog. She has positioned herself directly across from Mostly White Sheltie in order to keep the "prey" enclosed. She is in a classic Stalking position.

There are two dogs Targeting one dog, and that one dog is escaling Calming Signals. The intensity is ramping way up. Bandanna Dog notices this right away, and she and the dog on the far left turn to see what is going on.

#24 Top Photo: Mostly White Sheltie succeeds in Gathering or turning Spotted Dog. Very satisfying to those herding instincts!

Dark Herding Dog begins to circle to keep Spotted Dog "contained."

The dog on the far left is Looking Away from the action. You can see why in the next frame: another dog is approaching.

Bandanna Dog marches in with purpose. Keeping half-mast ears, with her tail confidently over her back, she orients and looks directly at the new action. She knows, by the body language and intensity, that this is not normal "play" victim-choosing; it is unsolicited-by-Spotted-Dog action. Spotted Dog asked these two to Calm Down, and, instead, Mostly White Sheltie and Dark Herding Dog ramped up on the intensity, opposite of what was requested.

#25 - Bottom Photo: Bandanna Dog moves in to take control of the action. She stops Mostly White Sheltie from chasing. You can see how she has placed herself in front of both dogs, but sideways - Splitting Up. And she has put her nose between the two dogs. Mostly White Sheltie acquiesces, albeit with a bark of frustration - thwarted! Spotted Dog, finding herself in Direct Eye Contact, uses lovely language skills. She uses it all: ears back, tail down, entire body slightly lowered, lips long and for good measure tosses in a Paw Lift. "Thank You for being in charge."

Side-kick (the dog right behind Bandanna Dog) looks on neutrally. Border Collie, far left, barks at everyone. No surprises there!

#26: Role Change! Dark Herding Dog engages the group by drawing near, then turning and running away in invitation. Spotted Dog gladly uses this as an opportunity to escape the closeness and intensity. Mostly White Sheltie falls in as well.

Bandanna Dog, Side-kick and Border Collie remain on the hill. If you go through this Photo Essay several times, you will see that this other Sheltie is like the classic Side-kick. Whatever Bandanna Dog is doing, this Sheltie just falls in with it.

It could be that Bandanna Dog is telling the other two to remain where they are. Because Border Collie was barking, Bandanna Dog is looking at him. Border Collie still uses great communication, he stops barking and uses an open mouth and long lips, along with a down tail to deal with Bandanna Dog's direct look, and up tail and ears.

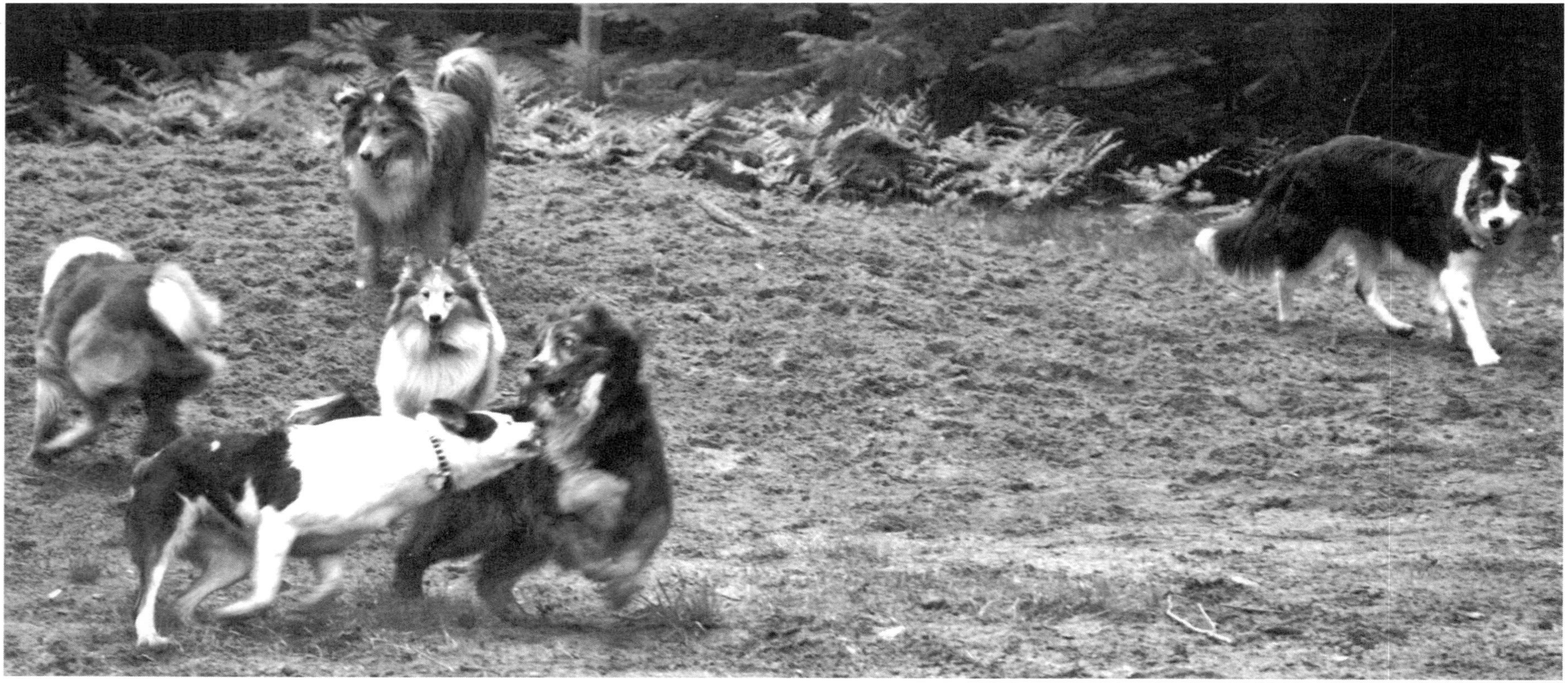

#27: Spotted Dog "heads" and moves in for the kill bite. The aim is low and for the neck area. Border Collie, to the far right, circles around the group; he is a good, sensitive herding dog!

Mostly White Sheltie is coming in from the rear.

Bandanna Dog and Side-kick are playing a game amongst themselves and are not involved with the "kill" at this time.

Bandanna Dog, who likes to control the action, is not controlling the main action at this juncture. She made her point of who is in charge and reminded the other dogs to "Play" at a certain specified and peaceful intensity. Dark Herding Dog and Spotted Dog are the main players at this moment.

Bandanna Dog is content to keep the attention of Side-kick, preventing him from participating in the main action. She is doing this in an appropriate and playful way, by saying: "You and I will play a game ourselves."

#28: As the group comes back around, Bandanna Dog Targets Mostly White Sheltie again. Bandanna Dog controls the movement of Mostly White Sheltie by orienting toward her, and lowering her head. Mostly White Sheltie happily complies, allowing Bandanna Dog to "move her feet" acquiescing to Bandanna Dog's status.

Spotted Dog, Border Collie, Dark Herding Dog and Side-kick all respond by forming a rough circle around Mostly White Sheltie. It is clear whose opinion is important.

#29: This is so interesting! The dogs keep a loose circle around Mostly White Sheltie, with Border Collie heading. She focuses on the dog in the middle and barks to "hold" her. Bandanna Dog Sniffs as a Calming Signal, to soften the intensity of correcting and controlling Mostly White Sheltie.

This group of dogs has excellent language skills. As you look through this photo essay, just think of how many times the dogs have taken a Break. As the intensity reaches a certain pitch, the dogs temporarily slow down the action or re-negotiate roles. Because of expert use of language, the peace is kept. Play continues instead of erupting into a dog fight.

#30 Above: Dark Herding Dog takes a Break to chew on a stick, Bandanna Dog takes a Break from controlling the action.

Mostly White Sheltie Targets Spotted Dog and attempts to get her to move by coming in closely, barking, "Move, you sheep!" Spotted Dog pretends Mostly White Sheltie does not exist by not only not looking at her, but also by not actively using a Look Away or some other signal of acknowledgement. She holds to a conspicuously neutral demeanor and looks right through Mostly White Sheltie. She can, because Bandanna Dog is nearby. Her presence reminds Mostly White Sheltie to keep intensity levels within the comfort zone requests from the other dog.

#31 Right: Spotted Dog moves away, with an open mouth, half-mast ears, and lowered tail. She is using neutral body language but has a slightly harassed look. See how she is glancing behind her, to keep Mostly White Sheltie in her vision?

Mostly White Sheltie takes advantage of the movement. Dark Herding Dog Targets - staring intensely at Spotted Dog, with lowered head and pricked ears. Dark Herding Dog has a "stalky" look. Mostly White Sheltie has a Driving or "moving the stock" look.

#32: Replace Spotted Dog with a gazelle. It is a very easy visualization! Mostly White Sheltie is Driving from behind, as the intensity picks up. Mostly White Sheltie has a lowered head and Stares at Spotted Dog with pricked ears.

Dark Herding Dog moves into a Header position, to cut the prey off at the pass.

Bandanna Dog leaves the action with a happy look. Tail up, and gently sweeping, not in a "bossy" position, ears pulled close to the head, slightly open mouth and squinty eyes - if I had to guess I would say a person she likes just said her name. She is moving towards some person with an acquiescent, respectful greeting carriage. Since she is so In Charge of the dogs (my interpretation, without actually being there) is that she is moving towards a human, not a dog.

In Summary

In this Photo Essay, we arrive during the middle of a Play Sequence and leave it while the Play continues on without us.

It is fascinating to see the dogs set up a prey/predator scenario and play it out.

What this photo essay shows well is the series of Conflict/Break cycles that are evident and so necessary in peaceful play.

Even in the Break periods you can see that although the intensity is lowered, communication about status, roles and control of the play still goes on. A similar example for humans is if you are working with someone doing an intense task, when you take a coffee break, you still chat about the completion of the task. During a softball game the team breaks. While they are on the break they reaffirm their camaraderie, plan their strategy in preparation to returning to the game and take a breather from the concentration required for the playing of the game.

If you look back through the photographs, you will see a pattern of behaviour with Bandanna Dog. If any dog enters after having left the main group temporarily, she has to "okay" it, or has "something to say about that." She makes sure the returning dog "notices" her. This is "top dog" or controlling behaviour.

The "other sheltie, Side-kick, is usually near Bandanna Dog and if not in the "prey" role, is always behind Bandanna Dog, taking Bandanna Dog's lead.

Mostly White Sheltie can barely play, for reverting back to herding instinct. This same intense herding behaviour holds true for Dark Herding Dog.

Spotted Dog is a middle-ranking, easy going type with the other dogs. She gives the impression of being of sound temperament, comfortable in social situations and a master of language. This dog has a level of self-confidence that is very high. She never gets rattled, never stops playing and participating and never gets irrational when irritated. She would rise high in politics or negotiation of corporate contracts!

Border Collie does not like rough play, intensity or wrestling. Like many herding dogs, he wants everyone standing still in a peaceful group.

All of what was described here was played out by the dogs in probably about ten minutes.

In this photo essay, there is a preponderance of herding dogs. If this had been a group of Labradors playing, the play would have a much different flavour. More wrestling and physical contact would be present for sure. With the herding dogs there is much more Chase and set up of definite prey/predator roles, with the predatory sequence carried out meticulously.

If there were Terriers present, the prey sequence and set ups would be evident, but the intensity would likely get out of control much more quickly, and there would be more physical contact as well. The Chase sequences would end with a more physical contact in the way of bumping. With my own terriers, I also see many more Negotiation and Calming signals used as reminders: "We're playing - remember - we're playing." Terriers need to constantly reassure each other that the play is not going to become murder.

Here, of course, with all I say, there will be exceptions! Always! I am trying to provide you with some generalizations to begin your observations with. Then you can build your language skills from there.

> Training Tip: Play can quickly turn aggressive. A dog choosing another dog as a prey object or as a step on the hierarchy ladder can lead to dire consequences. It is important for us to watch and learn from dog play, so we can decide when it is time for play to end, or if particular dogs do not belong in the group. From careful observation we also can learn when to not interfere needlessly. Initiate Breaks for the dogs if they are not doing it themselves.

For fun, here is the background I received on these dogs after I had this chapter written. I had to satisfy my curiosity about the dogs involved, and I know you will enjoy this information, too. The majority of these dogs were rescued by their owner. All of the dogs in this sequence are house-mates.

Bandanna Dog is a mixed breed, female, spayed, (1997); her real name is Jane Doe.
Side-kick is a Sheltie, male, castrated, (1995); his real name is Snickers.
Spotted Dog is a Border Collie, female, spayed, (2001); her real name is Mecca.
Mostly White Sheltie is a Sheltie, female, spayed, (1996); her real name is Riva.
Dark Herding Dog is a Border Collie mix, female, spayed, (2001); her real name is Zeta.
Border Collie is a Border Collie, male, castrated, (1990); his real name is Tay.

Photo Essay by: Joanne Weber

49
Play Gone Wrong

#49.1: Play Gone Wrong - Photo Essay

The dog on the far left has an intense and predatory look. Her head and neck are extended forward, with her head held in a lowered position, as if she were running low to the ground. Her ears are forward, and she is Targeting. The effort to move through the water distorts this somewhat. Her mouth is closed, showing tension in her jaw. This dog draws my attention to her immediately as I look at this photograph. Keep an eye on her as you peruse this sequence.

The dog in the middle and the Lab on the right are in direct eye contact. The Lab looks mildly concerned. There is a ridge of tension under her eye and just around the top and back of her lips. It is not a lot of tension, and her mouth is still open. Probably she has just noticed the dog in the middle closing in quickly and tightly.

The dog in the middle is showing a piloerector reflex along her back. If you look closely, none of the other dogs have the hair on their back raised like this, so it isn't an effect of the water on the hair - it is the extreme excitement of the moment. This dog may be uncertain, or she may be adrenalized from the Play, which is beginning to get out of hand.

Physical contact has been made. At least it is not head-on, but side-on, which is significantly less threatening. The dog in the middle has an even more pronounced piloerector reflex on her back near her tail, as she closes into the other dog's space. The Border Collie-mix, on the left, is still closing in pursuit. Her intensity level looks about the same. Even though her body doesn't have the same extreme forward orientation her head is still lowered, and her mouth is still closed in concentration.

The Lab still has her eyes directly on the light-colored dog, looking at the incoming action. She is rising up out of the water to get ABOVE the light-colored dog. If you look closely you can see how wide her eyes are opened.

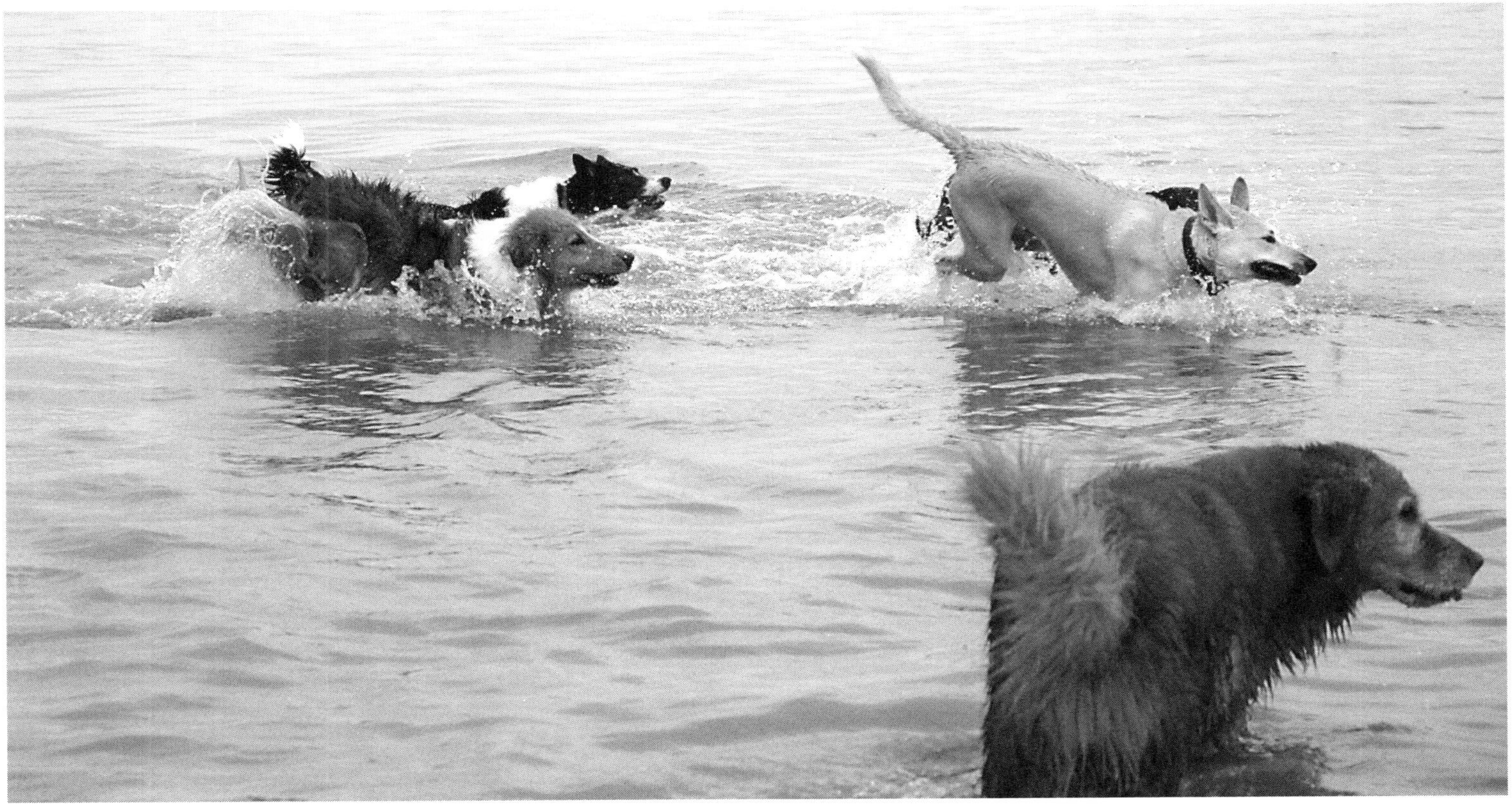

Two new players who have been nearby enter the picture. The Sheltie is deliberately moving into the action. He is in pursuit.

All of the other dogs have now moved into the proximity of the Golden. The Golden is doing a Look Away and a Lip Lick. He senses the building intensity of the dogs moving into his space.

The Border Collie-mix is maintaining a stable distance. Her intensity is starting to fade. She now has her mouth open. Instead of closing in pursuit, as she could have by now, she is hanging back.

The light-colored dog is now moving away from the Lab slightly. Her nose is now pointing straight ahead, which means she is not looking directly at the Lab anymore. Something in the Lab's demeanor is moving her away from him. Even though her nose is not oriented at the Lab, she is looking at him with her eyes.

We cannot see the Lab's face, but we can see he is crouching down and has lowered his body.

Now we see why the Lab lowered his body: he was gathering himself to pounce at the light-colored dog. The Lab opens his mouth and moves toward the light-colored dog who has been designated as "prey." It could be to seize the other dog in a Grab bite, or it could be a correction bite. In a Correction Bite, one dog hits the offender with an open mouth without closing the mouth down. The intent is to correct. It can be quite painful. Those teeth are hard!

The Sheltie is building in intensity as he gets closer to the "prey."

The Border Collie-mix, who looked so predatory at the beginning, has pretty much decided to drop out of the action. The Golden lowers his head and tail and remains still as the dogs move ever closer to him.

The Lab crouches down again. The light-colored dog has an even more pronounced piloerector reflex; her hair is up from the backs of her ears down to her tail. She still has her tail over her back in excitement. She is getting more than she bargained for: the Sheltie is closing in from the rear and the Lab is commanding her attention from the front.

The Border Collie-mix continues to ramp down. Her ears are drawn back. She is not looking toward the other dogs nor Targeting them any more.

This might have been just a correction until the Sheltie showed up. Then it quickly turned into a predation sequence. It may be a case of socially inept dogs interacting, not giving each other any signals that this is, indeed, "just play." Or, it could be a case of one dog giving the proper signals, but the other dog not receiving them. Without frequent use of such signals, play easily deteriorates into a fight or predatory behaviour.

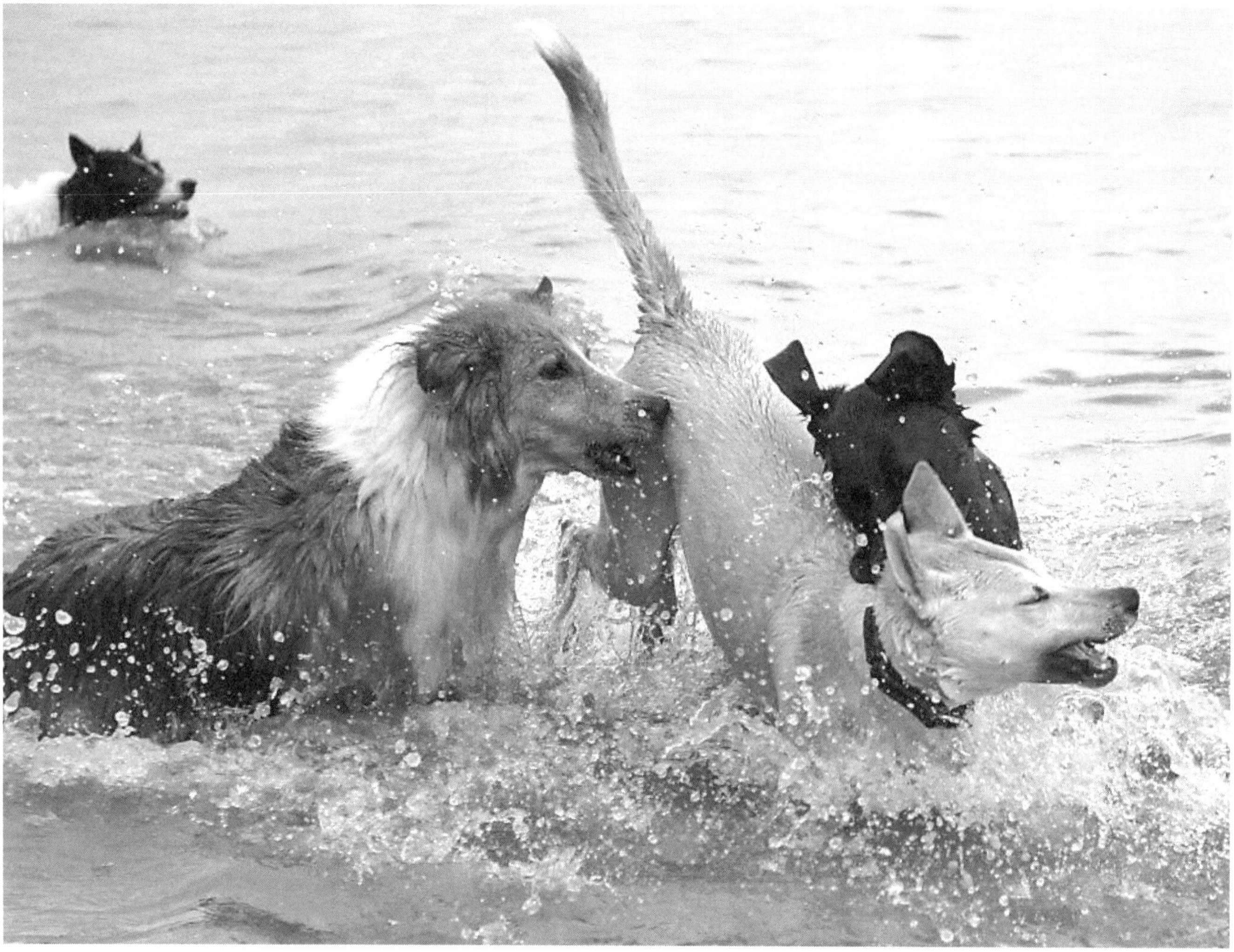

The Border Collie-mix is far back and is deliberately not even looking at these dogs now in order to stay out of the fray.

This is a fantastic example of predatory behaviour. This has gone from "Play" via a rapid rise in intensity to become something other than Play: Predation.

The Lab is grasping the neck/shoulder area. She is the "front man." The Sheltie is getting ready to do a Grab Bite on the rear of the "prey." This is typical of hunting canines. There will be a dog (wolf) on the front to do a Grab-Hold Bite on the neck, often the underside of the neck, to suffocate. There will be a second teammate to hold the rear legs or hamstring the prey. If there are others, the remaining animals will do belly-area bites to eviscerate the prey.

The "prey" dog, who started this, is now looking just to get out of her pickle.

Photo Essay by Joanne Weber.

The prey sequence continues. The Lab is crouching down for another neck bite while the Sheltie continues his attack on the rear.

The person in the background steps in and interrupts the dogs at this point. No injuries were sustained.

This shows so clearly how play can turn into something else entirely. The intensity gets a little too high; one animal invades another's space at this pitch of intensity. Sometimes one animal Targets another and begins to treat the "victim" as prey. This draws others into the hunt, as happened here.

Sometimes high adrenaline levels cause dogs to "unload" on each other. These same adrenaline levels can also account for playing too roughly. Reactive dogs cause dog fights.

Alternatively, when a Chase game is initiated, the chasers may become too intense. They do not use enough Calming Signals to reassure. This frightens the dog who has taken the "prey" role. As the "prey" dog becomes frightened, he begins to act like prey: looking back, tucking the tail, sometimes vocalizing. This can further incite the "predator" dogs, who begin to truly victimize the frightened dog. If the "prey" dog cannot hold it together and effectively stop the "predators" by using calm behaviour and Calming Signals, the play can get right out of hand.

> *Training Tip*: Interrupt play frequently. This serves two functions: First, it teaches your dog to come away from other dogs (always a major distraction). This is not just good obedience; it shows your dog that you have authority and that "Mom is watching." Second, interrupting the play can help to keep dog adrenaline levels down, thereby preventing dogs from becoming reactive. Reactive dogs "blow by" other dogs' signals. Play can easily segue into predation if the dogs become over-excited and ignore the "just playing" signals.
>
> In this instance, had the play been interrupted early on, chances are it would not have escalated into this reactive behaviour.

Section 7: It's the Quiz Section!

How Good Are You?

This section is designed to help you practice your new skills.

Before you begin, prepare. It might help you to gather some materials to take notes with. There is a chart at the end of this introduction that can guide you in your observations and notetaking.

The answers are in another section. Try not to peek until you have really worked at an interpretation. If you get stuck fast, go back through the other sections of this book and see if you can find a photo that reminds you of the one you are trying to interpret. Note that many of these photographs are not the *exact* situations shown earlier in this book. Some of these Quiz photos require a good deal of piecing together of things you learned from this book.

Take a couple of days for each photograph if you like. Look at it and think about it. If your experience with dogs is limited it will take you longer. Don't despair! Don't give up!

Try to think like a dog might. Simplify your thoughts. Think about the dog's sensory system, which is so very different from our own. What might be important to a dog, first and foremost? Safety is the answer. *Am I Safe In This Environment and In This Social Situation.* What next? *What Strategy Will Work Best So I Can Have The Most Resources.* Then maybe: *Is It Prey?*

As a reminder before you begin using the Quiz pages, I offer the following thoughts. How any dog might respond in different contexts depends so much on the inherited and experienced predatory "part" of that dog.

- How much prey behaviour is hard-wired in the dog and how that predation presents itself.
- The quantity and quality of the social interactions the dog has been able to experience.
- The kind of mother the dog had as a first role model.
- What kinds of experiences has the dog had?
- How much caution is hard-wired into the dog, or how much boldness?

Some breeds are so hard-wired that they respond in a very set manner - my Border Collie, for instance, filters EVERYTHING through sheep. Long before I began herding with her she did this. Tennis balls were sheep, other dogs were sheep (much to their annoyance!). When we ran agility, sometimes the obstacles became sheep, as she madly circled the A-frame I had directed her to climb. I was often a sheep. Rylie uses a lot of stalking and Eyeing behaviours when she communicates.

My German Shepherd bitch is very predatory. When she was younger I had to manage her very closely when she was watching other dogs go after a prey object, like a frisbee or ball. She was easily frustrated about being restrained. If she watched other dogs running in a fenced area, she was very prone to fence-fighting. Maeve, in those days, didn't use Negotiation language - she was very Reactive. She Targeted other dogs as prey if they were moving in a certain way. As she has recovered and developed her Native Language skills, she now uses endless Negotiation Signals and Calming Signals.

The Fox Terriers have a "hair-trigger." ANY kind of excitement may quickly cross over into predatory behaviour or frustration that is re-directed onto another dog. Because they have such hair-triggers, the terriers remind me a lot of watching captive wolves. They use lots of Calming signals and Negotiate the slightest of personal space infringements. If there is a status issue, the signals are very truncated.

What I am trying to say, in my circuitous manner, is that the breed or personality type of the dog will influence not just her own behaviour, but will also influence, in a subtle way, how that dog uses signals. It will also influence the types of signals that the individual dog uses most frequently.

Yet another component, in addition to breed-typical preferences, dogs are influenced greatly by the other dogs they have extensive contact with. Just as people pick up phrases and slang, even accents and dialect from each other, so dogs are affected by the crowd they "hang" with.

I could go on here forever, but you get the point. Even though individual dogs vary in how predatory (or anxious, or aggressive, or friendly...) they are, Native Language is a constant. All dogs display approximately the same sets of "words" as expressed by body language. Individual dogs may certainly have different "dialects." Some dogs are very wordy and expressive, and others could be poker players. If you are an excellent observer and good student, and you let the dogs be the teachers, you will learn fast.

On to the quiz! Try to interpret what the dog is "saying" with his or her body language. If there is more than one dog in the photograph, determine what each is saying. Have fun with this!!!

Line Drawings by Brenda Aloff.

Table 1: Worksheet for Observing and Interpreting Canine Signals

	NOTES
EYES: Shape Orientation (Looking At or Away)	
Pupil Dilation	
EARS: Shape Orientation Tension level	
Orientation of Nose	
Facial Tension	
MOUTH: length of lips shape of lips tongue	
Body Tension	
Tail	
Body Orientation	
Silhouette of the dog	
LEGS: Braced Relaxed	
Behaviour of the "other" dog, if applicable	

50
QUIZ

Background: The other dogs in class know each other because they come to class each week. The dogs are working in a circle around Larko, the Malinois, who is in the middle with me holding his leash. He is the "new kid" on the block.

Photo #3

Photo #4

See also 5-A, 5-B, 5-C, and 5-D which are close-ups of this photograph, and the tip after 5-D.

Photo #5-A

Photo #5-B

Observation Tip: If more than one dog is interacting, closely watch the behaviour of all of them. If one dog is easy to read, sometimes that dog can help you to interpret the situation.

Photo #5-C

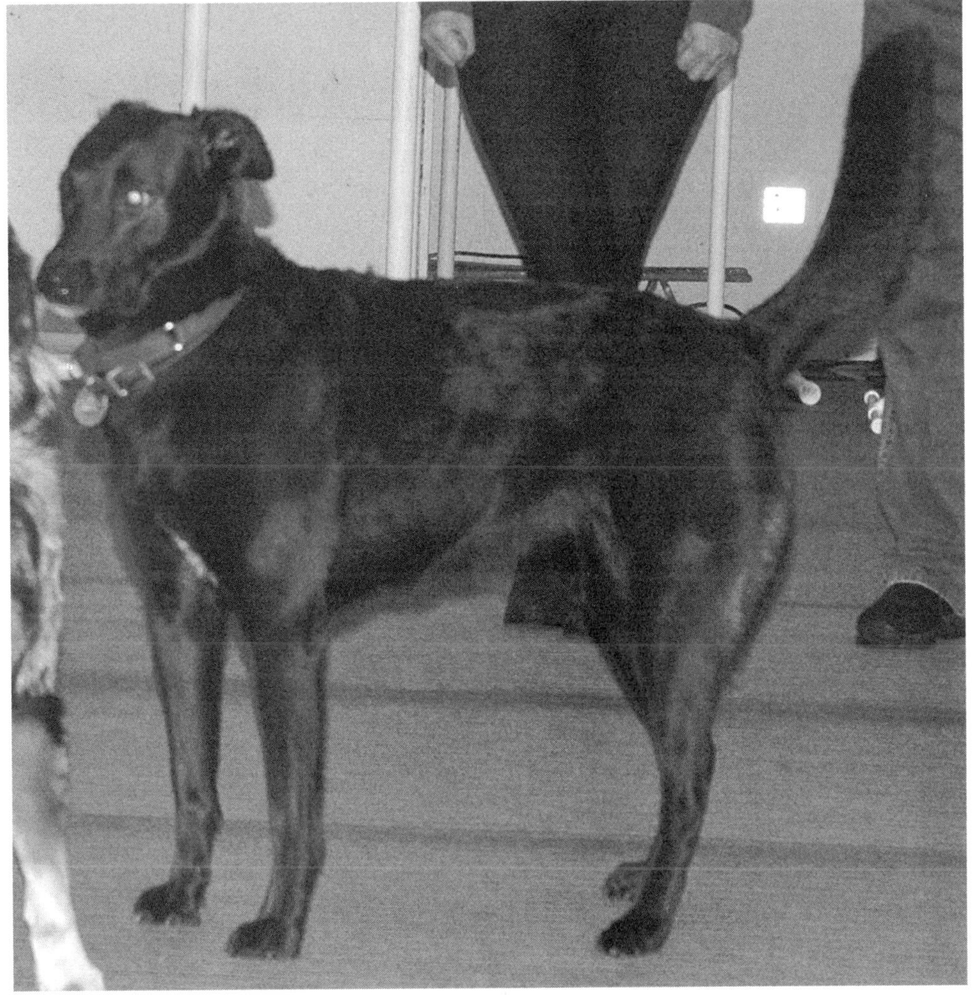

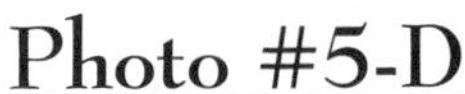

Photo #5-D

Photo #6

Photo #7

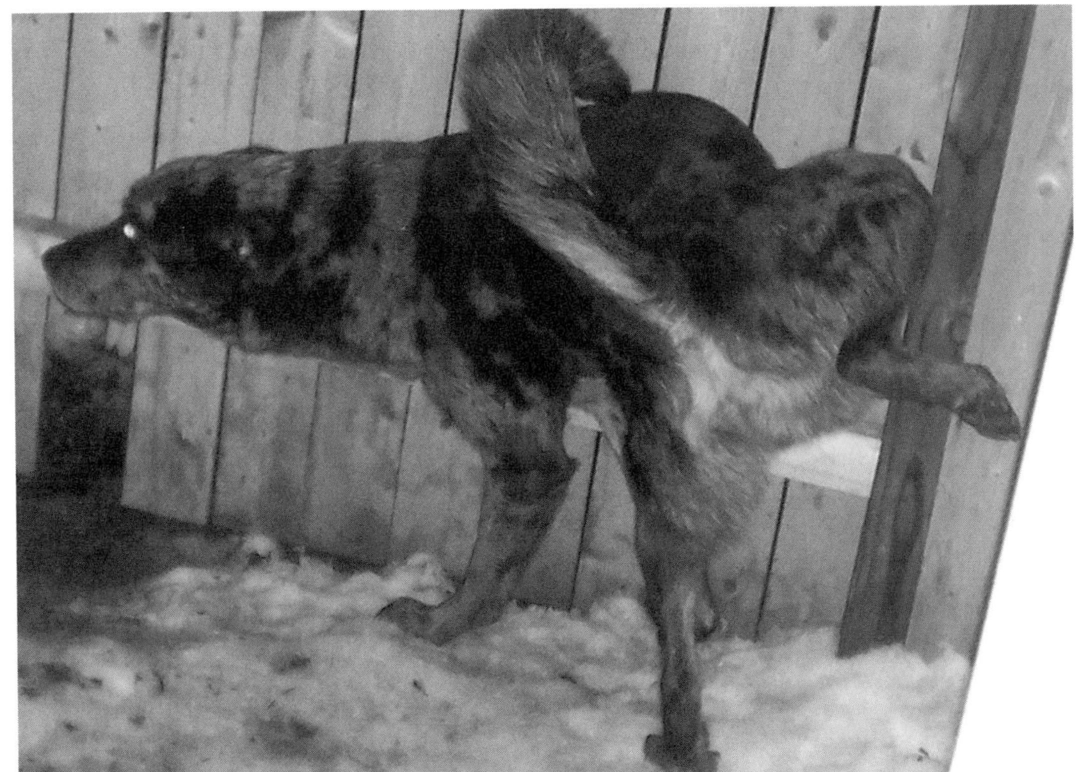

Photo #8

Photo #9

Photo Essay #10

Photo #10-1

Photo #10-2

Photo #10-3

Photo #11

Photo #12

Photo #13

Photo #14

Photo Essay - Photo #15-1

Photo #15-2

Photo #16

Photo #17

Note: Look Carefully! There are two dogs on the left, an Aussie in the foreground and a Coton in the background.

Photo #19

Photo #20

Photo #21

Photo #22

Photo #23

Photo Essay

Photo #24-1

Photo #24-2

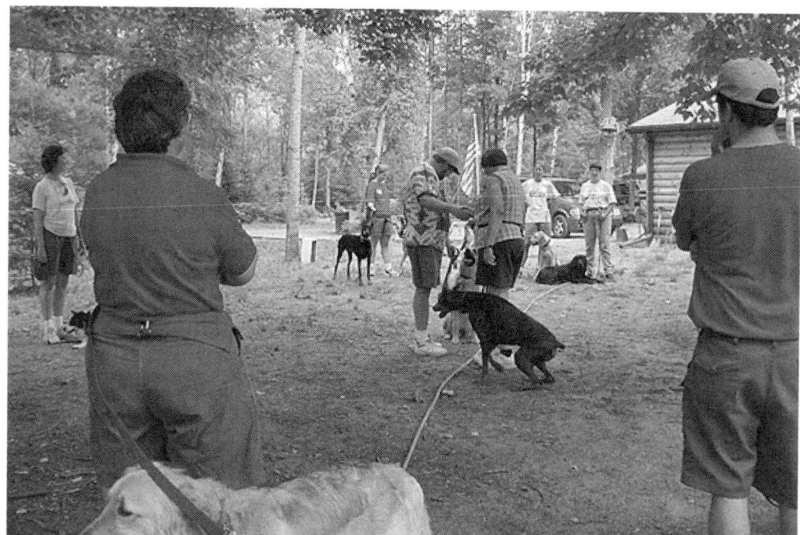

Same as Photo #24-2,

this photo just shows a view that includes more of the background and shows more of the surrounding dogs.

Photo #25

Photo Credits:
Photo #1, #2, #3, #4 & #5: Dave Schrader;Photo #6: Cherish DeWitt;Photo #7: Joanne Weber;Photo #8: Rachel Plotinski; Photo #9: Felicia Banys;Photo Essay #10: Cherish DeWitt;Photo #11: Rachel Plotinski;Photo #12: Joanne Weber; Photo #13: Sam Zieggenmeyer;Photo #14, Photo Essay #15 & #16: Joanne Weber;Photo #17: Sam Zieggenmeyer; Photo #18: Cheryl Ertelt;Photo #19, #20, #21, #22, #23, Photo Essay #24 & #25: Joanne Weber.

51 QUIZ ANSWERS

Photo #1: Two Neutral Dogs

How can you tell?

- half mast tails and ears
- dogs are not moving towards each other, as in lunging and violating personal space. Both dogs keep the leash loose.
- the Malinois is turned sideways to the Wire-haired Pointing Griffon
- lack of body tension
- dogs are Mirroring, (half-mast ears and tails) which indicates that nobody is seeking status, at least at this time. This also says, "I want to interact with you in a friendly or at least neutral way."

Photo #2: Body Inventory (Genital Check)

Background: The other dogs in class know each other because they come to class each week. The dogs are working in a circle around Larko, the Malinois, who is in the middle, with me holding his leash. He is the "new kid" on the block.

As the other dogs who come to class every week work around the outside of a circle with Larko in the middle, he performs a Body Inventory.

This is typically seen in the form of a Genital Check. Here, it is modified to a tail/anal gland check.

Body Inventories can be either Displacement Signals and/or a Calming Signals.

A similar signal is often seen in cats: the "When in doubt, wash," thing.

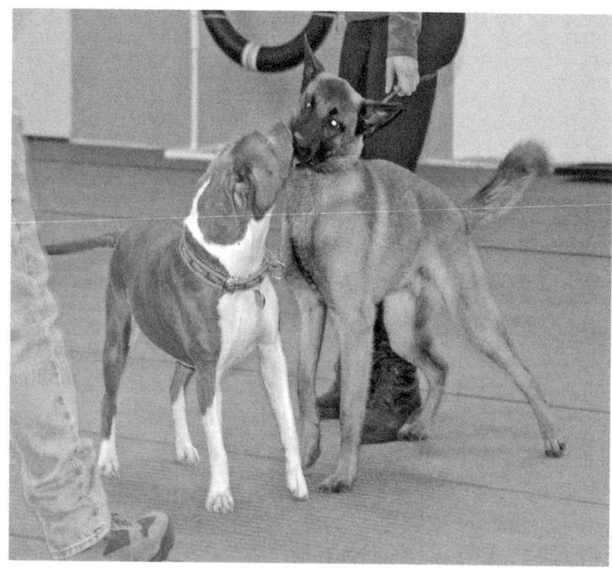

Photo #3: Friendly Greeting.
How can you tell?

- half mast ears
- half mast tail
- Mirroring - see the Paw Lift by both dogs.
- Emma is Puppy Licking.
- Even though both dogs are close together, see how they are orienting their bodies slightly away from each others personal space.
- The dogs are not approaching head-on: Emma, the AmStaff, is sideways to the Malinois.
- You can see I am restraining Larko slightly with the leash as he pulls towards Emma. This does give the impression he is standing up on tip-toe a bit, but the overall impression is still friendly. Emma is responding to his more upright posture by displaying a little bit of acquiescence. This may also be the response because Larko is a little bit excited by the greeting - see the pupil dilation?

Photo #4: Friendly Play-Fighting

How can you tell?

- not approaching head-on: the Malinois is sideways to the Aussie
- The Aussie's body language is oriented backwards, but not in an extreme way. If the dogs were really fighting, the Aussie would either be pulling away more to escape or she would be pushing harder and forward into the Malinois to counter-attack.
- Even though she has all her teeth out, there is a distinct lack of facial tension - there are no ridges around the lips or eyes.
- Both dogs have ears at half mast.
- The Malinois' tail is at half mast. (Cannot see the Aussie's tail. I dislike reading the body language on dogs with no tails....)
- The Malinois and the Aussie lack body tension. If you cut off the picture at the shoulder of the Malinois, he is very relaxed.
- The Aussie is lifting a paw.
-
- This is typical Play Biting of each other's necks and heads. Dogs love to play "Mouth Jive" games and will do so for long periods of time.

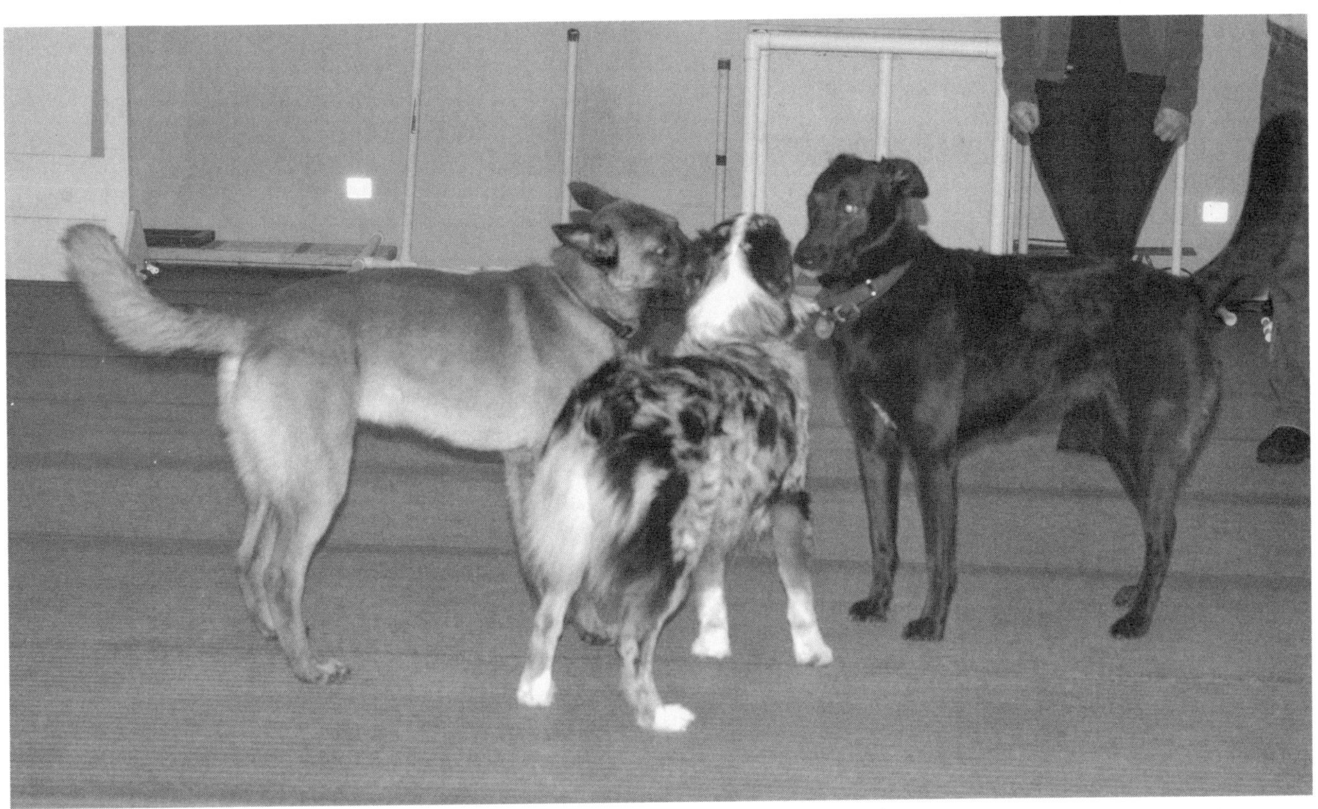

Photo #5: Greeting Behaviour

This Greeting has some tension in it.

Note, however, that not all the dogs are equally tense.

You can tell a lot just from the overall body postures:

- Zoey, the Aussie, is the most confident. She gives the impression of being fully "in her own space." Her body is oriented the most forward, and her feet are firmly planted. Her back is flat, not rounded like that of the other two dogs. Nicely, she is orienting her head away from both of the other dogs - a Negotiation Signal.
- Amanda, the Lab mix on the right, is the most anxious. Her body is oriented farthest backwards and her topline is the most rounded. Her feet seem awkwardly and tentatively placed, as if at odds with her body. Her tail is way up.

See also Photo #5-A, #5-B, #5-C & #5-D.

Photo #5-A:

Their faces tell interesting stories, too.
Larko, the Malinois, looks relaxed in body, but his face belies this, just a bit. His ears are drawn back rigidly, not at a relaxed half-mast. There is quite a bit of white showing around his eyes, and his expression is somewhat intense, with ridges below the eyes. He is pointedly sticking his nose into the middle of things, orienting his face fully forward towards Amanda. He acts as if he wants to be a big adult male, but doesn't quite know what he is doing. (Larko is the youngest dog at 6 months old and the only male in the group.)

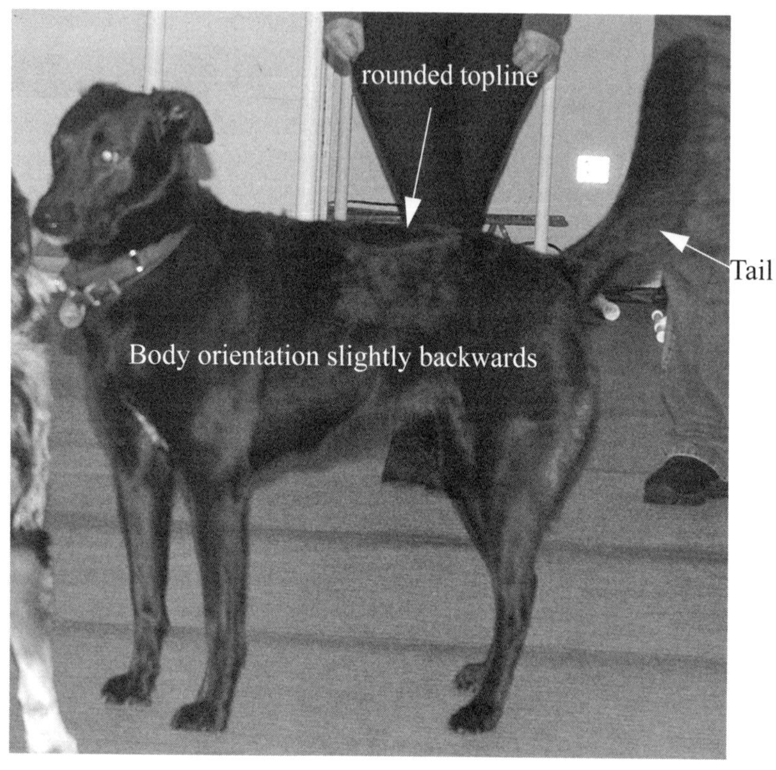

Photo #5-D

Look at Amanda's Silhouette and Body orientation. It provides more detail and validates the facial expression, which just adds more emphasis.

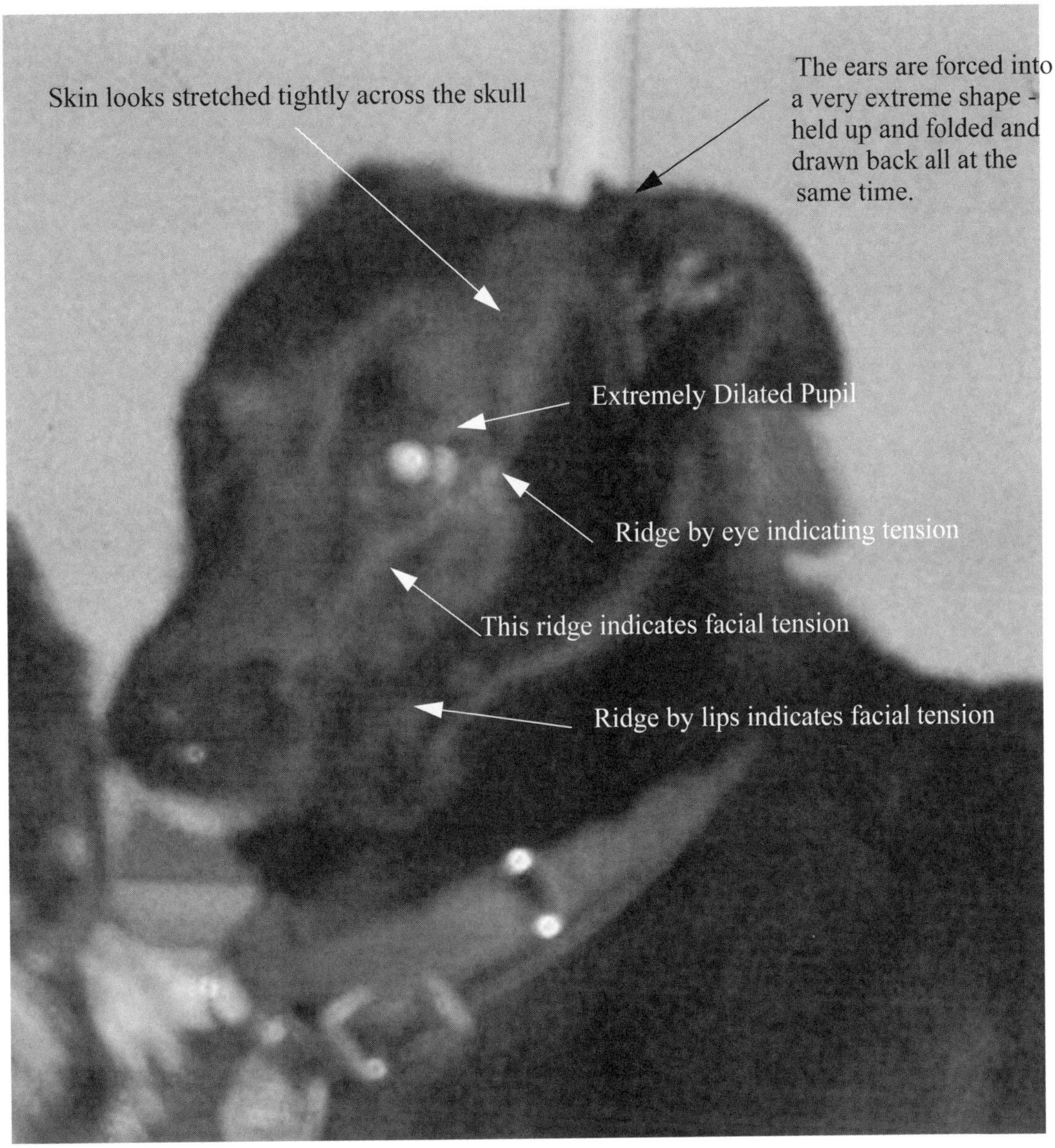

Photo #5-C:

Amanda's face is very tense.

- Her pupils are dilated and the whites of her eyes are showing.
- Her ears are drawn way up and back, so much so that her whole face is pulled taut.
- She is pulling her head slightly away from the other two, either as a bit of a Look Away, or as a physical avoidance maneuver. "You have both encroached on me and I am unsure about this!" It is significant that she is looking at the dogs, but her nose is pointed a different direction than her eyes.
- Her mouth is closed and tight.

What strikes you about this dogs face is how the skin looks as if it is very tightly stretched across the skull. Her ears are held in a very extreme position and they look "forced," as if they are being held in place very tightly.

It is hard to see the ridge around the mouth as I had to enlarge this photo and so there is some loss of quality, but I have pointed out where it is for you.

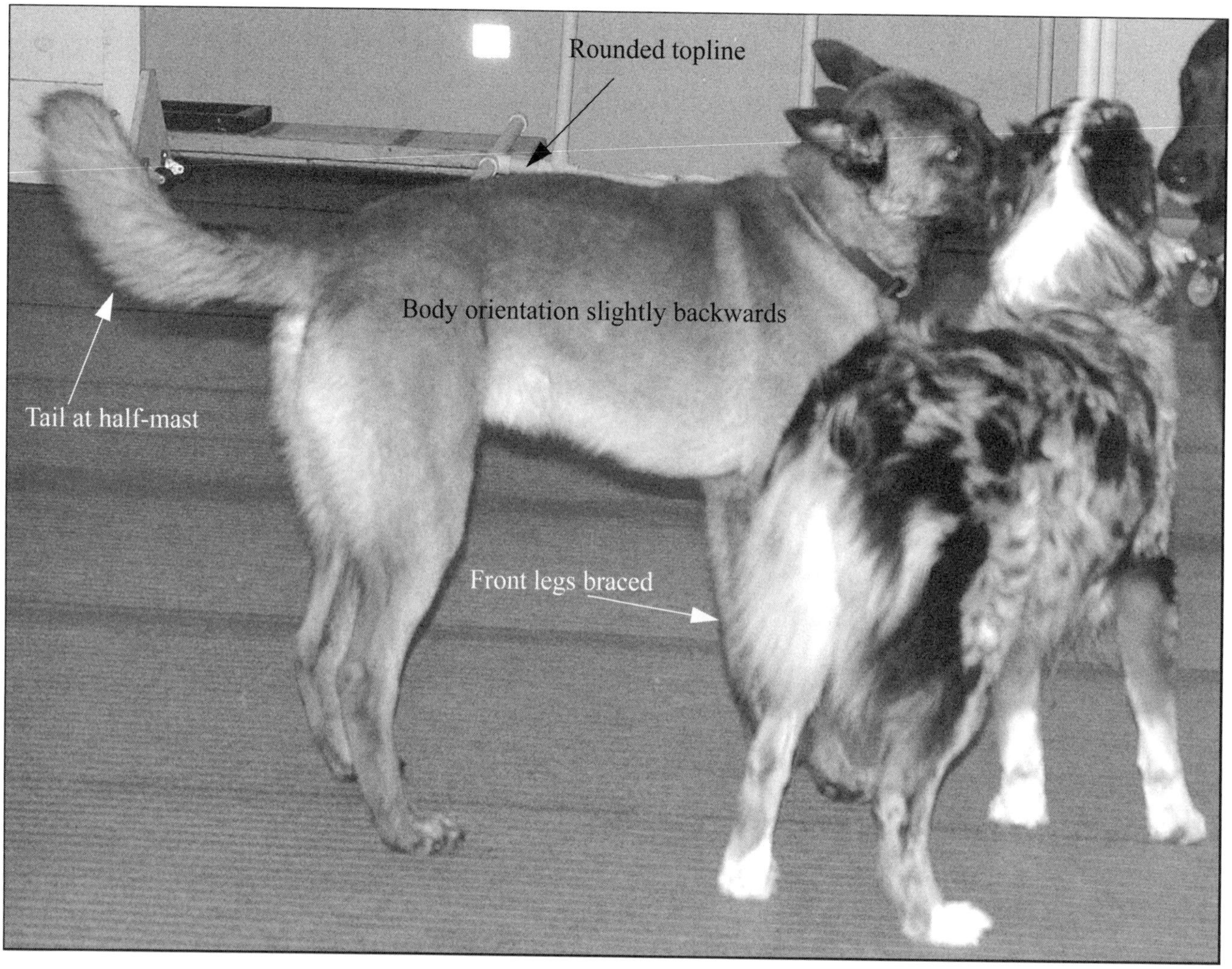

Photo #5-B:

Note the Silhouette of Larko, as noted in the photo above.

Despite some tension, there is no overt aggression here. However, if it were me, I would step in at this point with a brief interruption (Splitting Up), just in case one of the dogs decided the tension should be resolved in an unfriendly manner, and to prevent any of the dogs from becoming reactive.

Photo #6 - Greeting Stretch

This is not a Play Bow. You can tell because of the lack of intensity. This dog is greeting someone (dog, human, or other animal) in a friendly manner. This greeting is generally used only with known companions.

Photo #7 - Targeting

The dog on the right has Alerted and is Targeting on the prey object: the ball. (Or, perhaps, the other dog!) What we can see, is that the dog on the right is oriented and moving towards the other dog and the ball.

The overall Silhouette of the dog on the right says prey drive - attenuated, because the tail is up. When a dog shifts into high prey drive, he will lower his body and tail. He will also close his mouth until he is ready to bite. Thus, this particular Moment of Decision has a playful or non-confrontational feel to it because of the relatively low intensity of the dog on the right. The dog to the right has lowered her head, but she is otherwise keeping things light and playful. Her tail is up and her mouth is open. She has not Fixed On the toy or the other dog. In fact, she is not moving in the slow, deliberate pace of the serious Stalk. Her ears, although they are up, have a bit of floppiness to them which tells you that she is not so intense that she has become rigid. She has an opportunistic look, rather than a hard, serious, "I will fight to the death" attitude.

The dog on the left senses the intent of the Targeting dog on the right. The person is holding a ball - prey! The dog next to the person has a lot to think about. Her handler is in possession of a valued toy, and here is an intruder who has designs on the "prey." The dog to the left acknowledges the approaching dog; she uses a Calming Signal, a Lip Lick. The Lip Lick is combined with a Look Away from the approaching dog, but is also a Look At the ball. Regardless, whether you count this as a Lip Lick or a Tongue Flick, the signal indicates that this dog feels the invasion of personal space.

The dog to the left keeps her tail is up in a confident and happy way. Her ears, although up like those of the other dog, have a floppiness that shows she is not feeling personally threatened. She is only worried about who will get the ball. Notice that her Tongue Flick is aimed at the ball, not at the other dog. If she were only using a Lip Lick and Look Away, she would not be so deliberately focused on that ball, and her chin would be down. Were she worried about her safety, this would be indicated by a more defensive pose: body tension and rigidity. This dog on the left, then, is simultaneously using a Lip Lick as a Calming Signal and a Tongue Flick to show what she is most concerned about. Imagine that you have a twenty word vocabulary. You have to use these twenty words to communicate everything. Each word will have multiple meanings which will be determined by how you combine the words and by context.

The outcome will be determined by the way the dog on the left handles the intrusion and whether he decides to guard his owner or the ball. Also a factor is how the approaching dog acknowledges the signals given by the other dog.

I wish I knew exactly what happened next! The suspense is killing me! I found this photograph fascinating. A situation like this - an intruder coming in to take another's prey - is potentially volatile, but it is apparent that it will not explode here because the dogs are using such clear langauge and demonstating their awareness of each other. Being aware of another dog's personal space and displaying that awareness is a basic element of savvy dog language. Both dogs are keeping lines of communication open.

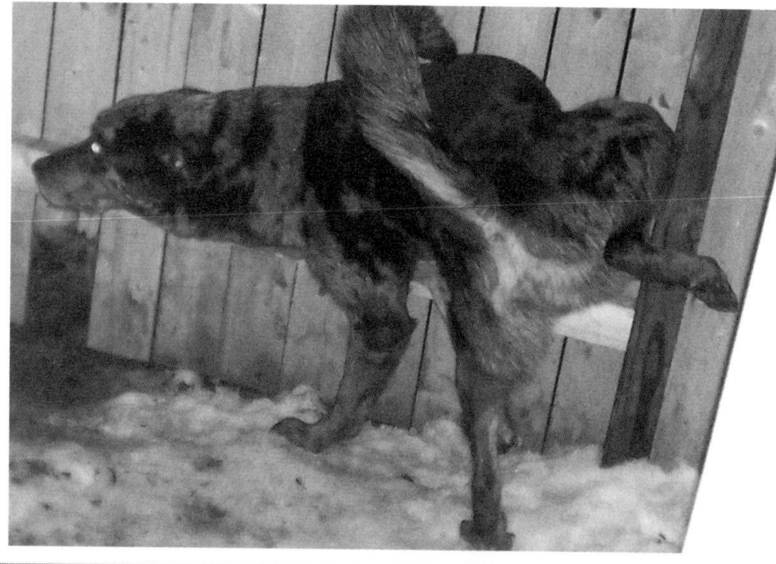

Photo #8: Urinary Marking

This dog is lifting his leg, probably as a territorial marking gesture.

Urinary marking can also be a Displacement behaviour.

It can be the start of a dog fight if two boys are staring at each other and then marking deliberately over each other's urine.

It can also be just plain, old peeing.

Dogs mark with urine and feces to keep track of each other and to send messages. All dogs love to read "Pee Mail."

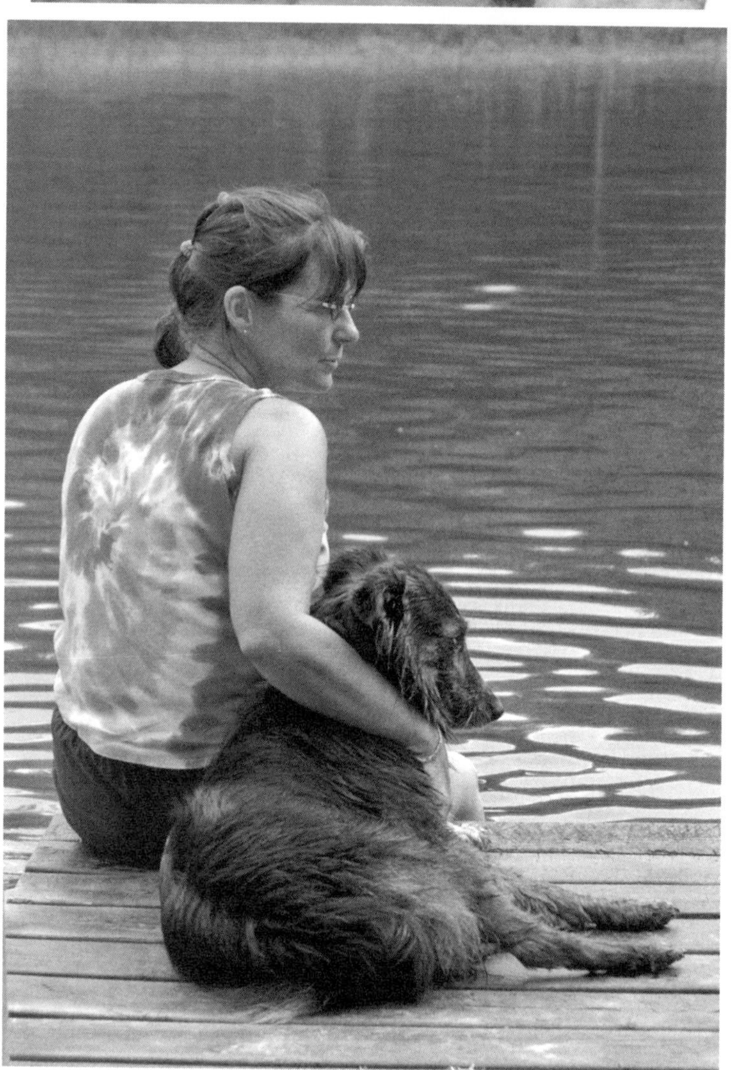

Photo #9: Mirroring Companionship

This photograph embodies what we all are looking for when we got a dog in the first place.

The obvious comfort that human and dog have with each other is the kind of communication that transcends species.

Dog and human are not just snuggled up, they are mirroring each other's position and body language. Fascinating!

Mirroring is tremendously significant because when it occurs, it means that the two parties (whether they be animal, human or one of each species), are in accord with each other. Communication is taking place on a deep and subliminal level. Sometimes Mirroring is meant to make another feel more comfortable, more understood.

Photo Essay #10

Photos #10-1, 10-2 & 10-3: Correction & Apology

Photo #10.1: Most notable about this sequence is that the puppy is in retreat, while, at the same time, in the first two photos at least, the older dog has a playful appearance.

Just before this sequence, the older dog had administered a Correction to the puppy for some infraction. This is a very typical, normal, uninterfered-with-by-humans dog-to-puppy Correction Sequence.

Don't assume that retreat always signifies panic. This pup is displaying the lowered head and rounded topline of a chastised dog. She also has her tail tucked between her legs. These can also signal appeasement behaviour, which usually does have a tinge of anxiety to it. Notice, in the first photo, particularly, how the puppy's back legs are spraddled, or carried far apart, as she slinks away from the older dog. This "slinking" is indicative of her moving in a slow, controlled manner - it is deliberate signalling. If the pup were panicked, she would be scrambling away in a frantic and speedy manner.

The pseudo-playful manner of the older dog tempers the correction to suit the age of the younger pup.

In Photo #10.2, the puppy has rounded her back further and keeps her tail tucked as she continues to move away.

The older dog decides to make sure the pup has been impressed by this interaction. To ensure understanding and Respect, the older dog follows the pup, not rushing into body space, but deliberately following until the puppy stops retreating.

In Photo #10.3, the puppy ceases her retreat, gives the older dog two eyes (undivided attention), and apologizes for the infraction. The older dog's point has been made: "Do you understand you were disrespectful? Good."

The puppy's posture here is typical of apology. Her back is slightly rounded, her tail still tucked. She is using two "big" signals: a Sitting position and a Paw Lift. She is also squinting her eyes and has drawn her ears back.

The specific way she lifts her paw is significant. If a dog is just curious or is waiting for you to toss a frisbee, you tend to see a low, "hanging" Paw Lift. In cases of appeasement or supplication, however, the paw will often be lifted higher, in this forced manner. This puppy's paw is not "hanging," but is tensely held up high and back.

The older dog acknowledges the pup's apology. The older dog's lips are further drawn back (compare with the first photo) and her body is now oriented backwards, not forwards into the pup's space. She has drawn her ears back and is also squinting her eyes: she is Mirroring the puppy. She has rounded her back and is looking quite a bit more friendly.

At this point the older dog would do one of two things: initiate play with the puppy, or just walk away, leaving the puppy both relieved and wiser about social propriety.

Photo #11: Personal Space

I love this photo - it is a hoot! The black dog is moving into the personal space of Bailey, the dog on the left. It matters a lot more to the black dog than to Bailey! The black dog is asking permission, using Negotiation Signals: mouth open, ears half-mast - but is orienting toward Bailey with wide-open eyes. "I am coming through!" Even though the eyes are wide open and looking at Bailey, the black dog manages to deliberately avoid direct eye contact. Smart! Savvy!

Bailey says, "Fine, with me. Whatever." See his relaxed body posture, open mouth, his really relaxed and loosely hanging lips? His eyes are squinty. Bailey is politely Looking Away to ensure there is no conflict.

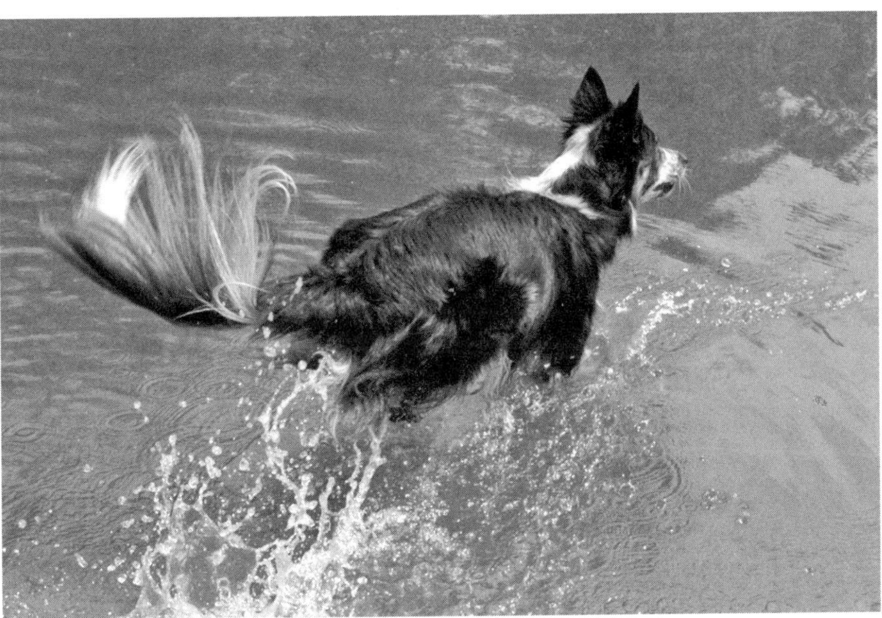

Photo #12: Alert & Pursuit

Past the Alert, past the Targeting stage, this dog has entered the Pursuit stage. The mouth is held *almost* closed in concentration, the tail is being used as a rudder, and the dog is moving toward a prey object.

When a dog first Alerts, the mouth may still be open. As the dog becomes more intense, the mouth will begin to close. By the time the dog begins the chase, the mouth will be mostly closed, although as the chase heats up the dog may pant again to cool off his body. Then as the dog gets close to the prey, the mouth will close again, in concentration, just prior to the Grab Bite.

Photo #13: Greeting

The Wire Fox Terrier is moving forward into the space of the Corgi in a very bold way. This is not unfriendly, but it is making the Corgi uneasy. The Corgi Sniffs, a Calming Signal. She is wearing drawn-back ears, in peace. Her topline is slightly rounded even though her rear legs are out behind her - this is evidence that her tail is tucked (remember to look at the topline to determine tail carriage with short-tailed breeds).

There is an element of Warning to the Corgi's expression. Even though she is Sniffing as a stress or a Calming signal, the Warning is apparent in the direction of her eyes. She is not using a Look Away but is, instead, directing her gaze straight ahead. This means that she is keeping the Wire well within her vision. There is also a horizontal ridge of tension just behind her eye.

The Wire is not returning a big Negotiation signal. He is leaning forward with ears and tail up, a typical pose for Terriers. He *is* offering a relaxed facial expression and squinting his eyes. These are definitely Negotiation or friendly signals, but they are very subtle. I get the feeling that this Corgi is anxious about the boldness of his approach and is looking for something more.

This is a good example of a personality clash. His style of approach is Very Terrier and hers is Very Not. The subtle signals given by some dogs are not Big Enough to suit the needs of others.

Photo #14: Caution

The Border Collie is approaching the water with a backwards orientation, down tail and braced front legs.

Photo Essay #15

Photo #15-1& 15-2: Alert & Prey Bow

Background: This dog is camping. This is his campsite. He is tied out.

Here is an Alert followed by a Prey Bow.

In this context, you can read this as: "Keep Away From My Territorial Boundaries!"

In the first picture, the Alert and Target, note the braced legs, direct stare, forced-up tail, closed mouth, and the Stillness.

In the second picture, the Prey Bow, note the gathered-under rear readying the dog to pounce forward, the tension in the set of the ears, and the forced-up tail.

Dogs, having only so many body parts to communicate with, often "cross over" with signals, as is evident here. The Alert and Target is directed at the interloping Victim. The next expression is often a defensive behaviour, such as a lunge and bark. In this case, though, the dog has chosen to direct the predatory language of the Prey Bow toward the victim. Despite the use of a predatory behaviour, the feel here is not of predation, but defense.

Both the lunge and bark and the Prey Bow would send the same message in this context: "Get out of here." The lunge and bark is more dramatic: "Leave so I don't have to do something about this," and so may hold more of a fearful element. The Prey Bow, which is a Ready position, is more confident, perhaps; it means, "Get out of here because I AM coming after you."

Photo #16: Proximity

The small dog is ignoring the larger dog's advances. The small dog is confident and is not moving away from the larger dog. The larger dog is coming in at a sideways approach and has squinty eyes in a friendly way.

I would say these dogs do not know each other well. There is a wee bit of tension in both dogs, shown by the larger dog with the slightly braced front legs. Both dogs have closed mouths, which can indicate tension in the jaw. Open mouths, overall, tend to be a friendlier signal than closed mouths. The ignoring of the small dog has a note of avoidance: "You are not even there."

Photo #17: Group Dynamics

Background: There are two dogs on the left, an Aussie in the foreground and a Coton de Tuliar in the background.

The Aussie is Butt Sniffing the Coton. The Coton is not entirely comfortable, but is maintaining very nicely. First of all, if you know Cotons, you know that the tail is held jauntily over the back, like a Bichon. No sign of a tail held jauntily, here. The tail is down. The Coton is looking up at his owner for support and has his ears held down. He is not being reactive, just a little uneasy.

The Labrador in the middle is attending to his handler. He is comfortable.

The Golden on the right is anxious. Her ears are drawn back, her back is rounded. She is panting and there are ridges of tension around her mouth. In light of the relative emotional states of the other dogs in the area, the tension of the Golden is out of proportion to the context.

This is a photo taken in one of my advanced Re-socialization classes. The Golden was in the class for anxiety problems.

Photo #18: Puppy Biting

These dogs are facing the same direction, there is no obvious conflict-oriented stance. There is no direct eye contact. The dogs are mirroring each other's body language closely. The lips of both puppies are long. Both the Flat Coat puppy, in the foreground, and the Golden are comfortable and relaxed about lying all over each other and wrestling. The Golden has squinty eyes. Looks like fun!

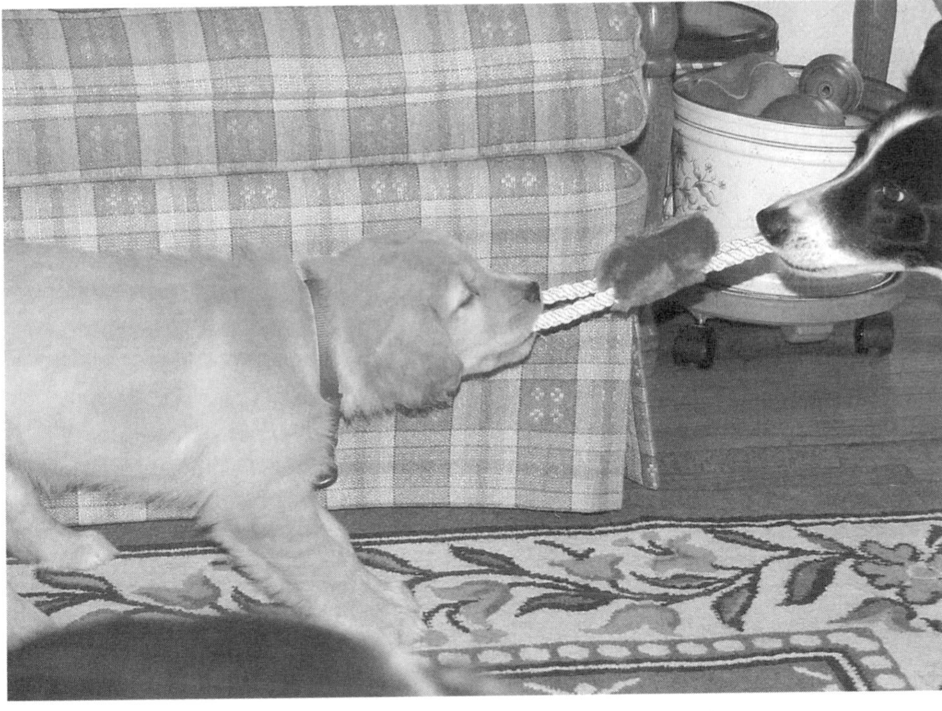

Photo #19: Tug Game

How do the dogs feel about this Tug-of-War game?

The Border Collie-mix is taking this pretty seriously. She is staring at the puppy with wide open eyes and has ridges of tension around and just below her eyes.

The puppy has squinty eyes. She is not about to let go of the toy, but is communicating "This is a game." Both dogs have a "Hold Bite" grip on the tug toy.

Some dogs do a lot of Warning/Guarding behaviour, but they never follow up on their threat. Other dogs figure this out pretty quickly and do not take the Warning/Guarding behaviours of this dog very seriously. Because of past experience they know: this particular dog never backs up the Warning with any action. In other words, that dog Talks the Talk, but doesn't Walk the Walk.

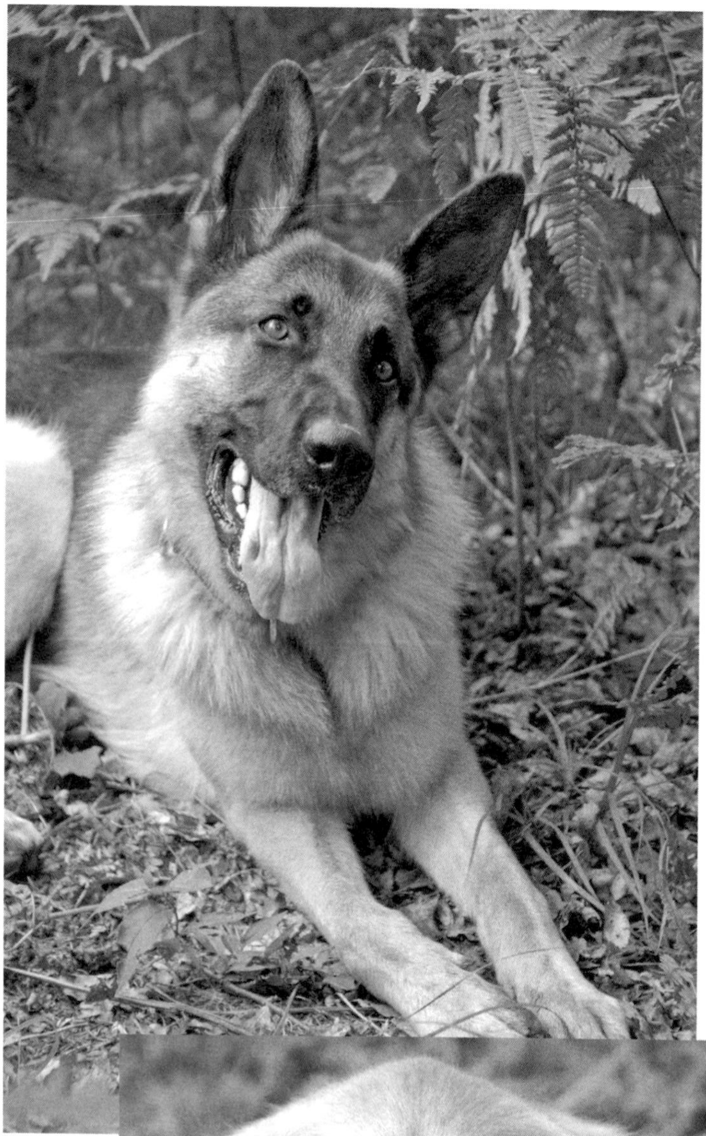

Photo #20: Head-tilt

Head-tilt of Curiosity. The relaxed jaw indicated by the open mouth and long lips, the erect ears and bright look of interest all show absorption.

Photo #21: Friendly

Can you pet this dog???? You betcha! Invitation to be interactive is written all over this dog. Squinty, blinking eyes, open mouth, ears held in a relaxed way, all say "I am comfortable and confident and friendly."

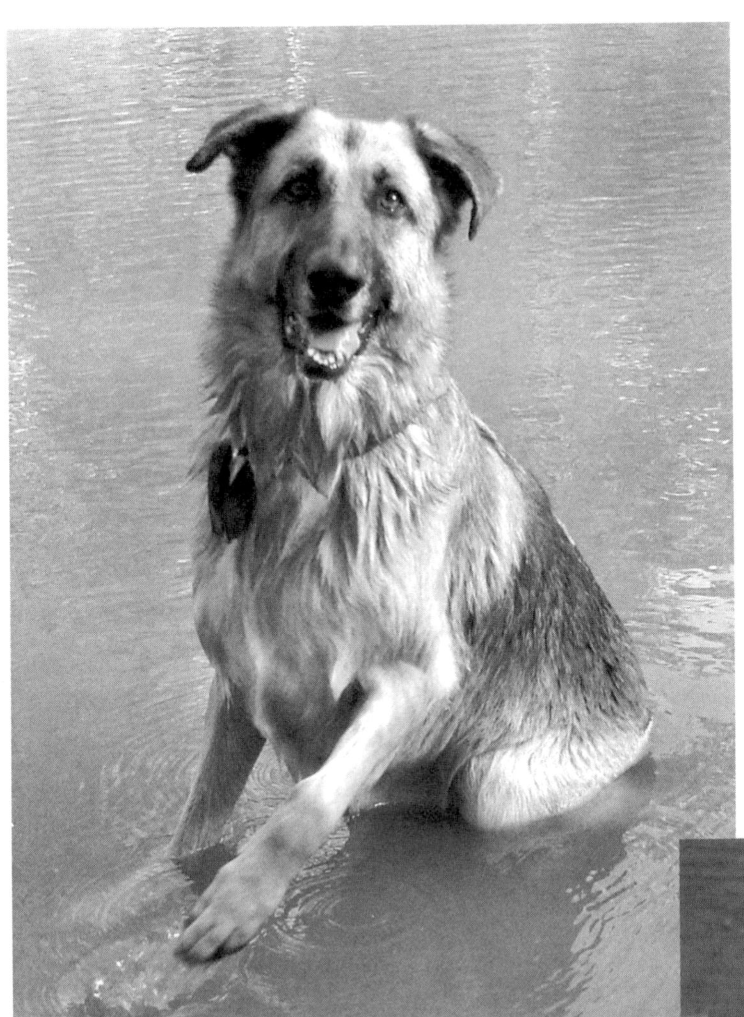

Photo #22: Paw Lift

The happy open mouth and alert look, combined with the insouciant demeanor show interest in something. This type of Paw Lift is not one of care-seeking or apology, but one of anticipation. Perhaps the owner is holding a ball to catch the dog's attention for the photo. This kind of Paw Lift has a slightly predatory feel, as if it is a precursor to a Point.

Photo #23: Confident, Relaxed

This Westie radiates confidence and self-assurance. The lack of tension indicated by the happy, open mouth, the tail held up and waving gently, the way he is propelling himself forward with jaunty steps, the pricked ears say, "I am happy in my world."

Photo Essay:

Photo #24-1 & #24-2: Conflict

In this kind of situation, nine times out of ten, the Reactive dog gets his butt kicked by his embarrassed handler. In this sequence, the dog who initiates and encourages aggression is the dog who is Targeting, the Doberman on the left. In the first photograph, the Doberman on the right notices the Doberman on the left, who is sending a clear message (Challenge) with a direct stare and forward body orientation, ears and tails up. The Doberman on the right uses ears back and a Paw Lift to tone the conflict down. In the bottom photograph, when she receives no Calming or Negotiation Signals back, she becomes Reactive, backing further around behind her handler in retreat, yet barking at the dog who is threatening her.

Further notice, that the Doberman on the right, is involved in doing a Pass By exercise, and is ignoring the Shepherd. The Shepherd knows what is going on, he is using a happy, open mouth, relaxed demeanor and Ignoring as Calming signals. The Shepherd, in trust, focuses on his owner

Bottom Photograph:
Fascinating is the Lab in the right background: he knows who the aggressor is, and is keeping an eye on the Targeting dog. The black dog next to him is remaining in a down with ears down and tail held close to the body. This is a Calming signal.

The Golden in the immediate foreground is using a Look away, lowered tail and squinty eyes, and the dog in the far left background is remaining in a down and ignoring the action also. These are not accidental, these actions all communicate "I am not involved."

Photo #25: Friendly

Look at these beautiful friendly dogs. We know these dogs are comfortable with each other because no one is Looking At anyone else. All the dogs have happy, open mouths and relaxed faces and bodies. The tails are confident, but gently waving. The dogs all have that goofy look on their faces that characterizes the dog that is relaxed and having fun.

References

Rugaas, Turid. (2005). *On Talking Terms With Dogs: Calming Signals*. Wenatchee, WA: Dogwise Publishing.

Ryan, Terry. (1998). *The Toolbox For remodeling Your Problem Dog*. New York, NY: Howell Book House.

Clothier, Suzanne. (1996). *Body Posture & Emotions: Shifting Shapes, Shifting Minds.* Stanton, NJ: Flying Dog Press.

Abrantes, Roger. (1997). *Dog Language: An Encyclopedia of Dog Behaviur.* Naperville, IL: Wakan Tanka Publishers.

Coppinger, Raymond and Lorna. (2001). *Dogs*. New York, NY: Scribner.

About The Author:

BRENDA ALOFF is a professional dog trainer. In addition to working with owners on the rehabilitation of fearful and aggressive dogs, Brenda also teaches puppy socialization, fundamental to competition obedience, conformation, tracking, back-packing, musical freestyle, and agility classes at Heaven On Arf Behaviour and Training Center, LLC, (say that fast ten times...) in Midland Michigan.

Brenda's childhood love was training and showing horses. Watching animal behaviour has always been a favorite activity. Her first Smooth Fox Terrier sparked culture shock and a fascination in dog behaviour.

As a natural progression of working with dogs with aggression and other behaviour problems, Brenda learned a lot about observing dog body language - the dog's own Native Language and primary means of communication. Brenda's understanding of canine language and social systems provides dog owners with effective means of communicating with their dogs and modifying their behaviour.

Brenda is currently sharing her living space with: Maeve, a rescue German Shepherd Dog; Rylie, a Border Collie; and beloved Smooth Fox Terriers Punch and Zasu (aka Zoomer). Abbey, her daughter, is currently studying creative writing in college.

Brenda's first book, *Positive Reinforcement: Training Dogs in the Real World*, was published in 2000. In 2001, this book was a finalist for the prestigious Dog Writers Association of America Award. She has also authored several magazine articles on dog training, produced a television program about canine behaviour, and been a guest on radio talk shows dealing with canine issues. Brenda's second book, *Aggression In Dogs: Prevention, Practical Management and Behaviour Modification*, was published in 2002.

She is a member of The National Association of Dog Obedience Instructors (NADOI), the International Association of Dog Behavior Counselors and several other breed and training organizations.

Brenda travels all over the United States and Canada, doing working clinics on canine aggression and learning theory, from short lectures to intensive week-long workshops. Body Language is always included, whatever the topic. People also travel to spend a week in Midland, and do a week of private and group sessions with dogs who have aggression problems.

This is my beloved Breanna and I sharing the joy of working as a team. I am forever indebted to her for all she has taught me. She is no longer here for me to cuddle with on the sofa...I miss her every day.

Photo by Kathy Mazur.

Brenda & Breanna. 2001.

Index

Index

Index

D

Index

Index

Index

Index

M

Index

Index

Index

Index

Index

Index

T

Index

Index